Adolescent Gambling

Mark Griffiths

London and New York

First published 1995
by Routledge
11 New Fetter Lane, London EC4P 4EE

Simultaneously published in the USA and Canada
by Routledge
29 West 35th Street, New York, NY 10001

© 1995 Mark Griffiths

Typeset in Times by LaserScript Ltd., Mitcham, Surrey

Printed and bound in Great Britain by Biddles Ltd,
Guildford and King's Lynn

British Library Cataloguing in Publication Data
A catalogue record for this book is available from the British Library

Library of Congress Cataloguing in Publication Data
A catalogue record for this book has been requested

ISBN 0-415-05833-3 (hbk)
ISBN 0-415-05834-1 (pbk)

Adolescent Gambling

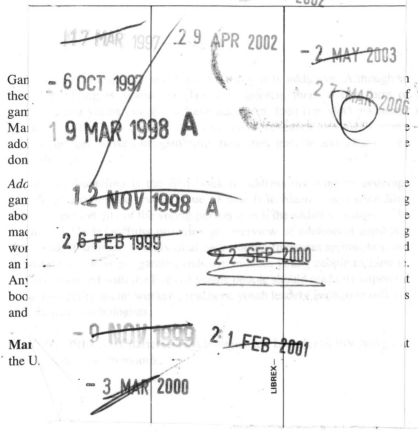

Gam...
theo...
gam...
Mar...
ado...
don...

Ado...
gam...
abo...
mad...
wor...
an i...
Any...
boo...
and...

Mar...
the U...

Adolescence and Society
Series editor: John C. Coleman
The Trust for the Study of Adolescence

The general aim of the series is to make accessible to a wide readership the growing evidence relating to adolescent development. Much of this material is published in relatively inaccessible professional journals, and the goals of the books in this series will be to summarise, review and place in context current work in the field so as to interest and engage both an undergraduate and a professional audience.

The intention of the authors is to raise the profile of adolescent studies among professionals and in institutes of higher education. By publishing relatively short, readable books on interesting topics to do with youth and society, the series will make people more aware of the relevance of the subject of adolescence to a wide range of social concerns.

The books will not put forward any one theoretical viewpoint. The authors will outline the most prominent theories in the field and will include a balanced and critical assessment of each of these. Whilst some of the books may have a clinical or applied slant, the majority will concentrate on normal development.

The readership will rest primarily in two major areas: the undergraduate market, particularly in the fields of psychology, sociology and education; and the professional training market, with particular emphasis on social work, clinical and educational psychology, counselling, youth work, nursing and teacher training.

To my father
Edward Thomas Griffiths (1936–1990)
– May you rest in peace

Contents

List of illustrations   viii
Preface   xi

1 The psychology of gambling: an overview   1

2 Adolescent gambling: an overview   34

3 Preliminary studies of adolescent fruit machine gambling
   and fruit machine addiction   75

4 The observational analysis of adolescent fruit machine
   gambling   96

5 The role of cognitive bias and skill in fruit machine
   gambling   129

6 The role of arousal and subjective moods in the
   maintenance of fruit machine gambling   149

7 Qualitative accounts and case studies of adolescent fruit
   machine addiction   169

8 Fruit machine gambling: the importance of structural
   characteristics   196

9 The treatment of pathological gambling   211

10 Fruit machine gambling: a final overview   240

Appendix 1   262
Appendix 2: Glossary   265
References   269
Name index   292
Subject index   297

Illustrations

FIGURE

10.1   A developmental model of a possible route from a
       television viewer to pathological gambler   260

TABLES

1.1   *DSM-III* criteria for pathological gambling   4
1.2   *DSM-III-R* criteria for pathological gambling   5
1.3   *DSM-IV* criteria for pathological gambling   6
1.4   Studies of arousal in gambling   18
1.5   Summary of heuristics and biases used by gamblers   25

2.1   Summary of questionnaire studies on adolescent gambling   36
2.2   Gambling among college students by state   41
2.3   Weekly gambling among college students by state   41
2.4   Maximum wager, pathological and problem gambling by
       state   42
2.5   Incidence of family gambling and alcoholism problems in
       pathological gamblers   45
2.6   Incidence of types of gambling in 15–19 year olds in the UK   54
2.7   Gambling incidence among schoolchildren as reported by
       school head teachers in the UK   55
2.8   Types of problems occurring as a result of gambling as
       reported by school head teachers in the UK   55
2.9   Summary of questionnaire studies on fruit machine
       gambling   66
2.10   Summary of UK research studies reporting signs of fruit
       machine dependency   72

3.1   Reasons for playing fruit machines as reported by players   85
3.2   Moods felt before, during and after playing as reported by
      players   86
3.3   Pathological gambling: percentages of players showing
      diagnostic criteria of *DSM-111-R*   88
3.4   Significant differences between pathological and social
      gamblers   89
3.5   Players' replies to 'Is there any skill in playing fruit
      machines?'   90
3.6   Skill factors in fruit machine gambling as reported by
      players   91

4.1   Breakdown of arcade observations by town, area, location
      and date   101
4.2   Total number of adolescents observed during observation
      sessions by time of year and location   103
4.3   Total number of male and female adolescents and ratios
      observed during observation sessions by time of year and
      location   103
4.4   Number of adolescents observed per monitoring session
      (inland)   104
4.5   Number of adolescents observed per monitoring session
      (coastal)   105
4.6   A comparison of observational methodologies   113
4.7   Differences between inland and seaside amusement arcades
      on numbers of fruit machines and video game machines   124
4.8   Differences between inland and seaside amusement arcades
      in marketing characteristics   125
4.9   Categorization of names of slot-machines   126

5.1   Key to the behavioural dependent variables   130
5.2   Means of fruit machine behavioural monitoring variables
      data   135
5.3   ANOVAs of fruit machine behavioural monitoring data   135
5.4   Utterance categorization used in content analysis coding
      scheme and percentage differences between regular and
      non-regular gamblers   136
5.5   Responses to the question, 'Is there any skill involved in
      playing a fruit machine?' by fruit machine gamblers   140
5.6   Responses to the question, 'How skilful do you think you
      are compared with the average person?' by fruit machine
      players   140

5.7   Skilful aspects of fruit machine gambling as reported by
        fruit machine gamblers   141

6.1   Percentages of gamblers meeting diagnostic criteria of
        DSM-III-R   151
6.2   Moods felt before playing fruit machines   152
6.3   Moods felt during playing fruit machines   153
6.4   Moods felt after playing fruit machines   153
6.5   Responses by regular fruit machine players as to why they
        are attracted to playing fruit machines regularly   155
6.6   Responses by non-regular players as to why people become
        regular fruit machine players   155
6.7   Comparison between non-regular and regular players'
        perceptions of attraction to fruit machines   156
6.8   Responses by non-regular players as to why they do not
        regularly play fruit machines   157
6.9   Responses by non-regular players as to their initial
        perceptions of the fruit machine they played on in the
        experiment   158
6.10 Means and standard deviations of the behavioural
        monitoring variables of gamblers   163
6.11 Means and standard deviations of heart rates before, during
        and after play of the total gamblers   164
6.12 Means of heart rates before, during and after play, and t-test
        comparisons of the total gamblers   165

7.1   Skilful aspects of fruit machine playing as reported by fruit
        machine players   174
7.2   Moods of fruit machine players before, during and after
        fruit machine playing   175

9.1   The twenty questions of Gamblers Anonymous   216
9.2   The twelve steps of Gamblers Anonymous   217
9.3   Types of behavioural therapy   221
9.4   Case studies of secondary fruit machine addictions   238

10.1 Summary of published studies by the author   241

Preface

Before explaining the structure and aims of this book I would like you to consider the following case studies. I have begun this book with these brief accounts in order to highlight the typicality of excessive adolescent gambling. I should also add that although the names have been changed, the accounts below are true cases.

Gary

Gary is 19 years old. He comes from an unsettled early life and had been in care and in youth custody for offences committed to feed his addiction to fruit machines. His gambling manifested itself in other forms such as horse-racing and the consequences were debilitating socially, financially and emotionally. He regularly followed the same pattern of spending. He would receive a payment of £80 in benefit, buy a large breakfast in the local cafe and a small amount of tobacco and then proceed to spend the remainder on a fruit machine in the cafe. He would always play until such a time as his money was gone, regardless of whether or not he had won anything. Although he experienced a 'high' when playing on the machines, he was unable to understand his behaviour. In addition, he would normally exhibit bouts of aggressive behaviour followed by a period of depression which would continue until the receipt of his next benefit payment. To survive the interim period, Gary would sell his possessions and borrow heavily from other people.

Brian

Brian is 17 years old. He comes from a stable background but is now serving an eighteen-month prison sentence for burglary offences to fund his fruit machine addiction. He began playing fruit machines from a very early age and even at 9 years old he was stealing £10 a time from his parents to play the machines. Brian was always being suspended from school for bad behaviour and was eventually taken into voluntary care. His parents blame themselves, particularly because they knew that he had played on the machines from an early age and never tried to stop him. Brian says he plays the machines because he gets a buzz from the lights, music and possible jackpot. During an average playing session he will spend between £50 and £80. On one occasion he stole £140 and then spent it in the course of one afternoon. He claims he just cannot stop playing.

Dave

Dave is 19 years old and is serving a youth custody sentence for theft. He is the second eldest son in a family of five and there is no history of gambling in his family. As a child, he played fruit machines at the seaside with money given to him by his parents. His problem became evident at 16 years of age with constant arrests for stealing to play the machines. To stop him playing the machines, Dave's parents escorted him to and from his place of work until they thought he was out of the habit. As soon as they stopped meeting him his gambling started again and he was then taken to Gamblers Anonymous (GA) by his mother. Although he enjoyed GA, his gambling did not stop and on one occasion when his parents refused to lend Dave some money to gamble he took a tranquillizer overdose. The shock of the attempted suicide renewed his family's efforts to help him. He got a job in a cinema but the foyer housed a fruit machine, and he was soon stealing from the till to play it. He has now served a number of custodial sentences but the pattern is always the same after release. He gets his dole cheque, cashes it and then goes and spends it all in one go down at the arcade in about two hours.

Jeremy

Jeremy is 18 years old and is an only child. He has been gambling on fruit machines since childhood. No one knew he had a problem until he burgled his school and was caught. His parents noticed he had changed from a 'happy-go-lucky lad' to a 'bad-tempered monster' but did not know why. He had started to develop a problem and as a consequence began to steal small amounts of money from the home, to use dinner money to play the machines and to play truant from school in order to go to the arcade. Over the years he repeatedly stole from home, including various valuables and the television set. He is now serving a sentence for credit card fraud.

These cases are typical of the many I have come across in the years I have been researching into the area of adolescent gambling. When reading these accounts, two things become clearly obvious. First, adolescent gambling appears to be very much a male activity. Second, when we talk about adolescent gambling in its most excessive forms, what we are really looking at is excessive gambling on one particular form of gambling, namely *fruit machine gambling*. It is no accident that the majority of this book concerns fruit machine gambling and fruit machine addiction, since it is this form of adolescent gambling behaviour which has the biggest impact on the lives of adolescents when compared with other forms of gambling. But what is it that makes someone become a fruit machine addict? Does fruit machine addiction *really* exist? Why do gamblers gamble excessively despite persistent losses? These are just some of the questions that this book will attempt to answer.

The book is split into ten chapters. Chapter 1 does not particularly concern adolescent gambling *per se* but covers an overview of gambling in general and highlights some of the theoretical issues. Chapter 2 features an overview of the adolescent gambling literature worldwide before discussing some of my own work in the later chapters. Chapters 3 and 4 outline some of my preliminary investigations into the area of fruit machine gambling using questionnaires, interviews and observational work before describing some of the experiments I have undertaken. In Chapters 5 and 6 I particularly concentrate on the psychology and psychophysiology of fruit machine playing. Chapter 7 outlines some of the qualitative work that I have carried out on fruit machine addicts and relies heavily on case study material. Chapter 8 examines how the gaming industry 'exploits' people who gamble on its machines and Chapter 9 outlines treatment approaches for problem gamblers. The final chapter integrates the research chapters and argues that fruit machine addiction is a bona fide addiction maintained by a combination of irrational thinking and psychophysiology. The main findings are that adolescent gambling – particularly fruit machine playing – is widespread, and that for a minority it is addictive.

This book is the first ever book published on adolescent gambling and is the culmination of many years of work towards gaining my Ph.D. It is essentially a series of my own studies that have been integrated with the contemporary literature on adolescent gambling – particularly fruit machine gambling. It also features treatment approaches, case studies and an insight into how the gaming industry induces people to gamble. The book has not so much been written up as "edited down" from the many papers that I have written over the last seven years or so. Anyone reading this book who has followed my work in the area of adolescent gambling since 1988 will not be surprised by many of the chapters in the book, since many of them are reworkings of papers published in journals such as the *British Journal of Psychology, Addictive Behaviors, Journal of Gambling Studies, Journal of Community and Applied Social Psychology*, etc. I have not identified these separately in the text as some chapters contain many extracts from many papers and to identify them in this way would spoil the flow of the text. For those who wish to refer to the original papers I have provided a list (see below) with identification of the original source (or version of the original source) and the chapter in which they appear.

This book could not have appeared without the assistance of many people. To name everyone who has been of help and inspiration would probably take up a page in itself but I would like to acknowledge a few individuals. My first debt of thanks must go to my Ph.D. supervisors – Stephen Lea and Paul Webley – who were the best academic supervisors I could have hoped to have had, and to Joan Fitzhenry who spent many years typing my manuscripts when I was at the University of Exeter. I would also like to thank a number of people from the field of gambling research who have given me much help over the years – particularly in the first few years as a postgraduate when I needed all the inspiration I could get. These include Sue Fisher, Paul Bellringer, Kenny Coventry, Gordon Moody, Iain Brown, Henry Lesieur, Mark Dickerson, Michael Walker, Robert Ladouceur, Alex Blaszczynski and Jim Orford. On a more personal level I would like to thank a number of people for just being there, including Phillipa Griffiths, Gail McMurray, Arlene Franklyn-Stokes, Rhona Magee, Freya Searle, Louise Rhodes, Catherine Nyman, Susan Wallace, Julie Munday, Dianne Wood, Joan Fitzhenry (again!), Bob Rooksby, Jonathon Smart and Kevin Thorpe. Finally, I would like to say thanks to all my family, but particularly to my father who died just before I received my Ph.D. and first lectureship. Without him I would not be where I am today and for that alone I am permanently indebted.

ORIGINAL SOURCE MATERIAL CONTAINED IN THIS BOOK

Chapter 2 contains material and extracts from Griffiths, 1989; 1991a; b.
Chapter 3 contains material and extracts from Griffiths, 1990; b; c; 1991.
Chapter 4 contains material and extracts from Griffiths, 1990d; e; 1991d; e; 1994a; b.
Chapter 5 contains material and extracts from Griffiths, 1993a; 1994c.
Chapter 6 contains material and extracts from Griffiths, 1993b; 1994d.
Chapter 7 contains material and extracts from Griffiths, 1993c; d.
Chapter 8 contains material and extracts from Griffiths, 1993e.
Chapter 9 contains material and extracts from Griffiths, 1991f; 1993f.
Chapter 10 contains material and extracts from Griffiths, 1989; 1991a; 1994e; 1995.

1 The psychology of gambling

An overview

Gambling is one of the few activities that cuts across all barriers of race, class and culture. In every day terms, 'gamble' is used to denote 'taking a risk' (Lea et al., 1987). For the purposes of systematic investigation into gambling, the preceding definition is clearly too vague. Although no one is in much doubt as to what gambling is (Lea et al., 1987), it is far harder to devise a formal definition than it is to identify specific forms of gambling activity (Herman, 1976), e.g. betting on horse-racing or playing the fruit machines. As early as 1950, Perkins classified gambling activities into four categories:

1 *Gaming* – the exchange of money during a game (e.g. fruit machines)
2 *Betting* – staking money on a future event (e.g. horse racing)
3 *Lotteries* – distribution of money by lot (e.g. National Lottery)
4 *Speculation* – gambling on stock markets (e.g. shares)

Even though some parties accept 'speculation' as a true form of gambling, most current researchers reject the category. In addition there are other dimensions to consider. For instance, some researchers (e.g. Cornish, 1978) have noted that some forms of gambling rely on pure chance (e.g. roulette) whereas others also involve a skill factor (e.g. poker). If, as it appears, there is no formal definition of gambling, there are a number of common elements that occur in the majority of gambling instances which distinguish 'true' gambling from mere risk-taking. These include:

1 The re-allocation of wealth, i.e. the exchange of money (or something of value) usually without the introduction of productive work on either side (Halliday and Fuller, 1974; Lea et al., 1987).
2 Winners gain at the sole expense of losers.
3 Exchange is determined by a future event, whose outcome is unknown at the time of the bet.

4   The result is determined (partly) by chance.
5   Losses incurred can be avoided by simply not taking part in the gamble (Devereux, 1968).

Many gambling activities also have other common factors, but these may not all be universal. For instance, Lea *et al.* (1987) noted that gambling is a social activity; however, this may not be the case with some people who play alone on fruit machines or those who individually gamble on the football pools. Finally it should be noted that most sources treat gambling as 'adult' due to its legal restrictions (Ide-Smith and Lea, 1988). However, this book will argue that acquisition and development of gambling behaviour in fact begins during childhood and adolescence. According to Ladouceur *et al.* (1986), the popularity of gambling has great 'economic, social, political and moral implications' (p.45) but the psychology of gambling behaviour has been the subject of relatively little systematic or controlled research, and consequently the variables which affect the acquisition, development and maintenance of gambling behaviour remain theoretical and largely unknown. From this brief opening introduction, it is clear that conceptually, gambling has progressed from being considered a unitary phenomenon to an activity that is currently regarded as multi-faceted and multi-dimensional in nature.

NORMAL AND SOCIAL GAMBLING

Although almost all national surveys into gambling have concluded that there are more gamblers than non-gamblers (e.g. Cornish, 1978; Kallick *et al.*, 1979), most of those participating are what might be termed 'normal' or 'social' gamblers who occasionally bet on a horse-race, play bingo or buy lottery tickets. Estimates based on survey data indicate that between 80 per cent to 94 per cent of British (Cornish, 1978), 24 per cent to 68 per cent of American (Culleton, 1985; Culleton and Lang, 1985; Kallick *et al.*, 1979) and 81 per cent to 92 per cent of Australian (Grichting, 1986; McMillan, 1985) adults have gambled at some time in their lives. Of these, approximately one-quarter to one-third gamble on a regular basis (Culleton, 1985; Culleton and Lang, 1985; Royal Commission on Gambling, 1951). Although Lea *et al.* (1987) have noted that some moralists hold the principle that it is wrong 'to benefit from avoidable chance events' (p.268), Cornish (1978) reviewed the relevant literature and concluded that there was no evidence that 'normal' or 'social' gambling causes interference with a person's job, marriage, day-to-day living, or that there are relationships between 'normal' gambling and crime. It would therefore appear that 'normal' or 'social' gambling is of no moral danger to most individuals in society because controlling the impulse to gamble is within their personal limits, i.e. money used for gambling is produced from their own disposable income on the basis of what they can afford to lose.

PATHOLOGICAL GAMBLING

Incidence and history of pathological gambling

Estimates of the number of probable adult pathological gamblers vary from 0.2 per cent to 1 per cent in the UK, (Dickerson, 1974; Royal Commission, 1951), 0.77 per cent to 3.4 per cent in the US (Kallick *et al.*, 1979; Culleton, 1985; Sommers, 1988; Volberg and Steadman, 1988; 1989) and 0.25 per cent to 1.73 per cent in Australia (Dickerson and Hinchy, 1988). These surveys have also indicated that pathological gambling is twice as common among males as it is among females, that non-whites have higher rates than whites, and that those with poor education are more likely to be pathological gamblers (Lesieur and Rosenthal, 1991). Further to this, Lesieur and Custer (1984) have estimated that between ten and fifteen people are affected by the typical compulsive gambler including spouse, children, relatives, friends and employers.

It should also be noted that most researchers believe that with an increase in the legalization of gambling activities there will be an increase in the number of pathological gamblers (Marcum and Rowen, 1974; Weinstein and Deitch, 1974; Skolnick, 1978; Dielman, 1979; Kallick-Kaufmann, 1979; Custer, 1982; Rosecrance, 1985) and, through legalization, the opportunity to gamble could stimulate participation and become more socially acceptable, leading to an increase in the number of pathological gamblers (Abt and Smith, 1984; Frey, 1984; Arcuri *et al.*, 1985; Moody, 1987). This would run parallel with the legalization and social acceptance of alcohol (Shaffer and Burglass, 1981).

In 1980, pathological gambling was recognized as a mental disorder in the third edition of the *Diagnostic and Statistical Manual* (American Psychiatric Association, 1980) under the section 'Disorders of impulse control' along with other illnesses such as kleptomania and pyromania. Adopting a medical model of pathological gambling in this way displaced the old image that the gambler was a sinner or a criminal.

Before the appearance of the *DSM-III* (1980), the subject of pathological gambling had produced an expanding body of literature by psychiatrists, psychologists, psychoanalysts and social workers (Knapp and Lech, 1987), and had appeared under a variety of labels including 'neurotic' (Greenson, 1947), 'compulsive' (Bergler, 1957), 'addictive' (Dickerson, 1977a), 'excessive' (Cornish, 1978) and 'pathological' (Moran, 1970a; b; c; d). There now seems to be an increased preference among professionals for the term 'pathological gambling' to describe individuals with severe gambling problems (Lesieur and Custer, 1984; Wolkowitz *et al.*, 1985; Allcock, 1986; Knapp and Lech, 1987) and this owes much to the consistent efforts of Moran (1967; 1970a; b; c; d) who argued that the phrase 'pathological gambling' is descriptive as opposed to such terms as 'compulsive' or 'addictive' which might suggest specific and homogenous etiologies.

In diagnosing the pathological gambler, the *DSM-III* states that the individual is chronically and progressively unable to resist impulses to gamble and that gambling compromises, disrupts or damages family, personal and vocational pursuits. The behaviour increases under times of stress and associated features include lying to obtain money, committing crimes (e.g. forgery, embezzlement, fraud, etc.), and concealment from others of the extent of the individual's gambling activities. In addition, the *DSM-III* stated that to be a pathological gambler, the gambling must not be due to Antisocial Personality Disorder (see Table 1.1).

As Lesieur (1988a) pointed out, these criteria were criticized for (1) a middle-class bias, i.e. criminal offences such as embezzlement, income tax

Table 1.1 DSM-III criteria for pathological gambling

The criteria state that maladaptive gambling is indicated by:

A. The individual is chronically and progressively unable to resist impulses to gamble.
B. Gambling compromises, disrupts or damages family, personal and vocational pursuits, as indicated by at least three of the following:

1. Arrest for forgery, fraud, embezzlement or income tax evasion due to attempts to obtain money for gambling;
2. Default on debts or other financial responsibilities;
3. Disrupted family or spouse relationships due to gambling;
4. Borrowing money from illegal sources (loan sharks);
5. Inability to account for loss of money or to produce evidence of winning money if this is claimed;
6. Loss of work due to absenteeism in order to pursue gambling activity;
7. Necessity for another person to provide money to relieve a desperate financial situation.

C. The gambling is not due to Antisocial Personality Disorder.

Source: American Psychiatric Association, 1980.

evasion were 'middle-class' offences; (2) lack of recognition that many compulsive gamblers are self-employed, and (3) exclusion of individuals with Antisocial Personality Disorder. Lesieur recommended that the same custom be followed for pathological gamblers as for substance abusers and alcoholics in the past, i.e. to allow for simultaneous diagnosis with no exclusions. In addition, the criteria leave out the 'problem gambler' who, by self-admission or by others' testimony, spends a disproportionate amount of time gambling but has yet to produce the serious consequences laid down in the *DSM-III*. The new criteria (see Table 1.2) were subsequently changed taking on board the criticisms and modelled extensively on substance abuse disorders due to the growing acceptance of gambling as a bona fide addictive behaviour.

However, in 1989, Rosenthal conducted an analysis of the use of the *DSM-III-R* criteria by treatment professionals. It was reported that there was some dissatisfaction with the new criteria and that there was some preference for a compromise between the *DSM-III* and the *DSM-III-R*. As a consequence, the criteria have again been changed for *DSM-IV*. The new criteria presented in Table 1.3 represent a combination of *DSM-III* (criteria

Table 1.2 DSM-III-R criteria for pathological gambling

The criteria state that maladaptive gambling is indicated by four of the following:

1. Frequent preoccupation with gambling or obtaining money to gamble.
2. Often gambles larger amounts of money or over a longer period than intended.
3. Need to increase the size or frequency of bets to achieve the desired excitement.
4. Restlessness or irritability if unable to gamble.
5. Repeatedly loses money gambling and returns another day to win back losses ('chasing').
6. Repeated efforts to cut down or stop gambling.
7. Often gambles when expected to fulfil social, educational or occupational obligations.
8. Has given up some important social, occupational or recreational activity in order to gamble.
9. Continues to gamble despite inability to pay mounting debts, or despite other significant social, occupational or legal problems that the individual knows to be exacerbated by gambling.

Source: American Psychiatric Association, 1987

Table 1.3 DSM-IV criteria for pathological gambling

The revised criteria now state that pathological gambling is indicated by at least four of the following:

1. As gambling progressed, became more and more preoccupied with reliving past gambling experiences, studying a gambling system, planning the next gambling venture, or thinking of ways to get money.
2. Needed to gamble with more and more money in order to achieve the desired excitement.
3. Became restless or irritable when attempting to cut down or stop gambling.
4. Gambled as a way of escaping from problems or intolerable feeling states.
5. After losing money gambling, would often return another day in order to get even ('chasing') one's losses.
6. Lied to family, employer or therapist to protect and conceal the extent of involvement with gambling.
7. Committed illegal acts such as forgery, fraud, theft or embezzlement, in order to finance gambling.
8. Jeopardized or lost a significant relationship, marriage, education, job or career because of gambling.
9. Needed another individual to provide money to relieve a desperate financial situation produced by gambling (a 'bailout').

Notes: ('Dimensions' for each of these criteria are: (1) progression and preoccupation; (2) tolerance; (3) withdrawal and loss of control; (4) escape; (5) chasing; (6) lies/deception; (7) illegal acts; (8) family/job disruption, and (9) financial bailout.)

Source: Lesieur and Rosenthal, 1991

6-9) and *DSM-III-R* (criteria 1-3 and 5) and the addition of 'escape' (criterion 4) which was added on the basis of recent research. According to Lesieur and Rosenthal (1991) this present wording appears to answer the critiques of *DSM-III-R*.

Typologies of pathological gambling

Although many researchers have recognized that there are differences between gamblers (e.g. Bergler, 1957; Fink, 1961; Sharma, 1970; Scimecca, 1971; Custer, 1977; Shubin, 1977), only two authors (Moran, 1970b; c; Kusyszyn, 1978) have outlined various psychological sub-varieties of pathological gambling. Moran's (1970b; c) classification was based on fifty male patients receiving psychiatric help for their gambling problems. After extensive interviewing of the patients, Moran evolved five sub-types of pathological gambler. These were as follows:

1 *Subcultural variety* (14 per cent) – Gambles excessively due to others in the same social environment gambling heavily. This type lacks independence and conforms to the social group.
2 *Neurotic variety* (34 per cent) – Gambles excessively as a means of relief from stress and emotional difficulties.
3 *Impulsive variety* (18 per cent) – Gambles excessively due to a 'loss of control'. Money is gambled until it runs out and 'symptoms of craving' appear. This variety of pathology is the most serious and produces an economic and social functioning disturbance.
4 *Psychopathic variety* (24 per cent) – Gambles excessively as part of general global disturbance, i.e. the psychopathic state. Criminality usually occurs but is on the whole unrelated to gambling.
5 *Symptomatic variety* (10 per cent) – Gambles excessively because of an associated mental illness (e.g. depression) in which the illness is primary and the gambling a secondary symptomatic manifestation.

As with most other typologies, Moran's classification may be clinically useful, but the distinctions between each group are not clear and many patients may have characteristics of more than one sub-type. Zimmerman *et al.* (1985) have found support for the 'neurotic', 'impulsive' and 'psychopathic' types during their research, although Allcock and Grace (1988) found their small sample of ten pathological gamblers to be no more impulsive than heroin addicts, alcoholics and controls.

Kusyszyn's (1978) classification of gamblers was based on four factors: money (won or lost), time devoted to gambling (a lot or a little), other people (negatively affected or not affected) and the gamblers' feelings (feel good or feel bad about their gambling). This model produced a logical multi-dimensional framework in which sixteen types of gambler can be generated, e.g. the archetypal pathological gambler (loses a lot of money, spends a lot of time gambling, feels badly and affects others negatively), the professional gambler (wins a lot of money, spends a lot of time gambling, feels good and affects no one), the millionaire happy-binge player (loses a lot of money, spends very little time gambling, feels good and affects no one) and the acute compulsive (loses a lot of money, spends very little time gambling, feels badly and affects others negatively). Kusyszyn's analysis is useful to the extent that it forces those interested in the study of gambling to consider the multi-faceted nature of gambling but many of the sub-types probably exist only theoretically.

Finally, it must be noted that sociologists too have considered pathological gambling sub-types and that their distinctions are primarily based on social class and group orientation. For instance, Livingston (1974) distinguishes between working-class and middle-class compulsive gamblers, while Lesieur (1984) differentiates between 'loners' (typically middle class), 'group-oriented' (typically working class) and 'action system players' (a twenty-four-hours-a-day action system devoted to hustling with other pathological gamblers). However, sociological distinctions are not as clinically useful when adopting a 'medicalization' model of gambling (Rosecrance, 1985).

Phases of the pathological gambler's career

The acquisition, development and maintenance of pathological gambling is an area that is continually disputed. The exact causes and reasons for continuing gambling behaviour seem to be dependent upon the individual, but there do seem to be some general underlying factors and recurring themes. Problem gambling generally begins in adolescence and may start following a major life stress (Wolkowitz *et al.*, 1985); for example, the death of a parent or birth of a first child. Such events may induce a need to escape from the problems of reality (Moran, 1970b). Prior to the age of 15, other predisposing factors may include serious family problems (e.g. divorce of parents), inappropriate school or parental discipline, exposure to gambling in childhood and/or adolescence (by family and/or peers), and even familiar emphasis on material symbols rather than savings (American Psychiatric Association, 1980). According to Custer and Custer (1981), there are several 'soft signs' of pathological gambling including a higher than average IQ, being lively and energetic, a risk-taker, a lack of hobbies and interests, low boredom threshold, episodic insomnia and 'workaholic' tendencies.

Lesieur and Custer (1984) in conducting independent research (Custer, 1982; Lesieur, 1984) have concluded that pathological gambling behaviour consists of three stages – the winning phase, the losing phase and the desperation phase. However, there is controversy as to whether it is the 'big win' (Lesieur, 1984; Custer, 1982) or a 'big loss' – termed a 'bad beat' (Rosecrance, 1986) that facilitates continued gambling in the losing phase. The winning phase normally begins with small but successful bets in adolescence. Early wins prompt more 'skilful' gambling which usually leads to larger winnings. Custer (1982) reports that most social gamblers stop at this stage. However, after a considerable big win which may equal or exceed the individual's annual salary, the gambler accepts the thought that the occurrence can happen again. The next stage – the losing phase – is characterized by unrealistic optimism on the gambler's part, and all bets are made in an effort to recoup losses (which has been termed 'the chase' by

Lesieur, 1984). The result is that instead of 'cutting their losses' gamblers get deeper into debt by preoccupying themselves with gambling, determined that a big win will repay their loans and solve all their problems. Family troubles begin (both marital and with relatives) and illegal borrowing and other criminal activities in an effort to obtain money usually start to occur. At this point in the pathological gambler's career, family and/or friends may 'bail out' the gambler. Alienation from those closest to the pathological gambler characterizes the appearance of the final stage – the desperation phase. In a last ditch frenzied effort to repay their debts, illegal criminal behaviour reaches its height and when there are finally no more options left, the gambler may suffer severe depression and have suicidal thoughts.

It is then, usually at the insistence of the family (if not the courts), that the gambler must seek help. Because the pathological gambler is impatient, requiring immediate results, Custer (1982) suggested that help should be aimed at priority areas, i.e. legal and financial difficulties, counselling to resolve family and marital problems, and most importantly hospitalization for desperate patients who are depressed and suicidal. More recently, Rosenthal (1989) has described a fourth phase called the 'hopeless' or 'giving up' phase. This is where the gambler knows they cannot possibly retrieve their losses and they do not care, leading to play for play's sake 'like laboratory animals with electrodes planted in their pleasure center, they gamble to the point of exhaustion' (Lesieur and Rosenthal, 1991, pp. 14–15).

Lesieur and Rosenthal (1991) also summarized a number of factors which they believe to be intrinsic and extrinsic to gambling situations and the progression of gambling. The intrinsic factors are (i) a big win (Custer, 1982); (ii) chasing behaviour (Lesieur, 1979; 1984); (iii) a bail out (Custer, 1982), and (iv) going on tilt (Browne, 1989). ('Going on tilt' is a gambling expression for an acute deterioriation in play or loss of control.) The extrinsic factors are (i) use of alcohol or other drugs; (ii) death of a close relative or divorce; (iii) birth of a child; (iv) physical illness or a threat to one's life; (v) difficulties in relationships and/or (vi) job or career disappointment and/or (paradoxically) success (Bolen and Boyd, 1968; Boyd and Bolen, 1970).

THEORIES OF PATHOLOGICAL GAMBLING

As a number of authors point out (e.g. Lesieur and Rosenthal, 1991), there is now a trend towards taking an eclectic approach to the study of pathological gambling. It is probable that sociological, psychological and biological processes are involved in an interactive and complex fashion in its etiology. The following section outlines both major historical and contemporary theories of pathological gambling, concentrating specifically on psychoanalytic theories, personality theories, learning (behavioural) theories, physiological theories, cognitive theories, and psychologically based addiction theories.

Psychoanalytic theories

Historically, psychoanalytic (psychodynamic) theories of gambling have been predominant, and many theories have emerged since Freud's original assertions in his paper 'Dostoevsky and parricide' (Freud, 1928). Without having met him, Freud analysed the novelist Dostoevsky and formulated a theory from this single case study in which he noted the apparent similarity between pathological gambling and masturbation. Freud argued that both are irresistible impulses, and promises to stop oneself performing the activity are often broken. Both are pleasurable acts, and both (according to Freud) lead to feelings of guilt on completion of the activity. Although the analysis was of a single case study, his theory was soon taken up by other psychoanalysts and generalized to others. By the 1940s, pathological gambling was seen by psychoanalysts as a masturbatory equivalent. Simmel (1920) had regarded gambling as a regressive infantile activity related to the pre-genital psychosexual phases, to obtain longed-for erotic satisfaction. He equated gambling with foreplay, winning with orgasm, and losing with ejaculation, defecation and castration. Part of the Freudian mechanism was the transfer of masturbatory guilt to the gambling activity, so that losing served as a punishment to cancel the feelings of psychic guilt. (Sexual metaphors were in fact abundant among psychoanalysts; see Griffiths (1990f) for a more detailed review.) Israeli (1935), Greenson (1947), Comess (1960) and Niederland (1967) all observed the depressive states that manifested themselves in habitual gamblers, although Israeli concluded that gambling relieved the 'bouts' of depression, i.e. he believed that the gambler was depressed to start with, whereas the other three saw gambling as an activity that warded off depression.

The most comprehensive psychoanalytic study of gambling was undertaken by Bergler (1957) who reported on 200 case studies. He used Freud's ideas about 'guilt relief in losing' and extended it in a somewhat different direction. Bergler argued that childish fantasies of grandeur were revived by gambling. The gambling act was a rebellious act, an aggression against logic, intelligence, moderation and morality. Ultimately it was a denial of parental authority, a denial of the reality principle. Even the gambler's parents (who symbolize logic, intelligence and morality) could not predict a chance outcome. Bergler's paradoxical 'unconscious desire to lose' formed the second part of his theory. This was the 'pleasure–pain' component, which arose when gambling activated forbidden unconscious desires. In essence, the gambler was paying for the aggression with the financial losses providing the punishment to maintain the gambler's psychological equilibrium. This line of thought was subsequently developed by Galdston (1951) and Harris (1964).

Having briefly reviewed the main psychoanalytic theories, we see that three major components are:

1 Gambling is an unconscious substitute for pre-genital libidinal / aggressive outlets.
2 Gambling involves an 'unconscious desire to lose' – a wish for punishment in reaction to guilt.
3 Gambling is a useful medium for continued enactments (but *not* resolutions) of the psychological conflict.

However, these theories have a number of shortcomings. Psychoanalytic interpretations of gambling do not account for the initial motivation to gamble or account for how a social gambler becomes a pathological gambler, and as with many psychoanalytic interpretations, a number of claims made are empirically untestable. Although there are some authors who claim that psychodynamic approaches still have much to offer the field of gambling – particularly in issues of treatment (e.g. Rosenthal and Rugle, 1994) – it could be argued that psychodynamic approaches provide little more than a useful historical perspective to the study of gambling.

Learning (behavioural) theories

By the early 1950s, the popularity of psychodynamic theories began to wane and the study of gambling became a topic for learning theory. Gambling was viewed as operant behaviour subject to various reinforcement schedules, i.e. behaviour tends to become strengthened (in this case gambling) when it is followed by reinforcement (e.g. winning money). Skinner (1953) argued that the individual's gambling behaviour is a function of their previous reinforcement history. For instance, when a person first gambles, initial successes lead to a greater chance that the gambling behaviour will continue, even if the reinforcement ratio declines. Although this hypothesis was based on his work from rats and pigeons, it is supported by some gambling research, such as Bolen and Boyd's (1968) concept of 'beginner's luck' and Custer's (1982) emphasis of the pathological gambler's predisposition by a 'big win' (see also Greenberg and Weiner, 1966).

A logical question to ask at this stage is what exactly is the reinforcement in the gambling situation? Is it purely monetary? Saunders (1979) has noted that money is quite obviously a reward. However, gamblers may win in the short run but most of them will eventually lose in the long run. Lea *et al.* (1987) pointed out that another potential reinforcer is activation ('the thrill of gambling'), and that this could play a role in all gambling situations. Further to this, Dickerson (1984) notes that there are multiple stimuli which can be perceived to be rewarding in gambling settings. Events such as the pre-race and race sequence at the race-track, the spinning roulette wheel and the placing of bets, can be reinforcing because they produce excitement, arousal and tension. It is obvious that common gambling situations, for instance, slot machines, have features in common with schedules of reinforcement. Both involve a probabilistic reward and both seem to produce very high and somewhat 'irrational' rates of behaviour (Lea *et al.*, 1987). While most researchers agree that most gambling can be adapted to a variable ratio paradigm, Dickerson (1979) argued that in the case of horse-race gamblers who gamble while watching regular races on television or listening to the radio in betting shops, a fixed interval schedule may be operating.

Apart from patterns of responding, the question of why people continue to gamble in the face of persistent losses is a question learning theorists have tried to answer. It is known that reward schedules that pay off only intermittently (as in gambling situations) produce a greater persistence after the reward is stopped than those in which there is a consistently high pay-off (Bijou, 1957; Keppel *et al.*, 1967). This has been called the partial reinforcement extinction effect (PREE). Another theory of the PREE that accounts for persistence is that persistence in some sense eventually pays off (Capaldi, 1966). Thus, eventually being rewarded after a long run of bad luck paradoxically strengthens (i.e. reinforces) the placement of losing bets.

Amsel's (1967) frustration theory can also be applied to gambling, as has been done by Reid (1986) and Lea *et al.* (1987). The basic proposition of the theory applied to PREE in gambling is that after a run of losses (i.e. no reinforcement) the person gambling becomes 'frustrated'. As soon as the next win occurs the frustration is dissipated, so the response that led to the frustration reduction becomes reinforced. In essence, this can account for the gambler who, despite a string of losses, can persist in gambling and feel good about it!

Learning theory provides a good account of some kinds of gambling, concentrates on the economic properties of gambling (Lea *et al.*, 1987), and supports the belief that since the behaviour is learned it can be unlearned. However, it does not account for why people who have given up gambling (say, after joining Gamblers Anonymous) and having extinguished the response, return to gambling years later after a long period of abstinence.

Psychometric studies and personality theory

It is logical to speculate that there might be a gambling personality; that is, a trait cluster that marks the gambler as a habitual or compulsive risk-taker (Lea *et al.*, 1987). However, psychometric data to date have not been promising and have been of limited value in identifying who are potential pathological gamblers, or in establishing specific guidelines in developing treatment programmes (Allcock, 1986). Walker (1992b) has extensively reviewed the literature on the psychometric studies of gambling and noted that most research in the area has been carried out on three personality dimensions – sensation seeking, extroversion and locus of control.

Sensation seeking is the 'need for varied, novel and complex sensations and experiences, and the willingness to take physical and social risks for the sake of such experience' (Zuckerman, 1979, p.10). This should mean that gamblers are higher than non-gamblers on sensation seeking measures. Studies in this area have provided contrasting results with one study supporting the hypothesis (Kuley and Jacobs, 1988), some studies showing no difference between gamblers and non-gamblers (Anderson and Brown, 1984; Ladouceur and Mayrand, 1986) and others showing gamblers to be lower on sensation seeking than normals (Blaszczynski *et al.*, 1986a; Dickerson *et al.*, 1987).

In studies on extraversion using the Eysenck Personality Questionnaire (EPQ) and its derivatives, the results have again proved contradictory. Since extroverts are highly sociable, crave excitement and enjoy noisy and active environments it would be predicted that gamblers are more likely to be extroverted. Although a couple of studies have found pathological gamblers to be more extroverted than normals, giving support for the hypothesis (Seager, 1970; Wong, 1980), some have found pathological gamblers to have lower extroversion scores than normals (Koller, 1972; Blaszczynski *et al.*, 1986a) and others have shown no difference (Moran, 1970b; McConaghy *et al.*, 1983; Ladouceur and Mayrand, 1986).

Research into locus of control has been more favourable. Walker (1992b) states that the central idea of the locus of control is that 'reinforcement which is perceived to be under the control of the individual will increase the habit of strength of the reinforced behaviour, whereas reinforcement which is perceived to be independent of the individual will not increase habit strength' (p.98). Therefore, in the case of gambling, gamblers would be expected to have a high external locus of control whereas those with a high internal locus of control would avoid gambling. The studies to date suggest that this may be the case as a number of studies have found gamblers to have a high external locus of control (Cameron and Myers, 1966; Moran, 1970b; Devinney, 1979; Wong, 1980; Hong and Chiu, 1988). However, a number of studies have found no difference (Malkin, 1981; Glass, 1982; Jablonski, 1985; Kusyszyn and Rutter, 1985; Ladouceur and Mayrand, 1986) and there has been one study which has found gamblers to have high internal locus of control (Huxley, 1993). However, as Walker points out, we do not know the direction of causality; that is, whether the external locus of control preceded the gambling or whether the gambling preceded the external locus of control.

The few studies comparing pathological gamblers to non-pathological gamblers using other personality tests have tended to find no significant differences or find that gamblers exhibited positive traits. For instance, McGlothin (1954) reported thirty female subjects who gambled to be better adjusted than normals on social, home and emotional scores on the Bell Adjustment Inventory. Morris (1957) showed that, in comparing gamblers and non-gamblers, his twenty-nine subjects were more 'secure, dominant and masculine' than the eighteen non-gambling controls. Kusyszyn and Rutter (1985) measured eleven personality characteristics in four different groups of people (nineteen non-gamblers, twenty-four lottery players, forty-two light gamblers and thirty-two heavy gamblers). Their results showed no significant differences in anxiety, depression, aggressiveness, defensiveness, internal locus of control, creativity or self-esteem on personality dimensions. In an earlier study, Kusyszyn and Rutter (1978) found no relationship between personality and gambling in a group of race goers whose gambling ranged from never to frequent.

Studies using the Edwards Personal Reference schedule have found pathological gamblers to have higher scores than normal on achievement, exhibition, dominance, heterosexuality, deference and endurance (Moravec and Munley, 1983) although a study by Taber *et al.* (1986) using the California Personality Inventory failed to show pathological gamblers had higher achievement motivation. Other studies (Livingston, 1974; Dell *et al.*, 1981; Taber *et al.*, 1986) have reported that pathological gamblers have low ego strength and a possibly higher incidence of narcissistic personality disorder.

One fairly consistent finding is that studies using the Minnesota Multiphasic Personality Inventory (MMPI) have found pathological gamblers to have elevated or 'spiked' scores on the psychopathic deviation (Pd) scale and clear signs of depression (Bolen *et al.*, 1975; Glen, 1979; Moravec and Munley, 1983; Graham and Lowenfeld, 1986; Adkins *et al.*, 1987). It is interesting that other addictive populations score highly on these two measures (Lesieur and Rosenthal, 1991) but it has yet to be established whether psychopathic traits and/or depression cause the pathological gambling or vice versa, i.e. the direction of causality is uncertain (Allcock, 1986).

It would appear from this brief overview that the utility and value of psychometric studies remains doubtful (Knapp and Lech, 1987), and the notion that pathological gamblers possess a unique set of variables or traits is, as Allcock (1986) asserted, 'a naive over-simplification and a fruitless direction for research' (p. 262). Gambling is complex and multi- dimensional, and personality factors are too 'global' to serve as the single cause. However, McCormick and Taber (1987) have outlined five major personality constructs which may have promise for future research and treatment. These are:

1 An obsessive compulsive factor (ranging from few preoccupations other than gambling to multiple compulsions).
2 A mood factor (ranging from depression to hypomania).
3 Presence of traumatic and major life stressors (from recent acute to remote chronic).
4 A socialization factor (from completely socialized to antisocial personality disordered).
5 Substance abuse or multiple addiction factor (from no other addictions to having multiple addictions).

Physiological theories

Physiological approaches to the study of gambling are becoming ever more prominent. At present there appear to be three main physiological lines of research, including (1) a search for a physiological disposition and/or an underlying biological substrate in pathological gamblers; (2) an examination of the role of arousal in gambling, and (3) speculation about endorphin related explanations.

The search for biological dispositions and substrates

Carlton and his associates (Goldstein *et al.*, 1985; Carlton *et al.*, 1987; Goldstein and Carlton, 1988) have performed a number of studies involving electroencephalographic (EEG) measurement (i.e. brainwaves).

Drawing on the theory that hemispheric dysregulation is related to failure of impulse control, they have looked for signs of differential hemispheric activation induced by different task requirements. It has been found that pathological gamblers (when compared against controls) showed deficits in degree of EEG activation produced by simple verbal versus non-verbal tasks. An interesting observation is that deficits such as this are not unique to pathological gamblers. Parallel deficits have been found in children with Attention Deficit Disorder (ADD).

ADD children are characterized by two primary symptoms (i.e. inattention and impulsivity) and a range of secondary symptoms (e.g. obstinacy and negativism) and show hemispheric differentiation analogous to pathological gamblers. Since ADD children have (1) an inability to sustain attention, and (2) are impulsive, it is not surprising that ADD is related to excessive behaviour, e.g. gambling and alcoholism (see Carlton and Manowitz, 1987). Logically, an important question to ask is, what normally active neurochemicals might be related to such inhibitory deficits? Fortunately, Carlton and Manowitz (1987) have pointed out that a large number of studies have directly implicated a naturally occurring substance in just such an inhibitory role, i.e. seretonin (5-hydroxtryptamine, 5-HT). Knowledge of a physiological disposition leads directly to treatment implications. If there is a 5-HT deficit among pathological gamblers, the logical step would be to see if increasing 5-HT activity alleviates gambling problems. Fortunately, 5-HT can be increased pharmacologically either by oral doses of tryptophan – an amino acid which is required for the production of 5-HT – or by the use of drugs which can directly increase 5-HT activity (Carlton and Manowitz, 1987). Much research needs to be carried out before such tentative findings and treatment implications can be confirmed.

Another team of researchers led by Roy (Roy *et al.*, 1987; 1988; 1989) have investigated the psychobiological substrates of pathological gambling by measuring levels of noradrenaline, monoamine metabolites and peptides in cerebrospinal fluid, plasma and urine. Roy and his associates have reported that pathological gamblers had a signicantly higher centrally produced fraction of cerebrospinal fluid level of 3-methoxy-4 hydroxyphenolglycol (a chemical substrate thought to underlie impulsive behaviour), as well as significantly greater urinary outputs of noradrenaline than controls. It has been postulated that pathological gamblers may therefore have a functional disturbance of the noradrenergic system, i.e. the system that is thought to underlie sensation seeking behaviours (see Zuckerman, 1979; 1984).

Finally, it should be noted that there has been one recent study by Comings *et al.* (1994) which has put forward evidence that there may be a genetic basis for pathological gambling in some people. They reported that a variant of the dopamine D2 receptor gene (DRD2) – which has been associated with other addictions including some severe forms of alcoholism – was found in 51 per cent of pathological gamblers (n = 171) compared with 26 per cent of controls (n = 714). This finding was highly significant. They also reported that the gene variant was found in 64 per cent of the most severe pathological gamblers. Further to this, the results suggested that pathological gambling itself was closer to the core effect of the DRD2 gene than any other (addictive) behaviour. The authors argued that the genetic variants at the DRD2 gene play a significant role in pathological gambling and support the concept that variants of this gene are an important risk factor for impulsive and addictive behaviours.

Arousal theories

'Excitement' has often been referred to as the gambler's drug (e.g. Boyd, 1982). From psychophysiological studies it has been shown that there is a significant correspondence between the arousal a subject feels and reports, and the arousal that is so-called 'objectively' measured (Brown, 1989a). Although there has been a much reported link between excitement and gambling, until recently there was little empirical evidence to substantiate such claims. In fact, most experiments involving the monitoring of heart rate (as a measure of arousal) during gambling have found no heart rate increases (e.g. Rule and Fischer, 1970; Rule *et al.*, 1971). However, in a pioneering study by Anderson and Brown (1984), the question of ecological validity was raised. Anderson and Brown studied a group of regular gamblers and reported that their heart rates did not increase in laboratory conditions but did in field conditions, i.e. in the casino. This perhaps explains why studies on arousal during laboratory gambling have failed to find heart rate increases above baseline levels.

There is now limited empirical support for this assertion that regular gamblers become aroused during gambling. These studies (outlined in Table 1.4), which have used either heart rate measurement or self report, suggest that gambling is very exciting and that some form of arousal or excitement is a major, or *the* major reinforcer for regular gamblers (Brown, 1987a). Additionally, it has been suggested that the excitement is subjectively experienced and an objectively verifiable state of arousal, not sexual, but probably autonomic and/or cortical (Brown, 1987a). There is also an assumption that the gambler is not striving to win a fortune but aiming to maintain a phenomenological state of excitement and/or escape, i.e. an optimum level of arousal. It is also assumed that the excitement or

Table 1.4 Studies of arousal in gambling

Researcher	Type of gambler	n	Methodology	Finding
Wray and Dickerson (1981)	Gamblers Anonymous members	51	Retrospective self-report	70 per cent of gamblers feel very/extremely excited during gambling
Anderson and Brown (1984)	Blackjack players and undergraduates	24	Heart rate	Regular gamblers' heart rate increased by 23 bpm on average
Leary and Dickerson (1985)	Poker machine players	44	Heart rate	High frequency players' heart rate increased by 13.5 bpm
Dickerson and Adcock (1987)	Poker machine players	43	State-Trait Anxiety Questionnaire	On subjective ratings persistent gamblers were significantly more excited
Dickerson et al. (1987)	Off-course betters	36	State anxiety portion only	On subjective ratings persistent gamblers were significantly more excited
Brown (1988)	Fruit machine players	12	Heart rate	Players' heart rate increased to an average of 26.7 bpm above base-line after 9 minutes
Griffiths (1990a; 1991c) (*1994d*)	Fruit machine players	50 (*60*)	Self-report questionnaires	Pathological gamblers significantly more excited during gambling
Coulombe et al. (1992)	Poker machine players	24	Heart rate	Both regular and non-regular players increased heart rate by approximately 3 bpm during gambling
Huxley (1993)	Fruit machine players	38	Heart rate	Both regular and non-regular players increased heart rate by approximately 5 bpm during gambling
Griffiths (1993b)	Fruit machine players	30	Heart rate	Both regular and non-regular players increased heart rate by approximately 22 bpm during gambling

euphoria is addictive and that, since it is short-lived, it needs to be repeated (Boyd, 1982).

Endorphins and gambling

'The term endorphin (a combination of endogenous morphine) is used to designate the entire group of peptides found in the brain and pituitary that mimic the biological properties of opiates' (Blaszczynski and Winter, 1984, p.111) Recent studies have shown that pathological gambling may be opioid mediated. Pratt *et al.* (1982) measured the electrodermal activity of sociopaths and controls in a cold presser test in which subjects were asked to keep their feet immersed in ice cold water for as long as possible. Since all the sociopaths were recruited from Gamblers Anonymous, the study was as much a study on pathological gamblers as sociopaths. Pratt *et al.* found that pathological gamblers showed longer mean immersion times than controls and that they were less physiologically responsive to noxious stimulation. Pratt *et al.* concluded that endogenous opioids may underlie the effect.

In a more systematic experiment using radio immunassay techniques, Blaszczynski *et al.* (1986) measured baseline ß-endorphin plasma levels in pathological gamblers. In the experiment, blood samples were taken from thirty-nine pathological gamblers and thirty-five controls at various intervals in the day before, during and after gambling. It was found that pathological gamblers did not differ from controls on baseline ß-endorphin. However, when Blaszczysnki *et al.* differentiated the pathological gamblers according to gambling activity, it was found that horse-race addicts had significantly lower levels of ß-endorphin than poker machine players and controls. Blaszczynski *et al.* (1986) considered the possibility that horse-race gamblers may reduce dysphoric mood or intolerable stress-related tension by increasing ß-endorphin levels. This notion has some validity in that depressed patients have been treated successfully by ß-endorphin administration (Gerner *et al.*, 1980) although the evidence is not conclusive (Blaszczysnki and Winter, 1984). For poker machine players on the other hand, Blaszczynski *et al.* suggest that motivation may be related to a coping style allowing temporary escape from stress situations rather than the need to elevate deficient ß-endorphin levels. The failure of ß-endorphin levels to increase during gambling was explained by the failure of the relatively small bet (2–10 Australian dollars) to generate high arousal. This finding has two implications. The first is that pathological gamblers are probably not a homogeneous group and are unlikely to have the same psychological and biological disposition. Second, if pathological gambling *is* opioid mediated, it suggests that treatment of pathological gamblers might be helped by the pharmacological use of opiate antagonists. Although physiological explanations of pathological gambling are not the complete story, any comprehensive theory must be multivariate in nature and account for physiological factors and influences.

Psychiatric disorders among pathological gamblers

Having reviewed the physiological theories of pathological gambling, it is perhaps worth mentioning that there have been attempts to explore co-morbidity with other psychiatric disorders. It was mentioned in relation to psychodynamic theories that depression may be a major factor involved with gambling disorders (Israeli, 1935; Greenson, 1947) and again by Moran (1970c) as one of the five types of pathological gambler (i.e. the symptomatic type). However, it was not until a study by McCormick *et al.* (1984) that incidence of co-existent affective disorders was monitored. They found in a study involving fifty pathological gamblers that 76 per cent had a major depressive order, 38 per cent were hypomanic, 8 per cent manic and 2 per cent schizoaffective. The main problem involving the link between gambling and depression is the direction of causality; that is, which came first, the gambling or the depression? The study could not answer the question but it did indicate that gambling appeared to function as an 'anti-depressant', and showed that gambling was the only thing which could 'lift' the patients out of depression. Linden *et al.* (1984; 1986) reported in a study of twenty-five male GA members they interviewed that eighteen of their subjects (72 per cent) had experienced at least one major depressive episode and that eighteen subjects (72 per cent) had recurrent major affective episodes. There was also a fairly high rate (20 per cent) of panic disorder.

Further evidence that depression is a major problem for pathological gamblers appears in a number of studies by Blaszczynski and his associates using psychological measures of depression (Blaszczynski and McConaghy, 1988; 1989; Blaszczynski *et al.*, 1990). There are also a number of studies which have reported suicide attempts in approximately one in five pathological gamblers (Moran, 1969; Livingston, 1974; Custer and Custer, 1978; McCormick *et al.*, 1984). Logically, if pathological gamblers have co-existent depressive disorders, the use of anti-depressants could be utilized in treating pathological gambling. Both Mostkowitz (1980) and McCormick *et al.* (1984) have reported pharmacological success by giving lithium to pathological gamblers to reduce their impulsiveness and excitability.

Lesieur and Rosenthal (1991) have additionally pointed out that the high rate of other psychiatric disorders in pathological gamblers suggests a possibility that some of them had been treated for these disorders prior to the recognition that they had a gambling problem. Evidence from a number of studies does indeed suggest that between 24 per cent and 40 per cent of pathological gamblers have previously visited mental health professionals prior to their gambling. This finding has been reported among both male (Custer and Custer, 1978; Nora, 1984) and female populations (Lesieur, 1988b). Such findings suggest the need for screening of general psychiatric populations to locate individuals with gambling problems. One study by Lesieur and Blume (1990) found seven patients out of 105 (6.7 per cent) to be probable pathological gamblers.

Cognitive theories

Besides the psychoanalytic, behavioural, psychometric and biological approaches to behaviour, gambling can also be viewed from a cognitive standpoint. Although a single theory of the cognitive psychology of gambling is as unlikely as the other approaches outlined to fully explain persistent gambling, a number of recent studies show there may be a strong cognitive bias involved in gambling behaviour (e.g. Gilovich, 1983) and that gamblers may suffer from illusion of control (Langer, 1975) and other erroneous perceptions, i.e. reference to factors other than chance (Gaboury and Ladouceur, 1989). Psychological variables such as belief in luck and skill are also considered important (Furnham and Lewis, 1983; Wagenaar, 1988).

The illusion of control

Probably the most single influential contribution to the cognitive psychology of gambling was Langer's (1975) series of experiments on the illusion of control. Langer's hypotheses were based on the observations that some people treat chance events as controllable. For instance, Goffman (1967) reported that Las Vegas dealers who experienced runs of bad luck could easily lose their job. Further to this, Henslin (1967) studied dice-players and noticed they behaved as if they were controlling the outcome of the toss. This was confirmed when players threw the dice softly for low numbers and hard for high numbers. In an experimental investigation, Strickland *et al.* (1966) reported that when playing with dice, people bet less money and were less confident if asked to bet after someone else had thrown the dice rather than throwing it themselves, even though the probability of success was the same in both situations. Langer argued that these behaviours were rational if the player believed their game was a game of skill.

The illusion of control was defined by Langer (1975) as being 'an expectancy of a personal success inappropriately higher than the objective probability would warrant' (p.316). This was tested for experimentally in a series of studies which supported her original hypothesis, i.e. under some circumstances people will produce skill orientations towards chance events. Langer reported that subjects bet more when cutting cards against a 'nervous' competitor than against a 'confident' one, and that subjects would sell previously bought lottery tickets for a higher price if they had picked it themselves as opposed to having the ticket 'assigned' by someone else. Other experiments showed that certain factors such as the nature of the competition, the familiarity of the task and the degree of personal involvement influence the belief that skill is a controlling force. In essence, Langer's basic assumption was that in some chance settings, those conditions which involve factors of choice, familiarity, involvement and/or competition may stimulate the illusion of control to produce skill orientations. In a later study involving the prediction of 'heads' or 'tails' after a coin was tossed, Langer and Roth (1975) reported that early wins during chance games induced a skill orientation. A similar finding was reported by Reid (1986) using a rigged slot-machine.

Biased evaluations and erroneous perceptions

Oldman (1974) reported that some roulette players see their game as skilful and offer explanations of why they failed. This observation was later tested experimentally by Gilovich (1983) in a study of the biased evaluations in gambling behaviour. In three studies using people who bet on football games, Gilovich demonstrated that subjects transformed their losses into 'near wins'. Subjects pinpointed random or 'fluke' events that contributed to a loss but were unaffected by identical events that contributed to a win. It was also reported that subjects spent more time discussing their losses and discounting them in addition to 'bolstering' their wins. The same effects were also found in gambling activities (e.g. computerized bingo) in which losses could not easily be explained away (Gilovich and Douglas, 1986).

More recently, Gaboury and Ladouceur (1989) reported on the erroneous perceptions people produce while gambling. In two studies they evaluated the cognitive activities of subjects while they played either slot-machines or roulette using the 'thinking aloud' method. Analysis of the verbalizations revealed that erroneous perceptions of the games (80 per cent) far outnumbered the adequate perceptions. For instance, people attributed their success to personal factors such as skill, whereas external factors (such as bad luck) accounted for losses. Similar findings have been reproduced in other experiments by Ladouceur and his associates (Ladouceur and Gaboury, 1988; Ladouceur et al., 1988).

Cognitive regret and the psychology of the near miss

Reid (1986) noted that near misses, i.e. failures that are close to being successful, are believed to encourage future play, and that some commercial gambling activities (e.g. fruit machines and instant lotteries) are formulated to ensure a higher than chance frequency of near misses. Reid argued that at a behaviouristic level, a near miss may have the same kind of, conditioning effect on behaviour as a success. For example, a fruit machine pays out money (and thus reinforces play) when three winning symbols are displayed. However, a near miss e.g. two winning symbols and a third losing one, is still strongly reinforcing at no extra expense to the machine's owner. Thus, at a lower cognitive level a near miss could produce some of the excitement of a win (i.e. cognitive conditioning through secondary reinforcement). Reid pointed out that the near miss can also be explained in terms of Amsel's (1958) frustration theory. Basically, failing to fulfil a goal produces frustration which (according to the theory) strengthens ongoing behaviour. According to Kahneman and Tversky (1982), the frustration produced by 'nearly winning' induces a form of cognitive regret. Loftus and Loftus (1983) elaborated on this idea and suggested that the elimination of regret may be achieved by playing again, thus encouraging persistent play.

Heuristics and biases: an overview

Corney and Cummings (1985) pointed out in a review of information processing biases among gamblers that humans tend to exhibit rather consistent biases when cognitively processing information. Researchers interested in the cognitive psychology of gambling have traditionally worked on a single cognitive variable like those outlined above, but in seminal work by Wagenaar (1988) on gamblers' heuristics and biases, such researchers 'can probably never live in the same intellectual world again' (Brown, 1990; p.421). Wagenaar examined gambling within the context of a theory of cognitive processes comparing normative decision theory (and its derivatives) and heuristics and biases.

The basic postulate of normative decision theory is that every decision problem can be modelled as a choice among gambles. The theory claims that it can predict a rational decision maker's preference for gambles (Wagenaar, 1988). However, there are some major considerations. Although hypothetically such a theory can predict future choices, in reality it rarely does – probably because most regular gamblers are in some way irrational. Furthermore, the theory would predict that people would not gamble in the first place (Wagenaar, 1988)! Massaro (1990) has additionally pointed out that normative decision theory is based on long run expectancies which do not make sense for single gambles. Wagenaar's thesis is that gamblers are 'motivated by a way of reasoning, not by defects of personality, education or social environment' (p.30) and that 'gamblers gamble, not because they have a bigger repertoire of heuristics, but because they select heuristics at the wrong occasions' (pp.116-17). Heuristics have the effect of reducing uncertainty and Wagenaar outlines an inexhaustive summary of sixteen such cognitive distortions which he believes can operate in gambling situations (see Table 1.5). Probably the most salient cognitive distortions are those outlined already in the work of Langer ('illusion of control') and Gilovich ('hindsight bias' and 'flexible attributions') as well as those to be outlined below such as the 'availability bias', 'the representativeness bias', 'illusory correlations' and 'fixation on absolute frequency'.

Representativeness (sometimes called 'the gambler's fallacy') applies to random samples of data and is where people expect to find a representative relationship between samples drawn from a population and the population itself (Tversky and Kahneman, 1971). For instance, when subjects are asked to create a random sequence of imaginary coin tosses, they tend to produce sequences where the proportion of tails in a short segment is closer to 0.5 than chance would predict (Tune, 1964). The erroneous processing of information by means of the representiveness bias leads to a number of improper judgements listed below (cf. Corney and Cummings, 1985):

1 Small samples are highly representative of the populations from which they come (Tune, 1964; Tversky and Kahneman, 1973).
2 Samples that have come from a restricted setting or environment are representative of data that come from a larger setting or environment (Jones and Nisbett, 1971).
3 Deviations of results from expectancies have a causal explanation; i.e. sampling variability does not exist (Tversky and Kahneman, 1971).
4 Extreme values generated from a purely random sequence will be cancelled by future values (Estes, 1964).

The availability bias occurs when a person evaluating the probability of a chance event makes the judgement in terms of the ease with which relevant instances or associations come to mind. For instance, pools winners are highly publicized to invoke the idea that big wins are regular and commonplace, when in fact they are rare. Illusory correlations are superstitious behaviours where people believe variables co-vary when in fact they do not. A good example of this was the study by Henslin (1967, mentioned

Table 1.5 Summary of heuristics and biases used by gamblers

Heuristic	Brief definition
Availability	The ease with which specific instances can be recalled from memory, thus affecting probability judgements
Problem framing	When the context in which the problem is framed determines the choice of strategy
Confirmation bias	Seeking information that is consistent with one's own views and discounting disconfirming information
Fixation on absolute frequency	Using absolute rather than relative frequency is used as a measure of success
Concrete information bias	When concrete information such as that based on vivid memories or conspicuous incidents dominates abstract information such as computations or statistical data
Illusory correlation	Variables that seem to co-vary when in fact they do not
Inconsistency of processing	The inability to apply a consistent judgemental strategy over a series of cases
Non-linear extrapolation	The difficulty in estimating joint probabilities of simple events
Reliance on habits	The choosing of alternatives because it is customary to do so
Representativeness	The judgement of the likelihood of an event made by estimating its similarity to the class of which the event is supposed to be an exemplar
Justifiability	When the justifiable rule is preferred over a rule for which no justification can be given
Reduction of complexity	When complete decision problems are reduced to simple ones before a decision can be made
Illusion of control	When uncertain outcome of an activity can by itself induce in a person feelings of control over the uncertain outcome
Biased learning structures	When observed outcomes yield incomplete information concerning predictive relationships
Flexible attribution	The tendency to attribute successes to one's own skill and failures to other influences
Hindsight bias	When retrospectively people are not surprised about what has happened and even believe they predicted the outcome

Source: Adapted from Wagenaar, 1988

previously) on dice-players who rolled the dice softly for low numbers and harder for higher ones. Fixation on absolute frequency refers to when people measure success using the absolute rather than the relative frequency of wins. Such people do in fact win a lot compared with most other people, but because they gamble so much they actually lose more than they win.

These cognitive 'bags of tricks' (Wagenaar, 1988) do give some insight into why gamblers do not learn from their past losses and help to explain supposedly 'irrational' behaviour in the gambling process. However, unlike normative decision theory, heuristics and biases have no predictive value. It is almost impossible to know which heuristic will be applied in a given situation and it is quite possible for the same person to use a different heuristic in the same situation on different occasions.

Psychologically based addiction theories

As Dickerson (1989) points out, it is not hard to understand the initial resistance to classifying pathological gambling as an addiction. A number of authors (e.g. Walker, 1989; Rachlin, 1990) have questioned how a behaviour can be addictive in the absence of a psychoactive agent. Many people's conceptions of what constitutes an addiction come from the term 'drug addiction' (Walker, 1989) and most traditional definitions verbalize this distinction, for example, 'an addiction is the state of being given up to some habit, especially strong dependence on a drug' (*Standard Medical Dictionary*). However, many leading authorities now view non-drug habitual behaviours (e.g. pathological gambling, overeating and compulsive sexuality) as bona fide addictions (Peele, 1979; Miller, 1980; Mule, 1981; Levison *et al.*, 1983; Orford, 1985). Perhaps one of the best definitions of addictive behaviour is that of Marlatt *et al.* (1988):

> a repetitive habit pattern that increases the risk of disease and/or associated personal and social problems. Addictive behaviours are often experienced subjectively as 'loss of control' – the behaviour contrives to occur despite volitional attempts to abstain or moderate use. These habit patterns are typically characterized by immediate gratification (short term reward), often coupled with delayed, deleterious effects (long term costs). Attempts to change an addictive behaviour (via treatment or self initiation) are typically marked with high relapse rates.
>
> (p.224)

Although the *DSM-III* and *DSM-III-R* definitional diagnoses of pathological gambling come under the heading 'disorders of impulse control', the updated *DSM-III-R* criteria were specifically modelled after those for psychoactive substance dependence. All the criteria (see Table 1.2), with the exception of criterion 5 ('chasing losses'), have their counterpart in the diagnosis of alcohol, heroin, cocaine and other forms of drug dependence (Lesieur and Rosenthal, 1991). While pathological gambling does not involve the ingestion of a substance, numerous researchers have noted its similarity to other addictive behaviour, e.g. withdrawal symptoms on the cessation of gambling (Wray and Dickerson, 1981), dependence (Moran, 1970b) and tolerance (Dickerson, 1984). Custer (1975) has gone as far as calling pathological gambling the 'purest addiction' because no external drug is administered to the biological system.

It is reasonable to assume that many aspects of physical substance abuse (e.g. alcohol/other drugs) and habitual activities (e.g. gambling, overeating) might have common biological, psychological and/or social roots (Jacobs, 1985). Although many people disagree over matters such as exact causation and treatment, many agree that low self regard or rejection by others is an important factor in substance addiction (Milkman and Sunderworth, 1983; Jacobs, 1985). They may also play a part in gambling addiction.

To date, only two studies (Blaszczynski *et al.*, 1985; Hickey *et al.*, 1986) have compared pathological gambling with pharmacological addictions on psychological measures. Blaszczynski and his colleagues used Gossop and Eysenck's (1980) thirty-two item addiction scale (derived from the EPQ) and hypothesized that pathological gamblers would show similar profiles to substance addicts (in this case heroin users). Their hypothesis was confirmed. Male addicts showed significantly elevated addiction, neuroticism and psychoticism scores as compared with controls, while female addicts showed significantly elevated addiction and psychoticism scores as compared with controls. They concluded that as items on the addiction scale are loaded with anxiety and depression components, the similarities obtained between substance addicts and pathological gamblers may have reflected a general factor of affective disturbance. Their finding that pathological gamblers showed a similar profile to heroin users strengthens the 'gambling as an addiction' argument. As mentioned earlier in the chapter, elevated 'psychopathic deviate' and 'depression' scores have been found on the MMPI (Bolen *et al.*, 1975; Lowenfeld, 1979). They also occur in heroin addicts (Craig, 1979), alcoholics, criminals and shoplifters (Beck and McIntyre, 1977), again supporting the notion that an affective disturbance links gamblers and substance addicts.

Hickey *et al.* (1986) looked at the commonalities between pathological gambling and psychoactive drug abuse using the Addiction Research Center Inventory (ARCI) (Haertzen, 1974). The basic idea was to compare the subjective effects of pathological gambling with the subjective effects of drugs. The ARCI (a 600 item true / false questionnaire) was administered to nineteen pathological gambling volunteers. They were then asked to complete the test, (a) while at rest and then (b) while simulating how they felt during winning at gambling. Their main finding was that simulated winning at gambling produced immediate subjective effects similar to the effects of drug abuse, particularly psychomotor stimulants. Again the conclusion was similar to that of Blaszczynski *et al.* (1985), in that pathological gambling shared critical commonalities with drug dependence.

Neuropeptides have been implicated in the acquisition of addictive behaviours (Snyder, 1975; Van Ree, 1983), and Blaszczynski *et al.* (1985; 1986b) noted that the body's own endogenous opioids (endorphins) can produce effects similar to exogenous opioids such as morphine, producing analgesia, euphoria, tolerance and physical dependence. Blaszczynski and his colleagues hypothesized that the reinforcing 'high' (euphoria) that is associated with gambling could be related to endorphin release and that therefore on cessation of gambling withdrawal effects occur due to an endorphin deficiency (see page 18 for a more detailed account).

Anderson and Brown (1984), unhappy that Skinnerian reinforcement theory could not account for the phenomenology of pathological gambling (especially relapse after abstinence), postulated a model concentrating upon individual differences in cortical and autonomic arousal in combination with irregular reinforcement schedules. This neo-Pavlovian model, in which arousal has a central role, plays an important role in the addiction process. According to Anderson and Brown (1984), this model accounts for reinstatement after abstinence and allows for the maintenance of the behaviour by internal mood / state / arousal cues in addition to external situation cues.

Although there are many theories of addiction, it is interesting to note that some of these theories are being developed from experiences with pathological gamblers. For instance, Jacobs' (1985) 'general theory of addictions' has hypothesized a general dissociative state common to all addictions and he and his researchers have found support for it (Jacobs, 1988; Kuley and Jacobs, 1988). Anderson and Brown (1987), employing arousal and reversal theory in explaining gambling addiction and relapse, put forward another general addictions approach. The basic proposition is that pathological gamblers switch from highly aroused to highly anxious states during the course of gambling (and vice versa). These states of arousal and reversal occur in telic (goal orientated) and paratelic (playful) states, in which cognitive processes (telic) and physiological processes (paratelic) are both considered. Anderson and Brown (1987) hypothesize:

The pathological gambler who, having begun with high arousal in an unpleasant telic state, may continue to gamble in the face of the most distressing anxiety. This may be because he has learned to associate the high arousal in the telic state of losing with the anticipation of the subsequent powerful reward in pleasurable excitement when eventually that high arousal will be interpreted after a win and a reversal to the paratelic state.

(p.189)

The theories outlined in this chapter are by no means exhaustive but do cover the main areas of psychological concern. The other main types of theory that the reader may be directed to are those from either a sociological perspective (e.g. Oldman, 1978; Hayano, 1982; Lesieur, 1984; Rosecrance, 1986; Ocean and Smith, 1993) or an economic / decision-making perspective (e.g. Eadington, 1987; Mobilia, 1993).

Gambling: the eclectic approach

It is clear that for any model or theory of gambling to be complete it must not only feature the sociological roots, the underlying physiological mechanisms and the psychological factors, but also provide a framework from which a non-gambler may eventually become pathological, and yet most importantly, be able to differentiate 'normal' or 'social' gamblers from those who gamble to excess. There have been a number of universal models of gambling (e.g. Moran, 1970c; Abt *et al.*, 1985) but perhaps the most comprehensive is that of Brown (1986a), who incorporated components from psychoanalytic, behaviouristic, physiological, sociological and psychological theories into an integrated eclectic model.

Brown (1986a) believes that any model should consist of a cross-sectional view, i.e. 'important groups of variables or "components" in the development and maintenance of gambling behaviour, whether addictive or not' (p.109) and a longitudinal view, i.e. the stages of acquisition and development of gambling behaviour in different 'sub-types' of gamblers. Brown lists eight cross-sectional variables (subcultural conditions, psycho-physiological arousal needs, behavioural reinforcement schedules, internal fantasy object relations, cognitive variables, affective factors, significant external relationships and social and institutional determinants) and four developmental stages (induction, adoption, promotion and addiction), all of which will now be briefly discussed (see also Table 1.5).

Cross-sectional variables

Subcultural conditions

This group of variables is basically made up of the sociological components which determine whether a person will gamble in the first place. Factors include the available opportunities to gamble (either during the individuals' occupation and/or leisure, etc.); social pressures to gamble from relatives, friends and work colleagues; an absence of a better alternative way of spending time; whether gambling provides a better opportunity for material gain than other options; the attitudes towards gambling not only from individual referents and groups, but also from the society itself. As Cornish (1978) notes, the initial decision to gamble is nearly always due to sociological motives.

Psychophysiological arousal needs

This group of variables stems from the work of Anderson and Brown (1984) in which the adoption of gambling depends on the individual's arousal level preference. Given Brown's (1986a) view that individuals seek an 'optimum level of arousal', gambling provides a mechanism of arousal change that could be seen as self-regulating. Frey (1984) has also argued that gambling serves its purpose as a 'safety-valve mechanism', i.e. tension management in a socially acceptable manner ultimately relieving stress and strain.

Behavioural reinforcement schedules

This group of variables produces resistance to extinction from gambling behaviour. This is achieved by irregular reinforcements on variable ratio schedules, e.g. money (Skinner, 1953), regular reinforcements on fixed interval schedules, e.g. arousal in a simple fixed pattern of short-term events when betting (Dickerson, 1979) or even long-term reinforcement based on periods of high arousal at induction of gambling in which the individual tries to reinstate initial arousal effects (Anderson and Brown, 1984).

Internal fantasy object relations

This group of variables stems from the postulations of the psychodynamic theorists and includes the felt and imagined status of the gambler. In addition, psychic confrontation with parents or figures such as 'Lady Luck' apparently occur and attempts are made (through gambling) to test out, change or manipulate the relationship.

Cognitive variables

This group of variables is concerned with the ways in which gamblers distort the perceptions of their gambling (and are described in more detail in Table 1.5). These are sufficient to show that psychological factors can influence the way in which people gamble and continue to gamble.

Affective factors

This group of variables consists of negative emotional states including anxiety and depression. For instance, an anxious person may act in a chaotic and uncertain manner as if to 'justify' the anxiety in much the same way as a depressed person will go to funerals because 'their habitual feeling patterns become socially acceptable' (Brown, 1986a; p.1010).

Significant external relationships

This group of variables involves external relationships (e.g. spouse, children, friends, etc.) and uses gambling as a means to gain power, status, security and affection.

Social and institutional determinants

This group of variables has been extensively covered by Lesieur (1979), and consists of the gambler's ever more limiting and constricting 'spiral of options' of obtaining money to recoup his losses by gambling.

It is unlikely that the cross sectional variables outlined above have equal weighting in the acquisition, development and maintenance of gambling behaviour, and it is almost certain that every individual will be different in the details of which variables affect them the most in maintaining the behaviour. This implies that (i) gamblers are *not* a relatively homogenous group, i.e. there *are* sub-types of gamblers, and (ii) that the various factors mentioned do *not* have a constant relative importance, i.e. importance of variables changes at different times and in different people.

Longitudinal dimensions

From what has been reviewed of Brown's model so far, it should be obvious that the variables outlined above are more important at some points in a gambler's development than others. Brown has proposed that a gambler progresses through four stages: induction, adoption, promotion and addiction. Below is a brief summary of the relative importance of the cross-sectional variables in the context of this longitudinal view.

1 Induction

The initial decision to gamble, the age at which the gambler begins, the type of gambling activity, etc. are almost certainly most dependent on the sociological factors outlined under subcultural conditions (1).

2 Adoption

The rejection or adoption of gambling in an individual's behavioural repertoire probably depends most on psychophysiological arousal needs (2) and behavioural reinforcement schedules (3), but other components may begin to show influence at this stage.

3 Promotion

Dominance of gambling activity in one's leisure time will almost certainly be dependent on all the cross-sectional variables with the exception of the desperation variables (social and institutional determinants (8)).

4 Addiction

Again, all components in the cross-sectional outlook exert an influence in addiction to gambling, but it is hard to say exactly when a 'normal' or 'social' gambler becomes a pathological gambler. The most important variables at this stage of development are the social and institutional determinants (8) which highlight 'the chase' (Lesieur, 1979; 1984).

In summary of Brown's (1986a) postulations, it appears that the gambler is at first influenced by sociological factors, e.g. attitudes and habits of parents, friends, peer groups, etc. as well as a lack of viable alternatives to gambling activity. During the middle stages of development, any number of factors can heavily influence the maintenance of gambling behaviour, whether they be of physiological, psychological or social origin. Persistent gambling eventually leads to a desperate 'spiral of options' and the variables affecting behaviour become limited.

As we have seen throughout this chapter, gambling is a complex, multi-dimensional activity that is unlikely to be explained by any single theory. Although eclectic approaches to the understanding of various human behaviours are often criticized, it does appear that explanations of gambling behaviour (and particularly excessive gambling) are best served by an integrated biopsychosocial model which stresses the individuality and idiosyncratic nature of the development of gambling problems. The one major problem with most empirical research on gambling behaviour is that it has been primarily involved with adult populations. It could be that adolescent gambling is in some way different and that alternative explanations and accounts are needed. I base the book on this consideration. An overview of the adolescent gambling literature is discussed in Chapter 2.

2 Adolescent gambling

An overview

Until recently, most sources viewed gambling as an 'adult' activity because of its legal restrictions (Ide-Smith and Lea, 1988). However, adolescent gambling is widespread. There has been little systematic research into the area and those studies that have been reported have nearly all used self-report questionnaires. The literature concerning child and adolescent gambling falls into a number of general categories. These are:

(a) Prevalence studies and case studies concerning adolescent gambling in general;
(b) studies of the economic socialization of children;
(c) studies of 'gambling as play' and games as precursors to gambling;
(d) empirical studies of risk taking and gambling-like behaviour in children;
(e) studies of particular forms of adolescent gambling (almost all exclusively fruit machine gambling).

Each of these areas will be examined in turn in this chapter.

PREVALENCE STUDIES OF ADOLESCENT GAMBLING

At the time I began my own empirical work in this area, the prevalence of adolescent gambling had only been reported in six studies (i.e. Rosenstein and Reutter, 1980; Amati, 1981; Arcuri et al., 1985; Lesieur and Klein, 1987; Ide-Smith and Lea, 1988; Ladouceur and Mireault, 1988) and one of these (Amati, 1981) was concerned with juvenile delinquents only. In 1989, I published a literature review on adolescent gambling (Griffiths, 1989) almost simultaneously with one by Jacobs (1989). There was little cross-over between the two reviews, chiefly because Jacobs made heavy reference to four unpublished studies (mainly by his own research team) and largely neglected non-American studies. Since then, a number of other studies have been published and again the main findings of these can also be found in Table 2.1. Brief summaries of the major studies will be outlined.

In 1980, Rosenstein and Reutter reported the fact that there were no studies on the incidence of adolescent gambling. As a consequence, they subsequently administered a questionnaire to 164 students (eighty male and eighty-four female American high school seniors) on adolescent gambling involvement and attitudes towards gambling. They found that, overall, 78 per cent approved of legalized gambling, and that 61 per cent of males and 38 per cent of females had gambled at some point in their lives. Only 41 per cent of males and 65 per cent of females described themselves as non-gamblers. Twenty one point seven per cent of males had once bet more than US$50 at one time. Significant sex differences were found in all gambling factors, the main one being that males gambled more than females. The main types of gambling reported by Rosenstein and Reutter are outlined in Table 2.1.

Amati (1981) investigated the recreational activities in a group of 136 Indian 7 to 16-year-old male juvenile delinquents. He noted that the distinction between recreation and deviance is somewhat blurred, and that so-called adolescent deviant behaviours (e.g. smoking, drinking and gambling) tended to appear in a cluster rather than occur singly. Amati's research suggested a pattern in which acquisition of gambling behaviour occurred primarily due to 'personal enjoyment', but that maintenance of the activity was sustained by a number of factors, most notably positive material gain and resentment and defiance of authority (both parental and institutional). Continued gambling also occurred when the losers were forced to gamble in the expectation of getting back the money they had lost ('the chase'). Amati reported that 39 per cent of his sample gambled regularly and that only 32 per cent of the boys said they *never* gambled. Fifty-six per cent of the boys reported that parents offered no objection to these 'habits'.

Two types of gambling constituted nearly all the gambling activity, these being cards (57 per cent) and an individualized number game called the *Matka* (30 per cent). Those who played cards carried with them a pack at all times, as they were necessary at any time or any place. Material gain was the most potent factor in maintenance of card-playing behaviour. The *Matka*, however, provided an element of thrill and an intense expectation which was not experienced when playing cards, and it became clear to Amati that positive material gain was only a small factor in sustaining the behaviour. Finally, Amati described gambling as a 'group activity' and a 'group phenomenon', asserting that gambling was a recreational activity

Table 2.1 Summary of questionnaire studies on adolescent gambling

Researcher(s)	Place of study	Age(s) of sample	No. in sample	% Gamblers (last 12 months)	Regular gamblers %	Main types of gambling	% Gambling at type	Comments
Rosenstein and Reutter (1980)	USA	High school students	164	49.3	22	Card games Sporting events Horse racing	56 49 39	
Amati (1981)	India	7–16	136	68	39	Card games Number games	57 30	Delinquent males only
Arcuri et al. (1985)	USA (Pennsylvania)	14–19	332	64	9	Slot-machines Blackjack	66 21	Casino gambling only
Jacobs et al. (1985)	USA (California)	14–18	843	20	4	(Not reported)		
Jacobs et al. (1987)	USA (California)	14–18	257	45	6	Card games Lottery Skill games	40 40 33	
Jacob and Kuley (1987)	USA (Virginia)	14–18	212	40	10	Card games Skill games Lottery	36 30 27	
Leiseur and Klein (1987)	USA	High school students	892	86	32	Card games Casino gambling Lottery Sporting events	49 46 45 45	5.7% showed characteristics of pathological gambling
Steinberg (1988)	USA (Connecticut)	14–18	573	60 (ever)		Card games Bingo Lottery	66 66 51	9% committed illegal acts to pay gambling debts

Study	Country	Sample/Age	N	%	%	Games	Comments
Frank (1988)	USA (Pennsylvania)	College students	200	59		Slot-machines 64 Blackjack 24	Casino gambling only
Ide-Smith and Lea (1988)	England (Devon)	13–14	50	89		Slot-machines 81 Card games 53 Wagers 51 Coin games 26	
Ladouceur and Mireault (1988)	Canada (Quebec)	14–19	1612	65	23	Lotteries 60 Sporting events 45 Card games 35	5.6% admitted they could not stop gambling even if they wanted to and 1.7% self confessed pathological gamblers
Lesieur et al. (1991)	USA (5 states)	16–57	1771	85		Slot-machines 54 Card games 51 Casino games 49 Sporting events 46	15% experienced 'gambling problems'. Rates of pathological gambling ranged from 4% in Nevada to 8% in New York
Winters et al. (1993a)	USA (Minnesota)	15–18	702	86	4.6–6.4	Card games 50 Skill games 40 Sporting events 37	8.7% classed as 'problem gamblers'
Winters et al. (1993b)	USA (Minnesota)	15–18	1101	89	8.3	(Not specified)	This study includes the data from the study above
Deverensky et al.	Canada (Quebec)	9–14	104	70	53	(Not specified)	This study was part of a larger experimental study
Oster and Knapp (1994)	USA (Nevada)	University students	544	92	22	Video poker 83(m)/72(f) Cards/horses 82(m)/46(f) Slot-machines 78(m)/77(f)	11.2% classed as pathological gamblers using the South Oaks Gambling Screen (SOGS)
			350	91	24	Video poker 81(m)/71(f) Casino gambling 80(m)/0(f) Slot-machines 77(m)/76(f)	8% classed as pathological gamblers using the SOGS; 5.7% classed as pathological gamblers using the DSM-III-R (1987) criteria

with social boundaries. Gambling (like most activities) was an activity to be learned, and in this case learned from within a peer group.

In 1985, Arcuri *et al.* conducted a survey in Atlantic City (USA) exploring the incidence of casino gambling by adolescents. Their main focus was an interest in the importance and impact of legalized gambling on the community's adolescents. Teenage gambling was explored to determine whether the activity was a dangerous behaviour that may escalate as an adult. Arcuri *et al.*'s (1985) sample consisted of 332 students from Atlantic City High School's 2,452 population. Students were selected from four grades and the results showed that 64 per cent gambled in the casinos, 21 per cent had visited the casino more than ten times and 9 per cent gambled at least once a week. As in the Amati (1981) study, parents showed little concern over their children's gambling and 79 per cent of students reported that their parents knew they gambled.

The two major types of gambling in adolescents were slot machines (66 per cent) and blackjack (21 per cent), and these were played because they involved the least cash outlay and were the least conspicuous. The authors concluded that the casinos in Atlantic City were a convenient temptation to teenagers and provided adolescents with a possible 'pathway out of poverty' in the form of obtaining a substantial win at the casino. Later that year Arcuri and his team of colleagues (Lester *et al.*, 1985) reported that a small percentage of students attended particular colleges because of their close proximity to gambling outlets, i.e. 4 per cent of 554 students at Stockton State College and 2 per cent of 216 students at Atlantic Community College attended these institutions because they were situated near to a casino. Further to this, Arcuri and his colleagues were also the first team of researchers to suggest that in some adolescents, gambling may be pathological. In conversations with the Atlantic High School counsellor, it was reported that the counsellor knew of forty-seven students who suffered a severe gambling problem and of these known cases 12 per cent used lunch money, 6 per cent shoplifted and 3 per cent sold drugs to raise money. In addition, most of the 'problem' gamblers missed school and were truants, and two students had lost thousands of dollars and had turned to crime to recover their losses.

Lesieur and Klein (1987) specifically looked at the problem of pathological gambling in adolescent teenagers. In a questionnaire given to 892 American high school students, they reported that 91 per cent of their samples had at some time gambled, that 86 per cent had gambled within the last year and that 32 per cent were gambling at least once a week. A worrying aspect was that 5.7 per cent of the students showed clear signs of pathological gambling (as outlined in the *DSM-III*) and that these signs were correlated with:

(i) *Sex*, i.e. 9.5 per cent of the males in the sample but only 2 per cent of the females were probable pathological gamblers.

(ii) *Parental gambling problems*, i.e. one or both of the pathological gamblers' parents had 'gambling problems' or 'gambled too much'.

(iii) *School grade average*, i.e. the pathological gamblers' grades were lower.

(iv) *Extent of gambling*, i.e. the pathological gamblers gambled at most opportunities.

It was also reported that social class, religion and schooling were weakly correlated to pathological gambling.

Ladouceur and Mireault (1988) administered a French translation of the questionnaire designed by Lesieur and Klein (1987) to 1,612 French Canadian (14-19 years old) from nine high schools in the region of Quebec City. The results revealed that 76 per cent had gambled once in their lifetime and that 65 per cent had done so within the last year. Twenty-four per cent of their sample reported that they gambled at least once a week, 5.6 per cent reported they wanted to stop playing but could not, while a further 1.7 per cent considered themselves to be pathological gamblers. The three most popular games were lotteries (60 per cent), sports betting (45 per cent) and card games (36 per cent). The gambling itself took place with both family members (61 per cent with parents, 57 per cent with siblings and 50 per cent with other relatives) and with friends (82 per cent), with a total of 8.9 per cent of teenage respondents reporting that they had committed illegal activities to finance their gambling (e.g. stealing money, selling drugs, etc.). In essence, many of their findings echoed those of Lesieur and Klein (1987).

A study carried out by Ide-Smith and Lea (1988) was the first British survey of adolescent gambling but used a very small sample of only fifty adolescents from an Exeter secondary school. The authors noted that a priori there are two routes by which gambling behaviour may be initiated. First, because of legislative change, children are constantly exposed to adult gambling by parents, relatives and older friends and frequently see betting shops, advertisements for commercial gambling (e.g. football pools) and low stake slot-machines. Second, gambling and its precursors may be present within the autonomous structure and culture of children's games. The second possibility will be looked at in greater depth later in this chapter.

Pilot work by the authors had indicated that gambling was widespread among adolescents but was virtually non-existent in 9 year olds; thus the questionnaire was given to a sample of young teenagers aged 13 to 14 years old. Results again showed a high percentage of adolescent gamblers. Ide-Smith and Lea reported that 89 per cent of their sample had gambled at some point in their lives (93 per cent of boys and 84 per cent of girls) and that the most common form of gambling was slot-machines (81 per cent) (as in the American study by Arcuri *et al.*, 1985) followed by card games (53 per cent), wagers (51 per cent) and coin games (26 per cent). Subjects reported gambling from a young age with boys starting at 8 years 3 months and girls starting at 8 years 9 months. Most of the sample claimed they had gambled by the age of 10 years old. In line with previous studies, sex differences were found in every type of gambling. Ide-Smith and Lea noted that boys might possibly tend to 'over-report' and girls to 'under-report', but argued that even such a reporting difference would mean that gambling is in fact part of a boy's culture and not part of a girl's. No significant differences were found in intelligence and social status in relation to gambling.

At the beginning of this chapter it was noted that a number of un-published US studies on adolescent gambling were reported in a review by Jacobs (1989). The three unpublished studies by Jacobs and his associates (Jacobs *et al.*, 1985; 1987; Jacobs and Kuley, 1987 – see Table 2.1) reported that between 20 per cent and 45 per cent of adolescents had gambled within the last year and that 4 per cent to 10 per cent did so on a weekly basis or more. Between 30 per cent and 41 per cent of these adolescents gambled before they were 11 years old, perhaps indicating that they did so with parental consent. The favourite games that teenagers played for money (in rough order of preference) were card games with families or friends (approximately 45 per cent), the state lottery (ap-proximately 43 per cent), games of skill, e.g. pool (approximately 34 per cent) and sports betting (approximately 30 per cent). This contrasts with the studies of Frank (1988) and Lesieur *et al.* (1991) – also outlined in Table 2.1 – who report slot-machines to be the number one gambling preference. However, it must be noted that Frank's study was concerned with casino gambling only, and therefore gambling activities such as lotteries and sports betting were not included.

The study by Lesieur *et al.* (1991) is the largest study to date in the US and surveyed students from six colleges and universities in five American states (New York, New Jersey, Oklahoma, Texas and Nevada). Although the study was not strictly concerned with adolescents it contained a large (unspecified) number of adolescents among its sample. The sample consisted of 1,771 students, of which 56 per cent were female and 44 per cent male. The main results of this study are reproduced in Table 2.2 (percentage of gambling among college students by state), Table 2.3 (percentage of weekly gambling among college students by state) and Table 2.4 (maximum wagers and percentages of problem and pathological gamblers by state).

Table 2.2 Gambling among college students by state (percentages)

Type of gambling	New York (n = 446)	New Jersey (n = 227)	Nevada (n = 219)	Oklahoma (n = 583)	Texas (n = 299)	5-State average
Playing cards for money	53	54	53	53	42	51
Bet on horses, dogs	29	41	30	32	22	31
Sports betting	28	35	31	23	28	29
Dice games	21	25	33	18	23	24
Casino games	39	75	84	27	20	49
Numbers or lotteries	69	66	42	30	20	46
Bingo	43	39	38	45	49	43
Stocks/commodities	15	23	19	18	18	19
Slot/poker machines	50	74	83	35	27	54
Pool, bowling, games of skill	40	51	41	43	42	44
Any gambling at all	90	92	91	78	75	85

Source: From Lesieur *et al.*, 1991

Table 2.3 Weekly gambling among college students by state (percentages)

Type of gambling	New York (n = 446)	New Jersey (n = 227)	Nevada (n = 219)	Oklahoma (n = 583)	Texas (n = 299)	5-State average
Playing cards for money	5	6	8	1.5	2	5
Bet on horses, dogs	3	2	1	1	0.4	1.4
Sports betting	5	3	5	2	3	3.5
Dice games	2	3	2	1	0.5	2
Casino games	3	6	29	0.5	0	8
Numbers or lotteries	14	12	4	1	1	6
Bingo	3	2	1	1	1	1.6
Stocks/commodities	3	4	7	2	2	4
Slot/poker machines	4	4.5	16	1	0.6	5
Pool, bowling, games of skill	12	11	8	7	8	9
Any weekly gambling at all	27	28	39	12	11	23

Source: From Lesieur *et al.*, 1991

Table 2.4 Maximum wager, pathological and problem gambling by state (percentages)

	New York (n = 446)	New Jersey (n = 227)	Nevada (n = 219)	Oklahoma (n = 583)	Texas (n = 299)	5-State average
Gambled with more than $10 in one day	41	57	55	36	33	44
Gambled with more than $100 in one day	12	13	19	8	6	12
Problem gamblers	18	16	16	11	12	15
Pathological gamblers	8	6	4	5	5	5.5

Source: From Lesieur *et al.*, 1991

Using the South Oaks Gambling Screen (SOGS) – a valid and reliable instrument for the identification of pathological gamblers – Lesieur *et al.* reported that 15 per cent of the students experienced some problems connected with gambling and that 5.5 per cent of the students scored in the pathological range of the SOGS (i.e. they scored five or more on the index). Those students diagnosed as pathological gamblers were significantly more likely to be male and to have parents who were problem gamblers or had other problems (e.g. drug abuse). Scores on the SOGS were significantly correlated with tobacco use, alcohol use, getting drunk, illegal drug use and arrests for non-traffic offences. Further to this, SOGS scores were negatively correlated with grade point average.

To date, almost all studies of adolescent gambling have reported gambling related problems among adolescents (e.g. harmed relationship with family, committing illegal acts to get gambling money or to pay gambling debts, disruption of school or work activities, truanting, etc.). However, these are admittedly in small minorities. A figure of 5 per cent or more probable pathological gamblers was found in the studies by Lesieur and Klein (1987); Ladouceur and Mireault (1988); Steinberg (1988); Frank (1988); Lesieur *et al.* (1991); Winters *et al.* (1993a; b); and Oster and Knapp (1994). These figures are much higher than the adult population but could be related to the fact that on the whole, chronological age is negatively related to gambling (Li and Smith, 1976; Kallick *et al.*, 1979; Mok and Hraba, 1991). Jacobs did not report if there were any sex differences in the review of his team's studies but other subsequent studies have all indicated significant sex differences with males gambling more often than females (e.g. Lesieur *et al.*, 1991; Winters *et al.*, 1993a; b; Oster and Knapp, 1994). Such a finding has even been found in younger children (e.g. Deverensky *et al.*, 1994). Other factors identified in more recent studies that have been linked with problem gambling in adolescents include poor grades at school, parents who gamble, regular drug use and history of delinquency (Lesieur *et al.*, 1991; Winters *et al.*, 1993a; Oster and Knapp, 1994). Such findings essentially confirm correlational data from earlier studies.

CASE STUDIES OF ADOLESCENT GAMBLERS

There have been only two other direct studies of adolescent gambling, both of which were essentially case studies and both over thirty years old. Kiell (1956) reported on 'The behaviour of five adolescents while playing poker'. In this study he observed the interactions of three 15-year-old and two 16-year-old boys while they were playing poker. His conclusions are perhaps best summarized by himself:

> The sub-surface habits, whether verbal or physical, which these ad-olescents brought to the poker table, are essentially those which they bring to the dinner table, the classroom, their other play. They are part of the maturative process. When the adolescent approached the card table, he brought his 'inner manliness' with him. It is in this kind of 'man-to-man' relationship, where adolescent striving for asserting maturity and achieving recognition thereof from his peers can genuinely be observed, stripped of fraud, of role playing his adolescence in front of his seniors. This is one large phase of the adolescent's real world.
>
> (Kiell, 1956, pp. 88-89)

Although these observations are from an old study, the notion of group interaction and social values among adolescent gamblers has also been reported more recently by Snyder (1986). Snyder noted that the chance to be a big winner among friends is often incentive enough for the 'typical 17 year old' to gamble. Once that player becomes involved, to quit is deemed as defeat from within his peer group, even when the prize is (financially) not worth the cost or the effort. Snyder went on to conclude that the adolescent gambles for his ego's sake and that the prestige of winning in front of one's friends or girlfriend keeps casual players interested beyond the limit that they would normally go. Second, adolescents seek to be part of a group to gain friends. Gambling can become the common link between members of the group and encourages others to play. This theme of gambling being a group phenomenon is fairly well supported in the more general group interaction literature, and it has been shown that people may take more risks in groups (Pruitt and Teger, 1969; Bauer and Turner, 1974). This has been explained in terms of the 'diffusion of responsibility' (Wallach *et al.*, 1964) and that risk has a cultural value (Brown, 1965).

The other study of adolescent gambling was by Harris (1964), who reported on the 'Gambling addiction in an adolescent male' (the title of his paper). In this paper, Harris outlined the case study of a 19-year-old male who had been 'addicted' to horse racing / dog racing gambling since he was 16 years old. The adolescent in question was in the eyes of Harris (a pro-Freudian psychoanalyst) suffering from a severe neurosis and was prone to depression because he was particularly fat and suffered from severe facial acne. The study gave little insight into the acquisition and development of gambling (except that gambling was symptomatic of other problems) but at least explained that gambling can be a problem even in adolescence.

Having outlined direct evidence of adolescent gambling, there are several studies which indirectly point to the existence of teenage gamblers. Retrospective self-report studies are the most common. For instance, in a study by Whitman *et al.* (1987) which examined patterns of poly addiction in alcoholic patients and high school students, they sampled 119 ninth graders (14 to 15 years old) of equal sex and found that 58 per cent of boys and 15 per cent of girls had gambled. Unfortunately, no other information on gambing behaviour was collected. More recently, Svendsen (1994) reported that 3 per cent of all the callers to the Minnesota Compulsive Gambling Hotline were under 18 years of age. However, the calls by adolescents may not necessarily have been in connection with themselves (i.e. they may have been ringing up for information or on behalf of a third party).

In another study Dell *et al.* (1981) asked thirty-five pathological gamblers about the onset of gambling. The mean reported age of gambling onset was 13 years old, and 37 per cent of their sample said they had gambled by the age of 10 years, 49 per cent between 11 and 19 years and only 14 per cent reported starting after the age of 19. Another interesting aspect of the questionnaire administered by Dell *et al.* (1981) was the reported incidence of gambling and alcoholism problems among the pathological gamblers' family members (see Table 2.5).

These findings are by no means isolated. Lorenz and Shuttlesworth (1983) reported that 25 per cent of compulsive gamblers' children had behavioural problems and engaged in drug, alcohol and gambling-related activities. Twenty per cent of their sample of pathological gamblers were raised in family environments in which gambling and/or other behavioural

Table 2.5 Incidence of family gambling and alcoholism problems in pathological gamblers

Family problem(s)	No. in sample	% Incidence
Parents with a gambling problem	12	34
Siblings with a gambling problem	5	14
Parents with a drinking problem	4	11
Siblings with a drinking problem	3	9

Source: Dell *et al.*, 1981

problems existed and suggests a 'continuity of experience from one generation to another particularly those which contribute to becoming involved in compulsive gambling' (Lorenz and Shuttlesworth, 1983, p. 71).

Mendelson and Mello (1979) have estimated that the children of alcoholic parents are four times as likely to become alcoholics as children of non-alcoholic parents. There is no reason why the same assumption cannot be applied to the children of gambling parents. Kusyszyn (1972) noted that 'the father of the compulsive gambler is also often a gambler and in many cases has been found to be an alcoholic' (p. 392). This assertion has been confirmed by Lesieur *et al.* (1986), who found that out of ninety-seven pathological gamblers, 38 per cent had fathers with gambling and/or alcoholism problems, and by Lesieur and Klein (1987) in a study mentioned earlier. Other studies outlined earlier in this chapter (e.g. Jacobs *et al.*, 1985; 1987; Jacobs and Kuley, 1987; Steinberg, 1988; Winters *et al.*, 1993a) have also confirmed such findings.

THE ECONOMIC SOCIALIZATION OF CHILDREN

Furnham (1986) has reported that it is likely that economic concepts (e.g. spending, saving, investing *and* gambling) are established in childhood and adolescence. However, gambling seems to be understood at a later developmental stage than most economic concepts (e.g. spending, saving, etc.). Therefore researchers may in fact be incorrect in trying to specify a general stage-wise process by studying more than one economic concept at a time.

Strauss (1952), Danzinger (1958) and Jahoda (1983) have all argued that the development through the stages of economic understanding is not simply a consequence of internal maturation but depends on experiental factors involved with money and economic exchange (Furnham, 1986). According to Furnham (1986), this may account for class, regional and national differences in the development of economic concepts and money-related habits (Cummings and Taebel, 1978; Stacey, 1978). Although Furnham has highlighted the three distinct factors involved in economic socialization – parental instruction and practices, formal schooling in economics and related topics, and personal experiences of the economy – it is less clear how these factors may accelerate economic understanding (Marshall and Magruder, 1960).

Furnham and Thomas (1984) noted that there have been several studies on children's perceptions of economic phenomena, e.g. labour and management (Haire and Morrison, 1957), debt (Miller and Horn, 1955), poverty (Furnham, 1982) and means of production and ownership (Berti *et al.*, 1982). It was also noted that very little research had been carried out on how children come to acquire these economic concepts. Fox (1978) argued that by the time children enter school they have already had experience of working, buying, trading, owning and saving. What should have become obvious by now is that gambling as an economic concept has almost totally been ignored by most researchers. There is no doubt that a person's initial decision to gamble is usually for monetary gain (Cornish, 1978), so the only conclusion we can draw from the non-inclusion of gambling in the economic socialization of children is that it has traditionally been thought of as an adult phenomenon.

The only researchers to have even considered gambling in the economic development of children have been Tan and Stacey (1981), who in a questionnaire posed three questions to 6 to 15-year-old Chinese children living in Malaysia:

1 Do you think people can make money from gambling?
2 What sort of gambling do you know?
3 Why are some sorts of gambling legal and some sorts of gambling illegal?

One surprising finding that Tan and Stacey reported was that most of the children (even pre-10 year olds) had gambled and that it was very popular and a part of the culture. Most of the children were indeed aware of the main types of gambling as well as its financial consequences from an early age. Up to about 10 years old, the children believed money could be made from gambling, but from the age of 10 upwards they believed that money is usually lost from gambling and only won under special circumstances. However, when asked about the legal aspects of gambling, the children possessed very little knowledge and replied with naive and moralistic answers. However, this corresponds with the western studies by Stacey

(1978) on legal socialization, which show that legal concepts are not grasped until well into the teenage years.

It may be that there are distinct cultural differences in acquisition of gambling behaviour on experiential grounds. Jahoda (1979) found that it was not until the age of 11 to 12 years that European children grasp the concept of profit, but in a later study (Jahoda, 1983) it was reported that African children acquire the concept of profit more quickly, presumably because of their trading and bartering experiences.

'GAMBLING AS PLAY' AND GAMES AS PRECURSORS TO GAMBLING

It is quite obvious that 'a person does not magically become a gambler at a certain age' (Abt and Smith, 1984, p.124). It has been hypothesized by a number of researchers (e.g. Herman, 1976; Abt and Smith, 1984) that the ritualized play of several childhood games provides 'training' in the acquisition of gambling behaviour and that some games are precursors to actual gambling. Some authors (e.g. Kusyszyn, 1984) hold the view that gambling is in itself 'adult play'. Freud (cf. Kusyszyn, 1984) was one of the first people to concentrate on the 'functions' of play and concluded that play (a) provides a wish-fulfilment; (b) leads to conflict reduction; (c) provides temporary leave of absence from reality, and (d) brings about a change from the passive to the active.

Since Freud, most psychologists have concentrated on the idea of 'conflict reduction' and in doing so have ignored his other three postulations. A more modern approach by Csikszentmihalyi (1976) has asserted that during play a person can 'concentrate on a limited stimulus field, in which he or she can use skills to meet clear demands, thereby forgetting his or her own problems and separate identity' (cf. Kusyszyn, 1972, p.132). In such terms, the idea of 'gambling as play' seems justified. As Caillois (1958) states, play is a 'free and voluntary activity', 'a source of joy and amusement' and 'bounded by precise limits of time and space' as well as being described by Goffman (1967) as a 'world building activity'.

Games provide the opportunity to prove one's superiority, the desire to challenge and overcome an obstacle and a medium by which to test one's skill, endurance and ingenuity. Games, unlike some activities (including life itself!), tell us whether we have won or lost. As has been observed by Abt and Smith (1984):

> in the context of a competitive and materialistic culture that has become increasingly regimented and standardized with little room for individual

creativity and personal achievement, games (including gambling) offer the illusion of control over destiny and circumstance.

(p.125)

Perhaps the best categorisation of game types was formulated by Caillois (1958) who listed four classifications – *agon* (competition), *alea* (chance), *mimicry* (simulation) and *ilinx* (vertigo). In the context of games involving gambling, *alea* and *agon* are crucial in that they offer a combination of skill, chance and luck. As was previously asserted, most people desire opportunities to test their strength and skill against an adversary, and those games which offer a component of skill or talent combined with luck and chance provide the most favourable conditions. This is particularly prevalent in males who are deemed 'masculine' if during the socialization process they show (socially) important traits such as courage, independence and bravery. It also provides a factor which could explain the significant sex differences in gambling. (See Thompson (1991) for a further discussion of 'machismo' as a cultural value in gambling.)

It is quite clear that very few children have the money to gamble (although adolescents do find greater opportunity), and as such many children's games that involve gambling are played for 'fun' not money. However, children may soon learn that money is a good way of keeping score. It is easy to understand how children and adolescents 'learn to bet', as there are various cultural signals that can influence 'would-be gamblers'. The television media portray gambling heroes (e.g. Kenny Rogers in *The Gambler*, Robbie Box in *'Big Deal'*, etc.) in addition to countless television (gambling) game shows (e.g. *Gambit, Play Your Cards Right, Bullseye, Winner Takes All*, etc.).

It has been noted by Sutton-Smith (1972) that children's games that depend on chance only are very rare, and that the only time 'chance only' occasions arise are in the forms of guessing games played by 6 to 9-year-old children. None of these games however really involve gambling as the only thing to lose is the game itself. However, there are a number of games which bear a strong resemblance to gambling behaviour and could be argued to provide gambling experiences. Not surprisingly, most of the participants are boys and those girls who do take part are usually called 'tomboys'. Another interesting observation is that in games involving winners and losers the real prize is often status as opposed to positive material gain – a point also made by Snyder (1986) and reported earlier in this chapter. Opie and Opie (1969) claim that games involving a gamble help children to understand the concept of risk. Thus by taking risks, reputations are built and winners gain social rewards (as opposed to financial ones). Three such games that have been investigated by Abt and Smith (1984) are marbles, card-flipping and card-playing. These will be briefly examined in turn.

Marbles

The object of this game (subject to local variation) is for a player's marble to hit his opponent's, thus claiming the opponent's marble. Marble players have their own currency: for example, to win an opponent's 'big marble', two hits by a 'small marble' might be required. (For a more detailed account of marbles in 'the playground economy', see Webley and Webley, 1990.) Marbles is an activity that can be played almost anywhere, is portable and is popular in the playground. It is male-oriented (usually because boys' and girls' playgrounds are segregated) and the etiquette involved has developed in much the same way as real 'adult' gambling. Although there is no exchange of money, it should be noted that the marbles have to be bought in the first place. Beating the playground's 'star player' would immediately raise that person's status.

Card-flipping

There are many variations of this game, which can accommodate two (or more) players. The units of currency are football cards (UK) or baseball cards (USA) and are selected from the player's store of cards to provide the stake. Again, like marbles, the aim is to win your opponent's cards, and this can be done either in a pure chance game – in which a player has to match the heads or tails of his opponent's card by flipping them in the air (like a coin) – or in a skilful game in which cards are stood up against the wall and whoever knocks them down wins all the cards that have been used on missed attempts.

Card-playing

This develops at a much later stage than marbles or card-flipping as the rules involved in playing are more sophisticated. As was reported in the study by Amati (1981) in the early part of this chapter, card decks are portable and can be played anywhere (e.g. at school, summer camp, etc.) and cards are played predominantly by males. Ide-Smith and Lea (1988) reported that by the age of 12 years old large numbers of children play pontoon (also called 'twenty-one' or 'blackjack'), at which stage money stakes might begin to appear. This is often a child's first non-commercial exposure to 'real' gambling and is usually acquired from playing with the family. Within peer groups, the card game provides an arena where skill is displayed and an adolescent's fantasies are lived out (Abt and Smith, 1984).

The three examples of children's games outlined above could all be considered as precursors to gambling if not actual gambling itself. These games bear marked similarities to adult gambling and fall into the bracket of competitive games. The flip of a card is as random as the toss of a penny, yet children and young adolescents truly believe that matching the face of the card in play is skilful. As Abt and Smith (1984) observe, 'the games of children . . . are steeped in ritual. Each is surrounded by its own subculture. A marble game may be the passage for status in the school yard' (p.132).

STUDIES OF RISK-TAKING AND GAMBLING-LIKE BEHAVIOUR IN CHILDREN

There have also been a few empirical studies that have investigated the antecedent and maintaining variables of risk-taking and gambling-like behaviour in children which were overviewed by Kearney and Drabman (1992). The first of these was by Kass (1964) who examined risk-taking behaviour on slot-machines in forty-two children aged 6 to 10 years. The children could choose any of three machines with low risk (1: 1), intermediate risk (1: 3) and high risk (1: 8) payouts to play on. The payouts were in the form of pennies that could be exchanged for prizes. The number of choices made per machine on the final thirty of the 210 trials was the dependent variable. Results indicated no age differences but girls preferred the high-risk machines and boys preferred the low-risk and intermediate-risk machines. The experiment was partly replicated by Arenson (1978) using different probabilities (1: 2, 1: 4, 1: 8) but no sex or age differences were found.

In 1966, Slovic evaluated 1,048 children aged 6 to 16 years on a game to win sweets at a county fair. Children could pull one of ten levers to earn a spoonful of sweets. However, one of the levers was a 'disaster switch'. If this lever was pulled, a buzzer would sound which meant that all winnings (i.e. sweets) gained by the child up to that point would be lost. The children were allowed to keep pulling the levers for up to nine trials with the knowledge that each successive lever pull increased the chances of selecting the disaster switch. In this experiment, the percentage of children who stopped playing the game at different levels was the dependent variable. Results generally indicated that boys continued to play the game (i.e. take more risks) but this was only significant at ages 11 years and 14 to 16 years. At younger ages (6 to 8 years) girls took slightly more risks. Again, the experiment was replicated at a later point by Kopfstein (1973) but failed to find the effects outlined by Slovic.

The results of the studies outlined here do not really add much to our understanding of adolescent gambling, although they do partly suggest that sex differences found in other studies of gambling are socially determined as there is little evidence of a difference in these experiments in the younger age groups. Where there is a difference they go in an opposite direction to what might be expected (i.e. girls being more risky at a younger age). Further to this, Kearney and Drabman (1992) pointed out that neither of these studies examined variables that possibly contribute to the etiology of gambling-like behaviour and no studies have examined pre-school populations. As a consequence they designed a study to investigate the role of social learning in a risk-taking/gambling-like situation. Subjects were eleven boys and ten girls, all of whom were 4 or 5 years old. Prior to playing a risk-taking game, children in an experimental group were exposed to a peer model who had ostensibly won a large prize (the 'big win' was in fact a large stuffed animal), whereas children in the control group were exposed to a peer model who had won nothing. Results indicated no age or sex differences but those children who were exposed to the 'winning' peer initiated more risks to win the large prize. An experiment by Frank and Smith (1989) has also demonstrated that like adults, 9 to 11-year-old children can develop an illusion of control on an activity as simple as predicting coin tosses. These two experiments suggest that cognitive and behavioural antecedents may be important in the acquisition, development and maintenance of gambling behaviour and that gambling-like experiences may be precursors to real gambling experiences.

FRUIT MACHINE PLAYING: AN INTRODUCTION

In the UK, coin-operated gaming machines fall into three categories – amusement with prize machines (AWP), skill with prize machines (SWP) and video game machines. Although AWP machines have become increasingly complex, they usually comprise three reels each which spin on a random ratio schedule after money has been inserted. The reels contain differing numbers of symbols (mainly representations of fruit: for example, cherries, lemons, etc.) which spin on predetermined time cycles, i.e. the first reel spins for approximately 2-3 seconds, the second reel for 3-4 seconds and the third reel for 4-5 seconds. This results in a staggering of the reels and produces a large number of symbol permutations. 'Pay-out' rates of machines vary between 70 per cent and 90 per cent and money is won when the payline – the middle of a 3 x 3 symbol matrix window – shows a winning symbol combination, e.g. a row of three cherries.

There are two types of AWP machines. These are the fruit machine and the jackpot machine. Under UK law, fruit machines have a maximum stake of 20 pence with a maximum pay out of £3 in cash or £6 in tokens. They can be located in a number of different types of establishment including amusement arcades, public houses, restaurants, cafes, cinema foyers, etc. Jackpot machines have a fixed stake of 20 pence where the maximum pay out can be anything up to £200, but they can only be located in licensed gaming establishments or private clubs.

SWP machines usually involve a pre-programmed set of 'general knowledge' questions which is activated after the insertion of a coin (usually 10 or 20 pence). On answering a predetermined number of multiple choice questions correctly, successful players can win money. These machines are also known as 'trivia machines' and can legally be placed in any establishment since they do not require a licence. Video game machines offer no financial winnings. These machines comprise a pre-programmed electronic game using high resolution graphics which is again activated after the insertion of money (usually 10 or 20 pence). The player's aim is to play the game for as long as possible, accumulating as many points as possible during the session. In some cases, successful players are rewarded by free plays on the machine with the added bonus of being able to record their high scores electronically on the video game's 'hall of fame'. As with SWP machines, video game machines require no licence so they can be located in many different establishments. Although SWP machines and video game machines are also (i) 'amusement machines'; (ii) produce 'problem' players, and are (iii) conceptually very similar to fruit machines, they will not be focused on to any great extent in this book. (For those readers who have an interest in amusement machines *per se*, see Loftus and Loftus, 1983; Griffiths, 1991a; 1992; 1993g.)

Interest in adolescent fruit machine gambling has primarily arisen due to the concern that some children and adolescents become 'problem' gamblers and suffer negative consequences as a result of their play (Fisher, 1991). This is a fairly recent phenomenon resulting from unforeseen consequences of the 1968 Gaming Act which created a loophole in the law allowing children to gamble on fruit machines (the only commercial gambling activity in the UK allowed to those under 18 years of age). Fruit machines are very profitable for their owners and there was a steady increase in their numbers throughout the 1980s (Moran, 1987; Centre for Leisure Research, 1990). This mirrors an increase in the number of problem gamblers seeking help. For instance, Moody (1989) reports that 50 per cent of new members to Gamblers Anonymous in the late 1980s were fruit machine gamblers with about half of these being children and the other half being young people in their late teens or early twenties. Similarly, the thirteen beds at the Gordon House Association (the only UK residential hostel for problem gamblers) were until recently occupied by the 20-45-year-old age group, but a report has shown an increase in the number of fruit machine referrals (41 per cent of ninety-eight cases), most of whom were under 20 years of age (Griffiths, 1988a).

In the UK, fruit machines can be found almost anywhere – seaside arcades, cafes, sports centres, youth clubs, chip shops, etc. – and provide a favourable environment and opportunity for children to gamble. Since the UK is the only country in the world where children and adolescents can legally gamble on fruit machines and this is the only commercial gambling activity that children and adolescents can engage in, it is perhaps not surprising that there has been a major upsurge of research into adolescent fruit machine gambling and its alleged negative consequences. The over-use of fruit machines can produce excessive and irrational behavior in children and adolescents (as well as adults). It has been postulated by some authors that this is because (i) they are low stake coin-in-the slot machines within each person's limits; (ii) they are less conspicuous than other forms of gambling, and (iii) in the UK at least, they are the most easily accessible form of gambling available to children and adolescents, who are prevented by legislation from using licensed betting shops (Moody, 1987; Ide-Smith and Lea, 1988). The remainder of this chapter (and book!) is essentially about fruit machine gambling, as it is this gambling activity more than any other which has given rise to so much concern.

STUDIES OF ADOLESCENT FRUIT MACHINE PLAYING

In February 1986, a survey of gambling habits involving people in the UK was conducted by the British Market Research Bureau (BMRB). The 1,451 survey participants included an unspecified number of 15-19-year-old adolescents. Percentage results are reproduced in Table 2.6 and clearly show that the most popular gambling activity among adolescents is the playing of fruit machines.

The first widely publicized academic study of fruit machine playing in children was by Moran (1987), who reported his findings from a question-naire that had been sent to the head teachers of local authority secondary schools in four London boroughs. Of the thirty schools that replied to Moran's questionnaire, twenty-five reported known gambling incidence. The remaining five schools were 'all female', and thus gambling came to the attention of teachers only in 'all boys' or co-educational settings. The most disturbing findings concerned those schools which contained fruit machine gamblers. Tables 2.7 and 2.8 highlight the fact that fruit machines

Table 2.6 Incidence of types of gambling in 15–19 year-olds in the UK

Type of gambling	% Incidence in 15–19 year-olds
AWP fruit machines	39
Lottery tickets	24
Card games	13
Bingo	13
Horse racing	10
Football pools	10
Jackpot machines	8
Greyhound racing	4
All gambling	67

Source: BMRB, 1986

are the most common form of commercial gambling among schoolchildren and that most problems occurring from gambling are due to fruit machines. Although Moran based his findings on head teachers' reports many of his conclusions have since been echoed by other researchers using more direct methods, as we shall see.

Evaluating fruit machine research: some problems

Research into the effects of adolescent fruit machine playing was until very recently sparse but the late 1980s and early 1990s produced a sizeable number of studies (see Table 2.9) – probably initiated by the work of Moran in addition to various sensational media stories. Both I and other authors (e.g. Fisher, 1991) acknowledge the difficulties and limitations of evaluating existing research which employs a variety of methods, sampling procedures and population sizes. However, in a research field that is growing but is still relatively small, the existing findings require careful consideration.

Some of the major concerns include (i) the type of publication in which the research appeared; (ii) the representativeness and size of the research sample, including the geographical location (e.g. national versus regional and/or local sampling) and issues of research confidentiality and anonymity, and (iii) issues of research definition. Each of these will be discussed in turn.

Table 2.7 Gambling incidence among schoolchildren as reported by school head teachers in the UK

Type of gambling	No. of schools reporting	% of schools reporting gambling (25)	% of total schools (30)
Coins-up-the-wall	24	96	80
Fruit machines	14	56	47
Video games	14	56	47
Card games	9	36	30
Betting/wagers	4	16	13
Lotteries	2	8	7
Football pools	1	4	3
Bingo	1	4	3

Source: Moran, 1987

Table 2.8 Types of problems occurring as a result of gambling as reported by school head teachers in the UK

	Schools with any form of gambling	Schools with fruit machine gambling	Schools with gambling other than fruit machines
No. of schools involved	20 (100%)	14 (70%)	6 (30%)
Poor work	14 (70%)	10 (56%)	4 (20%)
Aggressive behaviour	10 (50%)	7 (35%)	3 (15%)
Truancy	9 (45%)	7 (35%)	2 (10%)
Emotional disturbance	6 (30%)	5 (25%)	1 (5%)
Stealing	4 (20%)	4 (20%)	0 (-)

Source: Moran, 1987

Publication outlet

Compared with other areas of academic research, the area of adolescent fruit machine gambling produces many reports which are either unpublished or self-published by the organization funding the research. As a consequence, a lot of research that is done in the area is not peer reviewed in refereed journals and/or is carried out by people who have little or no training in research methods. Both of these factors raise the question of the validity of the research undertaken. I am not suggesting that those teams or individuals who have produced non-refereed research did not carry out their research in a professional manner and to the best of their ability, but I am suggesting that these research reports need to be treated perhaps a little more critically than those studies that have been externally reviewed.

In terms of publication outlet, the studies listed in Table 2.9 fall into four categories. These are self-produced publications (i.e. Barham and Cormell, 1987; National Housing and Town Planning Council, 1988; Spectrum Children's Trust, 1988; Graham, 1988; Lee, 1989; Centre for Leisure Research, 1990; Walton, 1990; Leeds Polytechnic Social Science Unit, 1989; Mayne and Tyreman-Wilde, 1993); unpublished manuscripts (i.e. Ashdown, 1987; Wyatt, 1988a; 1988b; Beverly Area Management Committee, 1989; Rands and Hooper, 1990); non-refereed papers in newsletters or books (Waterman and Atkin, 1985; Brown and Robertson, 1993), and refereed journal papers (Huff and Collinson, 1987; Ide-Smith and Lea, 1988; Bentall *et al.*, 1989; Griffiths, 1990a; b; c; Trott and Griffiths, 1991; Huxley and Carroll, 1992; Fisher, 1992; 1993a).

Sampling and definitional issues

Obviously, when assessing and evaluating data from research studies, it is often wise (especially in prevalence studies) to attach more weight to representative data sets. Of the studies outlined in Table 2.9 it should be noted that:

1 Only seven studies have data sets with more than a thousand adolescents (National Housing and Town Planning Council, 1988; Spectrum Children's Trust, 1988; Graham, 1988; Lee, 1989; Rands and Hooper, 1990; Walton, 1990; Huxley and Carroll, 1992), which perhaps suggests that these studies should be given more weight when evaluating the overall data.

2 Seven studies have data sets containing a hundred adolescents or less (i.e. Ashdown, 1987; Huff and Collinson, 1987; Ide-Smith and Lea, 1988; Beverly Area Management Committee, 1989; Griffiths, 1990a; c; Trott and Griffiths, 1991), which perhaps suggests that less weighting should be given to these studies when evaluating the overall data.

3 Only two studies used ostensibly national samples of adolescents (i.e. National Housing and Town Planning Council, 1988; Graham, 1988)

with all the remaining studies using regional, local and/or single site samples. This perhaps suggests that the national studies should be given more weighting than the non-national studies.

4   Nine studies used non-schoolchild samples. Of these, four studies sampled fruit machine players (i.e. Bentall *et al.*, 1989; Griffiths, 1990a; c; Trott and Griffiths, 1991), one study sampled trainees from a youth custody centre (i.e. Huff and Collinson, 1987), one study sampled both schoolchildren and Youth Training Scheme employees (i.e. Lee, 1989), two studies used general surveys which included adults (i.e. Centre for Leisure Research, 1990; Mayne and Tyreman-Wilde, 1993) and one study did not specify where its sample was obtained (i.e. Beverly Area Management Committee, 1989). These studies should perhaps therefore not be generalized to the 'average' adolescent.

5   Three studies did not give a breakdown of sex distribution (i.e. Beverly Area Management Committee, 1989; Leeds Polytechnic Social Science Unit, 1990; Centre for Leisure Research, 1990) which is perhaps a problem in generalizability and means that identifying sex differences is impossible.

6   Three studies had male only samples (i.e. Huff and Collinson, 1987; Griffiths, 1990c; Trott and Griffiths, 1991) which makes generalizing to females impossible.

7   Two studies did not guarantee anonymity of respondents (Graham, 1988; Centre for Leisure Research, 1990). This is probably the most serious of methodological flaws when investigating such a sensitive area and will be discussed in more depth below.

8   Pathological gambling was assessed using a valid instrument in only two of the studies (i.e. Griffiths, 1990a; Fisher, 1993a) in which adaptations of the *DSM-III-R* and *DSM-IV* criteria for pathological gambling were used. Any studies that refer to 'addicted gambers', 'compulsive gamblers', 'problem gamblers', etc. without having included valid items to measure it must be treated with caution. Most of the studies have their own operational definitions of what it is to be a 'regular' or 'problem' gambler but since many of the definitions are individual to the study itself it makes cross-comparison difficult. For example, throughout my own research (e.g. Griffiths, 1993b; 1994c) I have defined regular gamblers as those who play *at least* once a week. Graham (1988) defines regular gamblers as 'those who play *more than* once a week'. At first sight these two operational definitions might appear to be so similar as to make no difference. However, a gambler who plays on a fruit machine just once a week would be defined as a regular player under my definition but would be someone who plays 'not very often' under

Graham's definition. Some authors loosely define regular players as those who 'play often' (e.g. Barham and Cormell, 1987; Ide-Smith and Lea, 1988), while others leave it open to the respondents themselves to decide if they are regular (e.g. Spectrum Children's Trust, 1988).

Although this is in no way a completely exhaustive list of the limitations of previous research, it does indicate that almost no study is immune to criticism in some way. One other factor that perhaps needs to be mentioned at this point is that fruit machine gambling is also a *political* issue. Many of the results cannot be looked at without thinking of the wider political and legislative implications. One way to demonstrate this *and* to explore some of the other methodological issues raised is to examine in more depth the study carried out by Graham (1988) for the Home Office. The analysis that follows provides a critical (some may argue over-critical) assessment of the Home Office study and combines my own previous writings on this subject (Griffiths, 1991b) with those of Fisher (1991). It will be assessed both on its own merit and in light of the research that preceded and that which has followed it. It should also be noted that it is this report on which the Government's position concerning fruit machine legislation is based.

The Home Office report: a critical analysis

Background to the study

Because of increasing public concern over the alleged excessive use of fruit machines by young people and to the alleged negative consequences it can cause, the Home Office Research and Planning Unit conducted research to consider whether legislation was needed to restrict access of young people under the age of 16 years to these machines. The report concluded 'that whilst for a small minority of young people public concern may well be justified, the scale of the problem does not appear to warrant legislation' (p. iii).

Since there has been little systematic research on the acquisition, development and maintenance of fruit machine gambling in young people, the Home Office report on the playing of 'amusement machines' should have been widely welcomed by those studying the effects of these machines on the lives of children and adolescents. However, there appears to be a consensus of opinion among those in the field of adolescent gambling research that the Home Office report clouded the issue rather than clarified it.

Analysis of the Home Office literature review

A number of comments need to be made concerning the Home Office summary of previous research on 'amusement machines'. Although the report admitted that previous research had yielded 'useful data', much of Graham's literature review was spent negatively criticizing the previous studies on methodological grounds. These included the studies of Moran (1987); Barham and Cormell (1987), and the Spectrum Children's Trust (1988), all of which have provided evidence of negative effects of fruit machine playing. Apart from Moran's (1987) study based on head teachers' subjective perceptions of gambling in children, these studies provided useful self-report data, and – regardless of alleged methodological flaws – all of these studies gave similar findings, i.e. that a small but significant number of young people use fruit machines excessively and that a number of behavioural problems (e.g. stealing and truancy) can be associated with their playing.

Barham and Cormell (1987) and Moran (1987) were heavily criticized as 'studies which set out to justify a pre-conceived standpoint'. Perhaps the same allegation of a preconceived position could be made against the Home Office because the UK Government derives an enormous amount of revenue from the playing of fruit machines. The authors of the criticized reports had nothing to lose or gain by their research findings (although some may claim they were seeking legislative change), but the Government does, namely, money from revenue.

Barham and Cormell's (1987) study of fruit machine-playing in Bognor Regis was also criticized as not being representative of the extent and nature of playing fruit machines in other inland or seaside towns, a criticism also made by Graham against the Spectrum Children's Trust of their survey conducted in Taunton and Minehead. Yet the Home Office report notes that the playing of fruit machines regionally only 'shows minor deviations from the national average' (p. 15).

A number of criticisms were made against the two biggest studies, those by the National Housing and Town Planning Council (1988) and the Spectrum Children's Trust (1988). A common criticism was that these studies took no account of the money spent on fruit machines by an individual against his/her disposable income, the argument being that if an individual can *afford* to lose large amounts of money there is no problem. This is clearly not the case. To take an extreme example, a millionaire who gambles at every opportunity and shows 'compulsive' behaviour can clearly have severe gambling problems even if they are not financial! In addition, arguing that previous studies should have measured the amount spent on fruit machines against an individual's disposable income would mean that money from less acceptable sources (e.g. the using of lunch money or stealing) would have been neglected.

Another criticism made by Graham pertains to questions about deviant activity, e.g. 'Have you ever stolen money to play on the machines?'. Graham argues that those individuals who answer 'yes' to this question may have only stolen once. This may indeed be true, *but* it does not take away the fact that the individual *has* stolen. Surely to steal once is wrong? In addition, the Home Office report argued that 'stealing from parents' is not as morally bad as 'stealing from a stranger'. However, one of the children interviewed in the Home Office study said, 'I would never steal off my Mum, oh god no! It's one kid in a hundred who steals off its parents.' Another factor involved in stealing money from parents is that it is probably due more to opportunity than anything else. Ultimately, 'stealing is stealing' – whoever it is from.

Although this is not an exhaustive analysis of each criticism made against the National Housing and Town Planning Council and the Spectrum Children's Trust studies, it does illustrate the sometimes inconsistent and contradictory remarks of the Home Office report. The one study that the Home Office report considers favourably is a survey by Waterman and Atkin (1985). One has to ask whether this is because it is the only study which concludes that fruit machine playing is an enjoyable activity and is of little problem to adolescents. In criticizing the National Housing and Town Planning Council and the Spectrum Children's Trust surveys, the Home Office report claimed that they were unrepresentative and failed to eliminate sampling error. However, these criticisms could have been (but were not) made against the Waterman and Atkin (1985) study as it only used subjects from two schools in Birmingham.

One important factor which the Home Office report failed to consider was when the studies were conducted. All of the research that the Home Office criticized was conducted and published within two years of their survey. However, the one survey that was viewed favourably (i.e. Waterman and Atkin) was conducted some five years before their own. Waterman and Atkin themselves admit that their study is probably dated, and of little relevance to fruit machine playing at present (personal communication with Karl Atkin).

Another interesting observation is the striking similarity between Chapter 2 of the Home Office report ('Previous research on amusement machines') and some of the gaming industry's literature produced by the British Amusement Catering Trades Association (i.e. *BACTA – The Real Facts*, 1988; *The BACTA File*, undated). This is especially noticeable on the criticism of studies which highlight negative effects of fruit machine playing, e.g. Moran (1987) and the 'singled out' support for the study by Waterman and Atkin (1985). Once again we must ask ourselves what BACTA (as with the Government) has to lose by research that concludes that fruit machine playing can cause harmful effect? The answer is (again) *money*.

Analysis of the research design

The title of the Home Office report ('Amusement machines: dependency and delinquency') is very misleading. 'Amusement machines' cover a multitude of game machines including video game machines, trivia machines *and* fruit machines. Although some authors have suggested and provided evidence for other gaming addictions (e.g. Griffiths, 1991a; Griffiths, 1992; Griffiths and Hunt, 1993; Fisher, 1994), to lump video games and fruit machines together probably blurs the issues in question. And let us not forget that when we talk about fruit machines as 'amusement machines', what we are really talking about are *gambling machines*. The word 'gambling' is rarely mentioned when one talks about fruit machines, as the word 'play' or 'playing' is more frequently used.

In a report that has undoubtedly influenced policy on fruit machine legislation, one would expect to find an in-depth survey and questions that at least relate to the title of the report and which probe the individual about the negative consequences of fruit machine play. However, this is not the case. The Home Office questionnaire itself had only nine questions on fruit machine use and there were *no* questions on dependency and *no* questions on delinquency. The only reference to dependency and delinquency was made to questions posed to thirty-six fruit machine players involved in small group studies. There was no reason why, for instance, the *DSM-III-R* (American Psychiatric Association, 1987) criteria for pathological gambling could not have been used, especially when the questions themselves are based on dependency criteria for psychoactive substance abuse. To assess the extent to which children are at risk of becoming dependent upon fruit machines, the Home Office survey asked school- children:

- how often they played fruit machines within the last month;
- how often they spent their own money on playing the machines;
- how long they played during a typical session;
- how much, as a proportion of their weekly income, they spent on fruit machines;
- how frequently players spent more than £5 during a session;
- at what stage during a session they decided to stop playing.

The answers to these questions say nothing about dependency – they only indicate how much time and money children spend on machines. With only a small number of questions on fruit machine use, the Home Office report can only produce limited information. In addition, a number of questions are open to criticism. For instance, the first question asks if an individual has played on a fruit machine in the last month. If not, the respondent did not have to answer any more questions on fruit machine playing. However, there may be a number of reasons why an individual may not have played within the preceding month. By using this question, it is possible that the number of young people who play fruit machines may have been under-estimated. Another question which asks how often children spent their own money on machines automatically excludes the instances when money was spent from other sources (e.g. school dinner money, stolen money, etc.).

Another factor which contributes to the underestimation of fruit machine playing in children is the inclusion of 10 to 12 year olds. Not only are children of this age less likely to play on the machines or have their own resources even if they wanted to, but it is likely that some of the young children did not fully understand the questions being asked. There is one study which reported that a significant number of pre-11-year-old school-children did not realize that fruit machine playing was even a form of gambling (Wyatt, 1988b).

Fisher (1991) additionally points out two further points. The first of these is that no systematic attempt was made to cross-tabulate the statistics provided from the answers. For example, Fisher states that it would be interesting to know how many of those children who gambled 'two or three times a week' or 'nearly every day' also spent 'more than £5' in a session and/or a large proportion of their weekly income. The second point is that Graham's method of reporting focused on those who *did not* participate frequently, *did not* spend much money or *did not* behave deviantly in the course of their play. Attention was thus systematically attracted away from the minority of children whose play has given sufficient cause for concern to warrant a Home Office enquiry in the first place. For example, 'only a small minority of young people are at risk of becoming dependent upon . . . fruit machines' (p.18). As Fisher (1991) states, 'Take away the word "only" and the statement which in its original form is almost dismissive of this group now focusses upon them' (p.229)

The main criticism of the questionnaire, at least in my view, is the question of confidentiality – an assertion also supported by Fisher (1991). During the survey the children were asked a number of questions that preceded the items on fruit machine playing. These included asking the children to give their name, their parents' names, their address *and* their telephone number. How many children would answer honestly and truth-fully if they thought the information they were giving 'confidentially' might somehow get back to their parents? In studies where sensitive issues are investigated, anonymity is an essential if not the most fundamentally important aspect of research such as this.

Analysis of the findings

From the information generated by the nine questions posed to the 10 to 16-year-old children, the Home Office report derived some useful statistics. However, many of the conclusions regarding the negative aspects of fruit machine playing are based on their small group interviews with twenty-four regular players and twelve occasional players. Although small group work is important, to generalize from this type of research can be dangerous. The Home Office report criticized some studies because their sample size was too small (e.g. Huff and Collinson, 1987 – 100 subjects). Surely the same criticism can be made against the Home Office's general-izations from thirty-six cases – especially in the case of Riley and Shaw's (1985) delinquency questionnaire which was only administered to those involved in the small group research. Further criticism could be made about the delinquency questionnaire which was borrowed from Riley and Shaw's study of parental supervision and delinquency. As Fisher (1991) points out, it is insufficiently focused on the study in hand to be of much relevance. For example, items include 'written or sprayed paint on buildings', 'broken windows in an empty house', 'dialled 999 for a joke', etc. Not surprisingly, Graham found little evidence of behaviour which could have been moti-vated by a need to fund the playing of machines.

Another problem inherent with using groups in research is that it produces group-oriented responses. For instance, in the Home Office report, the notion of the 'lone addict' was dismissed using group data. It is very unlikely that individuals will become 'lone addicts' if they belong to a peer group to start with. In the Home Office questionnaire, almost one in five individuals reported that they played fruit machines alone – a statistic which to some extent contradicts their own group data.

General comments on the Home Office report

The general conclusion that runs through the Home Office report is that fruit machine playing is on the whole an enjoyable social activity in adolescents and that only a small minority will face serious problems as a result of their excessive fruit machine playing. But what is this 'small minority' as a national percentage of 10 to 16-year-old children? The Home Office report also states that 'only the odd one or two will decline into a life of dependency, debt and deterioration'. But one or two out of how many? The report fails to clarify these matters. Another question is at what percentage of the national 10 to 16-year-old population is the risk of becoming dependent on fruit machines significant? Even if only 0.5 per cent of the child population was at risk (which is the report's own tentative figure), on a national level this would be tens of thousands of children. When exactly does the problem become significant? If there is a one in a thousand chance that a child will catch a serious disease, steps are taken to inoculate *all* the children, even when only one child may be at risk. Why should fruit machines be any different if one in a thousand suffers from severe behavioural problems due to excessive fruit machine play?

Other forms of gambling are legally restricted (i.e. to over 18 year olds only) so why are fruit machines morally different? It may be the case that many children and adolescents would not have any problem controlling money spent on horse-race betting and other 'hard gaming', so should the restrictions be dropped and children be allowed access to the betting shops? Having said that, the Home Office and BACTA have shown some concern about those individuals who have problems as a result of fruit machine playing and have both stated that they wish to help in the treatment and rehabilitation of these individuals. But who is responsible for funding such treatment? Perhaps a small percentage of the revenue made from fruit machine playing should be put aside to help treat and counsel affected individuals. One final point is that throughout the report, the Home Office stated that their study was only a 'preliminary investigation', that some of the findings were 'tentative' and that more research was needed. Many of us hoped that the Home Office would keep their word, but it now appears that the report is being used as the final Government statement on the state of adolescent fruit machine playing in the UK.

Fruit machines: who plays them and how much?

Demographic characteristics of adolescent fruit machine gamblers in the UK are fairly well established. Most surveys which have reported on the incidence of fruit machine playing among a general population have concluded that they are most frequently played by male adolescents with a mean commencement age of around 10 to 11 years. The effect of social class has proved generally insignificant (Fisher, 1991), although the studies by both Graham (1988) and Fisher (1993a) suggest an increase of adolescent participation in fruit machine gambling with declining social class. Table 2.9 outlines a comprehensive summary of UK research studies on amusement machine playing in adolescence. Incidence figures of ever having played amusement machines ranged between 20.5 per cent (Rands and Hooper, 1990) and 84 per cent (Wyatt, 1988b). Incidence figures for regular playing (roughly defined as those playing at least once a week) ranged from 6 per cent (Graham, 1988; Leeds Polytechnic Social Sciences Unit, 1990) to 38 per cent (Walton, 1990). (These figures do not include those studies which surveyed fruit machine players only and/or those studies which included non-schoolchild samples.) The great variability of these figures is probably due to a combination of the methodology employed, the sample chosen to survey, the ages of the sample chosen to survey and the operational definitions of the factors and concepts employed. They do, however, demonstrate that adolescent gambling is widespread and that gambling is an activity that is not restricted to adulthood.

Fruit machine playing – a social activity?

There has been very little systematic research into whether fruit machine playing is a largely social or non-social activity. Brooks (1983) reported in a survey of Los Angeles video game players (as opposed to fruit machine players), that less than half the time in the arcade was spent actually playing the machines and therefore concluded that machine playing was to some degree a social activity. In a similar type of study, Braun *et al.* (1986) surveyed arcades and reported that most of the activity that takes place is solitary. Of 498 clients observed, 297 were alone, sixty were couples, fifteen trios, six foursomes and two quintets. Dominick (1984) reported that over one-fifth (21 per cent) of males played alone but only a small proportion of females (6 per cent) did similarly.

There is a lot of research into the social nature of fruit machine playing, suggesting that for most children a visit to the arcade is a social event enjoyed with siblings and friends. Graham (1988) described fruit machine playing as a 'predominantly gregarious, peer group centred activity' (p.22) in which going to the amusement arcade was the central focus of a social event. Graham argued that this was in contrast to 'the concept of the "lone addict", the solitary player entrapped by the machine's irresistible pull' (p.21). Graham even went on to add that the peer groups themselves provided a powerful regulating mechanism for those in danger of becoming 'dependent':

> If the playing of fruit machines goes beyond the boundaries of a social event and begins to impose on the individual's or the group's life outside the arcade, then the peer group is likely to intervene.
>
> (Graham, 1988; p.25)

Table 2.9 Summary of questionnaire studies on fruit machine gambling

Researcher(s)	Year	Age(s) of sample	Sample size			% of gamblers (last 12 months)	% of regular gamblers (1 week)	Research methodology
			Total	Male	Female			
Waterman and Atkin	1985	14–18	451	(not specified)	(not specified)	77	9	Questionnaire to schoolchildren
Huff and Collinson	1987	15–21	100	100	0	35 (check)	24	Questionnaire to juvenile offenders at a youth custody centre
Barham and Cormell	1987	11–16	329	163	166	51	19	Questionnaire to schoolchildren
Ashdown	1987	11–15	71	40	31	70	23	Questionnaire/interview to schoolchildren
Ide-Smith and Lea	1988	13–14	50	30	20	81	(not reported)	Questionnaire to schoolchildren
National Housing and Town Planning Council	1988	13–16	9752	5184	4434	64	14	Questionnaire to schoolchildren
Spectrum Children's Trust	1988	11–16	2434	1223	1211	66	8.7	Questionnaire to schoolchildren
Graham (Home Office)	1988	10–16	1946	960	986	27	6	Questionnaire to schoolchildren
Wyatt	1988a	11–15	634	386	248	59	(not reported)	Questionnaire to schoolchildren
Wyatt	1988b	11–15	194	('roughly 50–50')		84	(not reported)	Questionnaire to schoolchildren
Beverly Area Management Committee	1989	14–20+	50	(not specified)	(not specified)	94	90	Questionnaire/interview to unspecified 'young people'
Leeds Polytechnic	1989	11–16	576	(not specified)	(not specified)	39	6	Questionnaire to schoolchildren
Bentall et al.	1989	15–51+	213	160 (3 unrecorded)	50	100	41	Questionnaire to fruit machine players

Lee	1989	9–18	1399	747	652	72	41	Questionnaire to schoolchildren and Youth Training Scheme employees
Griffiths	1990a;b	14–21	50	39	11	100	34	Questionnaire/interview to fruit machine players
Griffiths	1990b;c	19	8	8	0	100	100	Discussion and interview with 'fruit machine addicts'
Brown and Robertson	1990	11–18	380	(not specified)	(not specified)	21	4.7	Questionnaire to schoolchildren
Rands and Hooper	1990	11–16	2817	(not specified)	(not specified)	20.5	9	Questionnaire to schoolchildren
Walton	1990	13–16	2704	49%	51%	83	32	Questionnaire to schoolchildren
			567	48%	52%	76	29	
			146	53%	47%	66	9	
Centre for Leisure Research	1990	(all ages)	3297	(not specified)	(not specified)	54	38	Household survey and interviews
Trott and Griffiths	1991	17–24	40	40	40	100	62.5	Questionnaire/interview to fruit machine players
Huxley and Carroll	1992	11–15	1332	678	654	40	21	Questionnaire to schoolchildren
Fisher	1993a	11–16	460	52%	48%	62	20	Questionnaire to schoolchildren
Mayne and Tyreman-Wilde	1993	under 16	96	44	52	38.5	16	Questionnaire to members of general public
		16–21	372	200	172	35	13	Questionnaire to members of general public
		6–11	200	96	104	40.5	(not reported)	Questionnaire to schoolchildren
		11–18	736	357	373	81	24	Questionnaire to schoolchildren
		13–14	50	29	21	34	24	Questionnaire to schoolchildren

However, one-fifth of the sample claimed they played on their own, a finding which has been echoed in other studies (e.g. National Housing and Town Planning Council, 1988). The National Housing and Town Planning Council (1988) further reported that the more time and money an individual spends playing on a fruit machine, the more likely they are to be playing on their own. However, this finding was not confirmed by Huxley and Carroll (1992), which suggests that further research is needed to settle the issue.

Other research has tended to provide contradictory findings. For instance, in a survey by Bentall *et al.* (1989) it was reported that most of their respondents visited amusement arcades alone but reported that young males tended to go with their friends. However, a survey by Rands and Hooper (1990) suggested that typical adolescent males tend to play alone, whereas female adolescents tend to play with their friends. When evaluating the evidence for the social nature of fruit machine playing it should be noted that there is a major consideration in that all the data collected were obtained using self-report measures, and may not be a true picture of such activity.

One final point worth mentioning is that Selnow (1984) reported that video game players use the machines as 'electronic friends'. This assertion had been tested experimentally by Scheibe and Erwin (1979), who studied the conversations of people with video games while they were playing them. Out of forty subjects, spontaneous verbalizations were frequent and recorded in thirty-nine cases, averaging one comment every forty seconds. They reported widespread use of pronouns for the machine, i.e. '*it* hates me', '*he's* trying to get me' or 'you dumb machine', but interestingly no use of the pronoun 'she'. The remarks themselves fell into two categories – direct comments to the machine and simple exclamations or expletives. Scheibe and Erwin concluded that players were reacting to video game machines as if they were people. It could be the case that a similar process occurs in fruit machine players – at least for those players who play the machines on their own – and will be a theme returned to later in this book.

Psychological characteristics of fruit machine players

Although research into the personality of gamblers has been quite abundant (see Chapter 1), there has been very little on either adult or adolescent slot-machine players. However, there are the odd exceptions (e.g. Koller, 1972), but to date there has been only one (as yet unpublished) study by Huxley (1993) examining the psychological characteristics of adolescent fruit machine players. Using the Eysenck Personality Questionnaire, Huxley found that although there was no difference in the neuroticism and extroversion scores of twenty-seven dependent versus forty-one non-dependent fruit machine players, dependent subjects did have higher psychoticism scores (although this just failed to reach significance). Huxley asserted that such children try to make up for the lack of feeling by indulging in sensation-seeking 'arousal jags' without thinking of the dangers involved. It was also reported that dependent gamblers registered more 'internal' scores on the Locus of Control Scale, i.e. they believed their behaviour determined outcomes on the fruit machine. Since this is the only study, and the number of subjects small, few clear conclusions can be drawn.

Addiction and the negative consequences of fruit machine playing

Most of the surveys into fruit machine playing have essentially been of a sociological nature, and as such there has been little in the way of explanation concerning the theoretical underpinnings of 'fruit machine addiction'. This has meant that a vast majority of researchers have taken concepts such as 'dependency' and/or 'addiction' as given and used without further attempting to give an insight into their meanings. As we saw in Chapter 1, there are valid criteria for assessing pathological gambling, yet only two researchers (Sue Fisher and myself) have used bona fide criteria in their studies. However, as Fisher (1991) points out:

> Such reticence on the part of sociologists is not altogether surprising since their task is to offer explanations of social action. As such they cannot be expected to define *addiction* to gambling, or anything else for that matter, since any attempt to do so necessarily involves the inappropriate application of sociological theories to non social (psychological/ physiological) phenomena.
>
> (p. 227)

Accepting previous studies' shortcomings, there is still a lot of data that have been collected which help determine whether fruit machine addiction in its most excessive form is a bona fide addiction. These findings (along with my own outlined in subsequent chapters) will be looked at in greater detail in Chapter 10 when the issue of 'fruit machine addiction' will be discussed further. For now, we will consider some possible indications of 'dependency' (i.e. amount of time and money spent playing, borrowing money, using school dinner money, stealing money and truancy).

Evidence for signs of 'dependency' in the UK are still quite sparse but steadily growing. Nearly all the studies on fruit machine playing (outlined in Table 2.9) have shown that a small minority of individuals have severe behavioural problems as a result of their excessive fruit machine playing. The debate centres around how big the 'minority' is. Table 2.10 outlines those studies which have reported negative consequences of fruit machine playing which could be taken as possible indicative signs of fruit machine dependency.

Obviously, one measure of commitment to a given activity is the proportion of resources that an individual puts into it. With respect to the playing of fruit machines, time and money are the two most salient resources. However, as we have already seen, accurately measuring the frequency of the fruit machine playing using some kind of meta-analysis is problematic due to methodological flaws / problems and inadequate operational definitions of what constitutes 'regular' or 'addictive' play. However, Fisher (1991) and myself (Griffiths, 1991g) have both estimated that around 10 per cent to 25 per cent play once a week or more and that approximately 3 per cent to 6 per cent play at least four times a week. Although frequency in itself does not automatically imply negative consequences, when taken together with the research into expenditure, the consequences do appear to be more negative.

Fruit machine gambling can be a very expensive pastime for children and adolescents. In my own experiments (see chapters 4 and 5 for further details) it has been demonstrated that players spend approximately £3 every ten minutes on a 10 pence per play machine (including winnings from the original stake). Further to this, Fisher (1991) reported that she spent £30.60 in one hour with the aid of sponsorship from one of her local machine operators. Such findings suggest that even short playing times can lead to relatively large losses – at least for the typical child or adolescent. Many studies have found a strong correlation between the amount spent during a typical visit and the frequency with which children and adolescents gambled (e.g. Waterman and Atkin, 1985; National Housing and Town Planning Council, 1988; Spectrum Children's Trust, 1988; Huxley and Carroll, 1992). For instance, in the survey by the National Housing and Town Planning Council, there were 22 per cent of respondents who claimed they played fruit machines once a week or more. Of these, 15 per cent spent more than £3 per session and 10 per cent spent more than £5 per session. Further to this, over 33 per cent of respondents who played at least four times a week spent more than £3 per session, and nearly 20 per cent spent more than £10 per session. This latter statistic means that these particular schoolchildren (albeit a small minority) were spending at least £40 a week on gambling. It is very unlikely that these individuals had such a disposable income in a week which can only lead to the conclusion that they acquired the money through less acceptable means. Possible sources of money beyond pocket money or a part-time job include borrowing money, using money that was for other purposes (e.g. lunch money, fare money, etc.) and stealing money. These will be briefly examined in turn.

Borrowing money in itself is not necessarily negative behaviour. However, borrowing money to finance fruit machine playing may be symptomatic of gambling too much, as it implies expenditure beyond the means of the participant (Fisher, 1991). Research has consistently shown that the more frequent the fruit machine gambling the more likely players will borrow money to do so (e.g. National Housing and Town Planning Council, 1988; Graham, 1988; Huxley and Carroll, 1992; Fisher, 1993a). Additionally, a number of studies have reported the using of school dinner money to play on fruit machines. Again, this is more common among frequent players (e.g. National Housing and Town Planning Council, 1988; Rands and Hooper, 1990; Huxley and Carroll, 1992; Fisher, 1993a). This confirms more anecdotal reports from schoolteachers. For instance, one headmaster at a secondary school in Devon reported a decline in school meal takings of up to £50 a week when fruit machines were installed in a cafe near his school, a decline which subsequently halted when the machines were removed (Griffiths, 1988a).

Stealing to play fruit machines has regularly been reported by a number of authors and is again correlated with frequency of play (e.g. Barham and Cormell, 1987; Spectrum Children's Trust, 1988; Huxley and Carroll, 1992; Fisher, 1993a). A growing number of authors are beginning to distinguish between stealing from home and stealing from outside the home (e.g. Huxley and Carroll, 1992; Fisher, 1993a – see Table 2.10), evidence which indicates that stealing from home occurs more often than stealing from outside the home. Whether this is a useful distinction seems to be purely down to the researchers themselves. As was noted in the section evaluating the Home Office report, Graham (1988) asserted that stealing from the home is not as morally wrong as stealing from elsewhere. However, it could be argued that stealing from home is no less serious than stealing from other sources and it could further be argued that the higher figure for stealing from home is a consequence and function of opportunity and proximity.

In addition to possible financial indicators of 'dependent' play it has also been reported that a minority of players truant to play fruit machines and that this is again correlated with frequency of play (e.g. National Housing and Town Planning Council, 1988; Leeds Polytechnic Social Sciences Unit, 1989; Huxley and Carroll, 1992; Fisher, 1993a).There are also other behaviours (e.g. chasing losses, irritability when not playing, etc.: see Table 2.10) which may be indicators of potential fruit machine dependence. Although there is a dearth of hard data concerning 'fruit machine addiction'

Table 2.10 Summary of UK research studies reporting signs of fruit machine dependency

Researcher(s)	Year	Dependency sign						
		Borrowing (%)	Using lunch money (%)	Stealing (%)	Truancy (%)	Heavy playing (%)	Irritability (%)	Chasing losses (%)
Huff and Collinson	1987	–	–	28	18	–	–	54
Barham and Cormell	1987	16.4	–	3.2	0.9	3	–	–
National Housing and Town Planning Council	1988	35	16.7	7.4	6.2	5	–	–
Spectrum Children's Trust	1988	16.5	–	4.3	4.3	–	–	–
Graham (Home Office)	1988	anec	–	anec	anec	2	–	–
Beverly Area Management Committee	1989	–	–	4 (22)[1]	–	51	–	–
Leeds Polytechnic	1989	20	–	10	7	6	–	–
Griffiths	1990	24 (38)[1]	18	12 (18)[1]	18 (32)[1]	6	8	4
Rands and Hooper	1990	7.3	3.6	1.5[2] (0.8)[3]	1.6	2	–	–
Walton	1990	22	12	7	6	5	–	–
Huxley and Carroll	1992	30	24	12[2] (5)[3]	14	16	–	–
Fisher	1993	37	21	11[2] (2)[3]	–	7	–	–

Notes: 1 Only happened once
2 From family members
3 From outside the family

it is clear from the studies outlined that some individuals (and quite possibly a significant minority) have what can only be described as a gaming dependency.

Fruit machines: concluding remarks

From the summaries of adolescent gambling studies (Tables 2.1 and 2.9) it is evident that gambling is a popular activity among the young – especially the use of fruit machines in the UK. Although it is likely that most adolescents can control their gambling, it is a worrying fact that clear signs of pathological gambling have been found in a number of US studies (e.g. Arcuri *et al.*, 1985; Lesieur and Klein, 1987) with, in some cases, incidence figures of 5 per cent and above – higher than the adult population (e.g. Lesieur and Klein, 1987; Lesieur *et al.*, 1991).

Probably the most important aspect of research into gambling among the young is the need to realize that pathological gambling is *not* just an adult phenomenon, although existing findings need to be replicated and verified. The main problem with adolescent gambling dependence is that there are so few observable signs and symptoms and it is not as visible to the eye as drug/alcohol addictions (Arcuri *et al.* 1985; Lesieur and Klein, 1987). It has been reported that the adolescent fruit machine gambler may undergo a personality change (Moody, 1987) but parents may just think it is 'a stage they're going through' or put it down to the problems of 'adolescence' and 'growing up'. The only other typical external sign of gambling problems might be the arrest crimes involving stealing to procure more money to 'feed the addiction' (Arcuri *et al.*, 1985; Moody, 1989). This obviously means that the problem is only detected in extreme cases, i.e. when the addict gets into trouble – usually with the police. Another factor that may contribute to the addiction's hidden nature is that when it *is* detected from within the family, the family itself can be over-protective and may try to contain the problem without involving external parties. As we have also seen, many of the dependency measures used are subjective; therefore future research on adolescents should use established diagnostic criteria to measure pathological gambling objectively. In fact a 'junior' version of the new *DSM-IV* has just been validated by Fisher (1991).

As I said at the beginning of this chapter, at the time I started empirical work there were only six published (survey) studies on adolescent gambling. The research that *had* been published was mainly gained from data collected via self-administered self-report questionnaires and case studies. In-depth interview and observation studies were virtually non-existent. It was my aim to examine fruit machine playing in a number of ways, utilizing a number of different research methods (interviews, questionnaires, participant and non-participant observation and ecologically valid experimental studies).

Since so little information was known about fruit machine players, pilot work began in December 1987 in the form of informal discussions and interviews with a group of self-confessed 'fruit machine addicts', the results of which are contained in the first part of Chapter 3. Simultaneously, longitudinal observational research employing both participant and non-participant observation methodologies were begun, findings of which can be found in Chapter 4. Based on these early discussions and preliminary observations, a questionnaire was constructed and used as a semi-structured interview schedule for a study examining the acquisition, development and maintenance of fruit machine gambling in adolescence (second half of Chapter 3).

3 Preliminary studies of adolescent fruit machine gambling and fruit machine addiction

One of the first problems that a researcher must negotiate when examining an area is what methodology to employ in eliciting the desired information. It may be argued that the most important aspect of research work is knowing what questions you wish to answer. However, in an area where there is a dearth of literature, it is often useful to try and examine as many aspects of the research area as possible, at least at an exploratory level. One of the most disheartening aspects as a researcher is that nearly all research methodologies have inherent problems. This is one of the reasons why a wide range of methodologies was used in the studies in this book (questionnaires, semi-structured interviews, informal discussions, participant and non-participant observation, and field experiments). Methodological considerations and concerns of using these will be made in the appropriate chapters.

When I began empirical work in this area in 1987, little was known about the phenomenon of excessive fruit machine playing among adolescents; therefore some exploratory pilot work involving informal discussions with eight 'fruit machine addicts' was carried out. This was quickly followed by a questionnaire and interview study with fifty fruit machine players and a concurrent observational study. These next two chapters outline these preliminary studies on adolescent fruit machine gambling and concern themselves with factors that were seen as important in the acquisition, development and maintenance of fruit machine playing behaviour. Much of the data collected in the first and third study (outlined in the next chapter) were qualitative and do not lend themselves to quantitative data analysis. The approach in these particular studies was on the whole empirical and qualitative, and they can be regarded as field studies capable of suggesting hypotheses but not of confirming fact. The second study was essentially quantitative and was to some extent a more formal follow-up to the first study.

STUDY 1: AN EXPLORATORY STUDY OF FRUIT MACHINE ADDICTION AMONG ADOLESCENT MALES

The first half of this chapter contains the main findings that were obtained during informal discussions between myself and a group of eight self-confessed addicted adolescent fruit machine gamblers and observation at their local amusement arcade, i.e. a qualitative study of self-reports and observation rather than quantitative data derived from rigorous experimentation.

Method

The group was contacted via a fruit machine addict known to the author. Unfortunately, no female fruit machine addicts could be located. The group were fully aware that I was researching the area of fruit machine gambling. Although they were not tested for signs of pathological gambling using the *DSM-III-R* criteria (American Psychiatric Association, 1987) due to the study's informal nature, it was clear from initial conversation that the criteria would have been fulfilled had a diagnosis been undertaken.

All of the eight participants in the study were white English males (with a mean average age of 19 years) who knew each other as friends in so far as they met each other regularly at an amusement arcade in their home town of Loughborough. Only one of the group was employed, ironically working in the arcade where the group met. Factors involved in the onset of fruit machine playing were examined, along with their alternative gambling activities and associated problems. The role of 'skill' and 'excitement' components in persistent playing was also discussed. I based questions around the seven major headings outlined below and followed up questions where I thought appropriate.

Onset of fruit machine gambling

Fruit machines provided all eight participants with their first personal exposure to gambling, although three of them mentioned they had sometimes helped their fathers with the football pools. All of the group had begun fruit machine playing by the age of 11 years, five claiming they had first played on their own, two with parents and one with friends. The main reasons for initially playing the fruit machines were to win money, to have fun, because their parents did, because their friends did and for 'something to do'. Although the chance of winning money was a fundamental reason for initial decisions in playing, none of the group now played to win, but rather 'played for the sake of playing', a point that will be returned to later.

Alternative gambling activities

When they were asked about involvement in other forms of gambling it became apparent that all eight participants were only interested in fruit machine gambling. All of them gambled every day or most days whereas other commercial gambling activities, e.g. the football pools, sports betting, bingo, etc. occurred infrequently. Non-commercial gambling activities, e.g. playing cards and wagers between friends occurred on a more regular weekly basis, but little money was ever exchanged. The main reason expressed by the group for the reluctance to gamble on these activities was that the excitement experienced while playing fruit machines could in no way be matched by other gambling activities.

With regard to other gaming machines, e.g. video game machines, half of the group had played them at some point in their lives but all of them agreed that there was little or no correlation between fruit machines and video game machines, i.e. they claimed that just because one is addicted to one machine in no way reflects or produces similar behaviour on another. However, those who used to play video games claimed they started playing fruit machines as a result of the initial exposure to their being near (or next to) the video games in arcade and non-arcade surroundings.

Sociological factors

When asked about their early career and the social influences upon it, responses were vague. Gambling among parents was minimal except for the football pools in three cases, and 'the occasional flutter on the horses' in two cases, although as previously mentioned, two participants were introduced to fruit machines by their parents. Initial fruit machine playing began in non-arcade surroundings for five players who began their playing career in local cafes, chip shops and a leisure centre. This was because owners of these establishments made no attempt to stop them playing, whereas arcade owners either asked them to leave the premises or refused them admission in the first place.

Peer group pressure to play fruit machines only seemed to be relevant once the player was established in a group of other players. The amusement arcade provided the meeting place of all eight participants because 'there was nowhere else to go' and 'nothing else to do'. Paradoxically, fruit machine playing was not a social activity for these addicted players. While watching the group, I observed little or no communication between peers while they were gambling on fruit machines.

When asked about alternative leisure activities to gambling that they participated in, the general feeling among the group was that once an individual is addicted to playing fruit machines, alternative activities are 'near useless' in stimulating that person. All of the group acknowledged they were addicted to fruit machines by the age of 15 years, with five of them claiming they were addicted at 13 years. For these individuals, gambling on the fruit machines was better than, say, pool or table tennis and they believed that these activities would only be enjoyable if fruit machine gambling had been avoided in the first place. Gambling for this particular group was strictly male oriented. None of the group admitted to gambling with women or in front of women. None of the group felt that fruit machine playing provided a medium to impress women and typical reasons for the non-inclusion of females were 'gambling is a man's domain' and 'they [women] wouldn't understand'!

Additional factors

When asked whether there were certain circumstances when they played fruit machines more heavily than at other times, responses provided only a few commonalities. For instance, being unemployed made two of the group play less because they had less money but made three of them play more because they had more opportunity. One participant recalled that when he was in full-time employment, fruit machine playing would occur only once a week on pay-day, but the session would last all evening until he had spent all of his (£60) wages. Another factor that increased fruit machine playing in three cases was when they were 'depressed' or 'on a downer'. Fruit machine playing in these cases was described as 'an escape from reality' and 'relief of worry and tension'. Only one person highlighted a situation in which fruit machine playing was decreased, and that occurred when he had a girlfriend and needed the money to take the girl out regularly.

Excitement and thrill factors

By far the major factor mentioned in relation to persistence in fruit machine playing was the excitement experienced during play. According to the group, arousal levels increased because they could actually feel their heart-beats getting faster and faster, especially when they were either winning or near winning, i.e. a visual display showing two winning symbols and a losing third symbol with a chance to 'gamble up' their winnings.

When questioned about why fruit machine playing was exciting, the group unanimously stated that they experienced a 'high' while playing. When asked about the nature of the high, the replies were somewhat vague or non-existent but two of them mentioned that the nearest equivalent pleasurable experience was having sexual intercourse. However, the group did explain that the high experienced in relation to alcohol and other soft drugs was very different because alcohol/drug effects produce mood-altering behaviour over a long period of time whereas the high experienced during fruit machine playing was almost immediate. It also became apparent that other forms of gambling could not produce the same excitement or high for the group. Another interesting aspect of fruit machine gambling was that at least half of the group claimed they could get a secondary high by watching another person playing. (This happened most often when the players themselves had no money and would ultimately resort to watching others play.) In these situations a fellow gambler will 'feel for the other person playing' but the secondary high is (predictably) not as good as playing the fruit machine themselves. One final point in relation to excitement is that money paradoxically appeared to be the fundamental factor in producing high arousal levels because none of the group said they would enjoy playing a fruit machine if they had one in their bedroom which gave free plays at the push of a button.

From further discussions it appeared that fruit machine playing could produce at least three kinds of moods: (i) the high; (ii) the low (depression), and (iii) anger. The high only occurred during play and was increased by wins or near wins. The other two moods usually occurred after fruit machine playing had ceased. An extreme low or bout of anger were usually experienced after a severe loss of money to the player in one session (e.g. over £50). For instance, one of the group said he had put his fist through the fruit machine because of a big loss and this resulted in the realization that he needed help and thus sought out help from Gamblers Anonymous.

Skill factors

Probably the most interesting aspect of the discussions on fruit machine playing was that once addicted, fruit machine players claimed they were fully aware that they would spend every penny they possessed playing *with* money rather than *for* it. Although in their early careers winning money was the primary reason for playing them, the philosophy behind their addictive fruit machine playing was 'to stay on the fruit machine as long as possible using the least amount of money', in much the same way as a video game player. This statement implies that fruit machine playing has an element of skill, in that the time taken to lose all your money can be lengthened by skilful playing. However, it was explained that chance could still be an overriding factor because an 'experienced' player could lose £5 in as many minutes. However, even the use of the word 'experienced' implies that some players are better than others through their skilful play.

Because the addicted fruit machine gamblers know they will lose all their money in the long run, all winnings are put back into the machine. Ironically, the only time that the study's participants kept their winnings was when the arcade itself closed while they were ahead. In this situation, the addicted fruit machine player would return to the arcade at the very next opportunity, i.e. the following morning to spend the previous night's winnings.

Traditionally, fruit machines have been viewed as games of pure chance, but to the regular fruit machine player the activity is in part skilful. With the introduction of 'nudge' and 'hold' buttons (see Appendix 2 for a glossary of play features of fruit machines), elements of apparent skill have been introduced. Basically, this means the time taken to lose all your money can supposedly be lengthened by skilful playing. According to the group, the complexity of fruit machines has evolved over the last ten years and skilful playing involves good tactile, auditory and visual perception, and co-ordination.

During the discussion all the group commented on the supposed skilful aspects of fruit machine playing. Knowledge of reel positions was the single most important factor in skilful playing and was needed especially when using the 'nudge' buttons and to some extent when using the 'hold' buttons. None of the group used any kind of mathematical probability method when playing fruit machines but some of them sometimes watched others playing, noting pay-offs and pay-outs in addition to watching the machines 'fill up with other people's money'. By watching the machines fill up with money, regular players can get a rough idea of which machines will pay out the most and when, and perceive a longer play expectation.

Associated problems

The group as a whole had experienced a number of serious problems associated with their addictive playing of fruit machines. By far the major problem, which was apparent in all eight cases, was the constant need to play and spend all their own (and others' borrowed) money at every available opportunity. (For example, one of the group claimed he had actually spent all his money given as Christmas presents before midday on 25 December at the local arcade.) This had left them all in debt at some time in their adolescent lives and had forced two of them to seek help from Gamblers Anonymous.

All of the group wished they could stop gambling, and the assertion that 'fruit machines should be banned' because they are 'deadly' and 'life-destroyers' was reiterated a number of times during the course of the discussions. In addition, the fact that even an 'experienced' player could lose £5 in as many minutes was recorded as another reason for their banning. Even though at least five of the group had some kind of criminal record none of the group admitted to stealing to 'feed' their addiction. This however may have been coincidental. They did know a number of other fruit machine players who regularly stole in order to play the fruit machines (and I subsequently discovered that two of the group appeared before the courts on burglary charges). All the group admitted they constantly truanted from school in order to play the machines. None of the group left school with any qualifications and this is probably the reason why seven of them were unemployed at the time of the study.

STUDY 1: A DISCUSSION

As with the small number of previous studies of adolescent gaming machine use that had been published at the time of this study, results showed that fruit machine gambling among adolescents was predominantly male-oriented and confirmed the speculation that pathological gambling was not just an adult phenomenon. Why fruit machine gambling should be so male-dominated is difficult to answer in the light of this study, but it could be speculated that there is a certain 'machismo' about the playing of fruit machines and girls are unrewarded socially if they try to impinge on what this group called the 'man's domain'.

A number of interesting factors arose from this informal study which I thought could be followed up in future empirical research studies (some of which are described in subsequent chapters). For instance, physiological measures of arousal before, during and after play could prove rewarding in the investigation of the high experienced by players, as could physiological measures of the secondary high, i.e. the recording of physiological reactions of regular players while watching others playing on fruit machines. The group's description of the high they experience (i.e. the immediate high) supports the research of Hickey *et al.* (1986), who suggested that the high experienced during gambling was most similar to psychomotor stimulants. The results also support the findings of many researchers (e.g. Anderson and Brown, 1984), who have asserted that arousal is a major reinforcer in persistent gambling behaviour. The study also provided anecdotal evidence that fruit machines can in some circumstances (e.g. losing heavily) induce aggression (i.e. the group member who put his fist through a fruit machine). However, this might have been (and most probably was) a rare occurrence.

It is also important to note that three players increased their playing when they wanted to escape from their current situation – especially if they felt depressed. 'Escape' gambling in slot-machine playing has been reported by Adkins *et al.* (1987) and by Lesieur (1988b) in a study of female pathological gamblers. This is an area to which I will return a number of times throughout this book. The study also gave some support for the idea that some gamblers gamble because of depression, but can in no way give insight into the direction of causality.

The fact that most of the players had 'favourite machines' reflected the belief that they were better (through familiarity) on one particular fruit machine than other less familiar ones. It also appeared that cognitive variables may be important in the continued playing of fruit machines, and with the introduction of specialist play features (e.g. 'nudge' and 'hold' buttons), it could be that these might stimulate the illusion of control (Langer, 1975) through personal involvement, perception of skill and familiarity of a particular machine. The study also indicated that research into the role of skill in the playing of fruit machines should be examined, i.e. whether the skill involved is actual or perceived. This could be achieved by an experiment designed to test for significant differences in regular and non-regular players. If regular players can stay on the machines significantly longer than non-regular players, as measured by time and number of total plays on the machine, it would suggest whether there was an element of skill or not. (Results from such an experiment can be found in Chapter 5.)

Another factor which may prove crucial in understanding excessive fruit machine playing is what this author has termed the 'psychobiology of the near miss' (see Griffiths, 1991c). If the excessive fruit machine gambler becomes physiologically aroused when he or she wins or nearly wins, then in the gambler's terms, they are not constantly losing but constantly nearly winning, reinforcing further play through self-arousal. Although this may be speculative, it does provide a framework in which the hypothesis can be tested experimentally.

The study suggested that other links between fruit machines and video games should be examined. Four of the eight gamblers in this study had played video games earlier in their playing career. Does video game playing lead on to fruit machine gambling? This is speculative at the present time, but some studies (e.g. Huff and Collinson, 1987; Fisher, 1994) suggest that those who play fruit machines heavily may also be video game players. This study also suggested that video game playing led to fruit machine playing – but only because of their close location to each other in arcade and non-arcade environments. Another similarity between fruit machine players in this study and video game players is their playing philosophy, i.e. to stay on the machine for as long as possible using the least amount of money. On the surface it seems strange that in most gambling activities the gambler plays to win money, yet the gamblers in this study claimed they knew they would lose every penny they had. However, it does not seem so strange if the players view fruit machines like video games rather than gambling activities.

A number of authors (e.g. Graham, 1988) have claimed that fruit machine playing is a social activity and although this on first examination seems to be the case, i.e. friends meet each other at the arcades, this study suggested that fruit machine playing itself is a solitary activity with little (or no) social interaction taking place.

Finally, the study indicated that more research is needed to examine the impact of pathological gambling on school or job performance. In this study, the group left school with no qualifications, which may have been connected to their truanting, and were on the whole unemployed. There is also a need for more research into possible links between excessive fruit machine gambling and criminal behaviour. In this study, the group claimed not to steal to play fruit machines yet at least five of them had some kind of criminal record. Again, the direction of causality needs to be established. Do those with 'criminal tendencies' become pathological fruit machine players or do pathological fruit machine players develop criminal tendencies to fund their gambling?

STUDY 2: THE ACQUISITION, DEVELOPMENT AND MAINTENANCE OF FRUIT MACHINE GAMBLING IN ADOLESCENCE

Although the studies of adolescent gambling outlined in Chapter 2 are interesting, those already published as this study was begun (in 1988) provided little insight except the incidence of fruit machine playing and/or the incidence of the negative effects of excessive fruit machine playing. The following study was not only designed to examine the sociological, psychological and physiological factors in the acquisition, development and maintenance of fruit machine gambling behaviour, but was carried out with a representative sample of the 'user population' in an amusement arcade, i.e. the fruit machine players themselves. The study also examined the existence of erroneous beliefs about skill in chance settings (i.e. the illusion of control) in adolescents as most of the previous research examining cognitive biases in gambling behaviour had been performed in the laboratory with undergraduate students.

Method

Sixty-nine adolescent fruit machine players were approached as they came in or out of an amusement arcade in Exeter (a typical British amusement arcade) and were asked if they would participate in a face-to-face interview and questionnaire study examining factors in the acquisition, development and maintenance of gambling behaviour. The questionnaire consisted of fifty-eight questions, of which six were open-ended. All remaining questions were of a forced choice variety. Fifty players (thirty-nine males and eleven females with a mean average age of 16.2 years) agreed to take part. On the basis of their responses, nine of these (all male) were deemed to be pathological gamblers as measured by the American Psychiatric Association (1987) diagnostic criteria. The nineteen adolescents refusing to participate in the study declined mainly due to lack of time.

Acquisition and maintenance

Most of the fruit machine players first started playing with friends (48 per cent) or parents (28 per cent), although a few began playing with siblings (10 per cent), relatives (6 per cent), or on their own (8 per cent). The mean average starting age of players was 11 years old and the major initial reasons for playing were for fun (90 per cent) and/or to win money (70 per cent). However, reasons for continued playing were markedly different (see Table 3.1) except that fun (84 per cent) was still the major factor. Only 48 per cent now played to win money and many played because their friends did (58 per cent) and/or because there was nothing else to do (50 per cent). A large majority (82 per cent) viewed fruit machine playing as primarily a social activity. A small number of players (10 per cent) reported they could not stop. Fruit machines were usually played upon in amusement arcades (98 per cent) although some players also frequented public houses (42 per cent), cafes (25 per cent), seaside arcades (24 per cent) and fish and chip shops (8 per cent).

Alternative gambling activities

Most of the fruit machine players participated in other gambling activities. These included sports betting, e.g. horse-racing (54 per cent) and the football pools (46 per cent), both of which were mainly undertaken with the

Table 3.1 Reasons for playing fruit machines as reported by players (n = 50)

	Reason(s) for starting (%)	Reason(s) for playing now (%)
Parents did/do	26	0
Friends did/do	44	58
To impress friends	4	2
Nothing else to do	38	50
For a challenge	28	18
For fun	90	84
To win money	70	48
To meet friends	2	30
Miss if not	–	20
Cannot stop	–	10

Note: Most players gave more than one answer

co-operation of parents. Other gambling activities were pursued with their friends, these being card games (84 per cent), coin games (38 per cent) and wagers (88 per cent). However, it must be noted that gambling activities undertaken with parents rarely involved use of the adolescents' own money, i.e. they took part in the gambling process but the money belonged to the parents. In addition, many claimed that even when gambling with their friends during card games or with wagers, little money actually ever changed hands. It was also established that over two-thirds of the subjects (68 per cent) also played video games.

The cost of playing: time and money

Fruit machine playing can take up considerable time and money. Although 32 per cent played once a month or less, 34 per cent played once a week, 28 per cent played more than once a week and 6 per cent played every day. In actual 'playing time', 20 per cent played on average at least an hour a day, and 30 per cent played a couple of hours a week. However, 50 per cent played on average less than an hour a week.

Most players could control how much money they spent and 70 per cent of the players spent less than £5 a week (with 36 per cent in fact spending less than £1 a week). However, 14 per cent spent between £5 and £10 a week and 16 per cent regularly spent over £10 in the same period. In money spent per session, 44 per cent regularly spent over £3 with 10 per cent spending £6 to £10. Over one-third of the players (42 per cent) had on at least one occasion lost over £10 in one playing session.

The money to play fruit machines came primarily from two sources: pocket money (52 per cent) and/or a part- (or full-) time job (64 per cent). Other sources were less acceptable and included admissions of borrowing money from friends and parents (24 per cent), using school lunch money (18 per cent), using Christmas or birthday money (6 per cent) and stealing from friends and parents (12 per cent). Gambling debts had occurred at least once in 38 per cent of players.

Gambling and affective states

A number of questions were asked relating to the mood(s) of players before, during and after the playing of fruit machines (see Table 3.2). Before playing, a majority of players (60 per cent) felt in a good mood although others were either fed up (14 per cent) or in a bad mood (4 per cent). During play, 44 per cent experienced excitement, 38 per cent felt they did not want to stop playing and 10 per cent claimed they could not stop playing. After playing, only 34 per cent felt in a good mood whereas 18 per cent were in a bad mood and 28 per cent were fed up. A number of players (40 per cent) wished they were still playing (see Table 3.2).

Table 3.2 Moods felt before, during and after playing as reported by players (n = 50)

Mood[1]	Before playing (%)	During playing (%)	After playing (%)
Excitement	4	44	0
Good mood	60	64	34
Bad mood	4	0	18
Being fed up	14	6	28
Not wanting to stop playing	–	38	–
Wishing you were still playing	–	–	40
Cannot stop playing	–	10	–
Other moods[2]	28	10	20

Notes: 1   Some players gave more than one reply
         2   'Other moods' refers to those players whose general mood before, during and after could not be determined

Fruit machines: attractions and disadvantages

Despite financial losses, the fruit machine is still attractive to the adolescent gambler. The players reported a number of attractive features and qualities including the chance to win money (72 per cent), actually winning money (40 per cent), the flashing lights (30 per cent), the music and noise (30 per cent), the prevention of boredom (26 per cent) and the excitement and stimulation (24 per cent). Minor attractions were the chance to 'be your own boss', good fun, a test of skill, helping to forget problems, the opportunity to play alone and watching others lose!

The major disadvantages of fruit machine playing were either financial problems, i.e. losing money (35 per cent), using up too much money (22 per cent) and poor value for money (12 per cent), or its addictive nature (20 per cent). Minor disadvantages reported by some players included knowing you cannot win in the long run, knowing you cannot improve your game and being a distraction from other leisure activities.

Negative consequences

Although 54 per cent reported they had won a lot of money at least once (the amount of which was undetermined), on other occasions 96 per cent had lost more money than they intended and 68 per cent had spent all their money. Other negative consequences of fruit machine playing which occurred at least once included truanting (32 per cent), stealing (18 per cent), getting into trouble with parents or teachers over gambling (15 per cent), irritability when not playing (8 per cent), causing damage to arcade surroundings (4 per cent), poor schoolwork (2 per cent) and aggressive behaviour (2 per cent). However, it must be noted that a figure of 2 per cent for 'poor schoolwork' and 'aggressive behaviour' represents only one person.

A number of players reported they would go out of their way to gamble on fruit machines (20 per cent) and 66 per cent reported they could stop playing them easily (24 per cent did not know and 10 per cent said they could not). Probably the most disturbing finding was that 18 per cent of the players were pathological gamblers as defined by the diagnostic criteria of the American Psychiatric Association (1987).

Pathological gambling

Fruit machine playing appears to be predominantly male-oriented and all the nine players (18 per cent) diagnosed as pathological gamblers were males. This group differed from the forty-one non-pathological gamblers significantly on a number of variables. Not surprisingly, significant differences were found on most of *DSM-III-R* diagnostic criteria since they are a measure of pathological gambling (see Table 3.3). Pathological gamblers started playing fruit machines at a mean age of 9.22 years, significantly earlier than the others who began at 11.34 years (t = 3.25, $p < 0.01$).

Table 3.4 shows the reasons for the continued playing of fruit machines. The pathological gamblers were significantly less likely to play because their friends did, or to win money, and they were significantly more likely to view fruit machine playing as a non-social activity. They were also significantly more likely to have had a big win in their playing career. On other financial variables pathological gamblers were significantly more likely to owe money in addition to obtaining money by less socially acceptable sources (i.e. borrowing, use of lunch/birthday/Christmas money and stealing). They were also significantly more likely to get into trouble with parents and teachers over gambling and were significantly more irritable when not playing.

The pathological gamblers were more likely to be attracted by the 'aura' of the machines (i.e. the music, noise and flashing lights) and experienced significantly more excitement during play. No difference was found between the two groups on other gambling activities.

Table 3.3 Pathological gambling: percentages of players showing diagnostic criteria *DSM-III-R*

Criterion	% Sample	Fisher's Exact
Frequently gamble and obtain money to gamble	22	2.2 x 10***
Frequently gamble larger amounts of money	26	4 x 10*
Need to gamble more to be excited	18	5 x 10**
Restless if cannot gamble	20	1 x 10**
Return to gamble to win back losses	4	NS
Make repeated efforts to stop gambling	24	NS
Gamble instead of going to school/job	18	4 x 10***
Sacrifice other activities to gamble	20	7 x 10***
Continue to gamble, even when owing money	54	NS

Notes: * $p < 0.05$
    ** $p < 0.01$
    *** $p < 0.001$

Table 3.4 Significant differences between pathological and social gamblers

	Fisher's Exact
Reasons for playing now	
• Because friends play	2 x 10*
• To win money	1.6 x 10*
• Miss if do not play	7 x 10***
• Cannot stop playing	1.32 x 10***
Financial factors	
• Winning a lot of money	2.2 x 10*
• Borrowing from friends/parents	2 x 10***
• Owing money	3.7 x 10***
• Using lunch money	5.4 x 10*
• Using birthday/Christmas money	6.6 x 10***
• Stealing money	7.9 x 10***
Affective states	
• Excitement during playing	1.98 x 10***
• Not wanting to stop playing while playing	9.7 x 10***
• Cannot stop playing while playing	1.32 x 10***
• Wishing you were still playing after playing	6.7 x 10***
Negative consequences	
• Got into trouble with parents/teachers over gambling	4.4 x 10***
• Missed school or job	4.6 x 10***
• Stealing	1 x 10***
• Irritable when not playing	2.6 x 10***
• Self-confessed addiction to fruit machines	7 x 10***
Miscellaneous	
• Attractiveness of music and noise	1.5 x 10*
• Social activity (playing as a . . .)	3.7 x 10***
• Would go out of one's way to play on the machines	7 x 10***

Notes: * $p < 0.05$
** $p < 0.01$
*** $p < 0.001$

Cognitive variables with relation to skill

In response to the forced choice questions, 'Why did you first start playing fruit machines?' and 'Why do you play fruit machines now?', 28 per cent and 18 per cent of the sample respectively reported 'for a challenge' as at least one of their reasons (see Table 3.1 for other reasons). This answer implied that fruit machine gambling was an activity that could be mastered, although the higher 'reason for starting' figure (28 per cent) over 'reason for continuing' (18 per cent) was probably due to incorrect preconceived expectations, i.e. some players who originally started for a challenge eventually realized the fruit machine could not be beaten in the long run.

When asked the forced choice question, 'Is there any skill in playing fruit machines?' only 12 per cent reported there was no skill whatsoever, although 40 per cent reported that 'mostly chance' factors were present when playing. However, 48 per cent of the respondents reported there was some degree of skilful activity. Interestingly, all nine players who were diagnosed as pathological gamblers reported there was some skill in playing fruit machines (see Table 3.5). By collapsing the responses into two categories 'all/some skill' vs. 'all/mostly chance', the difference between pathological (n = 9) and non-pathological (n = 41) gamblers was significant using Fisher's Exact Test ($p = 0.00052$).

In an open-ended question asking specifically, 'What skill is involved in playing fruit machines?', the 48 per cent who originally reported that playing was in part skilful gave nine different answers (all the replies are recorded in Table 3.6 which I constructed inductively after going through all the responses). Six of the nine responses included a reference to 'knowledge' of some particular feature of the fruit machine. Some of the replies were quite elaborate, e.g. 'each machine has its own personality and you have to master it . . . you have to relate to it and know what its next move is going to be.' However, in simple terms it meant little more than knowing how to operate a particular machine. One player did not actually

Table 3.5 Players' replies to 'Is there any skill in playing fruit machines?'

	Nonpathological gambling sample (n = 41)		Pathological gambling sample (n = 9)		Total sample (n = 50)	
	No. of people	*%*	*No. of people*	*%*	*No. of people*	*%*
All skill	0	0	0	0	0	0
Mostly skill	15	36	9	100	24	48
Mostly chance	20	49	0	0	20	40
All chance	6	15	0	0	6	12
Total	41	100	9	100	50	100

mention a particular feature of skilful playing but he implied that skill existed by reporting, 'like any game, the more you play the better you get'. This was a clear example of someone who believed 'practice makes perfect'.

It was noted that 42 per cent of the players reported that they had lost over £10 in one playing session at least once and that a number of them spontaneously added comments like 'I had some bad luck', 'I was having a bad day' or 'I wasn't concentrating'. This indicated that they discounted big losses as due to external influences. These explanations could be viewed as flexible attributions in Wagenaar's (1988) terminology.

STUDY TWO: A DISCUSSION

Although the study involved only fifty fruit machine players, the results did suggest a number of underlying trends in the factors affecting acquisition,

Table 3.6 Skill factors in fruit machine gambling as reported by players (n = 24)

Skill factor	No. of people reporting	% Total of sub-sample (n = 24)	% Total of whole sample (n = 50)
Knowledge of reel positions and symbol displays	17	71	34
Knowledge of 'nudge' and 'hold' buttons in prolonging play	9	38	18
Knowledge of a particular machine and how to operate it	8	33	16
Knowledge of 'bank' buttons and 'double or quit' ('gamble') strategies	4	17	8
Knowledge of token pay-outs vs. money pay-outs	4	17	8
Quick reflexes and quick decisions re display	4	17	8
Hand–eye co-ordination	2	8	4
Knowing when the machine is 'full of money'	2	8	4
Probability of pay-outs	1	4	2

Notes: (a) Most players gave more than one answer
(b) Percentages are to the nearest whole number

development and maintenance of gambling behaviour. This study again confirmed that for some individuals, fruit machine playing absorbs a lot of time and money and that it appears to be a predominantly male activity. It was not surprising that all those players diagnosed as pathological gamblers were young male adolescents. Although anecdotally cases of excessive female fruit machine gambling are known they appear to be much less common.

Results indicated that most players' initial reasons for playing are to have fun and/or to win money but, as with the pathological gamblers from the first study outlined in this chapter, even many 'social' gamblers stop playing to win money. Other factors like 'playing because friends do' (i.e. peer pressure) seem to become more salient. Pathological gamblers were significantly less likely to play because their friends did, perhaps suggesting that fruit machine playing is a social activity for less regular players. Results also indicated that adolescents play fruit machines in a wide variety of places and that a sizeable proportion do so in public houses when they are under age. This suggests there may be some link between adolescent drinking and adolescent gambling.

The study again confirmed that pathological gambling is not just an adult phenomenon, and at the time it was published in 1990 (Griffiths, 1990a), it was the first study to give an incidence figure of pathological gamblers in an adolescent fruit machine 'user population' (i.e. 18 per cent). However, this figure is biased, as the sample was taken from an amusement arcade where the heavier users are likely to be encountered, and therefore larger surveys need to be carried out to give more reliable estimates. It must also be noted that although the *DSM-III-R* was not specifically validated on adolescents it does seem to discriminate very heavy players from the rest.

In this study there seemed to be little difference in the acquisitional factors between the pathological and non-pathological gamblers except that the pathological gamblers started playing on fruit machines significantly earlier. However, this may or may not be causal. Pathological gamblers were more likely to have had a big win earlier in their playing career which confirms the work of Lesieur (1984) and Custer (1982), who both suggested a big win may be a crucial factor in the development of problem gambling. This study also suggested that more pathological gamblers tend to first start playing with their parents or on their own as opposed to with friends. However, participation with someone does seem to be a critical factor in the initiation of fruit machine playing. In addition, peer pressure appears to be important in the maintenance of non-pathological 'social' gambling. Anecdotally it was noted that such groups look after the interests of other players in the group and try to stop any of their friends who they consider are playing too heavily. Lone players do not have this pressure to stop and can thus deteriorate into excessive playing.

It was clear that even within a fruit machine user population, most adolescents have control over their gambling, although occasionally a number of social gamblers (i.e. those who were defined as non-pathological gamblers) did lose some control by either losing more money than they intended or by spending it all. Other negative effects were also found in a minority of social gamblers who gave positive responses to some of the *DSM-III-R* criteria for pathological gambling (e.g. gambling debts, owed money, truancy, etc.). Almost all of those diagnosed as pathological gamblers admitted negative consequences of their excessive playing including stealing and truancy, with some of them also admitting to poor schoolwork, aggressive behaviour and damage to the arcade surroundings. For these people at least, excessive gambling caused serious problems in their lives, confirming many of the findings outlined in Chapter 2 relating to signs of dependency.

There appeared to be no similarities between fruit machine playing and other gambling activities, although all the psychological gamblers played video games. This was not significant and could be explained by the fact that fruit machines and video gaming machines are invariably next to (or in the vicinity of) each other in amusement arcades. However, it could also be (as was mentioned earlier in this chapter) that fruit machine players 'progress' from video games to fruit machine playing.

Results from this study suggested that fruit machine playing could be operating at two distinct levels with the social gambler participating for fun, money and its social focus, and the excessive gambler playing alone, 'playing for the sake of playing' (with money rather than for it), attracted by the 'aura' of the machine. Again there is further evidence from this study that the excessive fruit machine players' reinforcer may be physiological as opposed to financial, as the pathological gamblers reported significantly more excitement and arousal during gambling activity than did social gamblers. However, with such a small number of pathological gamblers this suggestion is still highly speculative.

The data reported on subjective physiological arousal can be used indirectly to support both the arousal and endorphin literatures (see Chapter 1). In these studies, arousal was only mentioned subjectively. However, as was previously mentioned, there is a significant correspondence between the arousal that a subject feels and reports and the arousal that is objectively measured. It could be that the arousal is endorphin related. If regular gamblers become aroused while gambling, they may be producing endorphins, i.e. the body's own morphine-like substances. The more players gamble, the more tolerance the gambler builds up and eventually he or she has to keep gambling more to get the initial desired effect. Such a view is again highly speculative and contradicts the findings of Blaszczynski *et al.* (1986a) who suggested that machine gambling may be maintained by more 'escapist' motives than physiological ones, but it does have immense treatment implications. If persistent gambling is in part due to the gambler's physiology, pharmacological intervention could be used along with more common psychotherapeutic treatments in gambling prevention programmes.

Self-report data also suggest that fruit machines could in some ways be viewed as 'mood modifiers' and that there may be two (or more) types of heavy regular player, one of whom is hypo-aroused (and seeks out excitement) and the other who is hyper-aroused (and seeks out relaxation) or even individuals who experience both states at different times. The application of reversal theory (Anderson and Brown, 1987) could be used to explain how the same activity can be interpreted differently in different individuals, i.e. hypo-aroused people seek paratelic states whereas hyper-aroused people seek telic ones. Further research might give some support to such a hypothesis.

It appears that those players defined as pathological gamblers had a greater skill orientation than other less regular players. This strengthens the argument that cognitive factors may be crucial in understanding persistent gambling. The observation that gamblers give biased evaluations (Gilovich, 1983), make erroneous perceptions (Gaboury and Ladouceur, 1989) and use a variety of heuristics (Wagenaar, 1988) towards their gambling behaviour was in essence supported – at least anecdotally. This was particularly apparent in the explaining away of big losses or in reasons for 'bad playing'. It also appears that statistical and probabilistic knowledge play little part in evaluating gambles made on the fruit machines and that regular players simplify judgements by focusing on prolonged play rather than winning money, maybe using a heuristic that Wagenaar (1988) describes as a 'reduction of complexity' (i.e. reducing complex decisions to simple ones).

If, as it seems, cognitive factors do play an important role in the development and maintenance of gambling behaviour, the knowledge of the gambler's own negative thoughts and feelings could provide potentially useful cues in cognitive behaviour modification (Stumphauzer, 1980) and, as Gaboury and Ladouceur (1989) conclude, recognition of biased perceptions may help not only in the treatment of the pathological gambler but also in future programmes of gambling prevention schemes (see Chapter 9 for a further discussion).

Although conclusions should not be drawn from such a small study, the pattern that emerges is one in which sociological factors appear to be important in acquisition of gambling behaviour (and in the development and maintenance of social gambling), whereas development and maintenance of pathological gambling appears to be sustained by psychological and physiological variables. More comprehensive research needs to be done into the interaction of the multi-determinants involved in both adolescent and adult gambling behaviour which could provide useful information for further education, prevention, intervention and treatment programmes.

4 The observational analysis of adolescent fruit machine gambling

To date there has been very little systematic observational fieldwork on fruit machine playing, mainly because the amount of information that can be gained is limited and the information that *is* collected invariably throws up more questions and hypotheses than can be answered. In addition, much of the data collected are qualitative in nature and they do not lend themselves to quantitative data analysis. This research has mainly concentrated on adolescent gambling – especially in the UK – because (as we have seen in Chapter 2) there has been great concern over the negative consequences caused by 'fruit machine addiction' in younger people. Research investigating the behaviour of gamblers in the arcade has tended to concentrate on who is gambling on fruit machines and whether those participating are gambling individually or in groups. Results from these studies (outlined in more detail in Chapter 2) have produced mixed findings. To briefly recap, Graham (1988) reported that fruit machine gambling was a peer group-centred activity in which going to the amusement arcade was the central focus of a social event, whereas a survey by Bentall *et al.* (1989) reported that most of their respondents visited arcades on their own. Further to this, Rands and Hooper (1990) reported that adolescent males tended to play alone but that females tended to play in the company of their friends. However, the problem with all three of these studies is that most of the data collected were obtained using self-report measures.

An observational study was carried out by the Gaming Board (1988) to look for evidence of fruit machine gambling in adolescents under 16 years of age. To do this, Gaming Board inspectors were required to visit six selected arcades on three separate occasions during the period of the survey. The three visits constituted one each of the following:

Visit 1   Midday – 2 p.m.   weekday
Visit 2   4 p.m. – 6 p.m.   weekday
Visit 3   Any time during Saturday

By the end of the survey period a total of 151 inland arcades and twenty-five seaside arcades had been visited. Their results indicated that 31 per cent of those present in seaside arcades were reported to be under 16 years of age compared with 11 per cent of those present in inland arcades. Of these, less than half were accompanied by a responsible adult. However, the results should be treated with some caution. The Gaming Board determined age groups by observation alone which can be exceedingly difficult because of the variation in the subjective perceptions of the observers and within the observers themselves. Another major consideration is highlighted by Fisher (1991):

> Seaside arcades were inspected both inside and outside of school holidays. During term time nearly 500 under 16 year olds were observed, 2 / 3 of whom were accompanied by an adult. Unfortunately there is no mention of how this number of children compares with that found outside of the school holidays in inland arcades. Neither is it possible to assess the impact on this number of 'holiday' use by children who live outside the area. Nevertheless, 500 children observed gambling during term time, in such a limited time for observation, provide, at the very least, a potential avenue for future research.
>
> (p. 226)

The aim of the study reported in this chapter was to observe the machine playing behaviour of individuals across a number of arcades and to give an insight into the social world of the players. To date, the few reported studies have focused on behaviour observed in one arcade only with little reference to the type of arcade, the time of the year the study took place and whether the arcade was an inland or coastal location. It was this study's aim to observe arcade clientele, their behavioural characteristics, and to examine motivation for playing. Before giving a more detailed account of the aims and methodology of the study a note on the practical considerations of observational analysis is given in the next section.

THE SOCIAL WORLD OF FRUIT MACHINE PLAYING: SOME PRACTICAL CONSIDERATIONS OF OBSERVATIONAL ANALYSIS

The boundaries between the qualitative methodologies of social anthropology, sociology and social psychology are diminishing. One of the main research methodologies in studying small groups in natural settings is that of observational fieldwork which can either take the form of participant or non-participant observation (Gold, 1958). Both of these methodologies have their advantages and disadvantages.

For the purposes of this chapter, participant observation will be used synonymously with the term 'auto-ethnography' since both methodologies employ similar research techniques and processes (see Hayano, 1979). This type of methodology has the potential to overcome the lack of information not always elicited in non-participant observation, but in many cases should not be used solely to the neglect of other research tools (e.g. questionnaires, structured interviews, field experiments, etc.). Technically, ethnography concerns itself with the data of cultural anthropology derived from the direct observation of a particular society (Conklin, 1968). However, the distinction between social sciences is becoming somewhat blurred due to the interdisciplinary nature of current research programmes; ethnography can therefore be viewed as a participant observation methodology.

Fieldwork can be ideal for studying 'social worlds'. Lindesmith *et al.* (1975) defined 'social worlds' as 'those groupings of individuals bound together by networks of communication or universes of discourse and who share perspectives on reality' (p.439-40). There are countless worlds frequently segmented into various subworlds (Strauss, 1952), many of which go unnoticed, so-called 'invisible worlds', because they may be problematic in some way (Unrah, 1983).

Auto-ethnography literally means the study of one's own group (Rosecrance, 1986) and concerns research processes as well as research methods (Burgess, 1984). It can have a number of advantages. For instance, there may be acceptance by the to-be-observed group, similar definitions, a longitudinal perspective and a development of tacit knowledge. According to Hayano (1979), the criteria for auto-ethnographic research are (a) knowledge of the people, culture and/or language and (b) the ability to pass as a 'native' member. Obviously the choice of fieldwork is dictated by the identity of the researcher and it is quite possible for researchers to use this type of methodology without knowing their approach was auto-ethnographic. However, the 'insider role' (Rosecrance, 1986) can result in a lack of objectivity, i.e. research bias in interpreting and reporting information. Hayano (1979) has countered this argument by stating that subjectivism and personal involvement may not be methodological problems but can be assets which deepen ethnographic understanding.

Non-participant observation usually relies on the researcher being unknown to the studied group. The one distinct advantage of non-participant observation is that the researcher can study a situation in its natural setting without altering the conditions – but only if the researcher can blend in naturally. The one obvious advantage mentioned previously is that non-participant observation relies on observing behaviour and *only* observing behaviour. Since the researcher cannot interact in the social behavioural processes, most data collected will be qualitative, interpretive and to some extent limited. However, by using other methodological research tools (e.g. structured interviews), suspicions, interpretations and maybe even hypotheses can be confirmed.

Researchers constantly have to monitor the activities in which they are engaged, and have to be flexible. For instance, if a researcher enters the field with certain hypotheses, misconceptions may result which will need rapid revisions and/or redefinitions of methodology and hypotheses on the basis of early observations (Burgess, 1984).

May help

Observing fruit machine gamblers

One of the lesser studied social worlds is that of the adolescent fruit machine gambler. The best place to observe such worlds is at an amusement arcade. The most important aspect of non-participant observation work while monitoring fruit machine players is the art of being inconspicuous. If players know they are being watched, they are increasingly likely to change their behaviour in some way. For instance, some players will get nervous and/or agitated and stop playing immediately whereas others will do the exact opposite and try to show off by exaggerating their playing ritual.

The questions of 'how?' and 'where?' access to the research situation can be gained raise ethical questions. According to Burgess (1984), access is usually determined by 'informants' (quite often an acquaintance of the researcher) or 'gatekeepers' (usually the manager of the organization, etc.). Blending into the setting depends upon a number of factors. If the arcade is crowded it is very easy to just wander around without looking too suspicious, but the researcher must work out quickly what type of clientele the arcade has. The researcher's experience, age and sex can affect the situation. Since arcades are generally frequented by teenagers and young men, the general rule is that the older the researcher gets, the harder it will be for him or her to mingle successfully. If the arcade is not too crowded then there is little choice but to be one of the 'punters'. The researcher will probably need to stay in the arcade for lengthy periods of time; spending money is therefore unavoidable unless the researcher has a job there – an approach which may have its benefits. If the researcher has to play on fruit machines to avoid being noticed it is important to be aware that the machines are potentially addictive and that it is impossible to win on them in the long run. The only way to make money out of a fruit machine is to own one yourself! It is also important not to make notes in the arcade itself. The best practical research tool for arcade observation is a small pocket tape recorder. Using this, researchers can either record their thoughts, reflections and observations while in the arcade, or come out of the arcade and record their thoughts and observations retrospectively but immediately.

What are relevant data?

In report, say first time I work home & then recorded.

When the researchers are in the arcade they cannot study everyone at all times, in all places; it is therefore a matter of personal choice as to what data are recorded, collected and observed. So what are the relevant data? Once again there are very few guidelines. Schatzman and Strauss (1973) suggest categorization of behaviour into (a) *routine events* in which activities are part of the daily round of life; (b) *special events* which are fortuitous but can be anticipated, and (c) *untoward events* which cannot be anticipated or predicted. Alternatively, Spradley (1980) suggests three different types of observation. These are (a) descriptive observations describing the setting, the people and the events that took place; (b) focused observations which give the descriptive observations a more detailed portrait, and (c) selective observations which link the questions posed by the researcher. As has been mentioned previously, many of the data collected during observation will be qualitative in nature and therefore will not lend themselves to quantitative data analysis.

One aspect of observational fieldwork that becomes apparent is that it invariably throws up more questions and hypotheses than can be answered. Similarly, the researcher can make an observation, form a hypothesis but can find no way to test it empirically. For instance, I was on a ferry returning to England from France which housed five jackpot machines. There was a school trip on board and two young boys aged about 10 or 11 years old were playing on the machines. During my opportunistic observation of the boys' gambling behaviour, one of them won a £70 jackpot. Within minutes the winner was a 'hero' being carried upon the shoulders of all his friends. In addition there was a sudden rush of children to the five machines. All the children thought that they too could win the jackpot. It is easy to speculate that some of the children would have formed an irrational belief that there was more chance of winning on the machine than losing – they had just witnessed a big success with their own eyes. In addition, others wanted to emulate the young boy's success because he was now a 'hero'. However, to empirically test the observation that big wins and peer

Opposite- Once a machine payed out, No-one went on it.

Table 4.1 Breakdown of arcade observations by town, area, location and date

Town	Area of England	Location	No. of arcades monitored	Observation session dates	No. of visits to each arcade
Bradford	North	Inland	12	Dec 1988; Jan 1989; June 1989	3
Dawlish	South-west	Coastal	2	May 1988; Aug 1988; Aug 1989	3
Exeter	South-west	Inland	2	Mar 1988; Oct 1988; Feb 1989	5
Loughborough	Midlands	Inland	2	Dec 1987; Aug 1988; May 1989	3
Newton Abbot	South-west	Inland	2	May 1988; Feb 1989	2
Teignmouth	South-west	Coastal	2	May 1988; Aug 1988; Aug 1989	3
Torquay	South-west	Coastal	6	Feb 1989; July 1989	2

praise contribute to persistent fruit machine playing would prove difficult (although perhaps not impossible). Indirect empirical support for such a hypothesis might be possible through the use of interviews and/or questionnaires.

AN OBSERVATIONAL ANALYSIS OF ADOLESCENT GAMBLING IN AMUSEMENT ARCADES

The data used in this analysis were collected via the monitoring of thirty-three amusement arcades. Most of the data were collected from five towns in south-west England (Dawlish, Exeter, Newton Abbot, Teignmouth and Torquay), although data from two towns in the north of England (Bradford) and the Midlands (Loughborough) – which the author regularly frequented during the study period – were collected on an opportunistic basis. Of the seven towns, four were inland and three were holiday resorts. A summary of the gaming establishments monitored by town and geo- graphical area is given in Table 4.1.

Since these studies were of an exploratory nature there were no specific hypotheses. However, there were a number of basic aims underlying the monitoring:

1   To examine the level of adolescent gambling / machine playing within each arcade.

2 To observe the arcade clientele and examine their behavioural characteristics, and to examine the social nature of machine playing.
3 To examine motivations for machine playing.
4 To examine differences (if any) between inland and coastal amusement
arcades on the aforementioned aims 1–4.

Aim 4 was investigated because many authors have drawn attention to frequent
playing of fruit machines by those children who live in seaside resorts where
arcades tend to proliferate (Ashdown, 1987; Barham and Cormell, 1987;
Spectrum Children's Trust, 1988; Centre for Leisure Research, 1990; Fisher,
1991). Further to this, Graham (1988) reported that fruit machine playing was
slightly more prevalent in seaside resorts than in rural areas. The reason he
gave for this finding was the extent of opportunities to gamble in the respective
areas, i.e. seaside resorts have more gambling opportunities for the fruit
machine player. A further aim was to examine the marketing strategies and
characteristics of amusement arcades for their implications for adolescent
gamblers. Results relating to this area are reported at the end of this chapter.

The data were collected over a period of twenty-eight months using both
participant and non-participant observation methodologies. On occasion,
informal interviewing also took place. Each arcade was visited between
two and five times with each observation session lasting between thirty
minutes and three hours depending on how busy the arcade was and what
clientele were in the arcade. Most of the observations took place between
11 a.m. and 5 p.m., although evening observations (6-9.30 p.m.) were made
in Exeter, Loughborough and Torquay. The data were usually recorded on
to a pocket tape recorder, although on occasion immediate retrospective
notes were taken. The approach was on the whole empirical and qualitative,
and can be regarded as an observational field study capable of suggesting
hypotheses but not of confirming fact.

Adolescent use of amusement arcades

The results show that adolescents were observed in all but three of the
arcades. Table 4.2 gives a breakdown of the total number of adolescents
observed by time of year and location. It suggests that more adolescents
frequent arcades during the summer season, and that more adolescents
frequent arcades at coastal resorts than at inland ones. The data also suggest
that fewer adolescents frequent inland arcades during the summer.

Tables 4.3 (inland) and 4.4 (coastal) give a breakdown, arcade by
arcade, of the highest number of adolescents observed during each
observation session in addition to the time of year (summer/winter), the

time of day (daytime/evening) and the arcade size (as indicated by the total number of amusement machines). This suggests that the number of adolescents observed is related to the size of the arcade, i.e. the more machines the more adolescents, and the time of day, i.e. more adolescents are likely to be observed during the evening.

Table 4.3 gives the ratios of male and female adolescents who frequented arcades by time of year and location. (An exact breakdown arcade by arcade can be found in tables 4.4 and 4.5.) Results are quite clear-cut that males frequented arcades more than females by 3.3 to 1, a ratio that was higher in inland arcades (7.4 to 1) and in the winter season (5.1 to 1). The highest male to female ratio was in winter inland observations where males outnumbered females by 9.4 to 1. The ratio decreased to 5.2 to 1 in the summer but this was due to an overall decrease in males frequenting arcades, not an increase in females (see Table 4.5). Coastal observations of males and females had comparable ratios but in summer observations of total adolescents roughly tripled.

Table 4.2 Total number of adolescents observed during observation sessions by time of year and location

	Observation sessions (No. of adolescents observed)		
	Winter	Summer	Total
Inland	38 (135)	18 (93)	56 (228)
Coastal	10 (150)	14 (496)	24 (646)
Total	48 (285)	32 (589)	80 (874)

Table 4.3 Total number of male and female adolescents and ratios observed during observation sessions by time of year and location

	Observation sessions (No. of males vs. females observed ratio)		
	Winter	Summer	Total
Inland	122:13/9.4:1	79:14/5.6:1	201:27/7.4:1
Coastal	116:34/3.4:1	357:141/2.53:1	473:175/2.7:1
Total	238:47/5.1:1	436:155/2.8:1	674:202/3.3:1

Table 4.4 Number of adolescents observed per monitoring session (inland)

| Arcade | No. of adolescents observed per monitoring session (male:female breakdown); session no. | | | | | | Total ratio | Arcade size (no. of machines) |
	1	2	3	4	5	x		
LB1	6[a] (6:0)	9[b] (7:2)	7[ab] (7:0)	–	–	7.3	20:2	M (69)
LB2	12[a] (11:1)	16[b] (13:3)	12[ab] (8:4)	–	–	13.3	32.8	L (90)
BF1	0[a]	4[a] (4:0)	9 (9:0)	–	–	4.3	13:0	S (22)
BF2	5[a] (4:1)	10[a] (10:0)	12 (11:1)	–	–	9.0	25:2	M (52)
BF3	1[a] (1:0)	3[a] (3:0)	1 (1:0)	–	–	1.7	5:0	S (37)
BF4	2[a] (2:0)	0[a]	2 (1:1)	–	–	1.3	3:1	S (26)
BF5	15[a] (13:2)	15[a] (14:1)	13 (12:1)	–	–	14.3	39:4	S (27)
BF6	0[a]	0[a]	0	–	–	0	0:0	S (39)
BF7	0[a]	0[a]	0	–	–	0	0:0	M (75)
BF8	0[a]	0[a]	2 (1:1)	–	–	0.7	1:1	S (24)
BF9	0[a]	0[a]	0	–	–	0	0:0	S (26)
BF10	1[a] (1:0)	4[a] (4:0)	3 (3:0)	–	–	2.7	8:0	S (26)
BF11	9[a] (7:1)	7[a] (4:3)	3 (2:1)	–	–	6.0	13:5	S (27)
BF12	1[a] (1:0)	2[a] (2:0)	3 (3:0)	–	–	2.0	6:0	S (14)
EX1	4[a] (4:0)	0[b]	0[a]	5[b] (4:1)	2[a] (2:0)	2.2	10:1	M (63)
EX2	3[a] (3:0)	8[b] (7:1)	2[a] (2:0)	7[b] (5:2)	0[a]	4.0	17:3	L (82)
NA1	5[a] (5:0)	1[a] (1:0)	–	–	–	3.0	6:0	M (48)
NA2	1[a] (1:0)	2[a] (2:0)	–	–	–	1.5	3:0	M (51)
							201:27 (7.4:1)	

Key: LB = Loughborough; BF = Bradford; EX = Exeter; NA = Newton Abbot.

Notes: a = Winter observation (November–April)
　　　　b = Evening observation (6–9 p.m.).
If more than one count of adolescents per monitoring session was taken, only the highest number of adolescents per session has been recorded in the table.
S = small arcade; M = medium arcade; L = large arcade.

Table 4.5 Number of adolescents observed per monitoring session (coastal)

	No. of adolescents observed per monitoring session (male:female breakdown); session no.				Total ratio	Arcade size (no. of machines)
Arcade	1	2	3	x		
TQ1	16[a] (14:2)	10[b] (7:3)	–	13	21:5	S (27)
TQ2	10[a] (6:4)	17[b] (13:4)	–	13.5	19:8	L (86)
TQ3	8[a] (8:0)	32[b] (27:5)	–	20	35:5	L (121)
TQ4	6[a] (5:1)	28[b] (18:10)	–	17	24:11	L (97)
TQ5	9[a] (7:2)	57[b] (44:13)	–	33	51:15	L (139)
TQ6	4[a] (4:0)	26[b] (19:7)	–	15	24:7	M (66)
TM1	43[a] (27:16)	82 (43:39)	67 (41:26)	64	111:81	L (149)
TM2	11[a] (10:1)	13 (13:0)	11 (9:2)	11.7	32.3	M (54)
DL1	32[a] (24:8)	59 (47:12)	64 (45:19)	51.7	116:39	L (158)
DL2	11[a] (11:0)	16 (15:1)	14 (14:0)	13.7	40:1	S (36)
					473:175 2.7:1	

Key: TQ = Torquay; TM = Teignmouth; DL = Dawlish.

Note: Other abbreviations as in Table 4.4.

Amusement arcade clientele and behavioural characteristics

The clientele differences between inland and seaside amusement arcades were quite marked. Inland amusement arcades were predominantly frequented by 18–25-year-old males, apart from the morning 10–12 a.m. slot in which about a third to half of the arcade is occupied by middle-aged women, and the 6–9 p.m. slot in which as much as half of the arcade may be occupied with 14–18-year-old mixed sex teenagers. During informal conversations with the clientele, it was established that the middle-aged women frequented the arcades as a break in their family shopping to play cheap stake ('simple') fruit machines and/or bingo to meet people because they were socially and/or physically isolated.

Teenagers tended to use the amusement arcades as a meeting place for their social groups in which playing activity was predominantly male-oriented, usually playing video games as opposed to fruit machines, with girl(friend)s looking on in 'cheerleader' roles. However, while playing fruit machines there appeared to be minimal social interaction, with little or no talking (except at or to the machine) between players. Much of the fruit machine playing of the older male group (18–25 year olds) tended to be solitary or in duos, probably reflecting heavier use of the machine than their younger counterparts. Playing as a duo had the added advantage of a couple being able to monopolize certain machines when they (the machines) were in a 'good pay-out mood' or 'have been left with a good hold' especially if more change was needed from the cash counter, leaving one person to 'look after the machine' and stop other people playing it.

While playing on fruit machines a majority of regular players displayed similar behavioural characteristics. Playing at a very fast speed (up to a hundred times in ten minutes) – as if they were on 'automatic pilot' – was one example. The 'automatic pilot' behaviour was often temporarily halted when the 'nudge' feature came into play. It is at these moments when many regular players will crouch down and peer into the reel window and look up and down the three reels to see what symbols are coming up. Talking to (and especially swearing at) the machine was another common occurrence – especially when a player was losing money. A number of players left their winnings in the pay out tray during the play until they had either stopped playing the machine in question or until they needed more money to carry on playing. By leaving winnings in the pay-out tray, bystanders were given the impression that the player was winning. Another interesting behaviour pattern occurred when players knew they were being watched. Most players continued to carry on playing the same machine – even during a bad losing run – until they had won something. This was presumably to let the bystander know that they *can* win on the machines.

Many of the groups (usually three to six members) who frequented amusement arcades had a hierarchy. The belief of high skill in fruit machine gambling produces 'skilful' players who are given a higher recognized status by the remaining group members. Sometimes the high status individuals are just the older members of the group who, like the 'skilful' players, can interrupt the playing of subordinate group members to

[handwritten annotation: ↑ Players ask for advice]

give 'advice' (which often means actually playing for them). However, it is taboo for a subordinate to offer help to the 'experienced' players. Some groups will pool their money to give to the skilful player, who in turn tries to maximize the group's winnings which are then divided out among the group. Also, regular players who recognize other regular players but do not know each other as friends will sometimes call each other over to help to maximize winnings. For instance, one player who knows the reels can tell the other person almost instantly where the winning symbols are located. Such actions give the 'helper' a share of the winnings.

At seaside amusement arcades the clientele was somewhat different, which was probably due to (a) the wider choice of amusement games (e.g. video and fruit machines, pinball machines, coinpushers, rifle ranges, bowling, pool tables, etc.), and (b) a wider range of stakes on fruit machines (e.g. 1p, 2p, 5p and 10p as opposed to '10p only' machines in most inland arcades). Although more females were located in seaside amusement arcades, males still predominated by over two to one. Under 18 year olds appeared to account for approximately two-thirds of the clientele, the majority being male 10 to 16-year-old adolescents who played in small groups of between two and four people on video games and cheaper stake (2p and 5p) fruit machines. Most young females were under 10 years of age playing cheap stake (1p and 2p) fruit machines and coinpushers, usually accompanied by their parents. The few adolescent females who did use seaside arcades tended to play in couples next to each other on the cheap stake fruit machines or video games. Very young children (i.e. those under 7 years of age) tended to play non-gambling games watched by their parents. Girls tended to outnumber boys on the cheaper 1p and 2p stake machines by approximately four to one, whereas boys outnumbered girls on the more expensive 10p stake machines by approximately nine to two. It was also more likely that the high stake machines were played on by unsupervised adolescents.

It also appeared that different types of machines and games attracted different clientele. Coinpushers appeared to be played upon universally by all sexes and age groups except male senior citizens (who rarely frequent arcades anyway). Older women (i.e. middle to old age) tended to prefer cheap stake fruit machines like their much younger counterparts. Older adolescents and young men in groups (18 to 25 years) tended to play games of competition (e.g. table football, rifle range, video games), whereas those on their own played on higher stake fruit machines and pinball machines. Young couples in their late teens and early twenties tended to play games in which prizes could be won, usually played by the male to be won for the female.

Amusement machines: motivations for playing

During participant observation it was established that among adolescents, motivations for playing fell under a number of broad categories which the author defined as 'choice limitation', 'fun', 'control', 'social factors', 'atmosphere', 'escapism' and 'winning money'. It cannot be wholly certain that the groups and individuals who participated were representative of the machine playing population, although there is no obvious reason to suspect that they were not.

A majority of players congregated at amusement arcades due to choice limitation, giving reasons such as having 'nowhere else to go', a lack of age-related facilities and feelings of boredom. Social motivations included meeting friends, meeting new friends and assertions like 'everyone goes down there' (to the arcade) and 'there's always someone down here that you know'. The atmosphere and characteristics of the arcades were also considered to be important. To many adolescents, arcades have free entry, are warm, relaxed, friendly, and (on the whole) unsupervised. They also contain some of the 'latest technological developments'. They are places to 'have fun', 'have a laugh', 'mess around', to relax and 'be yourself'. Paradoxically, the machines themselves provide 'excitement', and for some are a way of 'letting out aggression' or 'relieving stress'. One of the most salient factors (and to some the most obvious) in motivation to play was the chance to win some money.

The heavier, regular players appeared to play more for 'control' and 'escapist' motives. For some of these players, the machines gave them a sense of mastery, control, competence and achievement, and for some they could be used as an escape, to 'take your mind off things', to 'forget about home' and to relieve depression. The motivation for a small minority of the players was either to 'beat the machine' or 'beat the system'. This could be achieved in any way possible including cheating (called 'fiddling' or 'strimming'). Such activities involved putting broken coathanger wire up through the pay-out slots of coinpushers to knock down overhanging coins or squirting jets of water into the pay-out slots (causing a short circuit) which sometimes activated an automatic pay-out by the machine. Since there are no rules of play on any of the machines, such players will also 'sell their expertise' to less experienced players by showing them 'how to play'. In actuality, these players were effectively obtaining free plays using novice's money and would then split any winnings.

In terms of motivation for regular playing on particular machines, video games were played mainly for competitive purposes and as a test of skill. This could be achieved by either beating someone else's score or by beating their own 'personal score'. Video game players were highly motivated to get their names, nicknames, initials or pseudonyms (in the form of three letters, e.g. GAZ, JOE, GOD, etc.) on to the 'Hall of Fame' which (usually) displayed a list of the all-time top ten scores on the machine between each playing session. Fruit machines were usually played to win money, to beat the machine, to 'get a buzz', for fun, to 'escape from reality' or because (as a few players claimed) they were 'addicted'.

GENERAL DISCUSSION

Although this study has an obvious sampling bias towards gaming establishments located in south-west England, it is unlikely that the amusement arcades monitored during the study were substantially different from those in other parts of the country. Accepting the study's limitations, the research did give a more detailed insight into the social world of fruit machine playing, the players' behavioural characteristics and their motivations for playing.

In general, the studies suggested that amusement arcades are frequented by a variety of individuals, and that a greater variety are found in seaside arcades as opposed to inland arcades, which tend to attract older teenagers and middle-aged women. Although the clientele of arcades differs depending on geographical location, the heaviest users of high stake fruit machines in any arcade appear to be predominantly young males (16 to 25 years old). These males tend to be solitary players who <u>develop special</u> relationships with certain machines, adhere to arcade specific fruit machine etiquette (whether alone or in a group), and spend comparatively large amounts of money even during one playing session. For non-heavy players the <u>arcade provides a social function.</u> For middle-aged women it provided an escape from the mundane aspects of life, for short stay seaside tourists it provided wall-to-wall entertainment, and for teenagers it provided a social meeting place and the opportunity to exercise their own autonomy.

Examining the studies in more detail, results showed that more adolescents frequented amusement arcades during the evening and the summer season, presumably because these are non-school/college times, thus increasing the opportunity to play on the machines. The fact that more adolescents play on machines in coastal areas could be explained by a mixture of various factors. For instance, (i) there are no age limit restrictions; (ii) coastal arcades are viewed as 'family entertainment' which might result in less stigma for adolescents playing the machines, and (iii) some adolescents might be holidaymakers who only play because their parents condone it or because it is something to do on holiday. Where arcades had no adolescent clientele, this was wholly explained by age restrictions (i.e. 'over 18s only').

As with nearly all previous studies of amusement machine playing, more males were found to play machines than females although there is no obvious reason why the total number of males playing inland should decrease during the summer. It may be that they get summer jobs or play summer sports instead of playing the machines. Whatever the reason, it might be useful to know for possible prevention or intervention strategies.

The question of whether machine playing is a social or solitary activity was not fully answered. For older women especially, the arcade did serve as a potential centre for social interaction, although many of the women played alone. Female adolescents frequented arcades in social groups but usually as a 'girlfriend' or 'cheerleader' to one of the male players. Solitary activity in the truest sense tended to occur in a few males, although there were still far more male adolescents who congregated in groups. However, during the playing of machines there was little verbal communication with other people, so it could be argued that machine playing itself is a solitary activity.

Many regular male players seemed to implicitly conform to certain rules, stereotypical behaviours and styles of etiquette. Many of the male groups were hierarchical where members 'knew their place', and behavioural characteristics like playing as if on 'automatic pilot' or crouching at machines to look at symbols at the back of reels were commonplace. Etiquette rules were very similar to those found in a previous study by Caldwell (1974), who studied the behaviour of poker machine players (the Australian equivalent to fruit machine players). He reported that there were a number of semi-formal rules of etiquette. For instance, if a player ran out of money on a particular machine and wanted to carry on playing it, the player would have a few minutes to return before other players could try their luck (which is similar to behaviours that occurred during this study, where playing in duos means that one person can 'look after the machine' while the other goes to get change, etc.). Caldwell also reported that there was a lack of aggressive behaviour with losses being calmly accepted, that expressive behaviour occurred in groups but not in solitary players, and that in groups there was humour present and encouragement for both winners and losers, except for the very regular players who would be taunted for failure. This picture of 'friendliness' and a relaxed atmosphere was not so prominent in this study. Observational research suggested that losses were not always accepted calmly and that many players, whether in a group or playing alone, became verbally aggressive towards the machine, often directing expletives at the machine. This is similar to the behaviour reported in a study of video game players' vocalizations by Scheibe and Erwin (1979).

Inland and coastal amusement arcades showed a marked clientele difference which was probably explained by coastal arcades having a wider choice of machines, games and stake sizes (resulting in wider age ranges particularly, and more equal sex distribution) and also by the fact that coastal arcades are primarily there for seasonal holidaymakers. At coastal arcades it was fairly clear that different types of machine attracted different types of people, although why this should be so is not so obvious. For instance, older women tended to play cheaper stake machines, perhaps because they considered it better value for money, whereas adolescent males tended to play competitive games and machines probably as a test of their 'masculinity'. However, more research is needed to ascertain the true function of such arcade machines.

Motivations for playing varied between individuals, although there were some persistent themes. Less regular ('social') players tended to play for fun, for money, for social reasons, for the atmosphere and because there is little else to do. However, regular and more 'heavy' players appeared to play for different motivating reasons and did not seem to be a homogenous group. At a simplistic level, there seems to be the heavy player who plays for excitement, to show off to friends and to demonstrate control, and the heavy player who plays to escape from something unpleasant in his or her life and who treats the machine as a kind of 'electronic friend' (Selnow, 1984).

Obviously much of the data reported here are inconclusive in nature and more research needs to be done to confirm the suggestions raised. One potential way of gaining behavioural data might be the videotaping of an arcade and its clientele. There might be some amusement arcade owners who use video cameras for security precautions and it might therefore be possible to study the playing behaviour of some individuals if owners such as these gave permission to use their video recordings for data analysis. It would also be useful to record the vocalizations of the interaction between machine and player in natural settings in an attempt to establish cognitive biases (see Chapter 5 for a further discussion of this). However, both these methodologies raise the ethical questions of informed consent and the invasion of privacy, and beg the question of whether the confined interior of the amusement arcade is a 'public' place.

ADOLESCENT FRUIT MACHINE GAMBLERS: A PSYCHOSOCIAL TYPOLOGY

Besides the study outlined above, there has been only one other longitudinal study on adolescent fruit machine gambling in the UK (i.e. Fisher, 1993b). The two studies were carried out independently of each other and had somewhat different aims. However, a closer examination of the two studies reveals a number of striking similarities in addition to a few subtle differences. This section attempts to integrate the main findings of the two studies with particular reference to the typologies explicitly reported by Fisher and implicitly reported by myself. Comparison will also be made between the data collection methods of the two authors in an attempt to discover whether the different observational methodologies contributed to differences in result findings.

FISHER'S (1993B) OBSERVATIONAL STUDY: A SUMMARY

Fisher's study from a sociological perspective involved non-participant observation supplemented with formal interviews of the arcade clientele carried out over a fourteen-month period while she worked as a part-time cashier in an unspecified seaside amusement arcade. (Its geographical location was kept deliberately anonymous to ensure confidentiality to those she interviewed and to avoid giving undue attention to the town after the publication of her findings.) Fisher's basic aim was to present a socio-logical account of arcade fruit machine playing among adolescents. Her analysis was presented in the form of a typology describing five different types of player (outlined below) differentiated by their primary orientation towards the fruit machine itself. The types emerged naturalistically, i.e. they were informed by, rather than informed, the fieldwork. She therefore had no specific hypotheses. A more direct detailed comparison of the methodologies used by Fisher and myself can be found in Table 4.6.

To compare the findings of the two studies, Fisher's player types (*Arcade Kings*, *Machine Beaters*, *Rent-a-Spacers*, *Action Seekers* and *Escape Artists*) are outlined and then contrasted with my own findings outlined earlier in this chapter.

The *Arcade Kings*

Fisher reported that *Arcade Kings* were males in their late teens or early twenties, possessed fruit machine playing skills, played in groups with younger 9–10-year-old boys (apprentices), were unlikely to have problems with their playing (i.e. 'addiction') and whose primary orientation towards fruit machine gambling was a positive gain in character. She reported that the groups were coherent and self-supporting with a shared sense of quasi-professional status and who shared losses and winnings, thus demon-strating group commitment and trust. In addition the *Arcade Kings* shared their 'skills' with the apprentices, who in return performed menial tasks for

Table 4.6 A comparison of the observational methodologies of Griffiths (1991d) and Fisher (1993b)

Variable	Griffiths	Fisher
Methodological details		
• Participant observation	Yes	No
• Non-participant observation	Yes	Yes
• Formal interviews	No	Yes
• Informal interviews	Yes	No
• Status as researcher	Punter	Arcade cashier (p/t)
• Primary orientation of researcher	Psychological	Sociological
Study details		
• Length of study	28 months	14 months
• Geographical location(s)	Bradford	Not specified
	Dawlish	
	Exeter	
	Loughborough	
	Newton Abbot	
	Teignmouth	
	Torquay	
• Type of arcade	Inland and seaside	Seaside
• No. of arcades observed	33	1
• No. of observation sessions	80	Not specified
• Length of observation sessions	30 mins – 3 hours	Not specified
• Time(s) of day studied	11 am – 9.30 pm	Not specified
• No. of adolescents observed	874	Not specified
• No. of adolescents interviewed (formal)	0	10
• No. of group interviews (formal)	0	4

the *Kings* (e.g. getting money from the change counter). A similar scene was reported earlier in the chapter on pp. 106–7 (and repeated here for direct comparison), although player types are described as either 'experienced'/'skilful' (i.e. the *Arcade Kings* in Fisher's terminology) or 'subordinates' (i.e. apprentices):

Many of the groups (usually three to six members) who frequented amusement arcades had a hierarchy. The belief of high skill in fruit machine gambling produces 'skilful' players who are given a higher recognized status by the remaining group members. Sometimes the high status individuals are just the older members of the group who, like the 'skilful' players, can interrupt the playing of subordinate group members to give 'advice' (which often means actually playing for them). However, it is taboo for a subordinate to offer help to the 'experienced' players. Some groups will pool their money to give to the skilful player, who in turn tries to maximize the group's winnings which are then divided out among the group.

It was also reported earlier in the chapter that 'experienced' players will sometimes exploit the younger players. Since there are no rules of play on a fruit machine, experienced players sell their expertise to less experienced players by showing them 'how to play'. In actuality, these players were effectively obtaining free plays using a novice's money. This exploitative behaviour was not reported by Fisher, who describes a scene where everyone was friendly and helpful towards each other.

The *Machine Beaters*

Fisher reported that *Machine Beaters* were males who played alone (because they do not like being watched) and whose primary orientation is asocial and to beat the machine. In addition, it was reported that *Machine Beaters* had a propensity to experience 'addictive' problems with their playing. Their determination to beat the machine at any cost required enormous resources of time and money and could lead to unsocial and/or illegal behaviours. Similarly, earlier in this chapter it was reported that the motivation for a small minority of players was either to 'beat the machine' or 'beat the system', and could be achieved in any way possible, including cheating. However, I believe these players to be a subset of 'experienced' players (i.e. *Arcade Kings*) who play in groups rather than alone and in which the machines give the players a sense of mastery, control, competence and achievement.

The *Rent-a-Spacers*

Fisher reported that *Rent-a-Spacers* were teenage females with no playing skills and little interest in acquiring them, and who gamble on fruit machines primarily to gain access to the arcade venue where they can socialize with their friends. Their preferred role is one of 'spectator'. Earlier in this chapter a similar picture was reported in which between 6 p.m. and 9 p.m. up to half the arcade may be occupied with 14 to 18-year-old mixed sex teenagers who tended to use the amusement arcades as a meeting place for their social group in which playing activity was predominantly male-oriented with girl(friend)s looking on in 'cheerleader' roles.

The *Action Seekers*

Fisher reported that the primary orientation of *Action Seekers* is the thrill and excitement of playing. She made no reference to typical age and sex of this type of player or to whether they usually played alone or in groups. As with the *Machine Beaters*, I believe *Action Seekers* to be a subset of 'experienced' male players in their teens or early twenties (i.e. *Arcade Kings*) and described a particular type of regular player whose primary motivating reasons for playing are for excitement, to show off their skill to their friends and to demonstrate control.

The *Escape Artists*

Fisher reported that *Escape Artists* can be either male or female, depressed, socially isolated and who gamble primarily as a means of escape from overwhelming problems. She also reported that the attraction of fruit machines for *Escape Artists* is found in both the game and the venue. The machine is both totally absorbing so that problems are temporarily forgotten and it also provides a source of non-human interaction. Citing my own work (Griffiths, 1991f), she thus describes the machine as an 'electronic friend'. She added that the venue fostered the escape from reality by providing a surreal environment and an opportunity to be among people without the need for intimate social interaction. I have also described this particular sub-type of player not only in relation to this chapter's observational study but also in other papers (see Griffiths, 1991g; 1993c). With reference to my own observational study, it was reported that for some players, the machines could be used as an escape to 'take your mind off things', to 'forget about home' and to relieve depression.

THE PSYCHOSOCIAL TYPOLOGY OF FRUIT MACHINE PLAYERS: SOME CONCLUSIONS

It has been demonstrated that the two independent studies by Fisher and myself are conceptually very similar despite the fact that they were approached from a different perspective, had differing methodologies and differing aims and objectives. The biggest difference in the typologies outlined by the two authors is that I believe *Machine Beaters* and *Action Seekers* to be hierarchical subgroups of *Arcade Kings*, although Fisher does admit that her categorizations may not be mutually exclusive. The 'experienced' player that I have described subsumes the aforementioned three types without trying to distinguish between each type, as I believe the motivations of action seeking, trying to beat the machine and the gaining of social rewards to be highly interlinked. It is also possible (and highly probable) that the differences were due to Fisher collecting her data from only one arcade.

Fisher's *Escape Artists* are almost identical to a type I describe as the 'secondary addicted' type (i.e. 'escape' being the primary motivation to gamble – see Chapter 7 for more details) and her *Rent-a-Spacers* match my description of 'cheerleaders' (i.e. female adolescents whose reason for being in the arcade is to be with their boyfriends, in male company, etc.). Since both authors independently identified what appear to be two distinct types (i.e. *Escape Artists* and *Rent-a-Spacers*), it may be that these particular types are mutually exclusive. It should also be noted that both authors identified a category of young boys which Fisher termed 'apprentices' and which I termed 'subordinates' and who knew their place in the arcade hierarchy. However, Fisher interpreted this hierarchy as a kind of training ground (hence the name 'apprentices') for the younger players, whereas my own interpretation is one of exploitation (hence the name 'subordinates'). These different interpretations may again have stemmed from the fact that Fisher collected data from only one arcade.

Considering that both of these studies were from a longitudinal perspective it is perhaps surprising that neither study gave an insight into whether players progressed from one particular sub-type of fruit machine player into another. For instance, do *Machine Beaters* ever go on to become *Escape Artists*? Fisher was perhaps in the best position to answer these types of questions, since she studied one arcade in depth and may have got a chance to know many of the arcade's regular punters, whereas I monitored many arcades but not often enough to follow individuals on a longitudinal basis. This is one area where more research may help answer questions regarding the acquisition, development and maintenance of fruit machine gambling and the mutual exclusivity of typologies.

Before concluding this chapter with the remaining results from my observational study (i.e. a brief analysis of arcade marketing methods and their implications for adolescent gamblers), there follows a short section on legal and illegal ploys in beating the fruit machine. This overview is placed here, as most of the data were informally collected during my longitudinal observation study.

BEATING THE FRUIT MACHINE: SYSTEMS AND PLOYS BOTH LEGAL AND ILLEGAL

If there is a system to beat, someone, somewhere will want to beat it. Fruit machines (by definition) are therefore no exception. It was reported earlier in this chapter that the motivation for a small minority of players was either to 'beat the machine' or 'beat the system'. This could be achieved in any way possible, including cheating (termed by players as 'fiddling' and 'strimming'). Such activities involved putting coathanger wire up through the pay-out slots of 'coinpushers' in order to knock down overhanging coins, or squirting jets of water into the pay-out slots (apparently causing a short circuit) which sometimes prompted an automatic pay-out by the machine. Such findings have also been echoed by both Barham and Cormell (1987) and the Centre for Leisure Research (1990), who report stealing from machines using a range of techniques.

This section examines the role and forms of beating the fruit machine, both legal and illegal. The sources it relies on are few (since there is little in the way of an established literature), but will attempt to integrate anecdotal type findings from my observational study with information gained from 'bandit beaters' (almost exclusively males aged between 16 and 25 years) who use 'underground' leaflets and booklets and other information in an effort to obtain more money from the machine. These publications used by 'bandit beaters' are generally unofficial, anonymously written and can be obtained through classified advertisments in various magazines (e.g. humorous and satirical magazines such as *Private Eye, Viz*, etc.). According to players, they usually contain little information but give themselves authoritative titles which are quite misleading. For instance, *'How to Beat the Fruit Machine'* (no author), *'Jackpot! The Bible'* (no author), *'Beat the Bandit'* (no author), etc. An analysis of the ways of beating fruit machines by the 'bandit beaters' reveals that beating the machine usually falls into three categories. These are 'credit mechanism fraud', 'coin fraud' and 'systems' all of which will be examined below. It should also be mentioned that the first two of these categories are illegal methods whereas the latter category is legal.

Credit mechanism fraud

When a gambler inserts a coin into a fruit machine, the machine will usually display the number of credits the gambler has. For example, if a gambler puts a pound coin into a machine which is 20p a go, the number of credits displayed will be five. This has led to a number of people to try to find ways to get themselves free credits without the insertion of coins. All the following examples allegedly involve ways of defrauding the 'credit' mechanism in fruit machines.

'Strimming' was one of the first methods of credit mechanism fraud. Machines were fitted with the 'design coin mechanism' which was a device that decided if the coin a player inserted was valid. A number of players soon realized that a piece of plastic cord (designed to fit a UK strimmer type grass cutter) could be strategically placed down the coin slot, thus generating free credits. It did not take long for manufacturers to discover such a practice. This led to devices that could determine the weight and composition of the inserted coin, thus preventing the practice of strimming. However, these new devices were not foolproof. It was not long before the introduction of *Coinmaster*, a small battery operated device which when switched on had the effect of temporarily interrupting the machine's electrical supply causing a sudden upturn in voltage and prompting the machine to give out free credits. Some people also discovered that the same thing occurred with a peizo crystal device (e.g. an electronic gas cooker lighter with the end removed). When used with the 'live' end in the proximity of a fruit machine's coin slot it produces free credits. This is because any form of electricity seeks the shortest route to earth which on many machines is through the coin mechanism. The machine 'thinks' it has been paid as the electrical spark travels down the coin slot and past the coin gate to earth. Static electricity also has the same effect. Some players have realized that if the amusement arcade has a nylon carpet, they can shuffle their feet on it, causing a build-up of static electricity. As with the lighter, if they touch the coin slot after a build up of static, they can prompt the machine to give them free credits.

The gaming industry's response was to install fruit machines with an electrical capacitor which absorbed any sudden increase in voltage, thus preventing free credits from being obtained. However, the fraudsters were not to be beaten. The next device to come to their aid was the *RF Jammer* (RFJ) which, like *Coinmaster*, was a small battery operated device. The RFJ emitted a radio signal with an audio 'squeal' which sent the fruit machines' electronics haywire and resulted in unlimited free credits. The gaming industry's eventual answer was to fit a ferrite ring around the main central processing unit, thus preventing external interference from electrical signals.

Coin fraud

Since the introduction of slot machines, gamblers have inserted a variety of coins and coin-like objects (low denomination coins, foreign coins, tap washers, metal tokens, etc.) in the hope that they might get a credit to play on the chosen slot machine. On the whole these simply do not work because the machine checks the coin for size, weight and composition. However, a few ploys to deceive the machine have emerged. The examples of coin fraud outlined below all stem from the UK and as such, all the coins mentioned are British unless otherwise stated:

1 According to 'bandit beaters', one of the most common types of coin fraud is to wrap aluminium foil around a 10p piece. This is known as 'potting'. If done correctly the machine is apparently fooled into thinking it is a 50p piece. The explanation given is that excess aluminium registers the inserted coin as a 50p piece on size, weight and composition. However, players report that this is very difficult to achieve. The problem is that the amount of foil used and way the foil is folded have a direct bearing on whether the 10p piece will be mistaken by the machine for a 50p piece. According to some 'underground' leaflets, a 10p piece wrapped in a 2.5 inch square piece of foil is enough to fool the machine. Other similarly reported practices involve wrapping insulation tape around the edges of a 10p piece to give it a similar weight to a 50p piece. Although this is a potential problem for the UK gaming industry, the number of successful instances of this form of coin fraud, according to the players, is probably quite low.

2 A second type of coin fraud that has been reported involves the use of an old 5p piece and a 1p piece. Players who read the 'underground' publications report that if a 1p coin and a 5p coin are glued together, followed by drilling a hole through the centre of the glued coins, the machine mistakes this combination of coins for a £1 coin. However, there are a number of considerations. According to players this is (i) fairly time consuming; (ii) the 5p coins are now out of circulation and difficult to get hold of (although there are apparently plenty of foreign coins which are the same size, weight and composition as a 5p piece), and (iii) defacing coins of the realm is illegal. It is highly unlikely that the UK gaming industry is too concerned about this particular form of coin fraud.

3 It has been noted by at least one underground publication that Swaziland has a coin (made by the UK Royal Mint) that is the same size, weight and composition as a £1 coin and that its exchange rate is only 20p. However, there is difficulty in getting hold of the coins because banks will not supply coinage – only paper money. Coin fraud in this case will only become a problem for the UK gaming industry if someone finds a regular way (legal or illegal) of getting large numbers of these coins into the UK.

Systems: genuine advice and tips on how to beat the machine

According to the 'bandit beaters', most of the leaflets and manuals which give advice on how to get the most from a fruit machine concern themselves with fraudulent (illegal) measures like the ones outlined above. However, some do give genuine advice such as featuring reel designs from popular machines. Knowing the reels is useful on a fruit machine when the 'nudge' feature comes into play. This enables players who know reel positions to move stationary non-winning symbols into winning positions after automatic play is over (see Appendix 2).

Some players also advocate that they have managed to win on machines due to a system called the 'winning loop'. The general philosophy behind any system of winning is that fruit machines are programmed by humans and therefore the machines rely on its punters to think like the person who designed the machine. A winning loop apparently occurs if the player gambling on the machine does not use the 'gamble' button at any time during the play sequence, even if it appears stupid not to. Apparently the machine has been programmed to induce the player into going down certain routes and if the player does not go down these prescribed routes the machine gets 'confused' and goes into a continuous pay-out cycle. However, evidence that such a system works appears to be limited.

BEATING THE MACHINE: A CONCLUDING COMMENT

There is no doubt that attempts to beat fruit machines do occur, although evidence as to whether such practices actually result in extra winnings appears to be limited. Comments by regular players appear to suggest that such publications are of little or no use and that cheating produces little in the way of extra money for the gambler. The fact that there are no rules of play on fruit machines may provide one reason why there seem to be a lot of underground 'Beat the Machine' type publications proliferating in the UK at the moment, although most people would perhaps like to think they can get 'something for nothing' and would buy them even if there were rules on the machines. The area of beating (and cheating) the fruit machine has been little explored empirically and is perhaps an area that would benefit from further research.

THE OBSERVATIONAL ANALYSIS OF ARCADE MARKETING METHODS AND CHARACTERISTICS

In addition to observing arcade clientele, their behaviour and characteristics, my observational study also informally monitored the arcades' marketing methods and characteristics. An analysis of UK slot machine marketing methods mainly falls into two categories, these being (i) situational characteristics which get the potential gambler into the arcades, and (ii) structural characteristics which either induce the gambler to play the machines or are inducements to continue playing. The first set of characteristics are primarily features of the environment and can be considered situational determinants of gambling. These include the location of the arcade, the number of arcades in a specified area, possible membership requirements and advertising effects. These variables may be important in the initial decision to gamble, even though they are external to the gambling activity itself. The latter set of structural characteristics are concerned with the gambling activity itself and can be differentiated into pure structural characteristics (i.e. what the owner/manufacturer puts into the machine) and psycho-structural characteristics (i.e. how an individual relates to the structural characteristic). See Chapter 8 for a more detailed analysis.

Since their are now approximately 2,000 amusement arcades in the UK (British Amusement Catering Trades Association, 1988) it will probably lead to arcades introducing more 'aggressive' marketing strategies to get people into their premises to play their machines. They also have the task of getting those people already in the arcade to stay in for longer amounts of time in the hope that they will spend more money. For instance, many UK arcades now have restaurant and/or snack facilities (Gaming Board, 1988).

According to Greenlees (1988), the variables that are crucial to machine success are floor location, coin denomination and pay-off schedules of the machines. In US casinos, restaurants are often positioned in the centre so that customers have to pass the gaming area before and after they have eaten. Another strategy is to use deliberate circuitous paths to keep customers in the casino longer, the psychology being that if the patrons are in the casino longer they will spend more money. Another important factor is the need to house machines which cater for all player preferences (Greenlees, 1988). However, in personal communications with members of the Gaming Industry, I (Griffiths, 1988b) noted that UK amusement arcade owners have realized that some forms of gaming machines (e.g. fruit machines) are more profitable than others (e.g. video game machines). I have further suggested (Griffiths, 1988a) that this has had two effects on marketing strategy. The first is that there tend to be far more fruit machines than video games in arcades; and second, the less profitable machines tend to be placed at the back of the arcade so that video game players have to walk past the more profitable fruit machines to get to their preferred choice of game. However, empirical support for such suggestions has been lacking.

The psychology of 'gambling advertising' and 'naming' is also important in attracting customers. According to Hess and Diller (1969), gambling advertising is usually aimed at the social (rather than the pathological) gambler. Gambling imagery is designed to make a person spend money, and in almost all advertisements there is a lack of reference to the word 'gambling'. Instead, guilt reducing statements referring to leisure are used, e.g. 'Try your luck', 'Test your skill', 'Get into the holiday spirit', etc. (Hess and Diller, 1969). With regard to naming, Costa (1988) notes that the names of slot-machines are important. For instance, the first slot-machine was called *The Liberty Bell* because it typified patriotism, being the symbol of American Independence. To date, only one category of names has been formally identified. This was by Hess and Diller (1969), who reported names were often given to imply a rendezvous with chance (e.g. *Fortune Trail*). Names such as this give the impression that the odds of winning are fair in comparison to the 'house'.

As we have seen, UK amusement arcades predominantly attract adolescents and recent studies (outlined in Chapter 2) have shown that a small minority of adolescents are pathological gamblers. It was also established earlier in this chapter that different machines attract different clienteles, with regular gamblers (usually male adolescents) preferring the more expensive stake machines. Since legislation has not been forthcoming, a number of arcades now have age restrictions and those arcades who are members of the British Amusement Catering Trades Association (BACTA) are additionally obliged to follow the BACTA code of conduct (see Appendix 1) which prohibits under-age gambling (i.e. no 'under 16s'). However, the BACTA code of conduct does not apply to seaside arcades, as these are deemed to be 'family entertainment' and approximately one in five arcade owners are not members of BACTA (BACTA, 1988). Additionally, some BACTA members may not adhere to the code of conduct because it is only voluntary. There is also concern that many arcade interiors are visually obscured by external characteristics (e.g. darkened windows) and this means that children who are inside are hidden from view and thus escape detection from concerned parties.

Since this study was of an exploratory nature (a more detailed account of the aims and methodology were given earlier in the chapter) there were no specific hypotheses. However, the study attempted to answer a number of questions in relation to the aforementioned points on marketing strategy. These were:

1 Do arcades house more slot-machines than video games?
2 Do arcades have a wide range of slot-machines which attract a wide ranging clientele?

3   Are video games situated at the back of the arcade, forcing people to walk past the more profitable slot-machines?
4   Are arcades introducing other services (e.g. snack bar / restaurant, bingo hall, selling of miscellaneous merchandise) to attract new customers?
5   Do arcades have age restrictions and / or display the BACTA code?
6   Are arcade interiors visually obscured by external characteristics?
7   Do arcades refer to 'gambling' in advertising their services?
8   Do slot-machines' names appear to be important?
9   Are there any differences between inland and seaside arcades on the above named variables?

The variables examined and compared were (a) the numbers of slot-machines versus the number of video games in each arcade; (b) the presence or absence of cheap stake slot-machines (as an indicator of slot range); (c) the positioning of video games in the arcade (i.e. are they located at the rear of the arcade?); (d) the presence or absence of a snack bar / restaurant, a bingo hall and/or selling of other merchandise; (e) the presence or absence of an age restriction notice and/or BACTA code of conduct, and (f) the presence or absence of an obscured view into the arcade's interior. Opportunistic observations about gambling advertising were also made. In addition, a small survey examining the names of slot-machines in two of the (Bradford) arcades was made. This simply involved the recording of every single different slot-machine name in two of the arcades under study. Where the same machine appeared more than once, only one machine name was recorded for the purpose of analysis. After all the names had been recorded, a coding scheme was intuitively constructed and a content analysis performed.

MARKETING STRATEGIES: FINDINGS

In both inland and seaside amusement arcades, the numbers of slot-machines heavily outweighed the numbers of video game machines (see Table 4.7). In addition, there was a significant difference in the ratio of slot-machines to video games in inland arcades (9: 2) and seaside arcades (9: 5). Results indicated that approximately half of the arcades had video games situated at the rear only and that customers at inland arcades had less choice in machine stake size than those at seaside arcades, with just over one-third of inland arcades housing cheap stake machines compared to two-thirds of seaside arcades. However, this result was not significant (see Table 4.8). Analysis of the remaining arcade marketing characteristics revealed that over a third of them had a snack bar / restaurant (nearly all of which were located at the rear of the arcade), approximately a quarter of them housed a bingo hall and a similar number sold other miscellaneous kinds of merchandise (see Table 4.8). It was also revealed that less than half the arcades had any kind of age restriction (although this did not necessarily prohibit the under-aged from being in the arcade as a number of establishments appeared to ignore adolescents playing the machines), that only five arcades displayed the BACTA code of conduct and that approximately two-thirds of the arcades had an obscured view of the interior (e.g. dark brown exterior windows, large posters and/or notices in the window, merchandise for sale blocking the internal view, etc.).

In comparing the marketing characteristics of inland and seaside arcades, three significant differences emerged (see Table 4.8). Inland arcades had significantly more age restrictions on children and adolescents, significantly more obscured views of the arcade's interior, and those inland arcades which housed video games were significantly more likely to have them situated at the rear of the arcade.

During the survey of amusement arcade advertisements (which were usually in the form of either posters in the arcade window or free-standing boards placed on the pavement outside the arcade), it became evident that the word 'gambling' in any form was non-existent. Many of the signs and slogans in seaside towns were geared specifically towards the young (e.g. 'children's entertainment', 'fun for the kids', etc.). Other advertisements, usually at inland arcades, could be considered to be those which attracted the 'twentieth-century child' with a thirst for technology (e.g. 'Come inside – all the latest machines') or humour (e.g. 'Come inside – slots of fun').

The mini-survey of slot-machine names revealed three basic categories and a fourth miscellaneous one, although not all the names were mutually

Table 4.7 Differences between inland and seaside amusement arcades on numbers of fruit machines and video game machines (n=28)[1]

	Inland		Coastal		All	
	Total	Average	Total	Average	Total	Average
No. of fruit machines	651	36.2	598	59.8	1249	44.6
No. of video game machines	147	8.2	335	33.5	482	17.2
Fruit machine: video game		9:2		9:5		13:5

Note: 1 No count was made at the five arcades at Dawlish Warren; therefore only twenty-eight of the arcades are included in this analysis

Table 4.8 Differences between inland and seaside amusement arcades in marketing characteristics (n=33)

	Inland	Coastal	All	Significance
Wide range of machine stakes in arcade	7/18	10/15	17/13	ns
Video games at rear of arcade	9/13	4/15	13/28	$p < 0.05$
Snack bar/restaurant in arcade	9/18	4/15	13/33	ns
Bingo hall in arcade	5/18	3/15	8/33	ns
Other merchandise sold in arcade	7/18	2/15	9/33	ns
Age restriction in arcade	14/18	1/15	15/33	$p < 0.001$
BACTA code in arcade	4/18	1/15	5/33	ns
Obscured view of arcade interior	17/18	4/15	21/33	$p < 0.001$

exclusive (see Table 4.9). By far the most common (53 per cent) were the machines which had a reference to money in their names (e.g. *Action Bank, Cashpoint, Cashline, Piggy Bank*, etc.). The second category of machine names (26 per cent) were those which mentioned skill or implied they were skill-based (e.g. *Skillcash, Fruitskill*, etc.), whereas the third category (6 per cent) implied they were chance-based (e.g. *Fortune Trail*). The remaining machines' names (15 per cent) either included reference to the word 'reel' (e.g. *Reel Money, Reel to Reel, Reel Crazy*, etc.) or could be described as acoustically attractive (e.g. *Nifty Fifty, Naughty but Nice*, etc.).

MARKETING STRATEGIES: A DISCUSSION

This part of the observational study, although on a relatively small scale, did demonstrate some clear findings. Since slot machines make more money per machine for the owner(s) it was perhaps not surprising to find high slot-machine to video game machine ratios in both types of arcade. There were, however, some differences. In general, seaside arcades had a significantly higher proportion of video games which were spread evenly throughout the arcade (as opposed to being located at the back of the arcade). In addition, seaside arcades had a greater diversity of machines in both type and stake size. This suggests that although arcade layout and machine profitability are important regardless of arcade type, they appear to serve different functions depending on locality. Seaside arcades (like their inland counterparts) primarily exist to make money; however, they appear to be less profit-oriented probably because they cater for the traditional family on holiday and do not wish to alienate potential clientele

Table 4.9 Categorization of names of slot-machines

Money	Skill	Chance	Miscellaneous
Action Bank	Circle Skill	Fortune Trail[1]	Naughty but Nice
Action Note	Classic Nudge	Just Fruit	Nifty Fifty
Bank-A-Note	Fruit Skill		Reel Crazy
Cash Attack	Go-for-Gold		Reel Money[1]
Cashline	Hit the Top		Reel to Reel
Cashpoint	Line-up		
Fortune Trail[1]	Nudge Fever		
Grab-a-Bank	Skill Cash[1]		
Grab the Bank	Super Line-up		
Hi-Lo Silver			
Money Belt			
Piggy-Bank			
Pound Sterling			
Pound Stretcher			
Reel Money[1]			
Skill Cash[1]			
Smash and Grab			
Swap-A-Note			

Note: 1 Three machines are located in more than one category

by housing a whole arcade with the new generation of more expensive stake (and seemingly more complex) machines which appear to attract only a small subsection of the population, i.e. male adolescents. On the other hand, inland arcades cannot rely on tourists to keep themselves in business. Their profits rely primarily on a smaller number of people who either have few day-to-day responsibilities and/or whose available leisure time is greater than the average person. Under these conditions it is perhaps not surprising that inland arcades (i) have higher slot-machine to video game machine ratios; (ii) house more expensive stake machines; (iii) have a less extensive range of machines; (iv) house the less profit-making machines at the rear of the arcade, and (v) cater primarily for a specific hardcore section of the population.

Since there is only a moral and/or voluntary obligation rather than a legal restriction preventing adolescents from frequenting arcades it is perhaps predictable that some arcades displaying age restrictions allow adolescent gambling to take place on their premises. BACTA estimates its members to comprise 80 per cent of all arcade owners; however, only 15 per cent of arcades in this study displayed the BACTA code of conduct which is significantly lower than would be expected (although as mentioned previously the code of conduct regarding age restriction does not cover seaside arcades as they are deemed to be 'family entertainment'). There is no reason to suspect that the arcades surveyed in this study were unrepresentative of UK amusement arcades, which suggests that a majority of BACTA members in this study did not display the code of conduct (for reasons unbeknown to the author) or that BACTA's membership estimate of all arcade owners (i.e. 80 per cent) is significantly higher than it actually is. The reason why inland arcades had significantly more obscured views of their interiors might be along the same lines as the reason why (until recently) betting offices in the UK had whitewashed exteriors, i.e. to limit the attraction of going into such places in the first place. It could be argued that although those already in the arcade are unlikely to be seen, it may prevent potential adolescent gamblers from going in in the first place. However, such an argument has yet to receive empirical support.

It would appear from the results that a majority of arcades are now offering at least one alternative service (e.g. snack bar) in a bid to either attract new customers or to detain those already in the arcade for as long as possible. Again (as with the location of video games), the majority of those arcades with a food facility positioned it at the rear of the arcade, thus forcing its customers to pass many machines that they may not have ordinarily done. This is similar to the restaurant positioning strategy of US casinos outlined by Greenlees (1988). The introduction of bingo into a quarter of the arcades studied has meant that a new clientele with available leisure time (i.e. middle-aged to older women) are exposed to fruit machines. However, earlier in this chapter it was indicated that this particular clientele played older, cheaper stake slot machines, i.e. traditional one-arm bandit type machines. This has led some arcades to deliberately place the cheaper stake machines adjacent to the bingo hall and/or away from the more complex looking machines (Griffiths, 1988a). The selling of other merchandise (e.g. ornaments, cigarette lighters, etc.) may not necessarily be a money-making marketing strategy but a way of ensuring that arcades get a licence to house slot-machines. Slot-machine licences are granted at the discretion of the local authorities, and in personal communications with one of these authorities, I was told that shops which apply for a slot-machine licence are invariably granted one. Therefore, some arcades may be submitting licence applications under the pretence of being a bona fide retailing outlet rather than an amusement arcade *per se*.

The assertions by Hess and Diller (1969) that gambling advertising relies on guilt reducing concepts and by Costa (1988) that the names of slot-machines are important were both supported. Interestingly, the most common category of slot-machine names which had a reference to money in their names (e.g. *Action Bank, Money Belt*) all suggested places where a person can get money from, *not* where a person can lose it. The second category implying some skill element were all 'modern' machines and are trying to attract those people who desire control in their games. According to some members of the gaming industry, this is what the new breed of players desires most (Griffiths, 1988b). The third category is what Hess and Diller would describe as 'a rendezvous with chance' implying a fair chance of winning. The survey of slot-machines was obviously not extensive but did highlight the fact that names do appear to be important in terms of the image a machine projects.

Results indicated a number of significant and subtle differences between the two types of amusement arcade. This suggests that the type of clientele which arcades attract may be determined by the marketing strategies employed. It is probable (although it cannot be confirmed from this study) that the management of inland arcades realize there is only a limited market for their product because it relies (essentially) on those individuals who have available free time (as opposed to seaside arcades who for large parts of the year can rely on tourists with an abundance of leisure time). Therefore, for inland arcades to make as much money as seaside arcades (which for most of the year have fewer customers than their inland counterparts) each individual in an inland arcade has to spend more per head. It is therefore somewhat predictable that inland arcades have greater numbers of higher stake slot-machines with bigger profit margins. However, since inland arcades are frequented primarily by adolescents there is a moral dilemma concerning (what some would say) the 'exploitation' of the more vulnerable individuals in our society. Freedom to promote one's product (in this case 'entertainment') does not appear to be the issue. The real issue is whether arcades should be consciously (or unconsciously) targeting their product at the young particularly when research has indicated that the younger a child starts to play slot-machines the more likely they are to develop pathological gambling tendencies (Griffiths, 1990a; Huxley and Carroll, 1992; Fisher, 1993b). Based on research findings in this and other studies (e.g. Fisher, 1992), the question of whether legislation is needed for the minority of potential gambling addicts at the expense of the majority's enjoyment is one issue that should be debated further at a governmental level.

5 The role of cognitive bias and skill in fruit machine gambling

It was reported in Chapter 3 that many regular fruit machine gamblers believe their actions to be, in part, skilful and that the introduction of specialist play features (e.g. 'nudge', 'hold' and 'gamble' buttons, etc.) may be stimulating the illusion of control through personal involvement and familiarity with a particular machine, in addition to such features being perceived as elements of skill. Paradoxically, it was also reported that some addicted fruit machine gamblers were fully aware that they would lose every penny they had in the long run (playing with money rather than for it) and their expressed philosophy behind gambling was 'to stay on the machine as long as possible using the least amount of money' in much the same way as a video game player. Such a statement implied that fruit machine gambling has an element of skill, in that the time taken to lose all one's money can be lengthened by skilful playing.

It was further reported that those fruit machine gamblers who were diagnosed as pathological gamblers had a greater perceived skill orienta tion than other less regular gamblers, thus strengthening the argument that cognitive factors may be crucial in understanding persistent gambling. The observation that gamblers use a variety of heuristics during their gambling behaviour was also supported. This was particularly apparent in the explaining away of big losses or in reasons for bad gambling.

In the study to be reported in this chapter, a number of factors and variables in the cognitive psychology of gambling were examined, including (a) whether the skill involved in fruit machine gambling is 'actual' or 'perceived' by comparing the success of regular and non-regular gamblers; (b) the cognitive activities of regular and non-regular fruit machine gamblers while gambling using the 'thinking aloud method', and (c) subjective measures of skill and skill perception in regular and non-regular fruit machine gamblers using a post-experimental semi-structured interview. (The semi-structured interview also asked questions about subjective moods, attractions and perceptions of fruit machines, etc., the results of which are reported in Chapter 6.). For the purposes of this experiment, fruit machine skill was defined as the ability of the individual to affect the outcome of gambling positively (e.g. more gambles with initial money staked and/or more winnings with initial money staked). Irrational verbalizations were those which were incompatible or contrary to reason (e.g. personification of the machine, use of heuristics). It was hypothesized that (i) there would be no differences between regular and non-regular fruit machine gamblers on objective measures of skill (i.e. on seven behavioural dependent variables that were monitored – see Table 5.1); (ii) regular gamblers would produce more irrational verbalizations than non-regular gamblers, and (iii) regular gamblers would be more skill-oriented than non-regular gamblers on subjective measures of self-report.

METHOD

Subjects

Sixty subjects (forty-four males and sixteen females; mean age 23.4 years) participated, all of whom had played fruit machines at least once in their lives. Most were recruited via a small poster advertisement circulated around the local university and college campuses. In addition, a number of regular players were recruited via a regular gambler known to the author. Regular gamblers (twenty-nine males and one female; mean age 21.6 years)

Table 5.1 Key to the behavioural dependent variables

Dependent variable	Operational definitions
Total plays	Total number of plays during the play session
Total time	Total time in minutes of play during one playing session
Play rate	Total number of plays per minute during the playing session
End stake	Total winnings in number of 10p pieces after the playing session was over
Wins	Total number of wins during the playing session
Win rate (time)	Total number of minutes between each win during the playing session
Win rate (plays)	Total number of plays between each win during the playing session

were defined as those who gambled on fruit machines at least once a week. Non-regular gamblers (fifteen males and fifteen females; mean age 25.3 years) were defined as those who gambled on fruit machines once a month or less. It would have been desirable to have comparable numbers of males and females in each group. However, as we have seen from earlier chapters, fruit machine gambling is very male-dominated and it was therefore not surprising that only one regular female fruit machine gambler was located.

Design

The study was conducted with the full support of the arcade's manager and was performed on an individual basis at a local amusement arcade as opposed to a laboratory simulation. This was because the ecological validity of experimental studies in the laboratory study of gambling behaviour has been seriously questioned (Anderson and Brown, 1984). However, it must be noted that a study by Ladouceur and his associates (Ladouceur *et al.*, 1991) suggests there is good ecological validity for the testing of slot-machine gamblers' erroneous cognitions in the laboratory.

Each subject was given £3 to gamble on a fruit machine, which gave them thirty 'free' gambles. All participants of the experiment were asked to try and stay on the machine for a minimum of sixty gambles (i.e. they had to break even and win back £3 from the money they had put in). If they managed to achieve sixty gambles with the initial £3 stake they were given the choice of either keeping any of the winnings or carrying on gambling. Although Leary and Dickerson (1985) have argued that a determining factor in producing excitement and risk-taking is gambling with one's own money, Ladouceur *et al.* (1991) have demonstrated that the crucial determinant in stopping subjects producing a disinhibiting effect when given money is allowing subjects to keep any money they have made.

Unless they made a prior objection, all subjects were asked to gamble on a particular fruit machine (i.e. 'FRUITSKILL') initially selected in the interests of experimental control. Regular and non-regular fruit machine gamblers were randomly assigned to one of two groups: 'thinking aloud' and 'non-thinking aloud'. Before looking at the results of the experiment, the 'thinking aloud method' will be examined.

The thinking aloud method

Throughout the history of psychology there has been considerable controversy over the validity of introspection and its surrounding methodology. In a much cited paper, Nisbett and Wilson (1977) argued that the introspective method was 'practically worthless' and at best 'unreliable'. They reported that on the whole, participants seem entirely oblivious of the mental processes involved in determining behaviour and argued 'to be unaware of the processes affecting behaviour is the rule'. Most cognitive psychologists were reluctant to agree with Nisbett and Wilson, and as a consequence they were attacked vehemently by a number of authors (Smith and Miller, 1978; Payne *et al.*, 1978; Ericsson and Simon, 1980; 1984). Accepting the criticisms of the introspective method, there are three points to bear in mind which relate to all introspective methodology:

1 The real question is not whether people have access to cognitive processes but more productively 'What are the *conditions* of access?' (Smith and Miller, 1978).
2 There are limitations in the introspective method for identifying cognitive processes, but it can be extremely valid in *some* circumstances (Ericsson and Simon, 1980).
3 The limitation of introspection is closely related to the limitations of the memory system (Eysenck, 1984).

As a consequence, Ericsson and Simon (1980) devised criteria with the intention of distinguishing between valid and invalid uses of introspection. These preliminary criteria were as follows:

1 It is preferable to obtain introspective reports during performance of a task rather than retrospectively. In view of the fallibility of human memory, retrospective reports may be incomplete due to failure of retrieval from long-term memory.
2 Subjects are more likely to produce accurate introspections when asked to describe what they are attending to, or thinking about, than when required to interpret a situation or to speculate about their thought processes.
3 It is clear that people cannot usefully introspect about several kinds of processes (e.g. neuronal events). The degree of involvement in attention is of much importance and it is assumed that only the information in focal attention can be verbalized. However, it must be noted that increase of experience in a task may take the process from a cognitively controlled one to an automatic one. Hence, what is available for verbalization to the novice may be unavailable to the expert.

One common criticism of the introspective method is that some researchers argue that by asking people to introspect while they are performing a task, the nature of the cognitive processes may be changed. Common sense suggests that the extent of any disruption of ongoing cognitive processes depends on what kind of information the subjects are asked to provide in their introspective reports (Ericsson and Simon, 1980). According to Ericsson and Simon, verbalizing information is shown to affect cognitive processes only if the instructions require verbalization of information that would not otherwise have been attended to.

Therefore, the best probable method for a precise evaluation of the cognitive activities of an individual during some specified activity is the 'thinking aloud method' (Ericsson and Simon, 1980). Basically, this method asks people to verbalize all thoughts they have during a specified activity without censoring their content. Payne *et al.* (1978) noted that in the studies by Nisbett and Wilson (1977), verbal reports were given after their experiments. This affords little comparison or insight into those results obtained by 'thinking aloud' *during* a task.

Ericsson and Simon (1980) point out that when subjects verbalize concurrently, they must do two things; namely, perform the task that is being studied and produce the verbalizations. Due to the limited capacity of short-term memory, time-lag and level of accuracy, only the most recently needed information is accessible directly. In 'concurrent verbalization' (i.e. the 'thinking aloud method') the additional cognitive load imposed by the instructions to verbalize may be negligible, as thinking aloud is different from *explanation*. The 'thinking aloud method' according to Ericsson and Simon (1980) should not change the course or structure of the task processes, although it may slightly decrease the speed of the task performance.

There have been many cases in which 'thinking aloud' has been found to have no systematic effect on the structure and course of the process involved in performing the task (e.g. Newell and Simon, 1972). In addition, a number of studies involving problem solving under 'think aloud' and 'silence' conditions have shown that verbalization does not affect behavioural manifestations of thought processes, only speed of performance (Roth, 1966; Karpf, 1973; Kazdin, 1976; Carroll and Payne, 1977; Perkins, 1979). A further hypothesis was thus added that thinking aloud subjects would take longer to complete the task than non-thinking aloud subjects. The thiry subjects who underwent the 'thinking aloud' condition were given the following additional instructions:

The thinking aloud method consists of verbalizing every thought that passes through your mind while you are playing. It is important to remember the following points: (1) Say everything that goes through your mind. Do not censor any of your thoughts even if they seem irrelevant to you; (2) Keep talking as continuously as possible, even if your ideas are not clearly structured; (3) Speak clearly; (4) Do not hesitate to use fragmented sentences if necessary. Do not worry about speaking in complete sentences; (5) Do not try to justify your thoughts.

(From Ladouceur *et al.*, 1988)

At all stages and in all conditions of the experiment, I was nearby recording the total time in minutes that each subject was on the fruit machine, the total number of gambles, the amount of winnings and the result of every gamble. The subjects assigned to the thinking aloud condition had their verbalizations recorded using a lapel microphone connected to a portable tape recorder. All verbalizations made during the gambling session of each subject were transcribed within twenty-four hours so that I could remember the context of the verbalizations.

RESULTS

Analysis of the behavioural data

Of the twenty-one possible differences on the seven behavioural monitoring variables, only two significant differences at the 0.01 level were found (see tables 5.2 and 5.3). Analysis of variance showed that regular gamblers in this study stayed on the fruit machine longer than non-regular gamblers using the same initial stake in terms of number of gambles (F (1, 56) = 4.27, p = 0.044) but this was not significant. In addition, there was no significant difference between the playing times of regular and non-regular gamblers (F (1, 56) = 0.35, p = 0.55). However, regular gamblers were found to have a significantly higher playing rate of approximately eight gambles a minute compared to six gambles a minutes of the non-regular gamblers (F (1, 56) = 7.96, p = 0.007).

There were no significant differences in the amount of total winnings after the gambling session had ceased between those gamblers who were in the thinking aloud conditions (which consisted of both regular and non-regular gamblers) and those who were not (F (1, 56) = 4, p = 0.05). Non-regular gamblers who were in the thinking aloud condition were found to have more wins than any of the other groups (F (1, 56) = 5.09, p = 0.028) but this again was not significant. Regular gamblers who thought aloud had a significantly lower win rate in number of gambles (F (1, 56) = 7.85, p = 0.007) but not as measured by time, i.e. the number of gambles (but not the time elapsed) between each win was significantly lower than for other groups.

Analysis of the verbalizations

In analysing the verbalizations of the thirty gamblers (fifteen regular and

Table 5.2 Means of fruit machine behavioural monitoring variables data (non-regular/non-think aloud [$N = 15$], regular/non-think aloud [$N = 15$], non-regular/think aloud [$N = 15$], regular/think aloud [$N = 15$])

Dependent variable	NR/NTA	R/NTA	NR/TA	R/TA
Total plays	47.8	56.3	55.7	65.6
Total time	8.4	8.5	11.5	9.9
Play rate	6.5	7.5	5.3	8.4
End stake	4.0	0	7.3	13.9
Win	6.1	8.0	8.3	6.0
Win rate (time)	2.0	1.0	1.7	1.8
Win rate (plays)	12.5	7.5	8.0	14.6

Table 5.3 ANOVAs of fruit machine behavioural monitoring data (regular/non-regular, think aloud/non-think aloud and their interaction)

Dependent variable	*F ratios for effect*[1]		
	Regular	Think aloud	Regular/think aloud
Total plays	4.27	3.73	0.03
Total time	0.35	3.47	0.50
Play rate	7.96[2]	0.05	2.33
End stake	0.09	4.00	1.53
Wins	0.03	0.01	5.09
Win rate (time)	1.67	0.66	5.61
Win rate (plays)	0.16	0.40	7.85[2]

Notes: 1   Degrees of freedom (1,56) in all cases
  2   $p < 0.01$

fifteen non-regular) who were in the thinking aloud condition, a content analysis was performed on the transcriptions. The coding scheme was intuitively constructed after all the transcripts had been collected. This yielded thirty utterance categorizations and a further miscellaneous category. A full list of the coding scheme with examples is shown in Table 5.4. Each type of utterance was tallied and subsequently given a weighting as a percentage of total utterances by each subject. Regular and non-regular gamblers were then compared on each utterance categorization using t-tests (see Table 5.4). Due to the large number of t-tests performed, the significance level for this study was set at p < 0.01. It must be noted at this point

Table 5.4 Utterance categorization used in content analysis coding scheme and percentage differences between regular and non-regular gamblers

	Non-regular	Regular	t	d.f.	Significance p
Irrational verbalizations					
1 Personification of the fruit machine, e.g. 'The machine likes me.'	1.14	7.54	-4.51	16	.0004[1]
2 Explaining away losses, e.g. 'I lost there because I wasn't concentrating.'	0.41	3.12	2.47	16	.026
3 Talking to the fruit machine e.g. 'Come on, aren't you going to pay out for me?'	0.90	2.64	-1.17	27	.25
4 Swearing at the machine, e.g. 'You bastard.'	0.08	0.60	-2.21	16	.042
Rational verbalizations					
5 Swearing/cursing, e.g. 'Shit', 'Damn', etc.	3.64	2.86	-0.06	27	.95
6 Reference to losing, e.g. 'I lost the whole pound there.'	4.77	5.79	-0.77	25	.45
7 Reference to winning, e.g. 'I won forty pence I think.'	6.77	9.79	-2.25	27	.042
8 Sarcastic reference to winning, e.g. 'Wow, I won ten pence.'	1.68	0.29	2.07	15	.06
9 Saying 'No' (including derivatives e.g. 'Nope', 'Nah', etc.) in response to the machine's reels	5.89	6.05	-0.08	25	.93
10 Saying 'Yes' (including derivatives e.g. Yeah, Yo etc.) in response to the machine's reels.	1.98	1.74	0.31	27	.76
11 Reference to the 'gamble' button, e.g. 'I'm gonna gamble this twenty pence up to a pound.'	1.98	3.36	-1.69	21	.11
12 Reference to gambling in general, e.g. 'I like a gamble on this type of machine.'	0.29	1.57	-1.95	15	.071
13 Reference to a near win, e.g. 'I just missed out on a pound win there.'	1.62	0.52	1.73	16	.10
14 Questions relating to confusion/non-understanding, e.g. 'What's going on here?'	13.24	1.56	6.65	19	.000[1]

No.	Utterance category				
15	Statements relating to confusion/non-understanding, e.g. 'I don't understand this.'	4.81	1.72	2.87	24	.008[1]
16	Reference to skill, e.g. 'I only won that because I was so quick.'	1.47	5.34	-2.46	19	.024
17	Humour reference/joke, e.g. 'Two melons – I like it when I get my hands on two melons.'	0.89	0.41	0.86	19	.40
18	Reference to chance, e.g. 'It's just chance if there's a big pay-out.'	1.28	1.09	0.31	24	.76
19	Reference to blank mind, e.g. 'My mind's gone blank – I can't think.'	2.18	0.00	–	–	–
20	Reference to 'holds'/'features'/'nudges', e.g. 'I'm gonna hold them.'	10.15	12.87	-1.33	24	.20
21	Reference to the 'number system', e.g. 'I got a '2' there.'	1.45	9.49	-3.53	15	.003[1]
22	Saying 'It's not worth it' in reference to 'holding' reel features.	0.54	3.00	-2.48	18	.023
23	Reference to sudden understanding, e.g. 'I see. Now I understand how that button works.'	2.27	0.37	2.88	16	.011
24	Reference to the machine being a waste of money/rip off, etc., e.g. 'This machine's a con.'	0.36	0.15	0.73	22	.48
25	Hoping/needing a certain feature to appear in the win line, e.g. 'I need an orange to win.'	0.77	3.28	-2.75	16	.014
26	Reference to frustration, e.g. 'This is so frustrating.'	0.26	0.00	–	–	–
27	Saying '(Let's) see what happens, (Let's) see what comes up.'	0.35	0.08	1.74	15	.10
28	Reference to luck, being lucky, e.g. 'My luck's in today.'	0.69	0.52	0.31	27	.76
29	Saying 'I can't do anything' or 'Nothing I can do' (to improve chances of winning).	0.14	1.16	-1.79	15	.094
30	General questions, e.g. 'Do you think it's raining outside?'	4.67	2.44	2.19	19	.041
31	Miscellaneous utterances, e.g. 'I think I'll get a bag of chips after playing this.'	25.53	11.73	4.58	26	.000[1]

Note: 1 $p < 0.01$

that the reliability of the coding scheme is unknown. Many of the verbalizations when transcribed contained terminology familiar to fruit machine gamblers and/or verbalizations which could only be understood in the context of gambling at that particular moment (and could thus only be coded by the experimenter). This meant that inter-rater reliability was low – but this was primarily due to the second rater's naivity of fruit machine gambling. An inter-rater reliability was also attempted using a regular fruit machine gambler, but this again proved difficult to code because they had no idea of the context having not been there themselves.

The results showed that regular gamblers made significantly more percentage verbalizations in only two categories. These were personifying the machine ($p < 0.001$) and referring to the 'number system' ($p < 0.01$). Non-regular gamblers made significantly more percentage verbalizations in questions relating to confusion and non-understanding ($p < 0.001$), in statements of confusion and non-understanding (p < 0.01) and miscellaneous utterances ($p < 0.001$). There were also two categories in which non-regular gamblers made verbalizations in which there was no verbalization equivalent in regular gamblers. These were referring to (i) their mind going blank and (ii) frustration. No significant differences were found in the remaining utterance categories outlined in Table 5.4, although many approached significance. For instance, regular gamblers made more percentage verbalizations in the categories 'swearing at the fruit machine', 'referring to winning' and 'explaining away losses'.

Although the majority of verbalizations of both regular and non-regular gamblers were rational, regular gamblers did produce more total irrational verbalizations (14 per cent) than non-regular gamblers (2.5 per cent), a finding which was highly significant ($p < 0.001$). Analysis of the transcripts revealed that gamblers use a variety of heuristics (e.g. flexible attributions, hindsight bias, reduction of complexity) although they did not appear to be abundant. For example, typical reasons for explaining away losses involved hindsight bias with gamblers predicting events after they had happened:

> I had a feeling it wasn't going to pay very much after it had just given me a 'feature' . . . . I had a feeling it was going to chew up those tokens fairly rapidly . . . . I had a feeling it had paid out earlier because it's not giving me a chance. (Subject 4, regular gambler)

There were also many flexible attributions:

> '. . . . two nudges, gotta be . . . oh, you son of a bitch, you [the machine] changed them, you changed them! You snatched the win.' (Subject 1, regular gambler)

'I'm losing heavily here . . . [the machine's] not giving me the numbers I want. I've just taken a quid off it so it wants its money back now.' (Subject 13, regular gambler)

'I'm not doing too well here . . . it must have paid out'. (Subject 11, regular gambler)

'This "fruity" is not in a good mood . . . someone's obviously won out of this before'. (Subject 5, regular gambler)

Some gamblers had completely erroneous perceptions:

'I'm only gonna put one quid in to start with because psychologically I think it's very important . . . it bluffs the machine – it's my own psychology'. (Subject 12, regular gambler)

Most of the above comments contain examples of personification (e.g. the machine that is in a bad mood, the machine that chews tokens, the machine that can be bluffed, etc.) but gamblers were usually far more direct, often swearing at the machine too:

'This machine doesn't like me . . . ooh it does, it's given me a number . . . hates me!! It's given me low numbers, I don't think it wants to pay out at all . . . . It probably thinks I'm a f**kwit – it's not wrong!!' (Subject 13, regular gambler)

'It's still not giving me a "hold" . . . I hope some other numbers drop in then I'll be able to get some kind of win . . . so harsh, it's really f**king me over . . . . Am I allowed to change machine? . . . I think this machine is not going to pay out happily . . . . It stitches me up every time . . . unbelievable.' (Subject 12, regular gambler)

'I thought there was a feature held . . . I had a feature held and then it stopped them . . . f**king conned . . . this is where it takes your money right at the end 'cos it's out of pocket . . . bastard machine. (Subject 2, regular gambler)

'Can I win more than 10p this time? . . . No!! . . . Obviously the machine's being a bit of a bastard at the moment. (Subject 10, regular gambler)

Analysis of skill variables

In the post-experimental semi-structured interview, a number of questions relating to skill were asked. In comparing the responses to the question, 'Is there any skill involved in playing a fruit machine?', using Fisher's Exact

Test, most non-regular gamblers said 'mostly chance' ($p < 0.05$) and most regular gamblers said 'equal chance and skill' ($p < 0.01$). The full results are outlined in Table 5.5. In response to the question, 'How skilful do you think you are compared with the average person?', there was a marked significant difference between regular and non-regular gamblers. Regular gamblers claimed they were at least of average skill, but more usually 'above average skill' or 'totally skilled' (see Table 5.6). Non-regular gamblers on the whole viewed themselves as 'below average skill' or 'totally unskilled' except for seven subjects who said that because fruit machines were 'all' or 'mostly' chance, they were as good or as bad (i.e. as average) as anyone else.

When asked 'What skill (if any) is involved in playing fruit machines?'

Table 5.5 Responses to the question, 'Is there any skill involved in playing a fruit machine?' by fruit machine gamblers ($N = 60$)

	Regular	Non-regular	Total	Significance p
All chance	0	3	3	n.s.
Mostly chance	10	19	29	n.s.
Equal chance/skill	18	7	25	<0.01
Mostly skill	1	1	2	n.s.
All skill	1	0	1	n.s.
Total	30	30	60	

Table 5.6 Responses to the question, 'How skilful do you think you are compared with the average person?' by fruit machine players ($N = 60$)

	Regular	Non-regular	Total	Significance p
Totally unskilled	0	12	12	<0.001
Below average skill	0	7	7	<0.001
Average skill	7	10	17	n.s.
Above average skill	18	1	19	<0.001
Totally skilled	5	0	5	<0.005
Total	30	30	60	

the subjects put forward twenty skills, many of which were 'knowledge' of some particular aspect of the machine. Although there was a lot of similarity between the skills listed by both the regular and non-regular gamblers (see Table 5.7) there were a few significant differences obtained using Fisher's Exact Test. Knowledge of the 'gamble' button was more likely to be viewed as skilful by regular gamblers than by non-regular gamblers ($p < 0.01$) as was knowledge of 'feature skills' ($p < 0.001$), knowledge of when the machine will (or will not) pay out ($p < 0.001$), and not playing if the fruit machine has just paid out ($p < 0.01$). This latter 'skill' is obviously important to regular fruit machine gamblers as they use it as a frequent excuse for not winning (see the quotes above).

Table 5.7 Skilful aspects of fruit machine gambling as reported by fruit machine gamblers ($N = 60$)

Skill	Non-regular	Regular	Total
Knowledge of the fruit machine	15	10	25
Knowledge of 'hold' buttons	8	13	21
Knowledge of 'gamble' button	2	11	13[1]
Knowledge of 'feature skills' (skill chances, etc.)	0	12	12[2]
Knowledge of reels	4	8	12
Knowledge of buttons/features (non-specific)	5	5	10
Knowledge of 'number system' and 'lighting up'	5	5	10
Knowledge of 'nudges'	4	5	9
Knowledge of when the machine will pay out	0	8	8[2]
Knowledge when to quit (and take winnings)	4	4	8
Light oscillation	1	6	7
Quick reactions to certain features	4	3	7
Not playing if the machine has just paid out	0	5	5[1]
Prediction/intuition of what is coming next	1	4	5
Hand eye co-ordination	2	1	3
Knowledge of probabilities and odds	2	1	3
Concentration and patience	2	1	3
Memory	1	0	1
Recognizing high pay-out symbols	1	0	1
Avoiding playing in the first place (!)	1	0	1

Notes: 1 $p<.01$
2   $p<.001$
(Most gamblers gave more than one response)

There were also a number of other indirect skill factors. Three regular gamblers objected to gambling on the chosen fruit machine because they were either not familiar with it or preferred gambling on another machine. Seven gamblers (again all regulars) began the experiment on the chosen machine but then changed to different fruit machines, each of them changing at least three times. It was also noted that of the fourteen regular gamblers who managed to break even on their initial stake (i.e. staying on the machine for at least sixty gambles), ten carried on gambling until they had lost everything. Of the seven non-regular gamblers who managed to break even after the first sixty gambles, only two carried on gambling until they had lost everything. This difference was highly significant using Fisher's Exact Test ($p = 0.0005$).

DISCUSSION

The behavioural data showed that the null hypotheses – that there would be no difference between regular and non-regular fruit machine gamblers – were on the whole supported. Although the results were insignificant, regular gamblers did stay longer on the machine, suggesting there are skilful aspects to fruit machine gambling. However, the skill appears to be little more than taking a few more gambles (approximately ten) to lose the same amount of money in approximately the same time as non-regular gamblers. Since there was no difference in total winnings but a difference in the number of 10p wins between regular and non-regular gamblers, the skilful element in fruit machine gambling appears to stem from the ability of a regular gambler to 'boost' or 'gamble up' smaller wins into slightly larger wins. It is very probable (although it cannot be confirmed from this study) that regular gamblers believe their activity to be far more skilful than it actually is. The hypothesis that gamblers who thought aloud would take longer to gamble on the fruit machine (in terms of time) was confirmed. They did take longer but the result failed to reach significance. It should also be noted that because regular gamblers play faster and more often, they can quite justifiably claim that they have more wins than the non-regular gamblers. However, this merely demonstrates a 'fixation on absolute frequency' bias, i.e. they do experience more wins but they also experience considerably more losses.

The fact that a few gamblers objected to gambling on the study's chosen fruit machine supports Langer's (1975) illusion of control through familiarity of particular machines; and the significant finding that most regular fruit machine gamblers play until they have lost all their money supports the self-report findings earlier in this book (Chapter 3) which reported that regular gamblers know that they will lose every penny in the long run and that they gamble with money rather than for it, staying on the machine for as long as possible using the least amount of money. It also supports an assertion by Daley (1987), who suggested that slot-machine players gamble 'to buy time'. Here, the gambler spends time on the machine not to win money but because it is intrinsically rewarding in itself. As Walker (1992b) points out, the function of the time might be social involvement, leisure, relaxation or escapism. He also went on to say that if a gambler starts with limited financial resources, then (all things being equal) gamblers would choose machines in a way to maximize their playing time. This again needs further confirmation but does suggest another reason why regular gamblers have favourite machines.

The hypothesis that regular gamblers would make more irrational verbalizations than non-regular gamblers during fruit machine gambling was supported. The results were markedly different from the previous work of Ladouceur and his associates (Ladouceur and Gaboury, 1988; Gaboury and Ladouceur, 1989; Ladouceur *et al.*, 1988), who reported that their subjects produced 80 per cent irrational verbalizations. In this study, irrational verbalizations constituted only 14 per cent of regular gamblers' thoughts and 2.5 per cent of non-regular gamblers' thoughts. Personal communications between Ladouceur and myself revealed that his coding scheme only included game-related categories whereas this study's coding scheme included all verbalizations. Accepting that the total amount of irrational verbalizations were significantly lower than the findings of Ladouceur and his colleagues, the study still supported the general postulations and the research into cognitive bias by Gilovich (1983), Ladouceur *et al.* (1988) and Wagenaar (1988).

It was not surprising that non-regular gamblers asked more questions and produced significantly more statements of confusion and/or non-understanding than the regular gamblers, as this was to be expected. However, these utterance categories are still important as 'manipulation checks' and demonstrate that the criterion used in this study to differentiate between regular and non-regular gamblers was valid. Despite the fact that a few non-regular gamblers verbalized that their minds had gone blank (i.e. they said things like 'I can't think of anything to say – my mind's gone blank') it was the regular gamblers whose minds went blank in behavioural terms because a number of them stopped speaking completely for periods of up to thirty seconds. This was probably because these regular gamblers were on 'automatic pilot' in that they could gamble on fruit machines without attending to what they were thinking about (a behavioural characteristic first outlined in the observational study of fruit machine players in

Chapter 4). It could also be the case that increased experience in the act of gambling on fruit machines took it from being cognitively controlled to automatic, and that what is available for the novice may be unavailable to the expert (Ericsson and Simon, 1980). Since a number of studies in this book (chapters 3, 4 and 7) have reported that some gamblers play for escapist reasons (e.g. to forget about a relationship, a broken home, etc.) it is perhaps not surprising that the more regular gamblers 'blanked out' going into what perhaps can only be described as 'escape mode'.

The study as a whole raises questions about the validity of the thinking aloud method. The behaviour of those gamblers who thought aloud did not differ substantially from those who did not, but the real question is not whether the cognitive behaviour was affected, but whether the data gained actually explains persistent (losing) gambling behaviour. In examining the verbalizations more closely it would appear that although regular gamblers do produce irrational verbalizations, the data gained were descriptive rather than explanatory. Although it is interesting that there should be a descriptive difference between the two groups of gamblers, it could be that the verbalizations produced are the 'symptoms' of a deeper underlying cause which may be a manifestation of a particular developmental phase or may be concerned with the gambler's psychological and/or physiological constitution. Wagenaar (1988) would argue that the difference between the two groups could wholly be explained through their selection of heuristics (and not 'defects in personality'). This is an area where more research needs to be carried out to ascertain the underlying causes of irrational gambling behaviour.

At present, it is difficult to predict when (or how) a heuristic will be used in a given situation, although further use of the thinking aloud method might give some insight. One way of experimentally testing such an idea might be to use a rigged slot-machine while subjects are thinking aloud and to manipulate the sequence of wins and losses. Such manipulations of wins and losses may reveal patterns in use of heuristics. It is thus unclear whether the use of heuristics depends on intrinsic factors (e.g. psychological mood states) and/or extrinsic factors (e.g. gambling history). For instance, I have suggested (Griffiths, 1993c) that big wins 'stimulate' irrationality. From an account of my own gambling experiences published a few years ago (see extract below), this appears to be a likely explanation:

> It wasn't long before I actually started to enjoy playing on the machines. In a way, I began to get a thrill of actually knowing what everything meant on the machine while I was playing . . . even if I didn't win. Not only would I play on the machines and watch other supposedly skilful

players, but I actually began to believe I was better than the average player . . . . The last three times I had walked away from the machines I had won – and won an amount far in excess of the money I had put in. However, these three wins made my fruit machine playing irrational. Big wins like these distort the reality of the situation. You know that you can't (on the whole) affect the outcome. Yet, somehow you believe that every time you put one pound into the machine that you're going to come out a winner.

(Griffiths, 1990g, pp.21–22)

Further to this, it is also worth mentioning a typical statement of players who in the post-experimental semi-structured interview said things like, 'I can't believe I keep coming back to play fruit machines sometimes'. This type of statement seems to imply that the machine was somehow pulling them into playing with no real conscious idea of why they were doing it. It also implies that when not playing fruit machines players can think rationally about their gambling behaviour but that when there is a fruit machine in front of them, some sort of irrationality 'takes over' consciousness and cognitive biases start to occur. It would be useful to know exactly when such biases start to occur. Is it when the player is actually in front of the machine? Outside the arcade? When the player first starts to think about playing the machine? Answers to such questions might provide a valuable insight for possible future cognitive-behavioural prevention programmes.

The hypothesis that regular gamblers would be more skill-oriented than non-regular gamblers was supported in both self-comparison ratings and in questions relating to skill factors in machine play. It may be that those skills reported by regular gamblers which were significantly different from non-regular gamblers' skills are the ones which enhance the number of gambles by 'boosting up' wins, i.e. there is little difference between regular and non-regular gamblers in terms of the total winnings but regular gamblers turn small wins into bigger ones by using the machine's 'nudge' and 'hold' buttons, thus extending their time slightly by re-investing their winnings. However, this would need to be confirmed in further studies. The perceived skilful aspects of fruit machine gambling were similar to those outlined in Chapter 3. It has yet to be ascertained fully which features of fruit machine gambling are truly skilful.

The role of skill in fruit machine playing has also been examined by Fisher (1993). Fisher reported that playing skills (or rather the lack of them) are inextricably interwoven with the various motivations to gamble, and she identified three major skills. These were 'choosing which machine to play', 'knowing the reels', and 'gambling' (i.e. using the 'gamble' button). In choosing which machine to play, players take into account how much money has already been put into a particular machine and how much it has paid out. According to the players, this can inform them whether or not it is worth playing. In this study such skills were listed individually but do support Fisher's findings. For instance, subjects in this study listed skills such as 'knowledge of a particular fruit machine', 'knowledge of when the machine will (or will not) pay out' and 'not playing if the machine has just paid out'.

'Knowing the reels' is a skill which Fisher reported as distinguishing the serious player from the others and basically refers to knowing the exact sequence of fruit machine symbols on each of the machine's reels. These differ on every single fruit machine; thus it is not surprising to find, as in this study, that players have 'favourite' machines (i.e. machines they are familiar with). Inextricably linked with 'knowing the reels' is 'nudging' which involves the free moving of a stationary symbol into a potentially winning position after automatic play is over (see Appendix 2). For example, if after gambling the machine displays three symbols (two 'oranges' and a 'cherry') and 'nudges' become available, a player who 'knows the reels' can use the 'nudges' to replace the 'cherry' with an 'orange' to win. In this study 'knowledge of the reels' and 'knowledge of nudges' were reported as separate skills.

As mentioned above, gambling refers to the use of the 'gamble' button on the machine. When some of the machine's graphics flash on and off, simultaneous pressing of the 'gamble' button while the selected graphics are lit will increase the player's winnings – at least, according to the players. However, in communications with the members of the gaming industry, I was told that the 'gamble' button – a feature whose operation is regarded by regular gamblers in this study as very skilful – operates purely by chance (Griffiths, 1988b). It can therefore be described as a 'pseudo-skill' feature, i.e. a structural characteristic that enables it to mimic skill-determined situations (see Chapter 8 for further details).

Fisher did not go beyond the three 'skills' outlined above, as they were the only ones she considered to be 'major'. Of the twenty skills put forward by fruit machine players in this study, many of these were minor and somewhat idiosyncratic (see Table 5.7). However, there were a few skills which could be considered as important – at least by the players – although it is still unclear which features of fruit machine play are genuinely skilful. For instance, if a player has just won on a fruit machine and has the opportunity to 'hold' (i.e. keep stationary any symbols before play has started), is it a 'skill' to hold them? By not holding what are obvious winning symbols, 'easy money' is lost. It could be argued that this is little more than what I have described as 'idiot skill' (Griffiths, 1991h) in that it would be stupid not to hold the winning symbols. 'Not playing when the machine has just paid out' is another example of what could be argued as 'idiot skill', since very few informed people would play after seeing the machine emptying its available money.

'Knowing the reels' does seem to be a genuine skill, as does 'light oscillation' and 'knowing the number system'. 'Light oscillation' involves the simultaneous pressing of a button when a light shines through particular symbols (usually a drawn representation of money) on the machine. Sometimes connected with this is 'lighting up', which involves the accumulation of points on 'the number system'. Many fruit machines have symbols which also carry numbers on the fruit machine symbol itself (e.g. a '1', '2' or '3' numbered on, for example, an 'orange'). If one of these numbers lands in the payline (i.e. in the middle row of the machine's 3 x 3 matrix) the value of the symbol lights up the appropriate number of letters of the fruit machine's name. For instance, on the machine in this study (i.e. 'FRUITSKILL'), a score of '3' would light up the 'FRU' of the machine's name. If the player is given the opportunity to 'hold' on the next play, a player can hold the '3' and light up the next three letters of the machine's name leaving 'FRUITS' lit up. The idea is to light up the whole of the machine's name to win money on the machine. This seems an easy way to win money but the catch is that the machine does not keep the letters a player has lit for more than a few plays (if at all). A player will often light up nine of the ten letters, only for the machine to wipe all the letters clear, e.g. a player might have 'FRUITSKIL' lit up and then the machine wipes it clear and the player must start again. This characteristic of the machine could thus be said to stimulate the illusion of control and/or the psychology of the near miss (see Reid, 1986; Griffiths, 1991c).

Other players may argue that intuitive feelings like 'knowing when the machine is going to pay out' or 'putting 10p in the machine to test its money bank' are genuine skills and that only certain players have these abilities, but these seem unlikely to be the sorts of skills that can be learned by everyone if they can be learned at all. Skill perceptions such as these are more rooted in superstitious behaviour or involve heuristics such as 'illusory correlations' (see Wagenaar, 1988), although such behaviour would make an interesting research topic.

Although there may be technically skilful elements in fruit machine gambling, they are probably of minor importance involving basic familiarity with the machine. The real difference between regular and non-regular gamblers is probably cognitive, i.e. the regular gamblers process information about skill differently and think there is more skill than there actually is. Further research would be needed to test this hypothesis. There also appears to be a cognitive difference in how regular gamblers react towards the machine itself. Compared with non-regular gamblers, regular gamblers personified the machine significantly more, adding support to the suggestion that some gamblers treat the machine as an 'electronic friend' (see Chapter 7). However, there may be a general tendency to personify machines with which people spend a lot of time.

It was suggested in Chapter 3 that knowledge of an irrational gambling bias may help in rehabilitating gamblers through cognitive behaviour modification. This would involve the attempt to modify the thought patterns of an individual in an attempt to moderate or stop their gambling. Using the design of this study, it might be possible to inhibit irrational bias in gambling by playing back tape recordings of a pathological gambler thinking aloud to highlight their irrational verbalizations. This I have termed audio playback therapy (Griffiths, 1993f). There is anecdotal evidence for such an assertion and will be returned to in the chapter on treatment of pathological gambling (Chapter 9). By knowing the detailed structure of the individual's gambling experiences (including their thoughts while gambling) a therapist can thus begin to moderate or eliminate the motivation to gamble. If cognitive biases do indeed stimulate persistent gambling it can only be concluded that cognitive therapies such as using audio playback might provide a way forward in the rehabilitation of problem gamblers.

6 The role of arousal and subjective moods in the maintenance of fruit machine gambling

Research outlined in this book so far has indicated multiple determinants in the acquisition, development and maintenance of fruit machine playing, and it has been argued that sociological variables appear to account for acquisition of gambling behaviour, whereas physiological and psychological variables appear to be particularly important in maintenance. This chapter reports the results of two studies and concentrates on the subjective mood states and psychophysiology in the maintenance of fruit machine playing. Each study will be reported in turn.

THE ROLE OF SUBJECTIVE MOODS IN THE MAINTENANCE OF FRUIT MACHINE GAMBLING

According to Carlton and Manowitz (1987), explanations involving the etiology of pathological gambling have tended to emphasize psychosocial factors. Accepting that these explanations are of major significance, the possibility that psychobiological factors are also important should not be ruled out. It is possible (and most probable) that such factors interact with psychosocial factors in the development of pathological gambling behaviour. Two psychobiological approaches to gambling that are actively being researched (and reviewed in Chapter 1) involve the role of (i) arousal and (ii) depression, as gambling reinforcers. It could further be the case that these two psychobiological factors are extreme ends of the same continuum.

The first study to be reported in this chapter analysed the subjective mood variables of non-regular, regular and pathological gamblers using self-report measures in an attempt to identify which mood states appear to be critical to gambling maintenance. Since the study was of an exploratory nature there were no specific hypotheses. A more detailed account of the methodology appeared in Chapter 5, since the data were derived from the larger experimental study examining the role of cognitive bias and skill in fruit machine gambling. After each subject had taken part in the experimental study, a semi-structured interview followed. During the interview, all subjects were screened for signs of pathological gambling using the *DSM-III-R* criteria (American Psychiatric Association, 1987) followed by a self-report measure developed in previous stages of this research programme which enquired about the the mood states of gamblers before, during *and* after gambling. Further questions were also asked relating to attractions and perceptions of gambling.

RESULTS

Analysis of *DSM-III-R* criteria for pathological gambling

Of the sixty gamblers, eleven (18 per cent) were diagnosed as pathological gamblers (ten males and one female), nineteen (32 per cent) were defined as regular (non-pathological) gamblers (all male) and thirty (50 per cent) were defined as non-regular gamblers (fifteen males and fifteen females). Table 6.1 displays each diagnostic criterion for pathological gambling and shows the percentages of non-regular gamblers, regular gamblers and pathological gamblers who answered 'yes' to each criterion. Since the *DSM-III-R* criteria diagnose pathological gambling and the pathological gamblers in this study were differentiated using the *DSM-III-R* criteria, the pathological gamblers *have* to have higher total scores on the criteria than the non-pathological gamblers. However, this does *not* necessarily mean they will definitely score higher on each individual criterion. The results show that the more a person gambles the more likely they are to experience signs of pathological gambling. For example, Criterion 1 ('Do you frequently gamble and obtain money to gamble?') was answered 'yes' by 7 per cent of the non-regular gamblers, 37 per cent of the regular gamblers and 91 per cent of the pathological gamblers. This order of ascendancy occurred in every one of the nine criteria.

The results also demonstrated that many regular (and a few non-regular) gamblers show signs of pathological gambling. For instance, over a half (58 per cent) of this sample returned to win back their losses (Criterion 5). In comparing *DSM-III-R* responses of regular versus non-regular gamblers, regular versus pathological gamblers, and pathological versus non-pathological gamblers, results (outlined in Table 6.1) showed that regular gamblers significantly outscored non-regular gamblers on four of the criteria, pathological gamblers significantly outscored regular gamblers on six of the criteria, and pathological gamblers significantly outscored non-pathological gamblers on all the criteria (see Table 6.1).

Table 6.1 Percentages[1] of non-regular gamblers (n = 30), regular non-pathological gamblers (n = 19) and pathological gamblers (n = 11) meeting diagnostic criteria of *DSM-III-R* for pathological gambling and significant differences between them

Criterion	NRG	RG	PG	Sig NRG vs. RG	Sig RG vs. PG	Sig NRG vs. PG
Frequently gamble and obtain money to gamble	7	37	91	$(p < 0.019)*$	$p < 0.007$	$p < 0.0001$
Frequently gamble larger amounts of money	0	5	55	n.s.	$p < 0.0005$	$p < 0.0001$
Need to gamble more to get more excited	7	11	45	n.s.	$(p < 0.03)*$	$p < 0.00096$
Restless if you cannot gamble	0	5	45	n.s.	$(p < 0.016)*$	$p < 0.0006$
Return to gamble to win back losses	3	58	91	$p < 0.0001$	n.s.	$p < 0.0001$
Make repeated efforts to stop gambling	0	11	36	n.s.	n.s.	$p < 0.0033$
Gamble instead of going to school/ job	0	5	36	n.s.	$(p < 0.048)*$	$p < 0.0033$
Sacrifice other activities to gamble	0	21	64	$(p < 0.019)*$	$(p < 0.047)*$	$p < 0.0001$
Continue to gamble even when you owe money	3	42	64	$(p < 0.011)*$	n.s.	$p < 0.0001$

Note: 1   All percentages to the nearest whole number

Key: NRG = Non-regular gamblers   RG = Regular (non-pathological) gamblers
         PG = Pathological gamblers   *Statistical significance at the 5% level

Analysis of subjective mood variables

A number of questions were asked relating to the moods the players experienced before, during and after gambling on fruit machines. Subjects were under no obligation to answer in any one particular way relating to the mood(s) they experienced. As a consequence, it was possible for some gamblers to report that during gambling they felt both aroused and depressed at differing times during the same gambling session. Tables 6.2, 6.3 and 6.4 display the percentages of non-regular, regular and pathological

Table 6.2 Moods felt before playing fruit machines: Percentages[1] of non-regular gamblers (n = 30), regular non-pathological gamblers (n = 19) and pathological gamblers (n = 11) and significant differences between them

Mood	NRG	RG	PG	Sig NRG vs. RG	Sig RG vs. PG	Sig NRG vs. PG
Good mood	60	63	63	n.s.	n.s.	n.s.
Bad mood/angry	3	5	9	n.s.	n.s.	n.s.
Excited	17	5	18	n.s.	n.s.	n.s.
Fed up/depressed	7	42	45	$p < 0.008$	n.s.	$p < 0.0096$
Other moods[2]	37	16	18	n.s.	n.s.	n.s.

Notes: 1   All percentages to the nearest whole number and some players gave more than one response
        2   Refers to those players whose general mood before could not be determined

Key: NRG = Non-regular gamblers   RG = Regular (non-pathological) gamblers
       PG = Pathological gamblers

gamblers who experienced various moods and subjective feelings. Most gamblers (approximately two-thirds) usually experienced good moods before, during and after gambling. Using Fisher's Exact Test, results showed that before gambling, both regular gamblers ($p < 0.008$) and pathological gamblers ($p < 0.0096$) were significantly more likely to report being fed up or depressed than non-regular gamblers. During gambling, results showed that there were no significant differences between regular and pathological gamblers but that regular gamblers were significantly more likely to experience excitement ($p < 0.01$) than non-regular gamblers, and that pathological gamblers were more likely to experience excitement ($p < 0.01$) than non-regular gamblers. After gambling, results showed there were no significant differences between either regular and pathological gamblers but that regular gamblers were more likely to feel in a bad mood or angry ($p < 0.027$) or to feel fed up or depressed ($p < 0.02$) than non-regular players (although these two findings again just failed to reach statistical significance), and that pathological gamblers were significantly more likely to feel in a bad mood or angry ($p < 0.0032$), to feel fed up or depressed ($p < 0.0058$) and to wish they were still playing ($p < 0.0004$) than non-regular gamblers.

Table 6.3 Moods felt during playing fruit machines: Percentages[1] of non-regular gamblers (n = 30), regular non-pathological gamblers (n = 19) and pathological gamblers (n = 11) and significant differences between them

Mood	NRG	RG	PG	Sig NRG vs. RG	Sig RG vs. PG	Sig NRG vs. PG
Good mood	43	68	55	n.s.	n.s.	n.s.
Bad mood/angry	3	21	9	n.s.	n.s.	n.s.
Excited	33	84	82	$p < 0.01$	n.s.	$p < 0.01$
Fed up/depressed	7	32	45	$(p < 0.043)$*	n.s.	n.s.
Not wanting to stop playing	17	32	45	n.s.	n.s.	n.s.
Cannot stop playing	0	0	18	n.s.	n.s.	n.s.
Other moods	37	5	9	$(p < 0.017)$*	n.s.	n.s.

Note: 1 All percentages to the nearest whole number and some players gave more than one response

Key: NRG = Non-regular gamblers   RG = Regular (non-pathological) gamblers
PG = Pathological gamblers   *Statistical significance at the 5% level

Table 6.4 Moods felt after playing fruit machines: Percentages[1] of non-regular gamblers (n = 30), regular non-pathological gamblers (n = 19) and pathological gamblers (n = 11) and significant differences between them

Mood	NRG	RG	PG	Sig NRG vs. RG	Sig RG vs. PG	Sig NRG vs. PG
Good mood	53	84	73	$(p < 0.034)$*	n.s.	n.s.
Bad mood/angry	3	26	45	$(p < 0.027)$*	n.s.	$p < 0.0032$
Excited	23	16	36	n.s.	n.s.	n.s.
Fed up/depressed	10	53	55	$(p < 0.02)$*	n.s.	$p < 0.0058$
Wishing you were still playing	7	32	63	$(p < 0.043)$*	n.s.	$p < 0.0004$
Other moods	33	21	0	n.s.	n.s.	$(p < 0.04)$*

Note: 1 All percentages to the nearest whole number and some players gave more than one response

Key: NRG = Non-regular gamblers   RG = Regular (non-pathological) gamblers
PG = Pathological gamblers   *Statistical significance at the 5% level

Analysis of attractions and perceptions of fruit machines

All the regular and pathological gamblers (n = 30) were further asked the question, 'What attracts you to gambling on fruit machines?'. A list of replies is outlined in Table 6.5 and shows that winning money (57 per cent), boredom / something to do (57 per cent), enjoyment / fun (33 per cent), excitement / 'buzz'/ 'high' (33 per cent), escape (27 per cent) and peer pressure / social activity (20 per cent) were the main reasons. Other lesser reasons (also in Table 6.5) included the machine looking attractive, being a skilful activity, winning the jackpot, etc. All the non-regular gamblers (n = 30) were asked the question, 'Why do some people become regular gamblers?'. A list of their replies is outlined in Table 6.6 and shows that like the regular gamblers, factors such as winning money (33 per cent), boredom / something to do (27 per cent), excitement / 'buzz'/ 'high' (23 per cent), escape (20 per cent) and enjoyment / fun (10 per cent) were popular perceptions. Using Fisher's Exact Test to compare regular and pathological gamblers' *actual* reasons for gambling versus non-regular gamblers' *perceptions* of regular gamblers' reasons for gambling revealed no differences. However, there were a few results which just failed to reach statistical significance. Gamblers' actual reasons were higher than the non-regular gamblers' perceived reasons on two factors, i.e. for enjoyment / fun ($p < 0.034$) and to win the jackpot ($p < 0.027$), and non-regular gamblers' perceived reasons were higher than gamblers' actual reasons on two factors, i.e. gambling for a challenge ($p < 0.029$) and because they get hooked / addicted / lose control ($p < 0.027$). A full comparison of responses can be found in Table 6.7.

Further analysis of non-regular gamblers

Non-regular gamblers were asked two further questions. The first of these was, 'Why do you not regularly gamble on fruit machines?'. There were a few popular answers, including the machines having no appeal (47 per cent), being a waste of money (40 per cent), hating the arcade atmosphere (23 per cent), not being able to afford the money to gamble (20 per cent) and the fear of becoming addicted (7 per cent). There were also a few singular reasons including 'because you can't win in the long run', 'because they're mindless', 'because it's a machine', 'because I'm embarrassed playing in front of people', 'because there's no point to them', 'because I'm a crap player', 'because they annoy me' and 'because I don't like the noise they make'. A complete list can be found in Table 6.8.

The final question asked non-regular gamblers about their thoughts and

Table 6.5 Responses by regular fruit machine players to why they are attracted to playing fruit machines regularly (n = 30)

Reason[1]	No.	%
Chance to win money	17	57
Boredom/something to do	11	37
Enjoyment/fun/entertainment	10	33
Excitement/buzz/high	10	33
To escape (depression/frustration/unfulfilment)	8	27
Social activity/peer pressure	6	20
Chance to win the jackpot	6	20
Good at playing/skilful	4	13
Machine looks attractive (lights/noises, etc.)	3	10
Have the money to gamble	2	7
To get rid of loose change	2	7
To chase losses	1	3
Challenge (to win/to beat machine, etc.)	1	3
The risk involved	1	3
Opportunity to play	1	3
Do not know	1	3

Note: 1 Some players gave more than one response

Table 6.6 Responses by non-regular players as to why people become regular fruit machine players (n = 30)

Reason[1]	No.	%
Chance to win money	10	33
Boredom/something to do	8	27
Excitement/buzz/high	7	23
Challenge (to win/to beat machine, etc.)	7	23
To escape (depression/frustration/unfulfilment)	6	20
They get hooked/addicted/lose control	5	17
Arcade atmosphere comforting/secure	4	13
Enjoyment/fun/entertainment	3	10
False sense of control/think it is skilful	3	10
Machines look attractive (lights/noise, etc.)	2	7
Social activity/peer pressure	2	7
Lack of confidence leads to machine friendship	2	7
To chase losses	1	3
They have the money to gamble	1	3
Do not know	1	3

Note: 1 Some players gave more than one response

Table 6.7 Comparison between non-regular fruit machine players' perceptions of attraction to fruit machines (n = 30) and regular fruit machine players' actual attraction to fruit machines (n = 30)

Reasons mentioned by both groups	Regular No. (%)	Non-regular No. (%)	Sig
Chance to win money	17 (57)	10 (33)	n.s.
Boredom/something to do	11 (37)	8 (27)	n.s.
Enjoyment/fun/entertainment	10 (33)	3 (10)	$(p < 0.034)$[1]
Excitement/buzz/high	10 (33)	7 (23)	n.s.
To escape (depression/frustration/ unfulfilment)	8 (27)	6 (27)	n.s.
Social activity/peer pressure	6 (20)	2 (7)	n.s.
Skilful	4 (13)	3 (10)	n.s.
Machines look attractive (lights/noise, etc.)	3 (10)	2 (7)	n.s.
They have the money to gamble	2 (7)	1 (3)	n.s.
To chase losses	1 (3)	1 (3)	n.s.
Challenge (to win/to beat machine, etc.)	1 (3)	7 (23)	$(p < 0.029)$[1]
Do not know	1 (3)	1 (3)	n.s.
Reasons mentioned by one group only			
Chance to win the jackpot	5 (17)	–	$(p < 0.027)$[1]
The risk involved	1 (3)	–	n.s.
Opportunity to play	1 (3)	–	n.s.
They get hooked/addicted/lose control	–	5 (17)	$(p < 0.027)$[1]
Amusement arcade atmosphere comforting/secure	–	4 (13)	n.s.
Lack of confidence leads to a machine relationship	–	2 (7)	n.s.

Note: 1 Statistical significance at the 5% level

perceptions about fruit machines, i.e. what was their initial reaction when they saw a fruit machine. There were a number of popular replies, many of which perhaps gave a better insight into why non-regular players did not gamble more regularly. The replies (outlined in Table 6.9) included feelings of confusion and not knowing what to do (53 per cent), feeling overwhelmed and anxious (47 per cent), and generally not liking the machine for some reason (27 per cent). These included responses such as, 'it looks cold', 'it's totally alien to me', 'it doesn't have much going for it',

Table 6.8 Responses by non-regular players as to why they do not regularly play fruit machines (n = 30)

Reason[1]	No.	%
Not interested/no appeal	14	47
Waste of money	12	40
Hate amusement arcade atmosphere	7	23
Do not have (or cannot afford) the money	6	20
Fear of the machine/becoming addicted	5	17
Lack of skill involved	3	10
Do not have the time to play	2	7
Never occurred to play	2	7
Cannot win in the long run	2	7
Better things to do	2	7

Notes: Miscellaneous answers from one person each are included in text
    1   Some players gave more than one response

'its stakes are too high', and 'the lights make you feel as if you've got to rush'. Alternatively, a small proportion (7 per cent) were more positive with comments such as 'it looks interesting' and 'it has pretty lights'.

Discussion

Results demonstrated that the more regularly gamblers gamble the more likely they are to display signs of pathological gambling as outlined in the *DSM-III-R* critera. Although it is virtually tautological that pathological gamblers answered 'yes' to each individual *DSM-III-R* criterion significantly more than non-pathological gamblers (since that is what is trying to be measured), it is interesting to note that regular gamblers also answered 'yes' to each of the criteria more than non-regular gamblers (and significantly so on four of the criteria), which suggests that some of these regular gamblers are potential pathological gamblers. Those criteria in which the pathological gamblers were significantly different from regular gamblers could be the most important factors that make a regular gambler become pathological (i.e. frequently gambling and obtaining money to gamble, gambling larger amounts of money, excitement during gambling, restlessness if unable to gamble, gambling instead of going to school / job and sacrificing other activities to gamble).

Significant differences between regular and non-regular gamblers on the

Table 6.9 Responses by non-regular players (n = 30) as to their initial perceptions of the fruit machine they played on in the experiment

Perception or thought[1]	No.	%
Feelings of confusion/not knowing what to do	16	53
Overwhelmed/panic/anxiety	14	47
Did not like a machine for a particular reason[2]	8	27
Was not daunted by the machine	5	17
Too much visual information/stimulation	4	13
Did not want to be in the arcade	2	7
Liked the machine for a particular reason[3]	2	7

Notes: 1 Some players gave more than one response
       2 Individual reasons are given in the text
       3 Reasons included 'It had pretty lights' and 'It looked interesting'

criteria also suggest that these factors are those which appear in the development of gambling from non-regular to regular (i.e. frequently gambling and obtaining money to gamble, returning to win back losses, sacrificing other (non-school / job) activities to gamble and continuing to gamble even when money is owed). What is clear from this study is that it would be useful for some kind of objective diagnostic criteria to be employed in all studies to make other studies findings' more comparable.

In analysis of the subjective mood variables, the main problem was that so many people consistently gave more than one answer, especially on what moods they experience subjectively after playing. However, most of these related to whether they had won, lost or had experienced a 'good' play, i.e. most people said they were in a good mood / excited if they had won a lot of money or had stayed on the machine for a long time, but experienced a bad mood and / or were depressed if they had lost a lot of money or lost what money they had quickly. Despite multiple answers to these questions a number of significant differences still occurred. Both regular and pathological gamblers experienced significantly more depressive moods than non-regular gamblers before and during gambling, which once again strengthens the findings of a causal or associational link between depression and gambling (e.g. McCormick *et al.*, 1984). Interestingly, both regular gamblers and pathological gamblers claimed they were still more depressed than non-regular gamblers after playing although it was only significant in the case of pathological gamblers versus non-regular gamblers. It could be that one of the reasons pathological gamblers gamble excessively is because their depression is relieved more (however temporarily) after gambling on fruit machines whereas in regular gamblers this is not the case.

Both regular and pathological gamblers experienced significantly more excitement during gambling than non-regular gamblers. This finding confirms other studies (e.g. Anderson and Brown, 1984) that excitement during gambling may be a reinforcing factor in facilitating regular and pathological gambling. Combined with the finding that regular gamblers do not need to gamble more to get more excited, it could be that regular gamblers are reinforced through excitement but develop no tolerance, whereas pathological gamblers do. Evidence for such an assertion is presented in this chapter's next study which uses objective psychophysiological data rather than subjective self-report data.

Not surprisingly, during gambling, pathological gamblers were more likely than non-regular gamblers to say they did not want to and/or could not stop gambling (although, again, this did not quite reach significance) and that after the session was over they were significantly more likely to wish they were still gambling. The finding that regular and pathological gamblers experience significantly bad moods after gambling can almost wholly be explained by the fact that these gamblers reported more big losses and/or bad runs on the machines.

The analysis of attractions and motivations for gambling on fruit machines agreed with the previous interview and participant observation work outlined in the earlier part of this book, i.e. winning money, social influences, boredom, excitement, escapism, etc. (see chapters 3 and 4). Non-regular gamblers produced the same kinds of reasons as to what attracts regular gamblers to the fruit machines, but fewer non-regular gamblers said regular gamblers gamble to win money, for enjoyment and because they are bored. In the case of 'winning money', fewer regular gamblers might report that it is not a significant factor in regular fruit machine gambling because so many gamblers (if not all) lose everything in the long run. It could be that non-regular gamblers interpret losses as something to be expected whereas regular gamblers interpret losses as near wins or explain them away. The fact that non-regular gamblers reported 'boredom' and 'enjoyment' less as factors in regular gambling than the regular gamblers might be in part due to them reporting that they are addicted (a reason not given at all by regular gamblers as a reason for regular gambling). Non-regular gamblers also thought that regular gamblers gamble for a challenge. This again is another reason that could have been put forward by non-regular gamblers as an intuitive reason for persistent gambling despite continual losses on the regular gambler's part.

The further questions to non-regular gamblers on why they do not gamble on fruit machines were asked in the hope that there might be some application to intervention and prevention strategies. In this respect the answers were disappointing. The reasons they gave, e.g. the machine having no appeal, being a waste of money, hating the arcade atmosphere, etc., are almost the exact opposite of why regular gamblers *do* gamble on fruit machines. The fear of addiction was enough in some people to prevent them from gambling regularly, and this was the only response which could in some way be used in an educational manner in some kind of prevention package. However, this does not help those already under 'the pull of the fruit machine'.

Not liking the fruit machine for some reason provided some interesting responses. There were those who did not like them because they considered them to be wholly chance determined (e.g. 'they're mindless', 'there's no point to them') and paradoxically those who did not like them because they considered them to be skill determined (e.g. 'I'm a crap player') as well as a number of responses which indicated that the machine put them in an uncomfortable mood (e.g. 'embarrassed', 'irritated', 'annoyed', etc.). It was probably these reasons along with their perceptions of fruit machines which gave a greater insight into their reasons for not gambling regularly. This was backed up by many non-regular gamblers who thought aloud while gambling on the fruit machine in the first part of the study (Chapter 5) and reported the feelings of confusion and being unsure what to do. This also implied that there is some skill involved in learning how to gamble on the machines.

Further to this, results suggest a very strong similarity between pathological gamblers and regular gamblers, i.e. when one group expresses a mood difference, so does the other one. The only difference is a matter of degree. Such an argument confirms the assertions that have been consistently put forward by Dickerson (e.g. Dickerson and Adcock, 1987; Dickerson, 1989) that excessive gambling has no clear-cut characteristics and that persistence in gambling is maintained by differing degrees of arousal and disturbed mood states.

In essence, the study indicated that the subjective moods of the gamblers do appear to have an effect on their gambling behaviour but that both 'depressed 'and (paradoxically) 'excited' states appear to be important in the maintenance of fruit machine gambling. The study was unable to determine which mood variable seemed to be the most important and concluded that more work is needed. Possible lines of research include the diagnosis of depression using clinical criteria rather than subjective reports and the objective measure of arousal using psychophysiological equipment. It is also unclear to what extent the current findings are applicable to other forms of gambling, indicating that research into other gambling addictions may also be necessary.

THE ROLE OF AROUSAL IN FRUIT MACHINE GAMBLING

The next study to be reported involved a more systematic monitoring of the psychophysiology of fruit machine playing at an *objective* level, i.e. the recording of heart rates (taken as an indication of arousal levels) in both regular and non-regular gamblers. Research to date (reviewed in Chapter 1) has indicated that explanations for persistent gambling may include a physiological component and it has been asserted a number of times throughout this book that a logical experiment to investigate the 'psycho-biology of the near miss' would involve relating physiological responses to behavioural events within a natural gambling setting. This study was designed to test for differences of heart rate between regular and non-regular fruit machine players (i.e. between subjects) and to investigate heart rate differences against the player's own baseline rates (i.e. within subjects) of both regular and non-regular fruit machine players. In addition to monitoring the physiological responses of these individuals, their behaviour was also monitored for number of plays, time on the machine, number of wins, etc. (i.e. a part-replication of the previous study). A more detailed methodology and list of hypotheses will now be given.

METHOD

Subjects

Thirty subjects (all male) with a mean age of 19.47 years all of whom had played a fruit machine at least once in their lives participated. Most were recruited via a small poster advertisement circulated around the local university and college campuses. In addition, the author recruited regular fruit machine players from the amusement arcade where the experiment took place. Regular players (mean age = 18.73 years) were defined as those who played fruit machines at least once a week. Non-regular players (mean age = 20.2 years) were defined as those who played fruit machines less than once a week.

Design

The study was again performed on an individual basis at a local amusement arcade as opposed to laboratory simulation, as the ecological validity of studies involving gambling arousal has been seriously questioned (Anderson and Brown, 1984). At the beginning of each session each subject was fitted with a portable heart rate meter next to their naked chest underneath their normal everyday wear. Since I was the only experimenter, females were excluded from the study. Each subject was given £3 to play a fruit machine of their choice which gave them thirty 'free' plays. All participants in the experiment were asked to try and stay on the machine for a minimum of fifty plays (i.e. their aim was to win back two-thirds of the money they had been given). If a player managed to achieve fifty plays with the initial £3 stake they were then given the choice of keeping any winnings or carrying on playing.

Before each playing session commenced, a baseline heart rate measurement was taken (the mean of twelve five-second recordings). A minute's heart rate baseline was also recorded after play had stopped. During play, the heart rate meter recorded the subjects' heart rates every five seconds. For the purpose of analysis, a mean heart rate during play was achieved by adding together all the heart rates recorded during the playing session and dividing by the total number of recordings.

At all stages and conditions of the experiment, I was again (as in the previous study) standing near the subject, recording total time in minutes that each subject was on the machine, the total number of plays, the total number of wins and the result of every play. I also recorded any instance of a particular kind of near win which involved gambling (i.e. using the 'gamble' button) and subsequently losing. At the end of the playing session and after all heart rates had been recorded, each subject underwent a semi-structured interview with the author which was developed in previous phases of the research project.

Hypotheses

This study basically consisted of two parts: (i) physiological data recording, and (ii) behavioural monitoring data recording. It was hypothesized that:

1 During the playing period, regular fruit machine players would have significantly higher heart rates as measured against baseline levels than non-regular players.
2 During the playing period *both* regular and non-regular fruit machine players would have significantly higher heart rates as measured against their own baseline levels.

3 Heart rates would significantly increase for both regular and non-regular players at times when they were winning or nearly winning and that these increases would be significantly higher in regular players against baseline than non-regular players.
4 There would be no difference between regular and non-regular gamblers in their behavioural monitoring data.

RESULTS

Analysis of the behavioural data

The mean scores and standard deviations of the behavioural measures for the thirty fruit machine players are shown in Table 6.10. Of the seven possible differences between groups (see Table 5.1, Chapter 5 for the behavioural monitoring variables), only one significant difference at the 0.01 level was found. Independent t-tests showed that there was no difference between regular gamblers and non-regular gamblers in terms of total number of plays, total time on the machine, number of wins, amount of winnings and number of plays per win. There was a highly significant difference in the number of plays per minute ($p = 0.0002$) with regular gamblers playing approximately ten times per minute and non-regular gamblers approximately eight times per minute.

Table 6.10 Means and standard deviations of the behavioural monitoring variables of the total gamblers (n = 30), regular gamblers (n = 15) and non-regular gamblers (n = 15)

| Variable | Total gamblers | | Regular gamblers | | Non-regular gamblers | | | |
	Mean	*S.D.*	*Mean*	*S.D.*	*Mean*	*S.D.*	*t*	*p*
Total plays	46.8	8.17	49.2	7.9	44.4	7.9	−1.66	0.11
Total time	5.58	1.23	5.33	1.2	5.83	1.25	1.11	0.28
Wins	5.56	2.45	5.87	2.33	5.27	2.6	−0.67	0.51
Endstake	3.43	7.3	2.33	6.23	4.53	8.3	0.82	0.42
Playrate	8.58	1.35	9.42	1.14	7.74	0.98	−4.31	0.0002[1]
Winrate (time)	0.97	0.33	1.08	0.29	0.87	0.34	−1.86	0.074
Winrate (plays)	10.1	5.0	9.25	2.45	10.87	6.66	0.88	0.88

Note: 1 $p < 0.001$

Analysis of the heart rate data

The data outlined in Table 6.11 shows the mean heart rates of the regular and non-regular gamblers before, during and after playing the fruit machine. Independent t-tests revealed no significant differences between the two groups although the heart rates of non-regular gamblers were higher after playing, a finding which just failed to reach significance ($p = 0.054$). An analysis of variance revealed there was no main effect in comparing the two groups (F (1,56) = 1.12, $p = 0.299$) and no significant interaction effect (F (1,56) = 2.39, $p = 0.101$).

The ANOVA also revealed that there was a highly significant difference between heart rates before, during and after playing (F (1,56) = 43.62, $p < 0.0005$). Further t-tests (see Table 6.12) revealed highly significant differences comparing heart rates before and during play in the total sample, and among the subsets of regular and non-regular gamblers (i.e. within group comparisons). The same finding was also repeated comparing heart rates before and after play. However, in comparing heart rates during play with those after play, it was revealed that there was a highly significant difference among regular gamblers but not among non-regular gamblers, i.e. non-regular gamblers' heart rates did not decrease significantly after playing whereas regular gamblers' did.

Further analysis of individuals' heart rates revealed that the mean difference from the lowest recorded heart rate to the highest during the playing period was 22.2 beats per minute (S.D. = 7.61). There was no difference between regular gamblers (mean = 21.6; S.D. = 8.5) and non-regular gamblers (mean = 22.8; S.D. = 6.86) using an independent t-test (t = 0.43, $p = 0.67$).

Table 6.11 Means and standard deviations of heart rates before, during and after play of the total gamblers (n = 30), regular gamblers (n = 15) and non-regular gamblers (n = 15)

Variable	Total gamblers		Regular gamblers		Non-regular gamblers			
	$\bar{x}$	SD	$\bar{x}$	SD	$\bar{x}$	SD	t	p
Before play	89.5	7.73	88.47	7.95	90.52	7.63	0.72	0.48
During play	97.99	7.76	97.5	7.73	98.48	8.02	0.34	0.74
After play	95.43	7.04	92.97	6.43	97.9	6.94	2.02	0.054[1]

Note: 1 $p < 0.01$

Table 6.12 Means of heart rates before, during and after play, and t-test comparisons of the total gamblers (n = 30), regular gamblers (n = 15) and non-regular gamblers (n = 15)

Heart rate variable	Total gamblers			Regular gamblers			Non-regulars		
	x	t	$p<$	x	t	$p<$	x	t	$p<$
Before play	89.5	-8.49	0.001^2	88.47	-5.55	0.001^2	90.52	-6.58	0.001^2
vs.									
During play	97.99			97.5			98.48		
During play	97.99	3.46	0.001^2	97.5	4.96	0.001^2	98.48	0.63	0.54
vs.									
After play	95.43			92.97			97.9		
Before play	89.5	5.44	0.001^2	88.47	-2.83	0.01^1	90.52	-5.07	0.001^2
vs.									
After play	95.43			92.97			97.9		

Key: 1 $p < 0.01$
     2 $p < 0.001$

In an effort to relate wins and near wins to increases in heart rate, a graph of each gambler's heart rate (taken every five seconds) was recorded. Although it appears that winning (and nearly winning) money is related to heart rate increases in some individuals, it is unclear whether this happens for all gamblers. Crude measures of counting the total number of peaks and comparing the peaks associated with events (i.e. winning and nearly winning) and the peaks not associated with events revealed no differences. In addition, the problem of the time lag in recording heart rate differences meant it was sometimes difficult to know which peak related to which event. As a consequence, it was decided that more sophisticated analysis would be unlikely to provide a clearer insight into the individual heart rate data.

DISCUSSION

Although this was a male-only study there is no reason to think that the results are not applicable to females, although further research on such an issue would be desirable. The behavioural monitoring data in this study suggested there was very little difference between regular and non-regular players basically supporting the null hypothesis. As in the study in Chapter

5 (see page 134), it was found that regular players do stay on the machine slightly longer in terms of number of plays, but again the finding was not significant. There were also no differences in terms of total time on the machine, the number of wins, the amount of winnings and number of plays per win. These results combined again suggest there are skilful aspects to fruit machine playing but that the skill appears to be little more than taking a few more plays to lose the same amount of money in approximately the same time as non-regular players. However, there was a highly significant difference in the number of plays per minute, with regular players gambling an extra two plays per minute (a finding also reported in the previous study).

Directly comparing the behavioural monitoring data of this study with the last one, it can be seen that although the results are relatively similar, players in this study played a mean of forty-seven plays in six minutes whereas the previous study produced a rate of fifty-six plays in nine-and-a-half minutes. This difference can be put down to three factors. In the study in Chapter 5, (a) players were asked to play sixty times before they were given the option of taking any winnings, whereas in this study players were only asked to play up to fifty times before given the option of taking any winnings; (b) half the players were asked to think aloud which slowed down their speed of playing, and (c) players were free to change machines, an option which was not available to those in this study. This meant that the time taken to swap to other machines was included in the total time subsequently divided by total number of plays. This led to the finding that in the study in Chapter 5, regular players and non-regular players played eight and six times per minute respectively, whereas in this study they played ten and eight times per minute respectively. Very fast playing was also observed in the observational study (Chapter 4, page 106) in which some players were reported to be playing up to a hundred times in ten minutes as if they were on automatic pilot.

The analysis of the heart rate data produced a number of interesting findings. The hypothesis that both regular and non-regular gamblers would have higher mean heart rates during gambling as compared with their baseline measures was supported. However, the hypothesis that during play the mean heart rates of regular gamblers would be significantly higher than non-regular gamblers was not supported. Both regular and non-regular gamblers experienced mean heart rate increases of approximately twenty-two beats per minute during the play period, and although the actual movement of playing a fruit machine may have contributed to some of the heart rate increases it is unlikely that this would have been more than a few beats per minute. It can therefore be concluded that gambling is objectively (i.e. physiologically) exciting/arousing for both these groups. These findings confirm previous studies of physiological measurement of heart rate in machine gamblers (e.g. Leary and Dickerson, 1985; Brown, 1988). Why the results of the two groups should be so similar is not obvious. It could be that because they had all played fruit machines at least once before, with many of the non-regular players playing a few times a month, their physiology responded to the machine in similar ways. It could also be the case that groups were not as distinctly different as they could have been. Although regular players in both this study and in Chapter 5's study were defined as those who played once a week or more, non-regular players in this study were defined simply as those who played less than once a week whereas in Chapter 5's study they were defined as those who played less than once a month.

The most interesting finding and the only significant difference between the groups was that after playing fruit machines, regular players' heart rates started to decrease at once, whereas non-regular players' did not change significantly. This suggests a reason why regular players might (a) play faster and (b) play more often. In terms of an addictive (endorphin related) model of gambling, both regular and non-regular gamblers get a 'high' physiologically when playing, but the non-regular gamblers stay higher for longer meaning they do not have to play as fast or as often to induce the arousal peaks. Regular gamblers, in contrast, could be seen as becoming more tolerant to the gambling 'highs', meaning they have to gamble either faster or more often to experience the initially desired effect.

The hypothesis that heart rate increases are related to wins or near wins was neither confirmed nor disconfirmed. Impressionistically, it did appear that wins and near wins caused heart rate increase in some players, and that bigger wins caused bigger heart rate increases, but there were many large heart rate increases which appeared to have no corresponding event during the behavioural monitoring. Since only one type of near win was being recorded (i.e. a loss after using the 'gamble' button) it would be useful in any replication study for there to be at least two (or more) experimenters recording wins, near wins (of all descriptions), times of wins and near wins, and behavioural characteristics of the player. Alternatively, the experiment could be videotaped and analysed retrospectively. It might also be useful to have some kind of 'rigged' fruit machine that did not have two consecutive win or near win events making relating events to arousal peaks easier. There is also the problem of what the gamblers themselves consider to be a 'near win'. A win is objective in that there is a monetary pay-out; however, a 'near win' is left up to each individual's cognitions. It could be that many of the arousal peaks on the heart rate data where I considered there was no behavioural event could have related to something cognitively. A future experiment could ask people to think aloud (as in the previous study) *and* record their physiological responses. It could be that relating internal cognitions rather than external events to physiological responses would prove more profitable in understanding persistent gambling.

The evidence in this study suggests that the 'psychobiology of the near miss' may still be a crucial factor in explaining persistent gambling despite constant losses. In examining individual heart rates it is clear that there are many 'arousal jags' during the play period of both regular and non-regular gamblers but that identifying the cause of the jags was beyond the boundaries of this experiment. Finally, in relation to measuring heart rates it must be noted that two subjects in this study (both regular players) smoked cigarettes during their gambling session. Both of these players were asked if they would refrain from smoking during the experiment and both gave the same reply that smoking helped them concentrate. Although this seemed to have little effect on their heart rate data it could be considered a confounding variable. It should also be noted from my own observations that many older male adolescents and young men (18 to 25 years old) who play fruit machines do smoke. Such an observation suggests that more research should be done examining the relationship between other addictive behaviours (e.g. smoking, drinking) and gambling, both psychologically and physiologically.

Throughout this book it has been suggested that cognitive and physiological components may be the most critical components in the maintenance of fruit machine gambling and there is no evidence to suggest they are not in this study, although it still cannot be ascertained how *exactly* these psychological and physiological mechanisms regulate such behaviour and whether it is regulated consistently and systematically across all regular and pathological fruit machine players.

7 Qualitative accounts and case studies of adolescent fruit machine addiction

It was noted in Chapter 2 that adolescent gambling is more widespread than is generally recognized and that there is a rapidly emerging literature which suggests that not only do a majority of children and adolescents gamble, but that in some cases it is pathological (Lesieur and Klein, 1987; Ladouceur and Mireault, 1988; Fisher, 1993a). To date, a majority of the research on adolescent fruit machine gambling has been survey type studies although observational qualitative findings have been reported (see Chapter 4). This has meant that most studies have concentrated on the incidence and demographics of adolescent fruit machine gambling (and pathological gambling) and the quantitative analysis of motivations, subjective feelings, negative consequences, etc. in fruit machine gambling. There has been very little detailed qualitative analysis of the phenomenon and few published case studies to date. This chapter outlines some of the qualitative research that I have carried out. The numbers of subjects involved are very small but the individualistic insights gained are as important as any large scale quantitative study. The chapter begins with the findings from a small postal study and then goes on to give detailed case studies of some fruit machine addicts.

A POSTAL STUDY OF REFORMED ADOLESCENT FRUIT MACHINE ADDICTS

This section outlines a postal survey of 'ex-fruit machine addicts' utilizing a questionnaire which asked particularly about their gambling pathology, the 'skill' factors in playing fruit machines, and how they felt (physiologically) before, during and after they had played fruit machines. Although the response rate was disappointingly low, self-written reports of individuals' fruit machine playing histories provided some 'rich' qualitative data supporting quantitative results from the previous chapters.

A questionnaire examining various aspects of fruit machine gambling behaviour in former (self-confessed) adolescent problem gamblers was administered. The questionnaire consisted of twenty-three questions, three of which were open-ended. In addition to demographic data, other information (e.g. reasons for playing, gambling pathology, skill factors if any during playing, and mood variables before, during and after play) was collected. At the end of the questionnaire, a blank sheet was provided for subjects to write a personal account of their fruit machine gambling history if they so wished and it is these personal histories that provide the substance of this chapter. The anonymity and confidentiality of the questionnaire were emphasized.

In this study, 150 questionnaires were sent, after preliminary negotiations, to the head office of the Parents of Young Gamblers (POYG) organization (a UK self-help organization for parents and guardians of young problem gamblers similar to Gam-Anon. (Gam-Anon is the, mainly female, support group which meets alongside Gamblers Anonymous and discusses the gambling problems of their partners.) The questionnaires were then given by POYG's head office to the local heads of six POYG groups to distribute among their members, who in turn were asked (via a covering letter) to pass on the questionnaire to their son or daughter.

Because there were a number of potential problems in the distribution chain, response rate was expected to be low. Of the 150 questionnaires distributed, sixty were returned immediately by two POYG team leaders who informed the author that their membership operated via a telephone network, and that they therefore had no addresses of their POYG members. Of the ninety remaining questionnaires, it was not possible to ascertain (a) how many parents actually received the questionnaire and (b) how many parents (if they did receive the questionnaire) passed it on to their son or daughter. Postmarks on the replies received suggests that the questionnaires only reached two POYG groups (Swansea and Birmingham).

In total, nineteen completed questionnaires were returned to the author from fifteen males and four females with an age range of 16-25 years (with a mean average age of 18.7 years). This gave a 21 per cent response rate (nineteen out of ninety). However, since postmarks revealed questionnaire returns from Swansea and Birmingham only, it could be argued that the true response rate was in the region of 40 per cent, as it appears that only these two POYG groups of approximately twenty-five members each actually received the questionnaires and distributed them to their members. At the time of the study, fourteen of the subjects were employed, two were unemployed and two were in higher education. Of the nineteen respondents, twelve provided a hand-written personal account of their fruit machine gambling. One questionnaire was completed by a parent because of a writing disability on the respondent's part.

Pathological gambling

Using the *DSM-III-R* criteria to confirm pathological gambling in the sample (American Psychiatric Association, 1987), sixteen of the nineteen respondents were deemed to be (or to have been) probable pathological gamblers, fourteen of whom were male and two female. Descriptions of such pathological behaviour became evident in the handwritten personal histories. Eight respondents wrote specifically about their financing of fruit machine gambling through criminal activity. These are a few typical admissions:

> 'The basic problem I had was that in order to feed my (fruit machine) addiction, I had to steal from anywhere I could, even if I knew I would get caught.' (Respondent 5, male)

> 'The reason I first started going to GA (Gamblers Anonymous) was that I had just committed a crime for the fifth time to feed my [fruit machine] addiction.' (Respondent 3, male)

> 'While I was playing fruit machines there were no good experiences, only bad, such as stealing money from my family and robbing chip shops, phone boxes and tills in shops.' (Respondent 2, male)

> 'As for obtaining money, I did this in any way possible no matter who I might hurt or what I may destroy. If I wasn't actually gambling I was spending the rest of my time working out clever little schemes to obtain money to feed my habit. These two activities literally took up all my time.' (Respondent 11, male)

> 'Any dinner, bus fare money went into fruit machines during school hours. When I started my full-time job . . . as a cashier, my weekly wages (£75) went . . . in a few hours. I needed more money therefore I stole from the cash till . . . I am now going to court.' (Respondent 1, female)

Most of the sample had clearly faced a number of problems concerning their fruit machine playing and were actively trying (or had succeeded in) giving up. This was reflected in the mean time since the subjects last played on a fruit machine of nearly eleven months. Their experience of fruit machine addiction was expressed in other negative ways:

> 'Gamble, gamble, gamble your life away . . . you might as well have put (the money) down the drain . . . you've got to face the truth that you're having a love affair, and it's with a machine whose lights flash, takes your money and kills your soul.' (Respondent 12, male)

'The only good experience of playing fruit machines is getting away from them.' (Respondent 7, male)

'I ate, slept and breathed gambling machines . . . I couldn't even find time to spend with the people I loved . . . . The machines were more important than anything or anyone else.' (Respondent 11, male)

'Other bad experiences I had were leaving home and falling out with my parents, and calling them things which deep down I knew weren't right. At the time I didn't give a shit.' (Respondent 2, male)

Motivations for fruit machine playing

The nineteen respondents were asked to specify what attracted them to playing fruit machines. The main reasons given were winning money or the chance to win money (twelve respondents) and the lights and sounds of the machine itself (six). Other attractions included an escape from depression (three), boredom (three), a challenge (two), excitement (two), chasing losses (one) and because friends play (one). These variables were expanded upon in the personal accounts:

'I normally started playing when I was depressed. The first time I gave [fruit machines] up, I was doing well until I split up with my girlfriend which triggered me off again.' (Respondent 8, male)

'Then came a series of family rows, not really severe, but things like this were amplified amidst my depression . . . I returned to the machines full time . . . whenever I felt depressed or maybe rejected, the urge to play machines became even bigger . . . I needed to counteract it by gambling.' (Respondent 11, male)

'[The initial attraction was] winnings, but this was gradually converted to lights, sounds, and I always received a great thrill from new machines with new ideas . . . I played on the machines to watch the wheels go round and could not come off them until I had put all the money I had on me into the machines.' (Respondent 10, male)

'I suppose that in England a person is aware of fruit machines from a very early age, and once tried they are never forgotten. For myself it was watching a disused launderette being transformed into a neon palace; entrance free, meet your friends, relax, smoke, bunk off school, stay in all afternoon in return for changing and spending all the money in your pockets . . . [and] what of that money? The cheap stake machines become boring so you play another big [expensive stake] one this time, after all, you've just seen somebody win off the next machine next to it and they win four pounds. Why not? you think.' (Respondent 12, male)

There are also those who 'blame' certain situations or events for their excessive fruit machine gambling. For instance, having a big win ('I won £120 in a pub' (Subject 5, male)) was viewed as one subject's downfall, and 'coming from a broken home as a child, living with mother and stepfather' (Subject 7, male) was seen as another. The mother who filled out her son's questionnaire wrote:

'My son is mentally handicapped. He first became addicted when he was about 14. We were initially quite pleased that he felt confident enough to go out by himself, and the [amusement arcade] owners were kind to him, and used to give him odd jobs to do. I think that whilst playing the machines, he felt 'normal' as the person on the next machine, and equally as good, if not better. He is in fact, pretty good at it!' (Mother of respondent 4, male)

Another subject blamed it on a false perception:

'I started gambling when I started on the Youth Training Scheme. I wasn't getting enough money to live on and pay lodgings so I started to gamble to try and win more money then I started to borrow and steal money for the machines.' (Respondent 6, male)

Skill factors

All nineteen respondents were asked how much skill is involved in fruit machine gambling and to rate themselves on how skilful they considered themselves to be compared with the average person. Just over a quarter of the sample (five) reported there was no skill in playing and a further one-third of the sample (six) reported it was 'mostly chance'. However, the remaining respondents (eight) viewed chance and skill factors as equally important in playing the machines. It was interesting to note that when subjects were asked how skilful they viewed themselves to be, no one reported being 'totally unskilled' or 'below average skill', only of 'average skill' (eleven), 'above average skill' (five) or 'totally skilled' (three). When asked what skill (if any) was involved in fruit machine playing, a small range of answers was supplied. Knowledge of the reels (four), knowledge of special features (four) and knowledge of the machine (three) provided the most popular answers (a complete list is given in Table 7.1). A typical view was given by Respondent 11:

Table 7.1 Skilful aspects of fruit machine playing as reported by fruit machine players (n = 19)

Skill	n	%
Knowledge of the reels	4	21
Knowledge of special features (e.g. skill chances)	4	21
Knowledge of the machine	3	16
Knowledge of holds and/or nudges	2	11
Knowledge of 'gamble' button	2	11
Quick reactions re visual display	2	11
Knowledge of when the machine will pay out	1	5
No response	2	11

Note: Some players gave more than one response

> 'Although there is never any guarantee that you will win by playing your machine, there is a fair bit of skill involved that can improve your chances.'

However, as Respondent 12 pointed out, the perceived skill may in fact be greater than the actual skill; thus:

> 'After you've been playing [fruit machines] some time, you get to know the reels, so you have (*or you think you have*) more chance of winning that elusive jackpot.' (*Author's emphasis*)

Mood factors

A number of questions were also asked about the moods of the gamblers before, during and after the playing of fruit machines (see Table 7.2). Results showed that before playing fruit machines a majority of the respondents often felt in a good mood (fourteen) but that some of them often felt other moods because a high proportion also reported often feeling depressed (eleven). During play, excitement increased and depression decreased whereas after playing good moods decreased and bad moods increased (see Table 7.2). Three-quarters of the sample (fourteen) claimed they could not stop fruit machine playing once they had started, and wished they were still playing when they had run out of money. One such mood cycle was described:

'I would always be looking forward tremendously to playing machines and [I] couldn't get to them fast enough . . . . [During play] I always got this kind of feeling – being "high" or "stoned" would be the best way of describing it. I was very often uncontrollable on my excitable actions, like a 5 year old at Christmas time . . . . Since becoming hooked I've never been able to stop playing a machine once I've started.' (Respondent 11, male)

Additional factors

During the analysis of self-written personal histories a number of other issues were raised. Three males reported they had graduated from fruit machine gambling to betting on horse-races and were attending Gamblers Anonymous. In addition, one female reported that she was addicted to video game machines as opposed to fruit machines:

'They are really the same thing as you have to put money in to achieve something. With me, I used to put money in [video game machines] to achieve a higher score. This led me to playing all the time and made me in a happy mood.' (Respondent 9, female)

However, much of the remaining verbal data concentrated upon problems in giving up fruit machine playing, realization of the seriousness of fruit machine addiction, and personal strategies in attempting to give up playing the machines.

Table 7.2 Moods of fruit machine players (n = 19) before, during and after fruit machine playing

	Before	During	After
		n	
Good mood/happy	14	12	7
Bad mood/angry	7	10	13
Excitement/'buzz'/'high'	8	12	7
Fed up/sad/depressed	11	6	10
Not wanting to stop playing	–	14	–
Cannot stop playing	–	14	–
Wishing you were still playing	–	–	14
Other	2	1	2

Note: Subjects were given the option to tick more than one box and most did

'No one knew of my addiction, but I wish I had had someone to turn to . . . and that's what many youngsters' problem is, they have no one to turn to for help.' (Respondent 9, female)

'[My mum] finally confronted me, and I did something which I'd never even thought of doing . . . . I told her everything and that was the first massive step towards reaching the light at the end of the tunnel. Now that she knew everything I was able to talk to her . . . enabling me to GIVE UP . . . it was sheer will power . . . with my family's backing to kick the habit. It took me three months to get it out of my system just like a drug. But it was after those three agonizing months I actually began to feel a person again . . . I only managed to stay away from the machines by doing other things, even if I didn't want to, just to stop me thinking of [fruit machines].' (Respondent 11, male)

'My parents forced me to go at first [to GA] but now I want to go. I stopped gambling for fourteen weeks after attending . . . and have saved over £500. Before, I would have spent this and stolen more. [However] I still face a possible six months in prison.' (Respondent 3, male)

'I have now given them up largely thanks to support from my parents and girlfriend.' (Respondent 8, male)

'[If I] became restless [from not playing fruit machines] I usually managed to overcome this by relaxing in a yoga orientated way I'd been taught at school – probably the only thing I ever listened to, and bothered to learn, at school.' (Respondent 11, male)

'The local arcade were quite co-operative and would phone if [my son] went over with a £10 note . . . I explained to them that he wouldn't have the money unless he'd stolen it . . . he doesn't go in the arcade regularly any longer, but he will play if there is a machine in the vicinity. I definitely think that the question of where the machines are sited . . . should be seriously reviewed.' (Mother of respondent 4, male)

DISCUSSION

Although the response rate in this study was low, and the sample was biased, the data collected are of existential value and do provide a valuable addition to a sparse literature. Response rate could have been very low for a number of potential reasons. Since the author had no control over the distribution chain it was hard to know where it had broken down and why. The POYG head office sent approximately twenty-five questionnaires to six POYG branches and two of them immediately returned the question-naires saying they could not help because their network was a telephone only set-up. At least two POYG branches produced no replies, which suggests that local branch leaders did not distribute the questionnaire to their members for some reason. There could also have been reasons why parents did not give the questionnaires to their sons or daughters, e.g. there may have been a bad relationship between them, etc. Finally, the gamblers themselves may not have wanted to take part in the survey because there was no particular incentive to do so.

Although there could have been a slightly more rigorous follow-up to this study it is unsure whether any more subjects would have taken part. Any survey on problem behaviour will cause difficulties in data collection. Since the data were collected via an organization concerned with giving help to problem adolescent gamblers and their families, it is not surprising that sixteen of the nineteen subjects (84 per cent) were diagnosed as (or had been) probable pathological gamblers using *DSM-III-R* criteria (American Psychiatric Association, 1987). They were probably also a biased sample in that they actively wanted to give up their fruit machine playing and concep-tualized the problem in the way that the POYG organizations did.

Allowing for the study's accepted shortcomings, the information pro-vided by the subjects was collected in a way which allowed for total anonymity and confidentiality from the researcher, a factor which has never been 100 per cent certain in previous questionnaire and interview studies in which subjects had some contact (however minimal) with the investigator. The reported research was also the first study of problem adolescent gamblers which has used written self-reported personal histories in its methodology. Anonymous personal accounts provide a detailed un-censored source of information which is often lacking in questionnaires and face-to-face interviews. Since most of the gamblers in this study were actively trying to give up gambling (or had succeeded), their accounts of their gambling behaviour may have been more truthful, rational and reflec-tive than if such a study had been performed using problem gamblers during mid-addiction.

It is obvious that reasons for gambling, and continued gambling, were given on a number of distinct conceptual levels. When the adolescent gamblers first started to play on fruit machines it was because their friends or parents did, or they were given the chance to be independent for the first time in their lives by participating in an 'adult' behaviour. As playing continued, early big wins may have produced irrational biases in their gambling behaviour, leading to heavy play. The core of the majority of the gamblers' reasons for excessive playing was escapism. In the 'sanctuary' of the amusement arcade players could forget about their broken home, their physical disability, their parents' arguments, their girlfriend leaving them, etc. In short, fruit machine gambling relieved the symptoms of a depressed state. At a different level the fruit machine itself was enticing: not only were players overwhelmed by a 'labyrinth of light and sound' but fruit machine playing provided an alternative way to get 'high' or 'stoned' which was exciting, challenging, relieved boredom *and* offered possible financial rewards.

As players become addicts, they become socially withdrawn and start to lose their friends – even the closest ones. So, at the final level, the fruit machine becomes the addict's *best friend*. To reiterate one player's claim – *'You're having a love affair, and it's with a machine'*. An addict can talk to it, shout at it, laugh at it – and it never answers back. It can make the addicts forget their problems, it can arouse them and occasionally even pays them money for being there. In essence, the hard core player 'worships' the fruit machine. They spend all their time either playing the fruit machine or finding ways to finance their playing. Since most adolescents have little income, they resort to using any money they can, i.e. lunch money, bus money, selling personal possessions, stealing from family members, and ultimately external illegal activity. From the personal histories it appeared that most of the gamblers spent up to £100 a week playing fruit machines, often in one playing session, with two individuals spending much more.

It would appear from the information provided that a majority of addicted adolescents lost total control over their lives, living in a 'blur' or a 'trance'. Such findings raise potential legal questions of responsibility of individual actions during criminal behaviour. Can the addicted gambler who commits a burglary plead 'diminished responsibility'? This is clearly an issue that both the legal and medical professions may have to investigate further.

A number of other issues from this study need to be followed up. As was suggested in the last chapter, more research is needed to confirm or refute the existence of depressive mood states *before* gambling, and heightened arousal states *during* gambling, perhaps by administering depression inventories to fruit machine players and measuring their physiological responses during gambling behaviour. This would add to the small body of findings which suggest that other forms of pathological gambling may be associated with depression (e.g. McCormick *et al.*, 1984; Taber *et al.*, 1987) and heightened arousal (Anderson and Brown, 1984; Leary and Dickerson, 1985).

It has previously been asked 'What happens to the adolescent fruit machine gambler?' (Griffiths, 1988a), since there are very few addicted players over the age of about 25 years. This study suggested that some players, three in this case, 'graduate' to betting on horses because they regard it as more skilful than fruit machine playing. However, this assertion is clearly tentative, and more longitudinal research needs to be carried out to establish a link between adolescent fruit machine gambling and other more 'adult' gambling activities. Alternatively, future retrospective studies using (say) Gamblers Anonymous members may reveal such links.

It has been argued earlier in this book that fruit machine gamblers may become physiologically aroused when they win or nearly win and that in the gamblers' terms, they are not constantly losing but constantly nearly winning, i.e. experiencing a psychologically rewarding situation although there is no financial reward (i.e. 'psychobiology of the near miss'). This study again gave indirect evidence that 'excitement' is a major motivation for some people for playing fruit machines, although not as much as the studies outlined in the previous chapters would indicate. It is also worth considering the differences between 'perceived skill' and 'actual skill', as results in this study suggest that although skilful elements may be present in fruit machine gambling, it may be that players think there is more skill than there actually is.

Finally, a number of important points concerning intervention and treatment appeared in the personal histories. One of the most salient themes in the prevention of further gambling was family communication and support (but this was probably due to the sample bias, i.e. the organization contacted was POYG). Adolescents may feel they have no one to turn to, especially if the relationship between themselves and their parents has deteriorated during their addiction. However, this must be overcome whether it be the parent(s) or adolescents who make the first move. Results in this study suggested that just *talking* about the problem was an important first step. Support from a girl – or boyfriend would also appear to be important especially in issues of adolescent identity and re-acceptance into the peer group. Other strategies were suggested by individuals in the study but they may not be applicable to everyone. Attendance at GA meetings was beneficial to a number of people even though they had initially been forced to attend; however, it must be borne in mind that there is a high drop-out rate of approximately 75 per cent to 90 per cent in GA, at least among adults (Stewart and Brown, 1988; Moody, 1990).

If adolescent gamblers are taught relaxation techniques (Markham, 1990) this may help overcome acute stress arising from not being able to gamble. Steps should also be taken to avoid amusement arcades and other fruit machine sites if they are regularly passed during day-to-day activity. As a final precaution – at least until the adolescent gambler seems to be moving towards recovery – parents could oversee the gambler's finances by looking after the adolescent's pocket money and/or part-time or full-time wages.

CASE STUDIES OF FRUIT MACHINE ADDICTS

The second half of this chapter focuses on three case studies in more depth. These are provided to allow the reader to get a feel about the lifestyle and consequences of fruit machine addiction. The first account was constructed from my own personal files, whereas the second and third accounts were written by the mother of a fruit machine addict and a fruit machine addict's clinical psychologist respectively. Despite the three different perspectives there are many common themes. For me personally, accounts such as these lie at the heart of why I do the research that I do. I make no apologies for the 'non-academic' style in some places.

Case study I: David

The data to be reported in this section were collected from a former adolescent pathological fruit machine gambler whose mother contacted me after the postal survey conducted with the Parents of Young Gamblers organization. (The gambler is in fact Respondent 11 in the postal study.) During a six-month period the author maintained regular contact with both the mother and son on an informal basis through both written and oral communication. Using the *DSM-III-R* criteria for pathological gambling (American Psychiatric Association, 1987) the subject concerned was confirmed as being a former pathological gambler.

The account that follows is very much based on the transcriptions from both the mother and son. As a consequence, the following section is far from academic in the traditional sense. A critical interpretation of the account will follow in the discussion. Before reporting the findings a number of points should be made. First, at no time did the author ever interview or engage in conversation with the mother and son simultaneously. All the data were collected independently. Second, some of the data were collected via correspondence (including the written personal history obtained from the above postal study) but this has not been separately identified in the account. This is purely to make the text easier to read. Third, the order of the account was determined by me in an effort to present the data in a chronological form. Fourth, since the account is highly personal, it was decided to give the subject a pseudonym ('David') in keeping with the text's informal and subjective nature. Finally, a couple of the quotes from the postal study are repeated where appropriate for the sake of clarity and completeness.

Background

At the time of the study, David was 18 years old. He was brought up in a seaside town with a younger sister (two years younger) by loving and understanding parents in a secure and stable background. Up to the age of 14 he had good reports from his school and was a member of the county swimming team. His mother described him as 'a loving, lively boy, clever at school and good at sports, someone I could be proud of'. However, over a period of four years he turned into 'a miserable, withdrawn and rebellious son'.

Discovering the problem

When David was 14 years old, two telephone calls alerted David's mother that her son might be having some problems in his life. The first was from his swimming club which wanted to know why the normally dependable David had started to turn up late or fail to turn up for his swimming practice. When David's parents asked him about it he became evasive and angry and accused the swimming coach of 'making it all up'. The matter was not pursued and David's parents put his problems down to 'adolescence'. The second came from David's school who informed his mother that David's work was 'going downhill' and that he did not seem to be trying. The school asked David's mother if he might be on drugs. Again, when David was questioned about his school work he became evasive, although he passionately swore that he had never taken drugs. David's parents had no reason to doubt him, especially because they could see no external signs of drug abuse. David's uncharacteristic behaviour carried on and he went out most evenings, often coming in very late with no explanations. His mother said:

'His change in lifestyle became obvious. He'd come in after school and leave the house. I'd plead with him to stay but it didn't seem to make any difference. He would just go. He seemed to have completely lost his respect for us. It was difficult to know what to do. We couldn't physically keep him at home, lock him in his room. Once I followed him, driving slowly behind him and watched him go into an amusement arcade . . . he was there with some of his friends playing on one of the machines. There didn't seem to be too much wrong in that. All sorts of awful things had been going through my mind. Perhaps he'd been out with a teenage gang who went robbing and mugging. Playing on the 'fun for all the family' machines as the arcade billed them, didn't seem too awful. He was doing a morning paper round and if he chose to spend his money with his friends it didn't seem too terrible.'

Like a lot of parents, David's mother and father had taken their children into the amusement arcades at the seaside (where, in fact, they lived). Lots of families did this and they could not see anything wrong in that because they felt it was 'harmless fun and doesn't cost much'. However, these early experiences coupled with exposure to fruit machines at David's swimming club were factors in David's acquisition of addictive fruit machine playing. But David's mother reported:

'I began to find money missing from my purse. We sat the children down and told them that money had begun to go missing. [David's sister] had seemed dreadfully upset by this . . . and David flatly denied he had anything to do with it. I asked [my daughter] later what was wrong. She burst into tears and said money had been stolen from her piggy bank too.'

The constant need to gamble

David provided an articulate account of life for him over this troublesome period:

'During four years of compulsive gambling I think I missed about six or seven days of playing fruit machines. Keeping in mind that four of those days were Christmas days and in my area Christmas Day was the only day it was impossible to gain access to a gambling machine it was impossible to leave them alone although admittedly, I never really wanted to try. I was unaware of the seriousness of my actions.'

'As for obtaining money, I did this in any way possible no matter who I might hurt or what I may destroy. If I wasn't actually gambling I was spending the rest of my time working out clever little schemes to obtain money to feed my habit. These two activities took up literally all my time. I even lost sleep from worrying about where I was going to get some money. When my financial sources ran out I would simply depend on somebody else's, no matter who or how close to me this person was.'

'Because I gambled every penny I had I would always gamble as large amounts as possible. I worked in a local restaurant and received about £60 every Friday, cash in hand. But there was a fruit machine by the door and my £60 was gone before I had left. Whilst I was working there

I recall going through a patch in my nightmare four years when things actually began to look up. I managed to save around £100 towards a motorbike by giving my mum a certain amount each week. Not a very large amount considering the wages I was earning but a great deal keeping in mind my constant need to play fruit machines.'

David's parents had opened a building society account for him and agreed to let him save the money towards a motorbike that he wanted. The bike seemed to signal a new beginning. As David explained:

'My new motorbike was a fine example of the things I could do with my money apart from gamble and lose it. Then came a series of family rows not really severe, but they were amplified amidst my depression and confusion. Hence, I returned to the machines full time. This led to me selling my motorbike after owning it for just three months. The £400 I received for the bike lasted just a day.'

Family distress

The more rows that David's family had, the more sullen David became. He refused to talk to any of his family and there was a general feeling of unhappiness in the home. David would constantly be in 'a world of his own'. When David did communicate it would only be to express his dissatisfaction with his parents, making comments like 'stop going on at me. You're always going on at me'. Occasionally, David and his father would end up fighting or at least David would lunge at his father, 'punching and kicking and biting while [David's father] tried to fend him off'. This would lead to David shouting and swearing and 'storming off to his bedroom'. David reported:

'As you have probably gathered already I ate, slept and breathed gambling machines which therefore meant that I never had time for anything else. I couldn't even find time to spend with the people I loved. This would hurt me very much but the machines were always more important than anything or anyone else.'

At this point, David's parents were considering divorce because they had so many arguments. David's mother felt the rows were upsetting David and driving him out of the house into the arcades to play on the machines. It was a vicious circle. David was driving his parents into arguments which led them to be worried and unhappy which drove David into the arcades which led to more arguments and so on. His parents did not know how to deal with the problem. They wondered whether they should give him the money (to stop the stealing) or turn him out of the house. As his mother said, 'the tension in the house was dreadful'.

Returning to win back losses, chasing, and excitement

David gave a number of insights into his motivations for continued playing:

> 'I never wanted to stop playing a machine. I couldn't even spend time to worry about the amounts of money I was pouring in, in fact it's hard to think of what was actually going through my mind, all I can remember is a total blank. Occasionally I wouldn't come round until I'd reached my home which is a good fifteen minutes walk from any machine. I'd arrive home and no matter how hard I'd try I couldn't remember the past few minutes walking from the arcade to my home. I was always very upset about losing all my money and I returned many times to try and win back my losses. But I was never convinced – I never believed that I would win it back, it was simply an effort to try and dig myself out of trouble and out of debt. Of course it was very rare I ever achieved this because if I ever did succeed in winning some back it would be put straight back in the machine anyway – I could never quit while I was ahead.'

> 'I would always be looking forward tremendously to playing machines and couldn't get to them fast enough. I always got this kind of feeling of being 'high' or 'stoned'. I was often uncontrollable . . . like a 5 year old at Christmas time. Although winning money was the first thing that attracted me to playing fruit machines, this was gradually converted to lights, sounds and excitement. I always received a great thrill from new machines with new ideas and new lights and sounds.'

> 'Since becoming hooked I've never been able to stop playing a machine once I've started. The only time I found possible to think about giving up was after leaving the arcade at closing time and vow never to return.'

The role of skill in fruit machine gambling

Initially, David liked demonstrating his skill because it enhanced his reputation among his friends and was an important part of maintaining his gambling. However, as his gambling developed he stopped playing with his peers and gambled alone. When gambling alone, the importance of skill was merely to prolong his time spent gambling on the fruit machines. When he first started playing the machines he would use his 'skill' to get a slightly lower win than the highest available so that his prize was paid out in cash.

As his addiction developed he preferred the higher token wins as he just wanted to stay on the machines as long as possible.

Addiction to gambling

For four years, David was addicted to fruit machines. As his mother stated:

'He couldn't wait for the doors of the arcades to open in the mornings. He hammered on them in frustration, wanting to get at the machines. He was obsessed by the lights, the noises. He was unable to concentrate on anything except his need to be there, playing them. He was so heavily hooked on them as anyone else might be on drink or drugs.'

'Apart from changes in his personality – the way he'd become so evasive and withdrawn, avoiding us or arguing with us about everything – David changed visibly. He didn't care what he looked like: he wouldn't wash, let alone bath. He would go to school looking as though he'd been pulled through a hedge backwards with his dirty, smelly jeans and T-shirt.'

This was all confirmed by David who made other comments about his addiction:

'Whenever I felt depressed (which was practically all of the time) or rejected, the urge to play machines became even bigger. Whenever I had to make a slight effort in my life I needed to counteract it by gambling. The biggest effort I ever seemed to make at one time was a half hour paper round every morning and this would result in my banging on the arcade doors in frustration waiting for them to open just so as I could spend my paper round wages. I find it very difficult to explain my feelings that I experienced during my addiction to fruit machines because now that I look back all I can remember is living in a trance for nearly four years. I was vaguely aware of the things I said and done and to this day have to rely on what other people have told me about what kind of person I was during my four year addiction. I simply can't remember, as if I had been drunk the whole time. I only ever did things which in some way or another would help fund my addiction whereas other important things just went down the drain. Things like washing and personal hygiene, eating and drinking, caring for my family and education. I sold a great deal of my possessions to subsidize my addiction despite two very well-paid jobs which I lost for being unreliable.'

Confronting the problems and recovery

The selling of David's motorbike prompted David's mother to get to the heart of the problem. She said to David, 'I'm not going to question you or tell you off. I just want to know one thing and you have to tell me. Where has the money gone?' David replied, 'The fruit machines. I had to have it for the fruit machines.' Shortly after, David's mother calculated that during the last two years he had spent £2,000. ('It was a shocking discovery.') Via a call to The Samaritans, David's mother got in touch with Gamblers Anonymous. David attended his first meeting and reported, 'It was marvellous . . . there are people there who I can talk to who know exactly how I feel.' David at last accepted that he had a problem. As David said:

> 'Despite all the heartache and depression I was suffering it never occurred to me to give up my gambling habits, I thought about it once or twice but never really got around to trying. It was after the 'motorbike saga' that things began to change. My mum knew how much I'd sold the bike for and managed to find out that most of the money had gone. She finally confronted me and I finally did something which I'd never even thought of doing in the past four years. I told her everything and that was the first massive step towards reaching the light at the end of the tunnel. Now that she knew everything I was able to talk to her instead of playing machines and enabled me to GIVE UP. There was no method, it was just sheer willpower and the fact that I wanted to give up was also very important too, probably crucial. It took me three months to get it out of my system just like a drug. But it was after those three agonizing months I actually began to feel a person again and it was then I realized all the terrible things I'd done and what I'd been through. The only way I managed to stay away from the machines was to do other things even if I didn't want to do them just to stop me thinking of them. I was always occupied but the only time I ever became restless was bedtime but I usually managed to overcome this by relaxing in a yoga orientated way I'd been taught at school – probably the only thing I ever listened to and bothered to learn at school since the age of 12.'

Through a combination of Gamblers Anonymous, talking about the problem, personally wanting to stop and not going near fruit machines, David managed to curtail his gambling. However, as his mother stated, 'There is no certainty that David is "cured" – a life crisis might trigger the need to go back to his addiction'. David himself still looks back to the 'lost four years' of his life and although he is now more positive in his outlook, negative feelings still predominate in his thoughts. This was particularly evident when he said:

'I lost a great deal of childhood with my parents and only sister which I can never replace. I still get very depressed when I think of the amounts I stole from family and close friends which are totally unrepayable. I could have had a car and a house by now if I hadn't have gone through such vast amounts of money. I lost my education which I am now having to start again to gain exams for the promotion I need in my current job. I will have to live with these mental scars for the rest of my life.'

Discussion

As with almost all case studies, it is hard to generalize to all such people affected by similar phenomena. However, this study highlights a number of findings which have yet to be reported in the general literature. As was reported in Chapter 3, gambling acquisition is usually a result of socio-logical (rather than psychological or biological) factors and this case appeared to be no exception. It was almost certainly the widespread exposure of fruit machines in the town where the subject grew up (i.e. a seaside town where fruit machines and amusement arcades were abundant) coupled with constant exposure to a single site machine (i.e. fruit machine playing with friends at his local swimming club) that accounted for the subject's acquisition of fruit machine gambling.

It is also worth pointing out here that the subject's gambling pathology only seemed to affect his immediate family (i.e. three people) although some friends may have also been affected. However, the number of people affected is significantly less than the constantly quoted figure of ten to fifteen people cited by Lesieur and Custer (1984). It could be that their figure relates to adult gamblers rather than adolescent gamblers although further research would need to be done to confirm this. The development and maintenance of the subject's gambling was due to psychological and physiological factors. Initial motivations for repeating gambling experiences were attributed to reasons such as winning money, excitement, to display skill, to have fun and because friends play. This would seem to confirm previous authors' findings (e.g. Chapter 3, this volume; National Housing and Town Planning Council, 1988; Spectrum Children's Trust, 1988). However, as the gambling developed, the reasons for playing were almost totally escapist. Gambling became motivated by feelings of depression, confusion and rejection. The subject vividly described his feelings of being in a trance and that his mind became a total blank.

Winning money was only important in that it meant longer on the machine (i.e. the subject played with money rather than for it). This was highlighted when the subject reported that as his gambling developed he gambled to win tokens rather than money (tokens having no monetary value except in the sole context of fruit machine playing). The role of skill changed as the gambling pathology developed. Initially 'skilful playing' was valued because it gained social rewards from the subject's peers and made him feel good about himself. However, in the later stages of his gambling career, the subject used skill to prolong the gambling period. The role of skill (or perceived skill) has been reported previously as being one of the possible critical factors in fruit machine gambling (see Chapter 5) but it has never been reported that the reason why skill is important in gambling pathology may change over time. The account presented here is one where skill is undeniably an important maintaining factor in fruit machine gambling but that its reason for importance is dictated by the context and/or stage of a person's gambling career.

There is little doubt that the subject was once 'addicted' to fruit machines. In addition to *DSM-III-R* classification as a pathological gambler (the revised criteria of which were based on the *DSM-III* criteria of psychoactive substance dependence), the subject displayed the classical features of substance addictions, e.g. salience (either gambling, thinking about gambling, engaging in behaviour which procured funds for gambling), tolerance (gambling more and more over the years using larger amounts of money), chasing (returning to win back losses) euphoria and dysphoria (getting 'high', then depressed after gambling), withdrawal (feeling irritable when not gambling, banging on arcade doors while waiting to gamble on the machines) and relapse (returning to full-time gambling after periods of non-gambling). There is however doubt as to whether the subject was 'primary addicted' or 'secondary addicted'. It would appear that the subject could fulfil both outlined types but at different stages of his gambling career. Up to about the first two years the subject appeared to have a primary addiction, i.e. he was addicted to the machine itself, whereas towards the end of the four years he appeared to be using the machine to escape the problems in his life (i.e. secondary addiction). It could be that the two types of gambler are mutually exclusive in time but not necessarily in the individual, i.e. a pathological gambler cannot simultaneously be primary and secondary addicted but can develop from one to another over time.

The subject managed to curtail his gambling through a combination of Gamblers Anonymous (i.e. knowing that other people existed who had the same problem), talking about the problem (particularly with his mother), yoga (i.e. a relaxation technique), behavioural self-monitoring (i.e. not going near a fruit machine) and – probably the most important factor – having the personal motivation to stop. This combination suggests that other addicted gamblers may benefit from a variety of approaches (rather than one therapeutic method) to treat their problematic behaviour. Since a critical factor in success appears to be 'wanting to stop', perhaps the most appropriate therapeutic application would be one in which the individual's motivation to stop is explored through motivational interviewing (Miller and Rollnick, 1991) and used as a foundation to help the client select other approaches (e.g. self-help groups, psychotherapy, behaviour modification) which they feel might benefit them.

In this particular case one of the most salient themes in the prevention of further gambling was family communication and support. The adolescent may feel they have no one to turn to, especially if the relationship between themselves and their parents has deteriorated during their addiction. However, this has to be overcome, whether it be the parent(s) or adolescent who make the first move. Results in this study suggested that just talking about the problem was an important first step.

Attendance at Gamblers Anonymous has been shown to benefit some people but interestingly, this study demonstrated that just one attendance at a meeting had a profound impact. The subject did not feel the need to go to Gamblers Anonymous again after the initial meeting. It appears that just seeing other people with the same problem was an important step in the self-recovery process. If other people benefit from brief attendance at Gamblers Anonymous it might partially explain why there is a 75 per cent to 90 per cent drop out-rate from Gamblers Anonymous, at least among adults (Stewart and Brown, 1988; Moody, 1990). The use of relaxation techniques advocated by Markham (1990) may also aid some gamblers in overcoming acute stress arising from not being able to gamble. The performing of yoga by the subject in this study was certainly seen as beneficial to recovery.

From my own personal research experience, the account presented above is typical of fruit machine addicts. I have collected many case studies over the years, all of which demonstrate the seriousness of fruit machine addiction for that particular individual. Although there is insufficient space to reproduce all the accounts in this book, two more case studies which I feel are typical are presented below. Just to reiterate, the first account was written by the mother of a fruit machine addict, the second by a clinical psychologist. Their accounts will not be discussed or analysed, since they are reproduced here to give credence to the typicality of David's account.

Case study II: a mother's account

'My name is Susan and I am the mother of a compulsive gambler. It is easier to start like this and to admit the sad, destroying truth. I don't know when the problem started but I do know that even at the very early age of

10 and 11 when we stayed at my parent's apartment at the seaside, my son didn't want to join his younger brother and sister on the beach, he just wanted to stay in the games room adjoining the apartment complex where there were machines and a table tennis game. He used to watch fascinated and talk excitedly, then I never gave him any money. He would make friends of a similar age standing around the machines. It was only at a later date that I realized that he had been helping himself to pesetas from the bedside table. As the years went by, we often queried amounts of money that went missing but always thought we had underestimated items, been given short change, had purchased building materials without making a note of it. There was also the possibility an au pair could be to blame. No one was ever accused but we became watchful.

'By the time James was 13 years old my husband was aware he could not account for large sums of cash and had to go to the bank more frequently. On one occasion he counted the money in the bedside drawer. He went out into the car but returned within a couple of minutes having forgotten something. He went to the drawer only to find half had already been taken. My son was the only one in the house. On confrontation he denied going into our bedroom. My daughter's money box had been raided on many occasions and I always said she must have miscounted and my youngest son who is now 11 years old had his hard earned pocket-money taken. Whenever questioned, James always swore on his life that he had not touched anything – he always put the blame on his brother or sister or au pair.

'He sold a collection of commemorative mugs from his bedroom. When I discovered their disappearance he accused his friends. I insisted on calling in the police and only then did he break down and say he had sold them to a local antique dealer. He had checked all the prices in the Miller's Antique guide book and had got a fair price for them. He promised never to do it again but within the first couple of weeks of his new school at 13 his watch was 'lost', his calculator 'stolen', etc. His paper round money 'fell out of his pocket', 'got lost' or was 'pickpocketed'. He became more touchy, bad-tempered, very low or too high as to be disruptive, uncontrollable and unpleasant in the home. He spent more and more time in his room and screamed at us if we went in or called him. He cut himself off from the family or any activity. I do remember one holiday we took a friend of his with us and rented a cottage in Somerset. He refused to come in the car on the journey down saying it would be too cramped for him. We gave him the fare money and took his friend down by car. We all eagerly waited at the village station that evening but he did not arrive on the London train. He 'missed the train'. The machines were too big a temptation for him. He did eventually arrive but the holiday was disastrous. He stayed in the cottage all week while we took his friend out each day. Only once did he agree to join us as we were going to a seaside resort. He and his friend went off on their own for the day. There were plenty of machines so he was happy. By this time his school work was suffering. He left for school on time and returned home on time but I now know there were many days he did not go to school. Some days he said he had borrowed £1 from a friend and had to pay back £2 because he had 'lost' his money, paid for a poor boy who couldn't afford to buy any lunch. On Friday morning at 3 a.m. at the age of 14 years James ran away. My 12-year-old daughter went to wake him at 7.30 a.m. and found his bed had not been slept in. There was no note and no clothes taken from his room (when he was found he had taken a toothbrush and a vest in a suitcase). I went to the police station. The police went to all the schools in the area to interview children he knew. One of the boys told me that James visited the local cafe every day before going to school. There were one or two machines in there. On showing a photo of James the owner said he had been in the day before asking to borrow £5.

'We had a very distressing weekend sitting by the phone. We still did not know what the problem was. We knew he was unhappy. He was found in Norfolk, in a small seaside resort, by the police that Sunday. When we collected him, the sergeant in charge said he had never come across a lad like him before. He was not the normal runaway from home kid. He said in the four hours of police custody he had answered every question with a question and the policeman was none the wiser to his problem. We drove him home. He was angry to be found. He did not want to go home and refused to go back to school. I still do not know why or what went on that weekend.

'He joined a small tutorial group of sixteen youngsters and I have never seen him happier. I felt he was free of the machines while he was there, perhaps I am being naive. He joined the lower sixth of a college but within a couple of weeks the head of the lower sixth informed me that he had not been attending classes. He left home on time and returned home on time but didn't attend school.

'Over the years we seemed to have misplaced so many things, the gold pen given to my husband, a gold sovereign pendant, many items we thought must be somewhere in the attic. Before the end of the first time we gave him an ultimatum, study or go out and get a job. He got a job within a couple of days to start in the January after the Christmas holidays. During the past couple of years he had disappeared for long hours. He had supposedly gone to friends but I never heard or saw any one of these friends. I thought he was on drugs because of his disruptive behaviour. We could not talk to him. Our family mealtimes were a nightmare. He never joined in conversations – just broke them up. He raided the children's bedrooms and flatly denied taking their chocolate and turning their drawers out. He raided the larder for sweet things. He put on weight, became spotty and more self-conscious and objectionable. He picked an argument for absolutely anything. He belittled his little brother calling him an idiot, thicket, fool, and ridiculed anything he did. My youngest became more morose and down-trodden.

'My husband found any communication with James impossible. He was coming home later from work. By now he was 16 years old and over six foot tall. I went to meet him at work one day to have lunch – I couldn't believe it – an amusement arcade was due to open the following day two doors from his office. During the next couple of weeks we discovered a prized collection of antique mechanical toys which had brought great joy to the children over the years, had depleted. He had been working his way through boxes of bric-a-brac, Dinky and Corgi toys, which had been carefully stored away.

'We called the police on him and he was taken into the police station. We refused to take him home as nothing seemed safe any more. I didn't want to lock my bedroom, hide my purse, empty my pockets any more. We helped him to find a room. He kept his job and phoned occasionally. Six weeks later after raiding the Dr. Barnardo's box and bouncing the cheque for his rent, he arrived on my doorstep saying 'I've decided to give you another chance'. His ultimatum was to go to Gamblers Anonymous and never touch anything in the house and go to work or back to college. He chose work.

'He is now 18 years old. He left home at 17- and-a-half to try and make a go of it. Now is the only time in our lives since James was 12 or 13 that we had a kind of peace. Only now do we realize what we have been through. We know he has had a lonely teen life of self-destruction and has nothing but a very bleak future unless he wants to help himself and go to Gamblers Anonymous.

'Psychiatrists, social workers, Child Guidance, Welfare Board, and the Teenage Walk-in Officer have all tried to understand the problem but don't. I have not been able to break the barrier and tell my parents. My father has angina and my mother is not a well woman. Up until now the shame and guilt we have carried has cut us off from society in general. I shy away from gatherings and the many activities I was once involved with. I know now it is not my problem, but I've protected him and my family and now it is more difficult to speak out. Putting this on paper has given me a lot of pain.

'I heard Gordon Moody on the radio one summer's day and I couldn't believe my ears. He was talking about my problem, my son. I could relate. We started a group of Parents of Young Gamblers and more and more groups are springing up over the country. The voice is one at the meeting. We all have the same son. A cancer in the midst which is self-destroying, breaks up families and destroys trust.

'I lost my son many years ago, when he was just a little boy, to a machine. He doesn't live with us but the house is full of him but empty. His bedroom was just a room containing a half-drunken cup of tea left amongst his handkerchiefs, dirty plates with dinner remains amongst his jumpers. Bank statements from two banks showing an overdraft of £2,500 at the age of 17. He had gone such a long way down the road to self-destruction before he was even old enough to be allowed into an arcade.

'I am the contact of the London group and I receive one or two phone-calls every week telling me of the new heartbreaking horror story of a young person's life through playing the machines. It has been difficult to write this but I want my voice to be heard. Do something to stop the machines being so easily available to young innocent children. We tell them don't talk to strangers, don't take sweets, don't go near the water, keep away from the railway lines but we don't say 'keep away from the machines'. We actually offer it as a prize. If it's raining we'll have a go. If you are good, here's 10p to have a go before the train comes, or while I finish my coffee here's 10p.

'Ten, 11, 12 year olds are so vulnerable, we must protect them. I have asked some of the parents with whom I am in contact to write their story. It is really too painful, too distressing for most of them. Please let their story be my story. At this moment in time, my son is living in a miserable lonely bedsit. He is one of the lucky ones. I have just spoken to one mother whose son is living in the embankment. My son earns anything from £120 to £180 but is still wearing the shoes he was wearing when he left school only now he is walking straight onto the pavement with no soles left on the shoes. He has no possessions but one pair of jeans for the weekend to change into. He walks with his legs close together so as not to show the holes worn through the trouser thigh.'

Case study III: a clinical psychologist's account

'My client is a 19-year-old man who was referred by his GP. He has been gambling on fruit machines for six years and is now in considerable debt to the tune of £1,500. He lives alone in rented accommodation, having been asked to leave his family home because of his gambling behaviour. He lives in deprived conditions having sold his furniture, stolen and run up further debt in order to finance his gambling. He is supported by a girlfriend who supplies him with food. He often spends his unemployment money on the same day that he receives it. He has been unemployed for several months now. In the past he has had unskilled jobs, although he is an intelligent, articulate person having left school with qualifications. He consistently underachieves.

'He says he started playing fruit machines for money when he was 13. However, as a young boy, his stepfather who was the manager of an amusement arcade used to give him tokens to amuse himself. His stepfather now has a very hard line on gambling and was depicted by my client as having been a hard disciplinarian in the past. My client can remain abstinent for up to four or five months and finds it easier if he has a job. He will gamble either when he is depressed, under stress, or in order to get a 'high'. He will spend up to £50 a session. If he has money in his pocket he says he must spend it. He described himself as excited and preoccupied whilst gambling. He has favourite machines, the more complex ones, which he describes as making him work harder, and these machines he describes as having a fascination for him to the extent that he cannot take his eyes away from them if he is sitting in a pub where they are. He describes his feelings when gambling as those of excitement and indeed describes himself as 'high'. His pattern of gambling tends to follow a binge and restraint model.

'At present he is depressed. Obviously this is as a result of his present circumstances, but I think there is an underlying depression concerning his family situation. He relies on either his mother or his girlfriend to control his money, although at the same time he will steal from them. He has some anger at his dependence on others to regulate his day-to-day finances. He has attended Gamblers Anonymous in the past but not found it to be useful for him. He feels he could stop gambling but describes himself as weak-willed. His typical retort is 'I cannot help it. I have no choice'.

'I have been seeing him for a number of sessions, exploring his family dynamics and also looking at behavioural control over his gambling. He can typically exert a lot of control in a restraint phase, but everything is overthrown by a binge. Any behavioural interventions suggested are not usually followed up and he invariably has some rationale for this. More recently he has obtained a job filling up supermarket shelves, and since then has not attended therapy. He had been pinning his hopes on the structure and increased finances that a job would give him providing an incentive for him to stop, but I have no way of knowing whether this is the case or not.

CASE STUDIES: A FINAL COMMENT

None of these three preceding case studies are sensationalist. They are typical accounts of the effects of excessive fruit machine playing. They highlight not only the effects on the individual but also on those people close to the adolescent gambler. They also indicate that there is a critical need for more in-depth case studies relating to fruit machine addiction. Quantitative studies highlight the generalizations of studied phenomena, yet it is the small differences which are critical, especially in the therapeutic setting. It is through such qualitative accounts that (a) the general public can be educated about the dangers of adolescent gambling to excess, and (b) therapists can identify and relate with their own clients and help in the formulation of strategies for therapeutic success.

8 Fruit machine gambling
The importance of structural characteristics

Determinants of the decision to gamble not only include the gambler's biological and psychological constitution and the situational variables, but also the structural characteristics of the gambling activity itself. As Cornish (1978) points out, the structural characteristics of a particular gambling activity are responsible for reinforcement, may satisfy gamblers' needs and may actually facilitate excessive gambling. By identifying particular structural characteristics it may be possible to see how (a) needs are identified; (b) information about gambling is presented (or perhaps misrepresented), and (c) cognitions are influenced and distorted. Showing the existence of such relationships has great practical importance. Not only could potentially 'dangerous' forms of gambling be identified, but effective and selective legislation could be formulated (Cornish, 1978).

The Royal Commission (1951) and Weinstein and Deitch (1974) have both attempted to construct lists of such structural characteristics and dimensions in which all gambling activities can be described, compared and contrasted. Weinstein and Deitch claim that analysis of the structural characteristics and their location on each of six dimensions produces a graphic representation of a gambling profile. The six dimensions are:

1 *Multiplier potential* – the way in which gambles can be made on one or a series of events; in particular, facilities for gambling at a variety of odds and/or stake levels.
2 *Pay-out interval* – the time elapsed before winning gamblers receive payment.
3 *Better involvement* – the extent to which gamblers are, or see themselves as taking an active part in gambling.
4 *Skill required* – an objective estimate of skill in the type of gambling; however, gamblers may have their own (incorrect) opinions.

5 *Win probability* – the probability of gamblers' winning an individual bet.

6 *Pay-out ratio* – the ratio of potential winnings to the gamblers' stake.

Cornish (1978) also outlined two further characteristics which although not given explicit names could be described as 'intrinsic association' and 'suspension of judgement'. Intrinsic association refers to the degree to which the gambling activity is associated with other interests and attractions. For example, betting at a sporting event which the gambler would normally attend anyway. Suspension of judgement refers to structural characteristics which temporarily disrupt the gambler's financial value system. For example, betting with chips instead of money at the roulette table where the money's true value can be disguised or seen as 'fun money'.

Although this list of structural characteristics is fairly comprehensive it should also be remembered that it is by no means complete, especially because some forms of gambling have characteristics which are unique to that particular activity. Abt *et al.* (1985b) have examined the structural characteristics of lotteries, pari-mutuels and casino games but a number of gambling activities have not been examined individually or in a culture specific context. One such form is fruit machine gambling. The Royal Commission (1951) said gaming (and betting) came closest to incorporating the largest number of gambling inducing characteristics. Such characteristics included a high pay-out ratio (i.e. jackpots), rapid event frequency, exercise of personal skills (real or imagined) and scope for beliefs about attractiveness of participation. In addition, heavy losses were viewed as a likely occurrence because gaming features structural characteristics which allow continuous gambling, although Cornish (1978) argued that the essentially solitary nature of this form of gambling prevented the competitive pressure to increase stakes which are present in other forms of gambling.

As we have seen in Chapter 2, a number of studies have shown that fruit machine gambling among adolescents is a popular activity in the UK (e.g. Ide-Smith and Lea, 1988; National Housing and Town Planning Council, 1988; Spectrum Children's Trust, 1988). Although most adolescents control their gambling activity, and the positive effects of gaming machines on adolescent development – particularly as a peer group social event and as an expression of individual autonomy – have been pointed out by some authors (e.g. Home Office, 1988), in some minority cases gambling behaviour can be pathological.

Accepting that for a minority of adolescents fruit machine gambling is a major problem, this chapter reviews the structural characteristics of the fruit machine which might promote persistent gambling, rather than the individual's psychological, physiological or socio-economic status. However, it must be noted that some structural characteristics are inextricably linked with an individual gambler's psychological constitution. This will be expanded below.

As we saw in Chapter 4, an analysis of fruit machine marketing methods mainly falls into two categories these being (i) situational characteristics which get the potential gamblers into the arcades and (ii) structural characteristics which either induce the gambler to play fruit machines or are inducements to continue playing. The former set of characteristics are primarily features of the environment and can be considered situational determinants of gambling. These include the location of the arcade, the number of arcades in a specified area, possible membership requirements and advertising effects. Although these variables may be important in the initial decision to gamble, may help clarify why some forms of gambling are more attractive to particular socio-economic classes, and could be considered structural characteristics, they are external to the gambling activity itself and as such will not be discussed here.

This chapter therefore concentrates on the latter of the two approaches by examining structural characteristics of the fruit machine itself and attempts to link behaviour and cognitions of gamblers to such characteristics. In addition to examining fruit machine gambling in relation to the structural characteristics outlined by the Royal Commission (1951), Weinstein and Deitch (1974) and Cornish (1978), other potentially important characteristics particularly salient to fruit machines will be discussed. These include symbol ratio proportions, the near miss, light, colour and sound effects, and naming. This is preceded by a brief history of structural characteristics which have been used by the gaming industry.

GAMING MACHINES: A BRIEF HISTORY OF STRUCTURAL CHARACTERISTICS

For almost eighty years, the gaming industry has used various inducements to entice people to play and to keep on playing fruit machines. As Hess and Diller (1969) point out, it is likely that many of the marketing 'ploys' used by the gaming industry have arisen spontaneously or fortuitously without psychological analysis. However, the effectiveness of these 'ploys' suggests there is much to be learned about the psychology of fruit machine gambling from an analysis of the marketing methods used by the gaming industry.

As early as 1902, some machines were designed to double up as a musical box, the thinking being that the person had to play the fruit machine to hear the music. Another marketing ploy which began to appear by the 1930s was the built-in vending machine. After playing the machine, players would receive items such as mints, bubble gum or candy (Holmes, 1985). Other enticing features highlighting the fruit machine's financial rewards began to appear in early fruit machine designs. In 1925, a 'guaranteed jackpot' was introduced and in 1944 the first fruit machine with a 'multiline pay' feature was introduced consisting of multiple reels which gave variable automatic pay-outs for differing reel combinations, i.e. a machine with more winning combinations. Some fruit machines were even concealed in the torsos of carved life-size cowboys and indians which were played by pulling the arms of one of these figures. According to Holmes (1985), this is where the term 'one-armed bandit' may have originated.

During the 1950s, a number of features were added to fruit machines, thus exploiting a loophole, by making them legally non-gambling devices at a time when anti-gambling legislation dominated (Costa, 1988). One such feature was the 'skill stop' button which gave each player the opportunity to stop any of the spinning reels independently. Thus, fruit machine playing was re-defined by the gaming industry as an act of skill and therefore was not a gambling machine by legal definition. Another inventive addition, also used to deceive the authorities, was known as the 'future play' feature. This became operational when a player had won the jackpot. The jackpot winnings would drop on to an internal platform but would not be released to the player until the next play was over. The machine also displayed the exact amount that the player had won. The logic behind such a feature was that if players knew how much money they were going to get before playing, and when they received it, the fruit machine could not be considered a gambling device since the reward was not a product of chance (Holmes, 1985). It must also be noted that throughout the last eighty years, promoters have used other techniques based both on appeals to expressive needs and the manipulation of situational factors to attract new custom or to increase their share of the market (Cornish, 1978), although such techniques have involved the manipulation of situational variables.

Having outlined a selective history of the importance of structural characteristics, the rest of this chapter discusses the role of pay-out interval, multiplier potential, better involvement, skill, win probability, pay-out ratio, suspension of judgement, symbol ratio proportions, the near miss, sound effects, light and colour effects, and naming and their relation to gamblers' behaviour and/or cognitions. Intrinsic association will not be discussed since it is considered to be a situational variable rather than a structural characteristic. It must also be noted that these characteristics could potentially be differentiated as either a pure structural characteristic (i.e. what the owner and/or manufacturer put into the machine) or a psycho-structural characteristic (i.e. an individual's relation to a structural characteristic).

PAY-OUT INTERVAL AND EVENT FREQUENCY

On fruit machines, the pay-out interval (the time between initial gamble and winning payment) is very short. Three factors are inextricably linked with such a characteristic. The first of these is the frequency of opportunities to gamble (event frequency) which some authors (e.g. Cornish, 1978) consider a separate structural characteristic. Logistically, some gambling activities (e.g. lotteries, football pools) have small event frequencies. However, in the case of fruit machines there are few constraints on repeated gambling – limits are set only by the speed of the machine's mechanisms involved and the players themselves. Such a characteristic may therefore be an inducement to gamble and an inducement to continue. The frequency of playing when linked with the two other factors – the result of the gamble (win or loss) and the actual time until winnings are received – exploit certain psychological principles of learning (Moran, 1987). This process (operant conditioning – described in more detail in Chapter 1) conditions habits by rewarding behaviour, i.e. through presentation of a reward (e.g. money), reinforcement occurs. To produce high rates of response those schedules which present rewards intermittently (random and variable ratio schedules) have shown to be most effective (Skinner, 1953). Since fruit machines operate on random and variable ratio schedules it is not surprising that high rates of response (i.e. excessive gambling) occur. Cornish (1978) notes that promoters appear to acknowledge the need to pay out winnings as quickly as possible, thus indicating that receiving winnings is seen by the gaming industry to act as a reinforcement to winners to continue gambling. Rapid event frequency also means that the loss period is brief, with little time given over to financial considerations and, more importantly, winnings can be re-gambled almost immediately.

THE PSYCHOLOGY OF THE NEAR MISS AND SYMBOL RATIO PROPORTIONS

Another related aspect to operant conditioning is the 'psychology of the near miss' (Reid, 1986) which can act as an intermediate reinforcer. Reid (1986) noted that near misses, i.e. failures that are close to being successful, are believed to encourage future play inducing continued gambling, and that some commercial gambling activities (particularly fruit machines and scratch card lotteries) are formulated to ensure a higher than chance frequency of near misses. Reid argued that at a behaviouristic level, a near miss may have the same kind of conditioning effect on behaviour as a success. For example, the fruit machine's pay-out line is horizontally located in the middle line of a 3 x 3 matrix. When three winning symbols are displayed, the jackpot is won (and thus reinforces play). However, a near miss, e.g. two winning symbols and a third losing one just above or below the payline, is still strongly reinforcing at no extra expense to the machine's owner (Skinner, 1953). Thus, at a lower cognitive level, a near miss could produce some of the excitement of a win, i.e. cognitive conditioning through secondary reinforcement (i.e. a psycho-structural characteristic). Therefore, the player is not constantly losing but constantly nearly winning (Griffiths, 1991c).

Reid (1986) pointed out that the near miss can also be explained in terms of frustration theory (Amsel, 1958) or cognitive regret (Kahneman and Tversky, 1982). According to Amsel, failing to fulfil a goal (not winning on a fruit machine, for instance) produces frustration which energizes ongoing behaviour. Subsequent wins then reinforce high rate behaviour. According to Kahneman and Tversky's theory, the frustration produced by 'nearly winning' would induce a form of cognitive regret. The elimination of regret can be achieved by playing again, and this in turn encourages future play.

Strickland and Grote (1967) drew attention to another design in fruit machines which has been experimentally shown to encourage repeated play and which Reid (1986) has argued produces a greater than chance number of near misses. They noted that the first reel on a fruit machine tends to have a larger proportion of winning symbols than the second reel, which has a larger proportion of winning symbols than the third reel. Since the reels stop in this order, the player is most likely to see a winning symbol early in the result sequence. Strickland and Grote investigated the effect by presenting players with frequent winning symbols either early or late in the fruit machine's result sequence. The former situation led to significantly longer play than the latter.

MULTIPLIER POTENTIAL

This structural characteristic basically equates to the range of odds and stakes that the form of gambling offers and can be viewed as a primary inducement to play. This means that gamblers can choose the rate at which their wins and/or losses multiply. In the US, this can be achieved on the same slot-machine and are called 'multipliers' (see Appendix 2), whereas in the UK the amount gambled per play is dependent upon the machine, i.e. each fruit machine has a constant gambling stake. Stakes to gamble on fruit machines can be 1p, 2p, 5p, 10p and 20p, with the general rule that the more money initially staked the greater the jackpot prize.

The research outlined in Chapter 4 showed that different stake fruit machines are generally used by different clientele. For instance, at seaside amusement arcades male 10 to 16-year-old adolescents play video games and cheaper stake (2p–5p) fruit machines and older adolescents and young men in groups (18 to 25 years) tend to play games of competition. Those on their own play higher stake fruit machines and pinball machines. Most females (young or old) played cheap stake (1p-2p) fruit machines. Why this particular structural characteristic should attract different clienteles can at present only be speculated, but as Cornish (1978) states, 'When the opportunity to use . . . higher stakes in order to multiply winnings or recoup losses rapidly is combined with high event frequency and short pay-out interval, participants may be tempted to continue gambling longer than they might otherwise do' (p.168).

BETTER INVOLVEMENT AND SKILL

Cornish (1978) states that to some extent better involvement (i.e. the degree of personal participation) and the exercise of skill are interrelated. To participate in fruit machine gambling, a player must not only be at the site of the gambling activity itself, but to some extent has to interact with the machine, i.e. a psycho-structural interaction in which the player is actively involved in making constant decisions in reaction to the machine's display after each separate gamble. Research has suggested that the more actively involved a person is with a gambling activity the more likely they are to believe that their actions can affect gambling outcomes, most probably through the illusion of control. As we saw in Chapter 1, the illusion of control was defined by Langer (1975) as being an expectancy of personal success inappropriately higher than the objective probability would warrant. Her experiments (also briefly outlined in Chapter 1) supported her basic assumptions that in some chance settings those conditions which involve factors of choice, familiarity, involvement and/or competition may stimulate the illusion of control to produce skill orientations.

The UK gaming industry has acknowledged that the current generation of fruit machine players desire control and skill in playing (Griffiths, 1988b). As fruit machines are based wholly or predominantly on chance, they preclude the players' abilities from significantly affecting the final outcome of play. However, in manufacturing and profit terms, to make the players think they are affecting the outcome is as good as if they actually are – and is at no extra recurrent cost to the operator.

With the introduction of specialist play features such as 'nudge', 'hold', and 'gamble' buttons (see Appendix 2), the creation of perceived skill has been achieved (i.e. the structural characteristics of a fruit machine enable it to mimic skill-determined situations). White (1989) has argued that specialist play features lead to longer play because there are no instructions on how to play or to use the features on the machines, and players have to spend money learning to 'master' the controls. My own research, particularly that outlined in chapters 3 and 5, has suggested that regular fruit machine players believe their activity to be skilful. It was also argued that the introduction of specialist play features stimulate the illusion of control through personal involvement, perception of skill and familiarity with a particular machine.

One of the contentions in this book has been that 'skill' appears to be a critical component in the maintenance of fruit machine playing and in the maintenance of group hierarchies of adolescent fruit machine players. Some group hierarchies are based on an almost universal 'group cognitive bias' (Griffiths, 1991h, p.97) in that regular players (in some cases) believe their fruit machine playing to be highly skillful and that the most 'skilful' players become group leaders with less 'skilful' players taking up subordinate roles. As we saw in Chapter 4, 'skilful' players are also in the position to 'sell their expertise' to other players (friends, novices, etc.) because non-regular players can be led to believe that 'the machine can be beaten'. This typology of players is almost identical to the sociological account reported by Fisher (1993b), who described these players as 'arcade kings' and 'slaves' (see Chapter 4).

There is very little skill involved in playing fruit machines and research outlined in this book has shown that there is little or no difference between regular players and non-regular players in how long they can stay on fruit machines in terms of time and money. At best, they take a few extra gambles to lose the same amount of money. In Chapter 5, sixty players were asked what skill was involved in playing fruit machines and the players put forward twenty-one 'skills' (many of which were knowledge of some particular aspect of the fruit machine). Interestingly, there was a lot of similarity between regular and non-regular players in the skills they listed although there were a few significant differences. It was also argued (again in Chapter 6) that many of the skills listed by players are what could be termed 'idiot skill'. For instance, if a player has just won on a fruit machine and the opportunity to hold (i.e. to keep stationary winning symbols before the next play has started), is it a 'skill' to hold them? By not holding what are obvious winning symbols, 'easy money' is lost, leading to a reduction of further playing. Since it would be stupid not to hold the symbols it is little more than 'idiot skill'. Fruit machine gambling thus combines active participation and personal skills (whether real or imagined), thus encouraging continuous gambling.

WIN PROBABILITY

Win probability and pay-out ratios differ in most types of gambling but are important structural characteristics (Royal Commission, 1951; Weinstein and Deitch, 1974). It is these basic risk dimensions which may help determine whether a person gambles on a particular activity in the first place. On fruit machines, these structural characteristics do not appear to be especially important to the gambler. The studies of adolescent fruit machine players reported in this book have indicated that winning money is only one of a variety of reasons for playing fruit machines. Other reasons for playing have included fun, boredom, social influences, atmosphere, escapism and excitement (see chapters 3 and 4). The studies involving pathological fruit machine players (chapter 3) have indicated that these gamblers play with money rather than for it and that their expressed playing philosophy is to stay on the machine for as long as possible using the least amount of money similar to video game play. Probabilities of winning on fruit machines are fairly high in comparison with other gambling activities, with most machines giving a 70 per cent to 90 per cent pay-out (i.e. on average 70 per cent to 90 per cent of the original stake is paid back to the gambler). New fruit machine gamblers may be attracted by machines displaying amounts that can be won on a fruit machine, although these amounts are fairly small in comparison with other gambling activities. It is also likely that the ordinary 'social gambler' does not think about the actual probability of winning but relies on heuristic strategies for handling the available information.

SOUND EFFECTS

According to White (1989), the sound effects (and flashing lights) of a fruit machine give a constant impression of fun and activity, as well as suggesting big money wins technically beyond the machine's capacity. Thus these characteristics could be argued to be psycho-structural. In addition, they can be viewed as gambling inducers and in some people may actually stimulate further gambling. In the questionnaire and interview study in Chapter 3, 30 per cent of the fifty adolescent gamblers interviewed claimed that the 'aura' of the machine (i.e. the music, lights and noise) was one of the fruit machine's most attractive features. It was also reported that the nine adolescents diagnosed as pathological gamblers on *DSM-III-R* criteria (American Psychiatric Association, 1987) were significantly more attracted to the 'aura' of the machines than the non-pathological gamblers.

Sound effects have also been used to give the impression that winning is more common than losing. This has been achieved in two ways. The first of these is that all fruit machines have metal pay-out trays (called 'wells') into which winnings fall. The sound of coins falling into a well means that everyone in the vicinity knows there is a winner. Further to this, it gives the impression of a bigger win than is actually the case because the fruit machine's winnings are usually paid out in small denomination coins (Caldwell, 1974; Greenlees, 1988). Second, a number of fruit machines buzz loudly or play a musical tune after a win. Since most machines (particularly in US casinos) are lined up in their hundreds (and sometimes thousands in the biggest Las Vegas casinos) you can always hear those who are winning (but never those who are losing!). This is similar to the 'ploy' used by Las Vegas and Atlantic City casinos who bang loud gongs to let the casino's punters know that winning individuals have 'beaten the house'. Like casinos, amusement arcades create an atmosphere resembling that of an exciting sporting event by generating a noisy, bustling environment with flashing lights and ringing bells (Hess and Diller, 1969).

Another effect that is used in fruit machines is pulsating sound. There are many times when playing a fruit machine that the pitch of the sound increases and the sound becomes faster. An example of this can be found on fruit machines after the 'gamble' button comes into operation. At this point, a cycle of two notes rather like a mini-siren begins, which tells the player a decision must be made (to either take the winnings or attempt to gamble up to a higher win). If the player takes the winnings, the sound stops. However, if the player gambles successfully, the sound increases speed and pitch and again the player faces the decision to take the winnings or gamble. As the prize on offer increases so does the sound's speed and pitch. This appears to increase the tension and also tends to make players react more quickly towards the machine. This particular use of sound has been termed 'perceived urgency' (Edworthy *et al.*, 1991).

LIGHT AND COLOUR EFFECTS

Light and colour are two variables (often interrelated) which affect behavioural patterns in a variety of contexts (Birren, 1978). For instance, Bornstein (1978) concluded that there is little doubt about the direct relationship between colour stimulation and activity of the central nervous system, although why this should be so is not clear. Lighting can affect performance and arousal levels. As light levels increase so does visual acuity, although this is only up to a critical point (Boyce, 1975). High levels of illumination can actually decrease performance by suppressing some information cues, e.g. visual gradients (Stevens and Foxwell, 1955; Logan and Berger, 1961); therefore, light levels and performance follow an inverted U-shape when plotted. It has also been found that dim lighting or reduced light levels lessen eye contact and increase verbal latency in conversations (Carr and Dabbs, 1974).

There is evidence that colour evokes affective states and influences behaviour. It has been suggested that some colours are associated with certain moods, i.e. red is 'exciting' and 'stimulating', blue is 'comfortable', 'secure' and 'soothing', orange is 'disturbing' and green is 'leisurely' (Odbert *et al.*, 1942; Wexner, 1954). In addition, variations in colour can affect human physiological reactions such as blood pressure and breathing rate (Acking and Kuller, 1972). Some researchers have found that colour may affect people's mood and arousal (Mehrabian and Russell, 1974) and their attitudes, and it has been speculated by Holohan (1982) that these differences may indirectly affect behaviour. By comparing people's galvanic skin responses, it has been shown that red induces higher levels of arousal than green (Wilson, 1966) and with reference to observed behaviour, red appears to be associated with increased frequency and intensity of response as compared with blue or green, while red and blue are usually preferred to green and yellow (Eysenck, 1941; Goethe, 1971). There is also some speculation that red can sometimes be connected with aggression, with green having a quietening effect (Birren, 1965), although it is probable that the indirect effects of colour on performance are probably related to cultural differences in the meaning and conventional uses of various colours (Holohan, 1982).

To date, there has been little research into the differential effects of colour stimulation on more complex behaviour in ecologically valid settings, and only one study by Stark *et al.* (1982) has examined the differential effects of red and blue coloured lighting on gambling behaviour. In this experiment, Stark and his colleagues hypothesized that if red was arousing, subjects exposed to red light were likely to gamble more frequently, stake more money and take more risks than subjects exposed to blue light. Their hypothesis was confirmed with red lighting having less of an inhibitory effect on gambling behaviour than blue lighting. Why this should be so was again open to question, although the most credible reason put forward was along semiological lines which stressed the cultural significance of the different colours for participants.

A study with one of my students (Griffiths and Swift, 1992) found that in an observation of five arcades in Plymouth (England), the general colour of all the arcades' interiors was towards the red end of the colour spectrum, that lighting was on the whole very dim and that the machines which they housed relied heavily on a series of flashing lights. It was reported that there might be two possible effects of dim lighting which might affect gambling profit. If visual acuity decreases as lighting levels decrease (Boyce, 1975), there is a possibility of poorer performance in both video games and fruit machines which both (to some extent) rely on visual ability. Such an effect over a long period of time will lead to more losing plays in a specified period of time, thus increasing profit for the management. A second more subtle effect may arise from the finding that dim lighting increases verbal latency and reduces eye contact (Carr and Dabbs, 1974). A number of researchers (e.g. Graham, 1988; Fisher, 1993b) have reported that playing is peripheral to social interaction for some adolescents. If dim lighting reduces social interaction with peers, there will subsequently be more gambling if such individuals stay in the arcade. It has also been pointed out that 'rows of dazzling neon lit machines bathed in soft lighting create an atmosphere which is probably conducive to gambling' (Caldwell, 1974, p.24).

THE PSYCHOLOGY OF NAMING

According to Costa (1988), the names of fruit machines are also important. It was noted in Chapter 4 that the first fruit machine was called *The Liberty Bell* because it typified patriotism in that it was the symbol of American Independence. Since identification of machine names probably produces different impression formations, these can be viewed as psycho-structural characteristics which are potentially gambling inducing. My own brief analysis outlined in Chapter 4 found that names of fruit machines fell into four categories. By far the most common were the machines which had a reference to money in their names (e.g. *Action Bank, Cashpoint, Cashline*). As you may recall, these names all gave the impression that the machines are places where a player can gain money, *not* where players can lose it. The second category of machine names were those which suggested that skill was needed to play the machines (e.g. *Skillcash, Fruitskill*) whereas the third category gave the impression the odds of winning are fair in comparison to that of the house (e.g. *Fortune Trail, Silver Chance*). The remaining machines' names included either reference to the word 'reel' (e.g. *Reel Money, Reel 2 Reel, Reel Crazy*) or were described as being 'acoustically attractive' (e.g. *Nifty Fifty, Naughty but Nice*).

SUSPENSION OF JUDGEMENT

In the introduction of this chapter, it was mentioned that suspension of judgement refers to a structural characteristic which temporarily disrupts the gambler's financial value system and is thus partly psycho-structural and potentially stimulates further gambling. In the case of fruit machines, money to gamble usually consists of low coin denominations (e.g. 1p, 2p, 5p, 10p), all of which make the gambler think there is little to lose on each gamble. However, if gamblers were to consider money staked per session rather than per gamble (i.e. the total amount of money spent and lost during gambling), they might not gamble as much. It should also be noted that many fruit machines pay out tokens of predetermined monetary value (see Appendix 2). Tokens (like chips at a roulette table) disguise the money's true value and are put back into the machine without hesitation because they cannot be exchanged back into money by the machine's owner. Such a characteristic also means that a player can experience the satisfaction of a (comparatively) big win but the machine's owner knows they have to put the winnings back into the machine, thereby decreasing the chances that the gambler will leave with any winnings.

CONCLUSIONS

It has been clearly demonstrated that various structural characteristics of fruit machines at the very least have the potential to induce excessive gambling regardless of the gambler's biological and psychological constitution. However, some structural characteristics (as have been shown) are capable of producing psychologically rewarding experiences even in financially losing situations (e.g. the psychology of the near miss) although there is no evidence to suggest that the gaming industry has used the psychological literature to 'exploit' gamblers. As Cornish (1978) noted, the development of exploitative practices is not easy to define, identify or prevent. However, personal communications between myself and the gaming industry (Griffiths, 1988b) indicates that some arcade managers and/or companies carry out their own research in the form of 'in-depth research' and 'hall tests'.

In-depth research involves the employment of a market research company to locate the heaviest machine players and to pay them to sit on a 'player panel'. Questions are then put to the player by the arcade machine company or its representatives about the attractiveness of machines, lights and colours, inducements to play, etc. Using the responses from the 'player panels', machines' features are updated to induce more players. Hall tests, on the other hand are still carried out by market research companies, but they generally use members of the public. In this type of research, volunteers are escorted from (say) their shopping to a nearby indoor room (the 'hall') in which they will then be shown, for instance, two particular flashing lights and asked which of these is more 'attractive', 'arousing', 'inviting', etc. Other questions relating to symbols, lights and colours are also asked. Again, results from this type of research are used in designing future machines. Such research would suggest that the gaming industry does not rely on general psychological research in designing its machines and arcades but does carry out its own research for profit-making purposes.

The examination of structural characteristics demonstrated that for many of the categorizations (e.g. the near miss, naming, light and colour effects, sound effects, skill, better involvement) it is difficult to separate the gambler's individual psychology from the situation. In all the named examples above, the success of the machine's structural characteristics (where success is defined as an increase in gambling due to the structural characteristic) depends upon the psycho-structural interaction. The importance of a structural characteristic approach to gambling is the possibility to pinpoint more accurately where an individual's psychological constitution is influencing gambling behaviour. Such an approach also allows for psychologically context-specific explanations of gambling behaviour rather than global explanations such as 'addictive personality'. Although many of the fruit machine's inducing structural characteristics are dependent on individual psychological factors (e.g. reinforcement) they are a direct result of the structural characteristics and could not have influenced gambling behaviour independently. It is for this reason above all others that a structural approach could be potentially useful.

This chapter has also demonstrated that previous categorizations of gambling's structural characteristics (e.g. Cornish, 1978) were incomplete because they have tried to be all encompassing, and that for fruit machine gambling at least, many more exist including the importance of light and colour effects, sound effects, the psychology of naming, the psychology of the near miss and symbol ratio proportions. It could be that fruit machine gambling has more 'gambling inducing' structural characteristics than other forms of gambling and could be the reason why large proportions of gamblers in the UK are 'addicted' to fruit machines (many of whom are adolescents). With its integrated mix of conditioning effects, rapid event frequency, short pay-out intervals and psychological rewards, it is not hard to see how fruit machine gambling can become a repetitive habit.

Knowledge about structural characteristics also provides information which may help in decreasing 'addictiveness' potential. Possible a priori steps that could be taken include limited use of arousing lighting on the machine, plastic pay-out trays instead of metal ones, notices on the machine which clearly state the pay-out rate, the win probability and a statement indicating that the machine is, on the whole, chance determined, a monitoring device which lets gamblers have a running total of how much they have put into the machine (actual amount rather than turnover), equal numbers of winning symbols on each machine reel, all pay-outs to be in money rather than tokens, 'neutral' names for machines and less choice in initial gambling stakes. The preceding list is by no means complete and the steps are only suggested as possible mechanisms for decreasing the number of people who experience problems with gambling by correcting cognitive distortions, false beliefs and false expectations. As this chapter has pointed out, there is plenty of evidence to suggest that a gambler's ignorance about probability or situational cues may encourage gamblers to think they have some influence over mainly chance determined activities, although as Cornish (1978) has pointed out, it is difficult to use such information directly in regulation of these activities. It should also be noted that educating the public about gambling may have the reverse desired effect and increase awareness. It may be that regulation is best carried out not through changing the structural characteristics but through such practices as prohibition of advertising, decreasing the number of outlets available to gamble and geographically locating gambling establishments (e.g. amusement arcades, bookmakers) away from sites where more vulnerable members of the population are found (e.g. schools, colleges).

Further work is needed to find out which structural characteristics are more likely to affect 'addictiveness' potential in particular forms of gambling. For instance, it may be that light, colour and sound effects are integral to increasing baseline levels of gambling among fruit machine players but not in other gambling forms (e.g. lotteries, horse-racing, etc.). Finally, it must be noted that nearly all theories of why people gamble take little account of the needs and motivations of gamblers and their interaction with environmental stimuli (including structural characteristics), although as we have seen throughout this book, individual predispositions (physiological, psychological and sociological) cannot be excluded as determinants in the decision to gamble and gamble excessively.

9 The treatment of pathological gambling

This chapter focuses on the various techniques that have been used in the treatment of pathological gambling. There is little in the way of specific treatments for adolescent pathological gamblers and it is therefore assumed that the accounts presented below are equally applicable to adolescents unless stated. Even though the medical model of gambling has only recently been adopted through its introduction into the *DSM-III*, 'cures' for the 'gambling illness' have been described in the gambling literature for over sixty years. Treatments have included psychoanalytic therapy, behavioural therapy, group and self-help therapy, as well as a number of miscellaneous treatments such as 'paradoxical intention'. These will be briefly reviewed in turn.

PSYCHOANALYTIC TREATMENT

It was noted in Chapter 1 that psychoanalytic theory predominated in the gambling literature in the earlier part of the twentieth century. It is therefore not surprising to find that the first recorded 'cures' for pathological gambling involved a psychodynamic approach. In the psychoanalytic situation, gambling is essentially viewed by the therapist as a neurosis (Bergler, 1957). The basic aim underlying psychoanalytic treatment is to show that the person's conscious thoughts about gambling are a cover for more important goals and beliefs and to uncover and confront the real reasons for gambling behaviour. The therapist's aim is to give the gambler insight into their unconscious motivations to upset their neurotic ritualized patterns of behaviour. Since the treatment can take a year (or more) of weekly sessions with the therapist, it could be argued to be very cost-ineffective.

There are a number of reported psychoanalytic treatment 'successes' in the literature and nearly all of them involve single case studies of males (i.e. Simmel, 1920; Greenson, 1947; Eissler, 1950; Lindner, 1950; Matussek,

1953; Harkavy, 1954; Comess, 1960; Reider, 1960; Harris, 1964; Laufer, 1966). Only Harris reported using psychoanalysis to treat an 'addicted' adolescent gambler. Bergler (1957) provided the most detailed analysis of pathological gambling treatment in his book *The Psychology of Gambling*. He reported a 75 per cent success rate but on closer examination this figure may be an overestimation. Allcock (1986) noted that of the 200 patients referred to Bergler, only 80 were included in his study. Of these patients, thirty-five dropped out because they had been coerced into treatment by relatives and friends. His success rate of 75 per cent is therefore based on only 30 per cent of his total referrals, thus reducing the significance of his findings.

Evidence for the utility of psychoanalytic treatment of pathological gambling is at best sparse and inconclusive, with some authors (e.g. Barker and Miller, 1968a) asserting that psychodynamic approaches to the treatment of pathological gambling appear to be of limited use. As with the psychodynamic theories and accounts mentioned earlier in this volume, it could be argued that psychoanalytic treatments are perhaps best viewed as part of the historical context, rather than in offering present day applicability. However, more recent writings have stressed that psychoanalytic treatment in conjunction with other treatments can be of great utility (e.g. Rosenthal and Rugle, 1994).

PSYCHOTHERAPY

There has been little published on the explicit use of group psychotherapy in the treatment of pathological gamblers, but it is the treatment of choice of professionals working with large numbers of clients presenting with addictive behaviours (Taber and Chaplin, 1988). There are many different forms of psychotherapy, almost all of which could be typically called 'talking cures' of some description. Psychotherapy can be utilized both in groups and with individuals and usually consists of regular sessions with a psychotherapist over a period of time. In this sense it is very similar to psychoanalysis. However, unlike psychoanalysis which tends to have distinct theoretical underpinnings, psychotherapy is often very eclectic by trying to meet the needs of the individual and helping the gambler develop coping strategies. Psychotherapy is also non-directive, and unlike psychoanalysis it does not aim to uncover deep-seated psychological neuroses. Taber and Chaplin (1988) reported that discussions concentrate on such topics as narcissism, manipulative behaviour, guilt, irrational thinking and low ego strength.

Group psychotherapy is popular in the treatment of pathological gambling particularly in conjunction with other therapies and activities in multi-modal treatment packages. These may include compulsory attendance at Gamblers Anonymous sessions, relaxation training and social skills training to help cope in everyday anxiety-provoking situations, and educational films about gambling. It is rare that psychotherapy is used in complete isolation as a treatment for pathological gambling. Group psychotherapy involves a small group of gamblers who recount their personal experiences relating to gambling while others may comment and react to what is being said. The psychotherapist's role is to facilitate the therapy session rather than verbally dominate it. According to Adkins *et al.* (1985), the 'spoken autobiography' is an important component in the gambler's overall therapy. It is claimed that success in psychotherapy is because people are looking for hope and there is group cohesiveness, common in any group that meets to discuss a mutual problem (Lieberman and Borman, 1979).

Individually, there are many aspects of the gambler's life in which they need help. This is neatly summarised by the acronym GAMBLING (Gambling Alienation Marital problems Behaviour problems Legal problems Indebtedness Needs Goalessness) formulated by Dr Robert Custer. Individual counselling helps the gambler practically to sort out some or all of these areas.

In terms of evaluating the effectiveness of psychotherapeutic techniques there is great difficulty because it is usually used as an adjunct to other therapies. It is therefore hard to establish whether 'success' is due to the psychotherapy, some other treatment intervention (e.g. Gamblers Anonymous) or an interaction between therapies. There is also the added problem of defining what a 'successful' outcome is. Although abstinence from gambling might appear to be a clear objective in the treatment of pathological gambling, many would argue that improvement in the lifestyle of the gambler – regardless of whether they have stopped gambling or not – is just as valid as an obtainable objective (Franklin and Richardson, 1988). Most evaluations of treatment involving psychotherapy have been done in the in-patient treatment programmes offered in the USA.

Since the first of these opened in 1972 by Robert Custer and Alida Glen at the Brecksville Division of the Cleveland Veterans Administration Medical Center in Ohio (Glen, 1976), other in-patient programmes have been developed in other VA medical faculties in Miami (Florida), Brooklyn (New York), Loma Linda (California) and Lyons (New Jersey) as well as programmes established in Maryland and Pennsylvania (Nora, 1989). Such treatment programmes usually last for twenty to thirty days and consist of medical evaluations, classes on addiction, relaxation therapy, assertiveness training, group psychotherapy, marital therapy, GA meetings and physical

exercise (see Taber, 1979 for a more detailed account). Reports of Brecksville's effectiveness have been published (Russo *et al.*, 1984; Taber *el al.*,
1987; McCormick and Taber, 1991). For instance, in the first evaluation
during a one-year follow-up, 55 per cent claimed complete abstinence on a
survey questionnaire and 21.5 per cent reported some gambling but had
been abstinent for at least one month prior to the survey administration.
Similar results for multi-modal treatment packages have been reported by
Politzer *et al.* (1985), Blackman *et al.*, (1986; 1989), Franklin and
Richardson (1988) and Schwarz and Lindner (1992).

Conjoint marital therapy

There are a number of reports in the gambling literature which note significant marital distress among problem gamblers (e.g. Darvas, 1981; Custer
and Milt, 1985; Lorenz and Yaffee, 1986; 1988; 1989) and that marital
distress can exacerbate gambling problems (e.g. Lesieur, 1984; Wildman,
1989; Bellaire and Caspari, 1992). Further to this, some authors (e.g.
Steinberg, 1993) advocate early interventions within the couple system for
those gamblers undergoing treatment. However, given these assertions, it
should be noted that (i) there are only two explicit psychotherapeutic
studies that have been reported in the literature that involve 'marital
therapy', and (ii) this form of therapy will be of little or no benefit to the
typical adolescent who will not have formed the type of relationship on
which therapy such as this is based.

This therapy is termed 'marital therapy' since it involves both the
gambler *and* their partner in the therapeutic process. In these cases, marital
therapy has been used instead of group psychotherapy (Boyd and Bolen,
1970) or as a supplement (Tepperman, 1985) to it. Couples may be seen
alone with the therapist or may take part in group discussions with other
similar couples but the general aim is the same: to allow couples to begin
working through their problems in a situation where each partner can be
less defensive and to face the problems in the relationship together at the
same time (Walker, 1992a). Other authors (e.g. Maurer, 1985; Fitchett and
Sandford, 1986) have also asserted that spouse involvement is a positive
factor in maintaining the involvement of gamblers in their treatment
programmes.

Boyd and Bolen (1970) believed gambling by married individuals
resulted from marital disharmony. If this is the case then therapy for the
gambler without their partner is likely to prove ineffective. Their main aim
was to treat both man and wife together and focused on getting the wives to
stop scapegoating their gambling husbands and to cease playing their

'martyr' role (Lester, 1980). Using an exploratory and fairly unstructured approach, results from their nine couples treated showed three had ceased gambling, five were near cessation and one couple had dropped out. Tepperman (1977; 1985) similarly treated ten pathological gamblers and their wives for twelve weeks based on the more structured twelve-step-recovery programme of Gamblers Anonymous but found no significant differences between this group and normal GA members on a number of psychometric scales (e.g. Beck Depression Inventory, Mooney Problem Checklist).

It is difficult to assess the effectiveness of both these studies as there is little in the way of standardized measures used. Further to this, and as Walker (1992a) points out, in the study by Boyd and Bolen, being 'near to cessation' is difficult to interpret and in the Tepperman study no statistics are given concerning continuance at Gamblers Anonymous and no details are given concerning the time and rate of improvement.

SELF-HELP TREATMENTS

Gamblers Anonymous

Gamblers Anonymous (GA) is a voluntary organization and is the most well-known self-help organization for problem gamblers, with over a thousand groups word wide. It uses a group therapy technique that is modelled on Alcoholics Anonymous (AA) and uses only ex-gamblers as helpers (Scodel, 1964; Antia, 1979). GA involves acceptance of personal responsibility and treats pathological gambling as an addiction that cannot be cured but merely arrested. It is thus an ongoing process and means that relapse into a life of *compulsive* gambling (the term preferred by GA) is just one bet away for the rest of that individual's life. To some it becomes a way of life both spiritually and socially (Stewart and Brown, 1988) and compared with almost all other treatments it is especially cost-effective (even if other treatments have greater 'success' rates), as the organization makes no financial demands on members or the community. For the therapy to work, GA asserts that gamblers must attend sessions voluntarily and must really want to stop gambling. Further to this, they are only allowed to join once they have reached 'rock bottom' and answer 'yes' to seven or more out of twenty questions given in a questionnaire containing twenty questions (see Table 9.1).

GA groups usually meet once a week and each member of the group talks about his or her personal experiences. (These testimonies are in fact

Table 9.1 The twenty questions of Gamblers Anonymous

---

1 Do you lose time from your work because of gambling?

2 Is gambling making your home life unhappy?

3 Is gambling affecting your reputation?

4 Have you ever felt remorse after gambling?

5 Do you ever gamble to get money with which to pay debts or to otherwise solve financial difficulties?

6 Does gambling ever cause a decrease in your ambition or efficiency?

7 After losing, do you feel you must return as soon as possible to win back your losses?

8 After you win, do you have a strong urge to return to win money?

9 Do you often gamble until your last dollar is gone?

10 Do you ever borrow to finance your gambling?

11 Have you ever sold any real or personal property to finance your gambling?

12 Are you reluctant to use 'gambling money' for normal expenditures?

13 Does gambling ever make you careless of the welfare of your family?

14 Do you ever gamble longer than you planned?

15 Do you ever gamble to escape worry and trouble?

16 Have you ever committed or considered committing an illegal act to finance gambling?

17 Does gambling cause you to have sleeping difficulties?

18 Do arguments, disappointments or frustrations cause you to gamble?

19 Do you have an urge to celebrate any good fortune by a few hours of gambling?

20 Have you ever considered self-destruction as a result of your gambling?

Source: From Custer and Milt, 1985

called *therapies*.) Meetings focus on the twelve steps to recovery which are based on those used by Alcoholics Anonymous (see Table 9.2). GA's therapeutic aims are to instil hope, openness and self-disclosure, develop social networks, focus on abstinence and loss of control, to rely on others for help and to develop spiritually. However, it should be noted that the spiritual development and references to a 'higher power' may detract some people from continuing with GA (Moody, 1989; and see, for example, steps 2 and 7 in Table 9.2). A recent study by Ciarrocchi and Reinert (1993) might help in this respect. They found that by using the Family Environment Scale (FES), GA members had a higher moral-religious emphasis (a dimension on the FES) than controls. Since it has good face

Table 9.2 The twelve steps of Gamblers Anonymous

1 We admitted we were powerless over gambling – that our lives had become unmanageable.
2 We came to believe that a power greater than ourselves could restore us to a normal way of thinking and living.
3 We made a decision to turn our will and our lives over to the care of this power of our own understanding.
4 We made a searching and fearless moral and financial inventory of ourselves.
5 We admitted to ourselves and another human being the exact nature of our wrongs.
6 We were entirely ready to have these defects of character removed.
7 We humbly asked God (of our understanding), to remove our shortcomings.
8 We made a list of all the people we had harmed, and became willing to make amends to them all.
9 We made direct amends to such people wherever possible, except when to do so would injure them or others.
10 We continued to take personal inventory and when we were wrong promptly admitted it.
11 We sought through prayer and meditation to improve our conscious contact with God as we understand him, praying only for knowledge of His will for us and the power to carry that out.
12 Having made an effort to practice these principles in all our affairs, we tried to carry this message to other compulsive gamblers.

validity, this FES subscale (or its content) might prove a useful marker for those who may or may not benefit from GA membership.

Outside of the meetings, members are free to call on each other whenever they get the gambling urge, and they adhere to the motto 'One day at a time'. GA claims to help fill the void left by not gambling by focusing attention on the demands of the next meeting and social rewards (i.e. praise from other members) for non-participation in gambling. GA's other major aim is to direct the gambler's energies towards work and leisure activities. For every year that members go without gambling they are awarded a pin which other members consider to be important milestones.

To date, there has been little systematic study of GA, but some researchers have offered qualitative observations (Scodel, 1964; Livingston, 1974; Cromer, 1978; Preston and Smith, 1985; Turner and Saunders, 1990). GA claims to be very successful but this is based on those gamblers who continue to come to the meetings. In GA's terms, those who drop out and resume gambling have not completed their treatment and as such are not included in their own informal accounts of treatment 'success'. This is clearly inadequate in rating GA's success, as it produces a figure close to 100 per cent effectiveness. Evaluation of effectiveness must include both 'continuers' and 'drop-outs' but there are a number of problems preventing this. Walker (1992a, pp.193–4) has noted the three major problems: anonymity, sample bias and criterion for success. These are outlined below.

Anonymity

No case records are kept, no attempt is made at objective evaluation, and the only evidence is the subjectively based self-report of the member. These self-reports are themselves not available to an outsider on the regular basis necessary for evaluation. (This, at least in the UK, is beginning to change, as GA is now starting to compile attendance records and to carry out some of its own evaluative research.)

Sample bias

GA accepts only those who come voluntarily and who meet the twenty questions criterion. Membership is continually changing and some members attend multiple meetings. These factors rule out the possibility of comparison with a control group.

Criterion for success

In GA this is complete abstention. Among those who drop out and among those who 'fall' there is no measure of the success that GA has achieved. It is quite possible that many of those who attended GA for a small number of meetings gained the strength to resist the urge to gamble compulsively without needing to attend further meetings. (This last point made by Walker is echoed by the case study of David outlined in Chapter 7 (see page 189). One GA meeting was enough for David to begin to sort out his problems and to eventually stop gambling.)

Despite these problems there have been two studies which have attempted to examine GA's effectiveness. Stewart and Brown (1988) reported that 50 per cent of members drop out in the first three weeks and that only 30 per cent are left after ten meetings. After one year, total abstinence from gambling occurred in only 8 per cent of members. Reasons for drop-out were inconclusive, but married men were more likely to continue than unmarried men. In a more in-depth study (again) by Brown

(1986b; 1987a; 1987b; 1987c) which examined differences between GA continuers and drop-outs, it was found that drop-outs reported significantly more 'strongly positive' reactions (e.g. 'I thought I was cured'), and changes in circumstances that prevented attendance (e.g. job prevented gambler getting to meetings). In addition, Brown reported that more drop-outs thought GA members were unsympathetic and punishing, that the GA handbook was poor, that there was too much time taken in administration and that the complete ban on gambling was too harsh. In conclusion, Brown suggested that GA may be better for excessive gamblers who had many problems (because it is inadequate for those still developing problems) and for those who had few or no relapses (because GA is better at avoiding relapses in the first place rather than dealing with them when they occur). Although this study provided valuable information about GA drop-out, it must also be said that all the data were collected using a comparison of only twelve 'continuers' versus twelve 'drop-outs' and that great caution must be taken in trying to generalize the results.

With regard to adolescents, Moody advises that that the parent should introduce the adolescent to GA with the minimum of fuss. However, anecdotal evidence suggests that the atmosphere of GA meetings can be very oppressive to a young fruit machine gambler surrounded by what are typically horse-race betters (Griffiths, 1990c).

Minimal interventions

Minimal interventions are a fairly recent treatment innovation and refer to those treatments which require a smaller amount of professional time and/or resources than are typical of the traditional face-to-face interaction between therapist and individual clients or groups (Heather, 1986; Dickerson *et al.*, 1990) As Dickerson *et al.* point out, such a definition includes a whole range of brief interventions including written self-help materials (with or without therapist contact). Heather (1986) further outlines five factors that have contributed to their growth:

1 The ever increasing cost of health services.
2 The emergence of the ideology of self-help.
3 An ethos and theoretical base in psychology supportive to such an ideology.
4 The erosion of illness models in areas of personal problems (e.g. alcoholism).
5 Evidence that some traditional treatments are ineffective.

Minimal interventions have been applied to other areas of addictive behaviour, particularly alcohol addiction (e.g. Miller *et al.*, 1981) and benzodiazepine addiction (Cormack and Sinnott, 1983; Cormack *et al.*, 1989) with success. More recently, a self-help manual for gamblers has been developed by Allcock and Dickerson (1986) which allows the gambler to choose whether abstinence or control is the preferred goal and gives advice accordingly.

There has been only one evaluation of a gambling self-help manual by Dickerson and his colleagues (Dickerson *et al.*, 1990). They evaluated the use of a self-help manual on twenty-nine problem gamblers with a six-month follow-up. The gamblers were divided into two groups, one of which received the manual and a set of questionnaires by post (sixteen gamblers) and one which received a manual and a structured interview (thirteen gamblers). Results showed that for both groups the expenditure and number of gambling sessions a week were reduced although there was no significant difference between the actual groups. Since there was no control group it is hard to know whether the amount of gambling would have reduced, as it could have been the case that the gamblers were thinking of trying to reduce their gambling anyway. Dickerson *et al.* (1990) concluded that the minimal intervention approach to problem gambling may be acceptable to some clients and may be associated with short-term reductions in gambling involvement. They also added that some form of self-help manual may well have a useful part to play in the provision of services for gamblers who seek help. As with self-help treatments like GA, self-help manuals – even if they are only partially successful – are still very cost-effective.

BEHAVIOURAL TREATMENTS

Compared with other accounts of treatments, the behavioural literature on pathological gambling 'cures' is fairly extensive. Treatment is based on the view that gambling is a learned maladaptive behaviour and can therefore be 'unlearned'. A wide range of behavioural techniques have been applied on this basis in the treatment of the problem gambler. These have mainly been based on the classical conditioning paradigm and include aversion therapy, *in vivo* desensitization, imaginal desensitization, systematic desensitization, relaxation therapy, covert sensitization, satiation therapy and behavioural counselling. Although it must be noted that none of these have been specifically used in the treatment of adolescent gambling, there is no reason to presume that such treatments would be any less successful than with adults. These treatments were recently reviewed by Walker (1992a) and are outlined in Table 9.3 and described in more detail below.

Table 9.3 Types of behavioural therapy

Aversion therapy:	Involves the pairing of an aversive stimulus (electric shock or emetic) with a specific gambling response or may be randomly interspersed throughout the gambling session.
In vivo *desensitization:*	Involves pairing cues for gambling with no gambling behaviour and feelings of boredom. Typically the gambler is taken to the gambling location and stands by without gambling for extended periods of time. The therapist suggests the whole situation is uninteresting.
Imaginal desensitization:	Differs from IVD by having the gambler imagine the cues for gambling and then pairing these imagined cues with a competing response such as feelings of boredom.
Systematic desensitization:	Refers to a gradient of increasingly powerful cues for gambling. At each step any arousal that the gambler is experiencing is extinguished by imagined scenes of tranquillity or direct muscular relaxation.
Relaxation therapy:	Consists of training in relaxation techniques which can be used when the urge to gamble arises.
Satiation therapy:	Involves presenting the gambler with no other stimuli and no other activities but those associated with gambling.

Source: Adapted from Walker (1992a)

Aversion therapy

The first major form of behaviour therapy to be reported for pathological gambling was electrical aversion therapy. In reviewing the aversion therapy literature, Lester (1980) noted that this form of therapy depends on the type of gambling activity. Electric shocks can be administered when gambling on one-armed bandits (Barker and Miller, 1968a; b), when reading the newspapers' betting pages (Goorney, 1968; Seager, 1970), while watching film of oneself gambling in a betting shop (Barker and Miller, 1968a; b), watching slides depicting roulette wheels, poker hands or betting shops (Seager, 1970), while actually gambling, e.g. when making bets by telephone (Goorney, 1968) and when making bets in a casino itself (Cotler, 1971). Other aversive stimuli used in case studies have included (i) the administration of apomorphine while gambling, thus producing unpleasant side effects, i.e. chemical aversion (Salzmann, 1982), and (ii) the playing of loud recorded female screams and aversive comments from the gambler's wife during race commentary (Fitchett and Sandford, 1976). Both of these latter case studies reported cessation of their client's gambling after treatment and at follow-up.

The timing of the aversive stimulus could be critical in treatment success. Theoretically, aversive responses should be paired to precede or coincide with the pleasurable arousal of gambling and should preferably be done in the gambling environment itself, otherwise 'the shocks will miss their mark' (Walker, 1992a, p.212). Many case studies have not taken these two factors into account. For instance, in many of the studies involving slot-machine players, the aversive stimulus was delivered randomly throughout the session (Barker and Miller, 1966; 1968a; b; Koller, 1972; Salzmann, 1982). With regards to the context, only two studies administered the aversive stimulus in the gambling environment (Cotler, 1971; Salzmann, 1982) as most studies were carried out in hospital rooms (Barker and Miller, 1966; 1968a; b; Seager, 1970; Koller, 1972; Fitchett and Sandford, 1976; McConaghy *et al.*, 1983).

In all the studies reported above, all shocks were administered by the therapists, except Cotler (1971) who let the patient administer the shocks to himself. One advantage that aversion therapy has over other forms of treatment is that it requires very few sessions before treatment is complete. These completion times have ranged from five hours (Koller, 1972) to twelve hours (Barker and Miller, 1968a; b). Success rates have been varied. Most of the single case studies reported success (e.g. Barker and Miller, 1966; Seager, 1970; Goorney, 1968) but there was little systematic follow-up. The most extensive study was by Seager (1970), who used electrical aversion on thirteen patients. Of these, only five people remained free of gambling.

It would seem that aversion therapy can curtail gambling behaviour in less time than other treatment techniques but to achieve a long-term improvement the patients must learn how to satisfy their needs in more adaptive ways (Lester, 1980). One could argue that if problem gambling is caused by some underlying psychological problem rather than a learned maladaptive behaviour, then aversion therapy would at best only eliminate the behaviour but not the problem. This therefore means that the gambling behaviour may well have been curtailed but as the problem is still there the person may well engage in other addictive behaviours (e.g. alcohol and/or drug abuse). It is also hard to evaluate treatment effectiveness in some studies because aversion therapy was used with other treatments. For instance, Seager (1970) gave supportive individual psychotherapy and also suggested joining Gamblers Anonymous. Cotler (1971) similarly used

individual psychotherapy in addition to reinforcement of alternative behaviours (e.g. visiting wife) as a positive reinforcer, self-recording of
gambling behaviour, covert sensitization, etc.

There are also other considerations. The first of these concerns the type
of therapy itself and the effect not only on those receiving the treatment but
other people's perceptions of it. Most laypeople would probably consider
the administration of electric shocks or emetics to be a cruel or barbaric
treatment regime even if the theoretical reasons for it were outlined to them.
Second, the psychologists must ask themselves whether this image of
'electric shock treatment' is the right kind of image we should be giving
members of the public. This second point has most probably been addressed and may in fact be one of the reasons that aversion therapies are
now seldom used in the treatment of problem gambling.

Desensitization therapies

Although desensitization therapies are popular in the treatment of many
behavioural disorders they have been used very infrequently in the treatment of pathological gambling. The use of imaginal desensitization has
been described by McConaghy *et al.* (1983), and by Blaszczynski (1988) in
his doctoral dissertation. McConaghy (1980) believes that everyone builds
up neuronal models for repetitive behaviour. If the behavioural sequence is
interrupted, then some form of unpleasant tension is experienced.
McConaghy believes this can only be dissipated by the completion of the
initiated sequence, i.e. a behavioural completion mechanism (BCM).
Gambling can thus be viewed as a repetitive behaviour maintained by a
BCM in which environmental cues (e.g. walking past a casino or amusement arcade) trigger the gambling urge. Imaginal desensitization therefore
tries to eliminate the BCM.

McConaghy *et al.* (1983) reported a controlled study in which patients
were assigned to a condition in which they learned to relax while reading
descriptions of scenes which prompted gambling responses (imaginal desensitization), while other patients were given unavoidable electric shocks
(aversion relief) which immediately followed the reading of similar gambling scenes and activities. An example of one such scenario is described
below which should increase the gambler's level of arousal if
McConaghy's assertions are correct. Immediately after the reading of the
scenario a relaxation procedure must be initiated:

> You are going home from work and you know your wife is away. You
> decide to go to the club and put a few dollars in the poker machines. You

enter the club and find a free machine, You are about to put a coin in but feel bored. You leave without gambling.

(McConaghy *et al.*, 1983, p.368)

Occasional relief scenes (i.e. activities incompatible with gambling) randomly occurred with no ensuing electric shock. After each group (of ten subjects) had received fourteen sessions, the State Trait Anxiety Inventory was administered in addition to a 'self-report of gambling incidences'. Significant differences were found in state anxiety with the imaginal desensitization group showing significant decreases (at one-month and one-year follow-ups) as well as decreases in urges to gamble. McConaghy *et al.* (1983) concluded that results support the theory that gambling behaviour is maintained by aversive tension. A further series of studies outlined by Blaszczynski (1988), in which he compared imaginal desensitization with a number of alternative behavioural therapies (*in vivo* exposure, relaxation therapy and aversion therapy) it was found at follow-up that 43 per cent of gamblers receiving imaginal desensitization had improved compared with 30 per cent for *in vivo* exposure, 30 per cent for relaxation therapy and 10 per cent for aversion therapy. However, it must be noted that of the 120 original subjects only sixty-three could be traced and thus the results should be treated with caution.

As with the use of imaginal desensitization, *in vivo* desensitization has been used sparingly in the treatment of pathological gamblers with only a few studies in the literature (i.e. Greenberg and Rankin, 1982; Blaszczynski, 1988). The basic idea is for the gambler to be immersed in the gambling setting (e.g. a betting shop) but to be prevented from gambling. Theoretically, from a conditioning perspective, the intervention is an extinction trial. However, the results have not been encouraging.

In the study by Greenberg and Rankin (1982) involving twenty-six patients, *in vivo* sensitization, covert sensitization and direct punishment with mildly aversive stimuli (rubber band snapping) were combined in an effort to teach the self-control of gambling urges. Instructions were often given in an attempt to prevent urges to gamble, for instance, using routes on which there were no betting shops, and in some cases the therapist actually accompanied the patient into the gambling situation itself. The outcome over a two-year follow-up showed that only five patients (i.e. 20 per cent) had gambling well under their control, seven had intermittent excessive gambling bouts and that most (fourteen patients) still gambled excessively. A similar outcome was reported by Blaszczynski (1988) in his twenty subjects who underwent *in vivo* desensitization. It was reported that at follow-up, two gamblers (10 per cent) were abstinent and that four gamblers (20 per cent) had improved. Walker (1992a) points out that even if the theoretical basis for the treatment is valid, the poor treatment results could be due to the short period of time in which the extinction trials are held, i.e. it could be that an over-learned behaviour like gambling would take months or years of trials before it was extinguished.

There has been only one reference to the treatment of problem gambling by systematic desensitization. Kraft (1970) reported that one of the forty patients he treated by this method was a compulsive gambler. His other patients included those with phobias, sexual disorders, alcohol problems, drug problems, stuttering problems and war neuroses. All were treated in exactly the same way using Wolpe's (1958) method of systematic desensitization. Unfortunately, the gambler was one of the five unsuccessful clients (along with the four heroin addicts) who showed no change in their behaviour following treatment. Since this involved only one gambler it is hard to evaluate whether such a treatment method has future utility.

Satiation therapy

The basic idea of satiation therapy is to eliminate the urge to gamble itself rather than the associational gambling specific cues (e.g. a casino) by allowing gamblers to engage in nothing but gambling until they become satiated. As Walker (1992a) has pointed out, satiation therapy is therefore a kind of 'reverse psychology'. If gambling is a learned drive to gamble, then theoretically it should be possible to extinguish the drive through satiation. There is only one isolated case of satiation therapy being used with gamblers. This is the treatment of five horse-racing betters by Peck and Ashcroft (1972). In this therapeutic setting, conditions are such that staff talk of nothing else but horse-racing, all reading material is about horse-racing and the gambler cannot do anything except think about, talk about and bet on races. Peck and Ashcroft claimed that for four of their five patients, gambling ceased to be a problem. However, the study reported does not provide any descriptions, measures or evaluations and as such little weight can be attached to the finding until further information or confirmation is provided.

Behavioural counselling and controlled gambling

In an unpublished paper by Montgomery and Kreitzer (1968) – referred to by both Dickerson (1984) and Walker (1992a) in their respective books on gambling – the authors specified the foci of behavioural therapies which aim to enable gamblers to exercise self-control over their behaviour. They report that therapies should aim at achieving change in three areas of the gambler's behaviour:

1 The gambler choosing not to gamble when the opportunity occurs.
2 Choosing to stop when losing.
3 Involvement with non-gambling activities.

(Dickerson, 1984, p.112; Walker, 1992a, p. 220)

Walker (1992a) goes on to say that while behavioural counselling involving change of this kind is probably common, there is little in the way of rigorous evaluation. Behavioural counselling usually involves the use of a contract not to gamble or not to gamble more than a certain amount, with rewards if the contract is kept (Walker, 1992a). The therapist attempts to arrange environmental contingencies so that the gambler's opportunity for coming into contact with both gambling venues and gambling friends or acquaintances are reduced. In addition, they want gamblers who find themselves in gambling venues to gamble less than they would normally do so. Behavioural counselling has been seldom used in published accounts of gambling treatments although two studies have used it in an attempt to control gambling rather than to eliminate it. This does not mean that a contract indicating gambling abstinence cannot be arranged between the therapist and the gambler, it just happens that the two published accounts in the gambling literature both focused on the issue of control rather than abstinence.

Dickerson and Weeks (1979) successfully controlled the gambling of a 40-year-old male by allowing the spouse to control finances and giving reinforcement both for incompatible behaviours and self-controlled bets through an intermediary. No gambling occurred during a one-year follow-up. Rankin (1982) employed a similar approach in which the goal of the treatment was controlled gambling rather than total abstinence. In treating a 44-year-old male gambler, he prohibited the reinvestment of his winnings and during a two-year follow-up period his patient deviated from this behaviour only three times. Although both of these cases were on the whole successful in their aims (i.e. to reduce and control gambling rather than eliminate it) it should be remembered that when generalizing from just two individuals, extreme caution is necessary.

These two case studies also raise fundamental questions about the nature and goals of gambling treatment. Controlled gambling (like controlled drinking for alcoholics) is a controversial treatment goal as most treatment agencies (particularly Gamblers Anonymous) stress abstinence as the only cure. However, a recent follow-up study by Blaszczynski *et al.* (1991) suggests that some ex-pathological gamblers can become controlled gamblers.

In their study, 120 pathological gamblers, who from between two and nine years earlier had completed a one-week behavioural treatment programme in a psychiatric unit, were re-contacted. Of the 120, sixty-three were located of whom eighteen were abstinent, twenty-five controlled and twenty un-controlled. The controlled and abstinent gamblers consequently displayed normal scores on scales of neuroticism, psychoticism, state and trait anxiety and depression. Prior to treatment, controlled gamblers showed a trend towards lower levels of assessed psychopathology which reduced follow-ing treatment. Blaszczynski *et al.* hypothesized that before treatment the post-treatment controlled gamblers were more psychologically adjusted and implied that controlled gambling may only be an option for relatively well-adjusted individuals.

COGNITIVE TREATMENTS

A more recent development in the treatment of addictive behaviours is the use of cognitive-behavioural therapies (e.g. Marlatt and Gordon, 1985; Harris, 1989). Despite the strong dominance of the cognitive approach within the field of psychology and psychological therapy, there have been very few applications to the treatment of gambling directly. This is very surprising considering that there is now a growing literature to suggest that gambling to some extent may be maintained by irrational thinking (e.g. Walker, 1992b; Griffiths, 1994c). In a review of the pathological gambling treatment literature, Walker (1992a) outlined two possible cognitively based treatment strategies – thought stopping and cognitive restructuring. There are also a number of other cognitively based therapeutic interventions (e.g. rational emotive therapy, cognitive behaviour therapy, motivational interviewing, relapse prevention) that have been used in the treatment of other addictive behaviours, in addition to one of my own (audio playback therapy) which may be of potential utility in the treatment of gambling. These will be briefly examined in turn.

Thought stopping

In describing the technique of thought stopping, Walker outlines what appears to be the only study by Maurer (1985). Walker explains:

> Typically, the patient monitors his or her impulses to gamble and when thoughts concerning the possibility of gambling are detected, one or more of a variety of thought-stopping or thought-replacement tech-niques is instigated. For example, a common thought-stopping routine

involves the use of a rubber band on the wrist. When the impulse to gamble is detected, the gambler snaps the rubber band and says aloud, 'stop'. The thought about gambling is then replaced by a previously rehearsed alternative. Thus the gambler might replace 'I'll go down to the club and make some money on the slots' by 'I'll go down to the library and borrow a really good thriller'. Similarly, the thought 'I'm so angry at my wife that I'm going to gamble for a few hours' might be replaced by 'I certainly am angry at my wife and after I have cooled down I will talk to her about my concerns'.

(Walker, 1992a, p.223)

Since Maurer (1985) also suggests this should be combined with a range of other interventions and therapies (i.e. attendance at Gamblers Anonymous, marital therapy, stress management techniques, relaxation training and self-hypnosis), it is hard to conclude that success would be due to the thought stopping alone. However, Maurer's approach does at least acknowledge that cognitive factors need to be addressed in therapy.

Cognitive restructuring

Walker (1992a) suggests that one way forward in the treatment of pathological gambling is the use of cognitive restructuring, although he acknowledges there are no reported case studies in the literature. It must therefore be noted that this approach is based on a theoretical, as opposed to an empirical, basis. Walker outlines what he considers to be the four most important steps in the successful treatment of gamblers:

1 The gambler must stop gambling (although it may be resumed at a later date).
2 Alternative activities to gambling are initiated or resumed.
3 A plan for repayment of debts must be initiated.
4 The motivation to gamble must be moderated or eliminated.

It is Step 4 that Walker sees as crucial in the cognitive restructuring approach. Cognitive restructuring attempts to change mistaken beliefs held by gamblers about their involvement in gambling rather than (say) eliminating personality or character defects, improving the relationship between the gambler and their partner, deconditioning the excitement associated with gambling or simply bolstering the gambler's resolve to stop gambling. Walker advocates that to achieve Step 4, a detailed account of the strategies, procedures and rituals used by the gambler in the gambling situation must be obtained. It is also assumed that the gambler is motivated by the belief that they will win in the long run. The therapist will then need to draw up a list of the most salient irrationalities of the gambler's situation and use them to adapt and change the gambler's belief system. Since this approach is hypothetical, Walker suggests some salient factors in the playing of slot-machines that may prove important in cognitive restructuring:

- a favourite place related to potential to win;
- a favourite machine or type of machine;
- rituals associated with playing the machine;
- prevent others from playing this machine until the gambler has finished with it;
- special methods of play (e.g. press quickly for a fast spin, etc.);
- ability to predict when a big pay-out will occur.

Such a treatment method does appear to have both intuitive and theoretical support. However, there is research to suggest that addicted fruit machine players do not gamble to win but gamble to stay on the machine as long as possible (see Chapter 3). This does not necessarily invalidate Walker's technique but does mean that the therapist has to concentrate on different false beliefs.

Audio playback therapy

One possible treatment technique for problem gamblers utilizing a cognitive approach that I have advocated may be potentially useful was briefly mentioned in Chapter 5 and termed audio playback therapy. In that study, I analysed the cognitive biases involved in fruit machine playing using the 'thinking aloud method' (Ericcson and Simon, 1980; 1984). As you will recall, this basically consisted of gamblers verbalizing every thought that passed through their minds while they were playing the fruit machines. These verbalizations were tape recorded and results showed that regular gamblers produced significantly more irrational verbalizations than non-regular gamblers, i.e. regular gamblers personified the machine (talking to it, swearing at it and giving it human characteristics), explained away losses by blaming external factors and claimed wins were produced by their own skill. Below is an edited example with my comments in italics:

> 'This "fruity" (*the fruit machine*) is not in a good mood . . . . Oh my, come on, PLEASE give me an "orange" (*talking to the machine*) . . . . Well done! (*congratulating the machine for giving him an "orange"*) . . . . Did you see that? The machine snatched the win – bastard machine . . . it's really laughing at me here (*the machine, that is*) . . . . Can I win

more than 10p this time? . . . . NO!! . . . Obviously the machine is being a bit of a bastard at the moment!'

After each subject was run, they were asked if they would like to hear the playback of their recording. Only four gamblers (out of thirty) wished to do so. To my surprise they all commented on how they could not believe what they had said and how they were thinking while gambling. None of these individuals was followed up formally. However, I recently met one of them by accident while out socially. This particular subject was a 19 year old male at the time of the initial study and was diagnosed as a pathological gambler according to the *DSM-III-R* criteria for pathological gambling (American Psychiatric Association, 1987). He had already attended Gamblers Anonymous before participating in my experiment but dropped out shortly after joining because he felt he did not fit into the group. In the conversation that followed with my ex-subject, it transpired that since taking part in my study his gambling behaviour had declined and subsequently ceased. He claimed that a large factor in the cessation of his gambling was hearing the playback of his recording. He claimed he could still remember some of the things he heard on the tape but reiterated his disbelief at what he had verbalized. He further claimed it was this disbelief that prompted him to examine and monitor his behaviour more closely. Through this self-introspective process he claimed he realized the futility of his gambling and eventually stopped playing; although I have no direct confirmation that he was telling the truth, I have no reason to believe he was lying.

I have previously argued both elsewhere (Griffiths, 1989; 1994c) and in Chapter 5 that knowledge of an irrational gambling bias may help in rehabilitating gamblers through behaviour modification. The method used in this research study (i.e the thinking aloud method) might be the best way to inhibit irrational gambling bias by using the audio playback as a treatment tool. However, this is not to say that other modes of treatment could not be used concurrently. It should also be remembered that although this technique involved fruit machine gamblers, there is no reason why this should not be extended to other forms of gambling addiction especially when the possible therapeutic implications are considered.

Rational emotive therapy

There has been one recorded case in the literature involving the use of rational emotive therapy (RET) based on the work of Ellis (1962). In this study, Bannister (1977) reported the treatment of a 46 year old male problem gambler using a combination of RET and covert sensitization. Over nine one-hour sessions, the main objective was to use RET to shift the gambler's perceived locus of control from external orientation over which he had little or no control to an internal orientation of control and responsibility. The second objective was to develop strong associations between negative consequences of gambling and gambling in general.

RET, like some other cognitive approaches, essentially focuses on irrational self-talk. For instance, Bannister described a gambling experience, i.e. the betting of US$200 on one team to beat another in a sporting final, and then examined what the gambler had to say about his actions:

Irrational self-talk: '(1) Although I knew I didn't have the money to spare, something came over me; (2) Besides, gambling is a disease with me.'

Rational challenges to the self-talk: '(1) Something didn't come over me. When I say that, I'm avoiding saying "I chose to gamble" and, therefore, I don't feel responsible for my actions. (2) Saying "gambling is a disease" makes me feel out of control. Diseases (urges, impulses) usually come without warning. If I view my gambling as an illness coming without warning in the past, what's to keep it from coming without warning in the future. Although it didn't seem like it at the time, I chose to gamble each time. I stand a better chance of not gambling in the future if I clearly see that I have a choice and am totally responsible for my choice.'

(from Bannister, 1977, p.225)

RET was then combined with covert sensitization which involved a highly individualized (and carefully rehearsed) imaginary scene. This scene involved four men plunging the gambler head first into rotting human waste. Vivid descriptions of the taste, olfactory and tactile sensations mixed with vomiting and fear of suffocation preceded the thought 'I'll never gamble again', whereupon the gambler escapes in the imaginary scene. Bannister reported that the gambler ceased gambling and continued to do so at two-year follow-ups. The gambler reported during follow-up that whenever he thought of gambling he automatically thought of the aversive scene which reminded him of the negative consequences of gambling listed in RET. Although it is difficult to establish in a case such as this case whether the RET, the covert sensitization or an interaction of the two was the most salient factor in the treatment success, it does suggest that such approaches should not be ignored in the treatment of problem gambling.

Cognitive behaviour therapy

A recent case study by Toneatto and Sobell (1990) reported the first published study using Cognitive Behaviour Therapy (CBT) in the treatment of a 47 year old male pathological gambler. The authors believed that gamblers may have distorted perceptions about their gambling and be biased processors of information. Based on the generic model of CBT outlined by Beck and Emery (1986), the treatment consisted of identifying major (false / erroneous) beliefs concerning several elements of gambling and submitting them to critical evaluation by examining antecedent and consequent cognitions during the gambling process. Three major themes became the focus of cognitive behavioural intervention.

1   The belief that the gambler could discover a foolproof betting system.
2   The belief that gambling losses could be balanced by future winnings.
3   The belief that the financial losses as a result of gambling were minor.

Toneatto and Sobell saw their patient for ten weekly sessions. At first consultation the patient was gambling ten times a month on average, and had been doing so for the past three years. It was reported that betting decreased and eventually stopped during a six-month follow-up and that in that time their patient had only gambled three times. Perhaps more importantly, the gambler reported that even though he had the resources to gamble he had no desire to so.

Motivational interviewing

The therapeutic approach of motivational interviewing (MI) has gained many adherents since its inception in the early 1980s. MI borrows strategies from cognitive therapy, client-centred counselling, systems theory and the social psychology of persuasion and contains elements of both directive and non-directive therapeutic approaches. Since the gambler is often coerced into therapy by a third party (Bolen and Boyd, 1968), the first task of a therapist is to motivate the client to change something about themselves. Miller and Rollnick (1991) are the main proponents of such an approach and advocate that MI is primarily about the motivational aspects of changing people's behaviour in the therapeutic setting, an area which Miller and Rollnick feel is most salient to those people who engage in addictive behaviours (e.g. alcohol and other drug use, gambling, eating disorders, etc.). The underlying theme of such a therapeutic approach is the issue of ambivalence, and how the therapist can use MI to resolve it and allow the client to build commitment and reach a decision to change.

Miller and Rollnick argue that motivation is not a personality problem and that there is little evidence for an 'addictive personality'. Such assertions are integral to MI's theoretical basis. The focus for MI highlights Prochaska and DiClemente's (1982) well-known six-stage 'wheel of change' which seeks to explain how people change either with or without a therapist. These stages consist of pre-contemplation, contemplation, determination, action, maintenance and relapse. The method employed in MI consists of using a mnemonically structured (A–H) list of eight effective motivational strategies (giving Advice, removing Barriers, providing Choice, decreasing Desirability, practising Empathy, providing Feedback, clarifying Goals and active Helping). This is intertwined with the five general principles of MI (expressing empathy, developing discrepancy, avoiding argumentation, rolling with resistance and supporting self-efficacy).

Such a cognitive client-centred approach does seem to hold clear possibilities in the rehabilitation of pathological gamblers but as yet there are no reported studies of utilization in this field.

Relapse prevention

A study by Cummings *et al.* (1980) suggested that many gamblers, like substance addicts, relapse into gambling following negative emotional states that they feel unable to avoid by other means. As a consequence of this, Harris (1989) outlined a treatment approach to pathological gambling based on the cognitive-behavioural addiction model and Marlatt *et al.*'s work on relapse prevention.

In Marlatt's terms, the gambler is an individual with low self-esteem, poor impulse control and limited stress coping skills (and thus uses gambling to counteract this). If therapeutic treatment focuses only on the gambling behaviour, the gambling itself may not be the problem. There are three stages involved in the cognitive-behavioural treatment of pathological gamblers. The first stage involves a thorough assessment of the gambler's cognitive and affective states. At this stage, the therapist must:

1 Establish the gambler's perceptions of gambling and their reasons for gambling.
2 Determine the accompanying maladaptive cognitions.
3 Locate the gambler's strengths of personality that might help in learning to better adapt to life situations.

In the second stage the therapist must address the gambler's lifelong problem in coping skills. The goal is to help stabilize mood and to develop and begin to practise new coping techniques (self-monitoring, thought stopping, relaxation training, stress inoculation techniques, etc.). The final stage directly assesses the cessation of gambling behaviours. The gambler should now be ready to learn about factors leading to relapse. A plan is drawn up between gambler and therapist (i.e. control or abstinence). The plan involves the identification of cognitive antecedents leading up to high risk relapse situations and the results of failing to cope with these situations. Although there are as yet no studies (at least in the reported literature) utilizing such an approach, it would appear that relapse prevention is perhaps one treatment method which needs to be further explored.

In summary, it would appear that relapse prevention, like other cognitive based treatments, is of promising potential and *may* be as effective as many of the alternative approaches. However, more research is needed to confirm such a speculative suggestion.

HYPNOTHERAPY

There is one case study by Griffiths (1982) – no relation! – which involves the treatment of pathological gambling by hypnosis. In this particular method, feelings of excitement (which is assumed to be maintaining the gambling) can be reduced or eliminated by hypnotic suggestion. The hypnosis aims not only to decondition the excitement associated with gambling but also to promote excitement associated with other activities. Griffiths used a standard hypnotic technique based on eye fixation with a progressive relaxation and deepening procedure on a 36 year old male who was described as having had a lifelong gambling problem. At the time of the treatment, the gambler was heavily in debt (pursued by creditors) and was being threatened with divorce from his wife. After only two sessions with Griffiths it was reported that no recurrence of the gambling had occurred. Although this is only a case study it does deserve further investigation as it is the kind of treatment method which would be extremely cost-effective if it were to work with other gamblers. There is, however, one limitation in that hypnotic susceptibility is 'normally distributed' throughout the population and as such this probably means that only those at the extreme end of the normal distribution curve would benefit. Griffiths did report that his patient was a good subject for hypnosis.

PARADOXICAL INTENTION

A case of treatment by 'paradoxical intention' on a 36 year old male pathological gambler was described by Victor and Krug (1967). They instructed their patient to gamble regularly during a period following seven months of group psychotherapy. The patient was also told 'how to gamble', i.e. making maximum bets, etc. The technique of 'paradoxical intention' (Frankl, 1962) makes the patient in question feel controlled by the therapist. At one level of explanatory analysis, being instructed to gamble may be assumed to diminish the anticipatory excitement (Walker, 1992a). At another level, if the patient rebels against the therapist, the patient loses the symptom (i.e. it is another technique which employs 'reverse psychology'). If the patient obeys, the patient loses the secondary pay-off of being 'bad' and punished. Victor and Krug reported that after 'several months' of follow-up (exact details were not supplied) the man's gambling had stopped. A recommendation to gamble regularly was similarly used by Eissler (1950) but with set limits on funding available. In some respects these studies are similar to the studies involving controlled gambling (e.g. Dickerson and Weeks, 1979; Rankin, 1982).

TREATMENT OF ADOLESCENT PROBLEM GAMBLERS: THE PRACTICAL APPROACH

As we have seen so far in this chapter, there has been little in the way of treatment approaches specifically geared towards adolescents. However, there is one programme that has been designed in the UK to specifically help in the treatment of adolescent gamblers. This is a non-theoretical approach called 'Ten key aspects' and is outlined by Bellringer (1992). The ten aspects come under two categories (*Preparation* and *Action*) and are described below.

Preparation	1	Understanding the issues
	2	Structure change
Action	3	Assessing the problem
	4	Providing counselling
	5	Developing trust
	6	Building self-esteem
	7	Providing support
	8	Managing finances
	9	Developing interests
	10	Measuring progress

1 *Understanding the issues* involves the practitioners asking themselves questions to get an idea of the adolescent gambler's situational context (e.g. How for some does gambling become a problem?, How can the danger signs be spotted?, Who else could help the gambler in their rehabilitation?, etc.). Some questions may have no direct answers but by asking the question, the practitioner can at least gain insight into some of the issues involved.

2 *Structure change* involves the setting up of a plan between the practitioner and adolescent gambler with realistic goals and measurable objectives. The exact mechanism for a structure for change is negotiated between the practitioner and the adolescent gambler but essentially involves three stages: (i) diagnosis (i.e. initial assessment of the problem, identifying objectives and ensuring that they are attainable and measurable); (ii) design (i.e. considering options available to meet objectives, discussing costs and benefits of options), and (iii) action (i.e. agreeing how objectives will be achieved, deciding on the strategy to be employed, carrying through the plan).

3 *Assessing the problem* is self-explanatory and involves a more in-depth assessment of the adolescent's gambling problem. The practitioner at this stage needs to assess (i) if the client's gambling really is a problem; (ii) who the gambling affects and how the gambler and significant others view the problem; (iii) the extent to which the gambler is motivated to stop; (iv) the underlying motives for their gambling, and (v) if the problem gambling is primary or secondary. Assessment (v) is quite important as this may save a lot of time in the therapeutic process. For instance, two case studies that I previously reported (Griffiths, 1991f) highlighted the theme of secondary addiction via 'escape' from a distressing environment to one of 'control' in another (i.e. the amusement arcade) in fruit machine addicts. These cases (see Table 9.4) highlight that the excessive fruit machine gambling was a secondary problem caused by the underlying main problem of feeling out of control in the family environment. By addressing the primary problem (i.e. the family environment), the secondary symptoms (i.e. the excessive fruit machine playing) disappeared.

4 *Providing counselling* has the object of empowering the adolescent gambler to effect change for themselves. Important considerations at this stage are agreeing the boundaries (i.e. staying within the boundaries of the agreed contract), creating the right atmosphere (i.e. counselling to be provided in a comfortable, interruption-free environment) and appropriate involvement (i.e. involving the family and other helping agencies where appropriate).

5 *Developing trust* is an important element of the programme and involves discussing the issue of trust and confidentiality with the adolescent gambler, helping the gambler to trust others and to be open and honest, empowering the gambler to change, avoiding hidden agendas or secret collusion with other people in the gambler's life and providing consistent support to the gambler.

6 *Building self-esteem* is important in restoration of confidence. The adolescent gambler's self-esteem will almost certainly be low, therefore the

practitioner must understand the gambling problem from the gambler's perspective and formulate short-, medium- and long-term goals. Where possible, the practitioner must attempt to turn negatives into positives and chart the adolescent gambler's progress, thus enabling them to feel a sense of achievement. Negative criticism should be kept to a minimum and each session should always end on a positive note.

7 *Providing support* is also important and should involve a support agency involving the practitioner, the practitioner's agency, other agencies and the adolescent gambler's family, friends and significant others. The family should be utilized at the earliest appropriate moment and should where possible take on an active role in providing additional support to the adolescent gambler. Support is particularly needed after relapses and after the main contact with the gambler has been terminated.

8 *Managing finances* (debt counselling) involves a thorough assessment of the adolescent gambler's financial situation and its object is to reduce the stress and despair of money problems. Such actions as talking to creditors, cutting up credit cards, drawing up budget plans, etc. are all useful in such situations. Getting another family member to take control of the adolescent gambler's expenditure may also be considered as a short-term option but the long-term aim is to gradually give back financial responsibility to the gambler.

9 *Developing interests* has the objective of replacing the destructive habit with a range of activities that are rewarding in themselves. By finding out what the adolescent gambler likes about gambling, the practitioner may be able to suggest similar alternatives which give the same kinds of physiological or psychological rewards. This is not as easy as it sounds but should be pursued. Some help may be required in the development of social and life skills.

10 *Measuring progress* is needed to provide effective feedback to the adolescent gambler. The use of graphs, checklists and diaries may be useful. Self-assessment and measuring success in the gambler's terms as well as the practitioner's may also be useful. The involvement of family and friends where appropriate should be encouraged. Objectives and goals should be revised and/or reset at regular intervals.

The ten key aspects can be used in conjunction with other therapies and viewed as either a supplement to other treatment techniques or a process of therapy in itself. Although this programme has yet to be evaluated, many of the aspects outlined are common sense actions, although formalizing them in a stagewise fashion may lead to a more coherent view of approaching the problem.

Table 9.4 Case studies of secondary fruit machine addictions

Case A

A 12 year old boy lived with his divorced mother, an 18 year old sister and a 17 year old sister (both of whom had a different father from the boy). The house was totally feminine with makeup, dresses and other female items scattered about the place, and the boy's mother and sisters all entertained different male friends on a fairly regular basis. In this environment the boy felt completely alien and sought solace in an environment in which he thought he could cope and have the power to control, namely a fruit machine. The mother was advised to let the boy live with his father, which she did, and the gambling problem stopped.

Case B

A 17 year old boy lived with his father and stepmother. The family home was in the six-figure bracket and the family had two cars. The boy did not want for anything material and the stepmother was also a magistrate. On entering the home he was afraid to walk on the carpet (the pile was so deep), afraid to put a cup on the table (it was so highly polished), etc. The boy felt completely alien to this sort of environment. Again it was an environment in which he had no control; therefore he sought out an environment to which he thought he could escape and have power over. Again it was a fruit machine. He was advised to leave home. Although he still visited his family on a social basis after moving into a bedsit, his gambling stopped.

Source: From Griffiths (1991f)

SUMMARY OF PATHOLOGICAL GAMBLING TREATMENTS

Although therapists have claimed a reasonable amount of success in most spheres of treatment, it is probably fair to say that gambling has been fairly resistant to therapy interventions and that the gamblers themselves may be reluctant and resistant (Harris, 1989). Walker's (1992a) thorough meta-analysis of gambling treatment outcomes claimed that only about one-third of gamblers (37 per cent) are still abstinent after two years. Psychodynamic 'cures' are at present almost non-existent (at least in the published literature) and aversive behavioural techniques are rarely used except in conjunction with other forms of treatment. The influence of the spouse of the adult gambler in successful treatment appears to be crucial and it would appear that the most potentially effective treatments are those which acknowledge the multivariant nature of and influences (e.g. cognitive, social and physiological) on pathological gambling and utilize more than one therapeutic approach. The only 'new' (and some might say radical) approach to the treatment of pathological gamblers could be in the field of psychopharmacology which perhaps might see the use of beta-blockers to decrease arousal levels during gambling (Brown, 1986a) or the administration of opiate antagonists to block euphoric ß-endorphin effects (Blaszczynski *et al.*, 1986b). For instance, there are already some published case studies on the success of treating pathological gambling using pharmacological agents including the use of lithium carbonate (Moskowitz, 1980) and clomipramine (Hollander *et al.*, 1992).

There is no doubt that some pathological gamblers can learn by a variety of means to abstain from gambling or continue in a controlled non-problematic manner (Dickerson, 1989) and, as Orford (1988) asserts:

> The general principles for treating compulsive gambling are the same for treating alcohol dependence or abuse: good assessment, individual and family counselling, and consultation or referral if necessary. As with alcohol problems, specialist treatments such as aversion therapy or psychotherapy do not confer any advantage in most cases. The emphasis is now on a less specialized approach that is more within the realm of general medical practice: recognizing the problem and addressing it openly and positively within an established and trusted relationship may be more valuable than the search for specialist treatment.
>
> (p.729)

Further to this, it has been demonstrated that there is little in the way of treatments directly aimed at the adolescent gambler and that this is an area for future expansion. A partial explanation for this state of affairs may be due to general non-acknowledgement that such problems in adolescence exist. However, there is now abundant evidence that adolescent problem gambling is an identified phenomenon and this needs both funds and ideas for its prevention, intervention and treatment.

10 Fruit machine gambling
A final overview

Fruit machine gambling is becoming an increasingly researched area. The aim of this chapter is to (i) assess and integrate the main research findings in this book on fruit machine gambling into a coherent framework (see Table 10.1); (ii) assess whether excessive fruit machine playing is a bona fide addiction, and (iii) to formulate a 'fruit machine addiction' risk factor checklist. The first aim will be attempted by examining the antecedents and consequences of fruit machine gambling and then outlining the implications for prevention, intervention and treatment. The second aim will be attempted by examining whether excessive fruit machine playing fulfils Brown's (1988) addiction components. The third aim will be attempted by integrating the main findings of the fruit machine literature to date.

FRUIT MACHINE GAMBLING: A FUNCTIONAL / BEHAVIOURAL ANALYSIS

The approach chosen to integrate this book's studies is along the lines of Miller's (1976) functional / behavioural analysis model which was originally formulated to deal with adolescent alcohol abuse but can be applied to the acquisition, development and maintenance of adolescent fruit machine gambling. Miller's model highlights the 'ABCs' of a behaviour, in this case gambling.

GAMBLING

ANTECEDENTS ⟶ *BEHAVIOUR* ⟶ *CONSEQUENCES*

Within this simple theoretical framework, the parameters of gambling can be best understood (and ultimately treated) by analysing the factors and events that occur before gambling (antecedents) and soon after (consequences). Stumphauzer (1980) outlined Miller and Mastria's (1977) approach in

Table 10.1 Summary of published studies by the author

Year	Methodology	Subjects	Main findings
1990c	Informal interview/participant observation with 'addicted' players	8	Excitement and skill appeared to be two main reinforcers among addicted fruit machine gamblers. Negative consequences of excessive play (crime, truancy, etc.) also reported.
1990a	Semi-structured interview/ questionnaire with players	50	Nine out of fifty (18%) were probable pathological gamblers and displayed serious consequences including debts, truancy and stealing. Sociological factors important in acquisition and psychological/physiological factors important in maintenance.
1991d	Participant and non-participant observation of thirty-three amusement arcades	874	Adolescent gambling depends upon time of day and time of year. Regular gamblers conform to rules of etiquette and display stereotypical behaviours. They gamble for fun, to win money, to socialize, to escape and for excitement. Males outnumber females by over three to one.
1991f	Case studies of ex-players	2	Two case studies which reported fruit machine addiction ceasing after primary life problems had been resolved.
1993c	Postal questionnaire to ex-players	19	Self-written personal histories revealed insights into overcoming fruit machine addiction. Confirmation of negative consequences and reasons for playing of previous studies above.
1993b	Psychophysiological analysis of players' heart rates in arcade	30	Regular and non-regular gamblers' heart rates increased by approximately 22 bpm during gambling. Non-regular gamblers' heart rates did not decrease significantly after gambling.
1993f	Case study of ex-player	1	Case study reporting that a pathological gambler decreased and stopped gambling due to hearing audio playback of himself 'thinking aloud'.
1994c	'Thinking aloud' experiment in arcade/semi-structure interview with players	60	Regular gamblers produced significantly more irrational verbalizations than non-regular gamblers when thinking aloud during gambling. Regular gamblers were significantly more skill-orientated than non-regular gamblers.

which five major classes of antecedents were identified (social, emotional, situational, cognitive and physiological). The same factors were utilized for consequent behaviour, whether they were of a positively or negatively reinforcing nature. For instance, gambling could be viewed at a simple behavioural level consisting of primary positive reinforcement (e.g. feeling better, more relaxed), social reinforcement (e.g. encouragement, companionship, praise) and negative reinforcement (e.g. termination of anxiety and other uncomfortable feelings).

In relation to alcohol abuse, Stumphauzer (1980) outlined a number of antecedents and consequences. With slight modification they are equally applicable to fruit machine gambling behaviour and are summarized below:

Antecedents

1 *Social setting events:* Identification and influence of those present at the scene of gambling.
2 *Modelling antecedents*: Influence of peer models and their teaching of gambling.
3 *Self-control antecedents*: Influence of cognitive factors such as belief about 'illegality' or 'wrongness'.

Consequences

1 *Physiological effects*: Reaction to gambling, changes in feeling (both immediate and at intervals after).
2 *Social reinforcement*: Level of approval by both friends and parents.
3 *Self-control consequences*: Influence of cognitive factors like 'worried about being caught gambling' or 'worried about financial well-being'.

'Learning' to gamble would thus be attributable to a complex set of antecedent and consequent events (Stumphauzer, 1980). Perhaps one of the most interesting implications is that if all the outlined variables above are simultaneously contributing to fruit machine gambling, they are in effect forming a comprehensive (perhaps even 'overlearned') system for continued (and possibly) increased gambling behaviour with little or no evidence for negative or counter controls (Stumphauzer, 1980). Having realized that there is an adolescent gambling problem, many would argue that we should proceed to develop a treatment programme specifically designed for teenage pathological gamblers. The implications in using the functional/ behavioural approach are self-explanatory. Any treatment programme would aim to modify each precipitating factor outlined in the 'ABC' model.

ANTECEDENT FACTORS IN FRUIT MACHINE GAMBLING

This section will discuss the social, situational, emotional, behavioural, cognitive and physiological antecedents of fruit machine gambling in relation to the studies outlined in this book. All of the studies discussed in Chapter 3 provided evidence that social and situational factors are critical in the acquisition of fruit machine gambling. These studies showed that there appeared to be little difference in acquisitional factors between pathological and non-pathological gamblers except that pathological gamblers (a) started playing fruit machines significantly earlier (9 years versus 11 years); (b) started playing with their parents or on their own rather than with friends and other relatives, and (c) were less likely to play because their friends did, viewing fruit machine gambling as a non-social activity. Although in all the exploratory studies it was reported that adolescents met up with their peers at amusement arcades, thereby supporting previous research (e.g. Graham, 1988), the actual playing behaviour was non-social with little social interaction except at or to the machine. The most salient situational antecedent which became apparent in all these studies was 'choice limitation', i.e. boredom and/or nothing else to do. Many young people played fruit machines because of a lack of age-related leisure facilities. It was also noted in the observational study (Chapter 3) and the case studies (Chapter 7) that some gamblers played fruit machines because they lived in a seaside town where the arcades were in some sense part of the town's adolescent subculture.

In addition to the sociological factors, another set of antecedents, namely emotional, would appear to influence acquisition (although they may be more important in maintenance). Some of the studies (particularly the findings in chapters 3 and 7) confirmed that depressive moods are antecedent to playing in pathological gamblers, thus paralleling the literature on the link between depression and adult gambling (e.g. McCormick *et al.*, 1984). None of the studies explicitly asked about the causes of the depressive moods, but spontaneous comments from gamblers in two of the studies (the interview and questionnaire study in Chapter 3 and the postal study in Chapter 7) suggest that they are depressed about personal and family relationships, and about life in general.

In all of the studies, having a big win was the only behavioural antecedent of fruit machine gambling, although almost all of the gamblers were motivated by the chance to win money at the outset. In the interview and questionnaire study (Chapter 3, page 92) it was reported that pathological gamblers were significantly more likely to have had a big win early in their playing career. This generalization was supported in the author's other studies and would appear to be an important antecedent if a quote from one of the subjects in a thinking aloud experiment is typical:

> 'I'm feeling lucky so I'm gonna gamble it . . . . YEAH! I WON, I WON. . . . God, I should have tried this gambling stuff ages ago . . . I've never been lucky on these things.'

Once a big win has occurred there is always the thought that it can happen again, and it should also be noted that a small win in adult terms may be a big win to a young child. Evidence from other authors also indicates that big wins are an important factor in the development of gambling behaviour (e.g. Custer, 1982).

As antecedents, the cognitive and physiological factors do not appear to be as important, at least based on the empirical evidence of these studies. Salient cognitions that may influence acquisition may include false belief systems (e.g. superstitious behaviour) and/or self-control antecedents such as beliefs about potential addictiveness. It could be the case that physiologically a player may be seeking an optimum level of arousal (being hypo-or hyper-aroused) and discovers that by chance a fruit machine can act as a 'mood modifier'. There is no direct evidence from these studies for such an assertion although the importance of consequent physiological factors (discussed below) provide some implicit support.

CONSEQUENT FACTORS IN FRUIT MACHINE GAMBLING

This section will again discuss the social, situational, emotional, behavioural, cognitive and physiological consequences of fruit machine gambling in relation to my own research. Most of the early studies (Chapter 3) provided evidence that for heavy or pathological gamblers, little contribution was made to the consequent maintenance factors by social or situational determinants, although some evidence was presented that many social/non-regular players gamble because their friends do. It was further reported in the observational study that social groups may facilitate non-pathological (i.e. 'social') gambling by 'protecting' those who appear to be playing excessively.

Many of the studies reported the emotional consequences of fruit machine playing in some excessive players. Tense and depressive moods were relieved by 'escapist' playing. Fruit machines were used by players to 'escape from reality' and to blank out the mind. Although it has yet to be confirmed, it could be that many of the players who appeared as if they were on 'automatic pilot' in the observational study (Chapter 3) and those who found it difficult to verbalize their thoughts as they played fruit machines in the thinking aloud study (Chapter 5) were in 'escape mode'.

The behavioural consequences of fruit machine playing were extensively monitored in many of the studies. As fruit machine gambling became more regular, financial reinforcement appeared to become less important although chasing behaviour did occur in some individuals, and returning to win losses is a common behaviour among pathological gamblers. It would appear that the behavioural consequences of fruit machine playing are highly integrated with the cognitive and physiological consequences.

A number of the studies investigated the cognitive consequences of fruit machine playing, demonstrating that regular gamblers have irrational biases concerning their gambling behaviour and that they use a variety of heuristics (e.g. flexible attributions, hindsight bias, illusory correlations, reduction of complexity, etc.). Reiteration of some of the quotes from the thinking aloud study demonstrate this. Typical explanations for explaining away losses involved hindsight bias with players predicting events after they happened:

'I had a feeling it wasn't going to pay very much after it had just given me a feature . . . I had a feeling it was going to chew up those tokens fairly rapidly . . . . I had a feeling it had paid out earlier because it's not giving me a chance.' (Subject 4, regular player)

We also saw that some players had completely erroneous perceptions:

'I'm only gonna put one quid in to start with because psychologically I think it's very important . . . it bluffs the machine – it's my own psychology.' (Subject 12, regular player)

Others personified the machine, usually swearing at it:

'This machine doesn't like me . . . ooh it does, it's given me a number . . . hates me! It's given me low numbers, I don't think it wants to pay out at all . . . probably thinks I'm a fuckwit – it's not wrong!' (Subject 13, regular player)

'It's still not giving me a hold. . .I hope some other numbers drop in then I'll be able to get some kind of win . . . so harsh, it's really fucking me over . . . Am I allowed to change to another machine?.. I think this machine is not going to pay out happily . . . It stitches me up every time. . .unbelievable.' (Subject 12, regular player)

'I thought there was a feature held . . . I had a feature held and then it stopped them . . . fucking conned . . . this is where it just takes off your money right at the end 'cos it's out of pocket . . . bastard machine.' (Subject 2, regular player)

Why the players should demonstrate these irrationalities is not so clear. It may be that there is a general tendency to personify machines with which people spend a lot of time. At present it is likely to be difficult to predict when a heuristic will be used, although further use of the thinking aloud method might give some insight. It is also unclear whether use of heuristics depends on intrinsic factors (e.g. psychological mood state) and/or extrinsic factors (e.g. gambling history). For instance, it was suggested earlier in the book (Chapter 5) that big wins might 'promote' irrationality.

Many of the irrational biases can be explained in relation to skill perception. The assertion that regular fruit machine gamblers are more skill-orientated than non-regular gamblers was supported many times during the studies. Although the thinking aloud study (Chapter 5) demonstrated that regular gamblers can and do stay on fruit machines longer than non-regular players, what it really demonstrated was the fact that regular gamblers took a few more plays (i.e. ten gambles) to lose the same amount of money in the same amount of time. Because regular fruit machine gamblers play at a faster speed when they play and play more often, they can quite rightly claim they have more wins than non-regular gamblers. However, as was previously mentioned, this merely demonstrates a 'fixation on absolute frequency' bias (i.e. they *do* experience more wins, but they also experience considerably more losses).

Although there are technically skilful elements in fruit machine playing, they are mainly low level, involving basic familiarity with the machine. This was labelled in Chapter 5 as 'idiot skill'. The real differences between regular and non-regular players is probably cognitive, i.e. the regular players process information about skill differently and think there is more skill than there actually is, although further research would be needed to confirm such an assertion. There also appears to be a cognitive difference in how regular players react towards the machine itself. Compared with non-regular players, regular players personified the machine significantly more, adding support to the suggestion that some players treat the machine as an 'electronic friend' (Selnow, 1984).

All the studies in this book have supported the hypothesis that arousal is a physiological consequence and a major reinforcer in persistent gambling behaviour. Informal interviews and participant observation (Chapter 3) suggested that many fruit machine players get a 'buzz' or 'high' from gambling, a finding which was confirmed in later studies (Chapter 6). All of these reported that pathological gamblers get significantly more excited during gambling and that they need to gamble more to get more excited. The psychophysiological study (Chapter 6) showed that fruit machine gambling for both regular and non-regular gamblers is an exciting activity confirming the work of others (Anderson and Brown, 1984; Leary and Dickerson, 1985; Brown, 1988). Quotes from non-regular gamblers in the thinking aloud study (Chapter 5) also suggest that for some of them fruit machine gambling is an exciting activity:

> '60p! I'm in the MONEY! I'll take it, I'll take it . . . . That was quite exciting.' (Subject 4, non-regular player)

> 'Tremendous . . . it's getting quite exciting now, isn't it? . . . I'm getting quite excited by this "Fruitskill" – don't know what the hell it's doing though.' (Subject 7, non-regular player)

The psychophysiological study also showed that non-regular players take more time for their heart rates to decrease to baseline levels, implying that they do not have to play as fast or as often as regular players to get a 'buzz', although any future replications should allow a longer period for recording post-gambling baseline levels. This also suggests that regular players become tolerant to the excitement. Without physiological evidence, Boyd (1982) noted that gambling euphoria is short-lived and therefore has to be repeated, possibly leading to addictive behaviour. This is consistent with the hypothesis that addiction to gambling may be endorphin related, i.e. gamblers get a 'buzz' when they win because the body produces its own morphine-like substances (endorphins). As the body becomes more tolerant to the endorphins, gamblers may have to gamble more to get the same initially desired effect, eventually leading to both physiological and psychological dependence.

One of the main contentions to emerge from the research outlined throughout this book is that the role of arousal and the role of cognitive biases are critical to the maintenance of gambling. One possible integrated account of the role of these two factors is what I have termed the 'psycho-biology of the near miss'. This model states that when gamblers win or nearly win they get physiologically aroused and that in the gamblers' terms they are not constantly losing but *constantly nearly winning*. Although there is a lot of indirect evidence from these studies, there is by no means a full confirmation. All of the research indicates evidence of a subjective feeling of excitement especially when winning during play. Transcripts of gamblers' verbalizations in the thinking aloud study revealed that many players turn losses into near wins and that some of them believe they are going to win and then do not, meaning they get excited and then there is no financial reward. For example, one such subject stated:

> 'Two nudges . . . yeah, gotta be (a win) . . . oh you son of a bitch, you changed them . . . snatched the win.' (Subject 1, regular player).

The psychophysiological study provides the strongest objective support that fruit machine gambling is an exciting activity and heart rate data impressionistically suggested that arousal was related to wins, size of wins, and near wins. The main problem with testing the model is that it relies on being able to link a gambler's physiology to what is in effect a subjective concept, i.e. a near win. One possible way around this problem is is to devise an experiment which gets players to think aloud while playing a fruit machine, while simultaneously recording their physiological responses. One such similar experiment has recently been published by Coulombe *et al.* (1992), who reported a significant positive correlation between erroneous perceptions and level of arousal in video poker players. A further problem with the model is that some players appear to play fruit machines excessively not because of their arousing capacity but because of their tranquillizing capacity.

IMPLICATIONS FOR PREVENTION, INTERVENTION AND TREATMENT

Although most adolescents control their gambling, it is a worrying fact that clear signs of pathological gambling by a minority of players was found in nearly all of the studies outlined in this book. Using *DSM-III-R* criteria for pathological gambling (American Psychiatric Association, 1987), results from three studies (the questionnaire and interview study in Chapter 3, the thinking aloud study in Chapter 5 and the psychophysiological study in Chapter 6) suggested that among fruit machine 'user populations' approximately one in six fruit machine players are pathological gamblers (18 per cent of fifty players, 18 per cent of sixty players and 13 per cent of thirty players respectively), and as a result suffered a number of negative behavioural consequences, e.g. stealing, truanting from school, poor schoolwork, irritability, etc. At present there is little in the way of help available to these adolescent problem gamblers. The rest of this section therefore examines some of the implications for prevention, intervention and treatment, suggesting possible ways forward using the 'ABC' model.

Since sociological factors appear to be critical in the acquisition of fruit machine gambling behaviour, prevention needs to be aimed at the social and situational antecedents. There are a number of levels that this can be approached from (e.g. societal, school, family, individual, etc.), some of which may be more practical than others. Since pathological gamblers start playing fruit machines at a significantly earlier age than non-pathological gamblers, a finding also reported by other authors (e.g. Huxley and Carroll, 1992; Fisher, 1993a), an obvious step would be for the UK government to legislate against young people playing fruit machines. A 'blanket ban' on using such machines would thus prevent acquisition until at least late adolescence. Another approach might be to raise educational awareness of the dangers of fruit machine gambling not only among children and adolescents, but also among those who have an influence over them (e.g. parents, guardians, teachers, etc.). Although this is unlikely to prevent fruit machine gambling in all young people, it might reduce (a) the total number of adolescents who start to gamble on fruit machines and (b) the amount of time an adolescent spends playing them.

Since many adolescents play fruit machines because of a lack of age-related facilities, it would seem practical to set up youth clubs that, like arcades, are perceived to be minimally supervised and allow adolescents to be autonomous. The fact that some players are socially rewarded for playing fruit machines cannot be altered directly, but more adaptive personal and social skills can be taught as responses to stress (i.e. emotional antecedents); for example, relaxation, assertion and social skills training (Stumphauzer, 1980). As gambling may be modelled by both parents and peers, the family's role in maintaining gambling behaviour should be addressed in therapy, and any prevention plan should aim to increase the gambler's contact with non-gambling peers.

Since one of the physiological consequences of fruit machine playing is excitement, alternative 'highs' could be encouraged, such as skiing (Nickel, 1975) or hang-gliding (Brown, 1986a), although these would be unavailable options on financial grounds for many people. One implication for treatment is that pharmacological intervention may be possible. As was briefly mentioned in Chapter 9, this could be in the form of beta-blockers to slow down heart rates, anti-depressants and anxiolytics to relieve depression and/or anxiety (although this may replace one addiction with another) or the use of opiate antagonists (e.g. nalaxone) if machine gambling is endorphin-regulated.

Finally, evidence or knowledge of a gambler's own negative thoughts, feelings about their behaviour, and irrational biases may provide potentially useful cues for behaviour modification (Stumphauzer, 1980). For instance, it was reported in Chapter 5 (and in an informal case study in Chapter 9) that playing back the gambler's own tape recorded thoughts during gambling after using the thinking aloud method might increase the chances of a gambler understanding their own cognitive biases.

By viewing pathological gambling as an addiction there are further implications for treatment, the studies suggested, that pathological fruit machine players are not an homogeneous group, and that there appear to be at least two sub-types. This would have major treatment implications. It has been speculated earlier in this book that the first type of gambler appears to be addicted to the fruit machine itself and plays to test their skill, to gain social rewards and most of all for excitement (i.e. they get a 'buzz' or a 'high'). This was termed a 'primary addiction' and would appear to be a mixture of Moran's (1970c) 'subcultural' and 'impulsive' types of gamblers. The second type of pathological gambler appears to play fruit machines as a form of escapism, where the machine is possibly an 'electronic friend'. These players are usually depressed, socially isolated and are those who fit the stereotypical 'lone addict' media image. This is what was termed a 'secondary addiction' in that the player uses fruit machines as an escape from a primary problem (e.g. broken home, relationship break-up, etc.). It would appear that this type of machine 'escape gambler' is not confined to the UK. A recent study by Kroeber (1992) in Germany compared machine gamblers with roulette gamblers. Kroeber reported the stereotypical machine gambler as follows:

> Game machine gamblers begin to gamble at about the age of 19; they come from lower class families where the father is missing or has addiction problems, and the situation is overcharging the mother; they have grown up under emotionally meagre conditions. They lack self-confidence and therefore do not feel capable of coping with the challenges of job and relationships which form part of adult life. They drift into anti-social groups that devalue work and relationships or they get into long-term depressive or sub-depressive states, especially when social difficulties such as unemployment occur. Here gambling serves as a means of retreat that diminishes fear and tension or as anti-dysthymic self-stimulation. In the case of early intervention the therapeutic possibilities are rather positive, as long as dissociality is not yet fixed.
>
> (p.90)

This type of gambler would appear to be a mixture of Moran's (1970c) 'neurotic' and 'symptomatic' types. If the primary problem is resolved the excessive fruit machine playing should disappear. (Two such case studies were reported in the previous chapter – see Table 9.4.) This distinction obviously has clinical usefulness and may also help to explain conflicting research, some of which states that fruit machine playing is a social activity and some of which states it to be a solitary activity.

A variety of methods have been used to treat adult pathological gamblers (outlined in Chapter 9) and as previously asserted there is no reason to assume that most of these cannot be applicable to adolescent gamblers (e.g. self-help groups, psychotherapy, etc.). However, the implications for intervention and treatment in this chapter have been based purely on findings from the studies in this book. The 'ABC' model could be highly relevant and potentially useful for further study of adolescent gambling, particularly because it provides a simple framework for examining antecedents, consequences and implications for treatment.

IS EXCESSIVE FRUIT MACHINE GAMBLING A BONA FIDE ADDICTION?

For many people, the concept of addiction involves the ingestion of a drug (e.g. Walker, 1989; Rachlin, 1990). However, there is now a growing movement (e.g. Miller, 1980; Orford, 1985) which views a number of behaviours as potentially addictive including many behaviours which do not involve the ingestion of a drug. These include behaviours as diverse as gambling, overeating, sex, exercise and computer game playing and has led to new all-encompassing definitions of what constitutes addictive behaviour. One such definition (from Chapter 1) is that of Marlatt *et al.* (1988) who define addictive behaviour as:

> a repetitive habit pattern that increases the risk of disease and/or associated personal and social problems. Addictive behaviours are often experienced subjectively as 'loss of control' – the behaviour continues to occur despite volitional attempts to abstain or moderate use. These habit patterns are typically characterized by immediate gratification (short term reward), often coupled with delayed deleterious effects (long term costs). Attempts to change an addictive behaviour (via treatment or self initiation) are typically marked with high relapse rates.

(p.224)

The way of determining whether fruit machine addiction is addictive in a non-metaphorical sense is to compare behaviour patterns against clinical criteria for other established addictions. This method of making behavioural excesses more clinically identifiable has recently been proposed for two other potential addictions – 'television addiction' (McIlwraith *et al.*, 1991) and 'amusement machine addiction' (Griffiths, 1991a; 1992). Brown (1988) has postulated that addictions consist of a number of common components. It is these components that will be used as the basis for determining whether fruit machine addiction is a bona fide addiction. These components are outlined below.

Salience

This is when the particular activity becomes the most important activity in the person's life and dominates their thinking, feelings and behaviour. For instance, even if the person is not actually engaged in the behaviour they will be thinking about the next time they will be.

Euphoria

This is the subjective experience that people report as a consequence of engaging in the particular activity (i.e. they experience a 'buzz' or a 'high').

Tolerance

This is a process whereby increasing amounts of the particular activity are required to achieve the former effects. For instance, a gambler may have to gradually increase the size of the bet to experience a euphoric effect that was initially obtained by a much smaller bet.

Withdrawal symptoms

These are unpleasant feeling states and/or physical effects which occur when the particular activity is discontinued or suddenly reduced, e.g. the shakes, moodiness, irritability, etc.

Conflict

This refers to conflicts between the addicts and those around them (inter-personal conflict) or from within the individuals themselves (intrapsychic conflict) which are concerned with the particular activity.

Relapse

This is the tendency for repeated reversions to earlier patterns of the particular activity to recur and for even the most extreme patterns typical of the height of the addiction to be quickly restored after many years of abstinence or control.

FRUIT MACHINE ADDICTION

As we saw in Chapter 2, a number of studies have examined the incidence of pathological gambling in adolescence with results ranging from 0.5 per cent to 6 per cent probable fruit machine addicts depending on the methodology and criteria for pathological gambling employed. Further to this, there is a problem with the identification of fruit machine addiction because there is no observable sign or symptom as with other addictions (e.g. alcoholism, heroin addiction, etc.). Although there have been some reports of a personality change in fruit machine addicts (e.g. Moody, 1987), many parents may attribute the change to adolescence itself. It is quite often the case that many parents do not even realize they have a problem until their son or daughter has been in trouble with the police. Despite the problems of identification and diagnosis of fruit machine addiction there is now an abundant literature which indicates that fruit machines are addictive. Using empirical evidence from the studies outlined in this book, in addition to the case study material, it will be argued that there is evidence that fruit machines are addictive, fulfilling each of Brown's (1988) addiction component characteristics.

Salience

There is no doubt that for some individuals fruit machine playing is the most important thing in that person's life. There are many studies which highlight that for a small minority of individuals, fruit machine playing is a high frequency activity (i.e. played at least once a day) and that even when they are not actually playing the machines they are thinking about the next time they do (Griffiths, 1990c; Huxley and Carroll, 1992; Fisher, 1993a). Some selected quotes from the ex-fruit machine addicts in the postal study (Chapter 7) highlight the case:

> 'If I wasn't actually gambling I was spending the rest of my time working out clever little schemes to obtain money to feed my habit. These two activities literally took up all my time.'

> 'Gamble, gamble, gamble your life away . . . you might as well have put it down the drain. You've got to face the truth that you're having a love affair, and it's with a machine whose lights flash, takes your money and kills your soul.'

> 'During four or five years of compulsive gambling I think I missed about six or seven days of playing fruit machines – keeping in mind that about four or five of those days were Christmas days where it was impossible to gain access to a gambling machine . . . . As you have probably gathered, I ate, slept and breathed gambling machines . . . I couldn't even find time to spend with the people I loved . . . . The machines were more important than anything or anyone else.'

Euphoria

There are now many studies which have reported that fruit machine playing is an exciting and arousing activity. These have included both subjective self-reports from interviews and questionnaires (Chapter 3, this volume; Dickerson and Adcock, 1987) and objective experimental studies which have measured heart rate as an indicator of arousal (Chapter 6, this volume; Leary and Dickerson, 1985; Brown, 1988). A typical retrospective self-report from a case study reported in Chapter 7 highlights the case:

> 'I would always be looking forward tremendously to playing machines and I couldn't get to them fast enough. During play I always got this kind of feeling – being 'high' or 'stoned' would be the best way of describing it. I was very often uncontrollable in my excitable actions, like a 5 year old at Christmas time.'

There are also self-reports of excitement from gamblers while playing on the machine. For instance, in the thinking aloud study in which players thought aloud continuously while playing, subjects reported such feelings as:

> '60p! I'm in the money! I'll take it, I'll take it . . . . That was quite exciting.' (Subject 4)

> 'Tremendous . . . it's getting quite exciting now, isn't it? . . . I'm getting quite excited by this 'Fruitskill' – don't know what the hell it's doing though!' (Subject 7)

Tolerance

Again, there are now a number of studies reporting cases of fruit machine players who have to gamble more and more and with increasing amounts of money to get the desired arousal level that they once got gambling with lesser amounts of money.

> 'The cheap stake machines become boring so you play another big (expensive stake) one this time, after all, you've just seen somebody win off the next machine next to it and they won four pounds.'

Most of the evidence is of a self-reporting nature as demonstrated in the above quote from Chapter 7. However, in the psychophysiological study (Chapter 6) it was reported that both regular and non-regular fruit machine players' heart rates increased significantly during the playing period by approximately twenty-two beats per minute. However, as was noted, the interesting finding was that after playing fruit machines, regular players' heart rates started to decrease at once, whereas non-regular players' heart rates did not change significantly. In terms of an addictive model of fruit machine playing, both regular and non-regular players get a 'high' physiologically when playing, but the non-regular players stay 'higher' for longer, meaning they do not have to play as fast or as often to induce the arousal peaks. Regular players, in contrast, could be seen as becoming more tolerant to the playing 'highs', meaning they have to play either faster or more often to experience the initially desired effect. It was argued that the psychophysiological study in Chapter 6 could be viewed as the first study to show an objective measure of tolerance in fruit machine playing.

Withdrawal

A number of studies have indicated that fruit machine addicts who cease playing on the machines experience 'withdrawal' effects such as irritability and moodiness (see Chapter 3). However, almost all of the evidence is self-report only and consequences such as 'irritability' and 'moodiness' may not in themselves be considered bona fide withdrawal effects by some people. This is perhaps one addictive component where more research is needed to confirm the existence of an identifiable withdrawal syndrome in fruit machine addicts.

Conflict

There is much evidence in the literature that fruit machine addiction causes interpersonal conflict, although there is perhaps less evidence for intrapsychic conflict. (This is perhaps because many fruit machine addicts do not admit they have a problem – even to themselves.) In addition to case studies showing parent–child conflict (chapters 7 and 9), there is evidence showing teacher–pupil conflict (Chapter 3, this volume; Moran, 1987). A typical parent–child conflict situation was reported in Chapter 7 concerning 'David' (a fruit machine addict) and his parents:

> David's parents were considering divorce because they had so many arguments. David's mother felt the rows were upsetting David and driving him out of the house into the arcades to play on the machines. It was a vicious circle. David was driving his parents into arguments which led them to be worried and unhappy which drove David into the arcades which led to more arguments and so on.

Relapse

Relapse is a common occurrence among fruit machine addicts. There are now numerous reports in the literature demonstrating that fruit machine addicts often return to their addictive pattern of playing after controlled periods of abstinence. Typical case study example quotes again come from the postal study in Chapter 7:

> 'I normally started playing when I was depressed. The first time I gave up (fruit machines), I was doing well until I split up with my girlfriend which triggered me off again.'

> 'then came a series of family rows . . . I returned to the machines full time. Whenever I felt depressed or maybe rejected, the urge to play the machines became even bigger . . . I needed to counteract it by gambling.'

Miscellaneous negative consequences

Like other addictive behaviours, fruit machine addiction causes the individual to engage in negative behaviours such as truanting in order to play the machines (e.g. Chapter 3, this volume; Huff and Collinson, 1987; Moran, 1987; NHTPC, 1988; Leeds Polytechnic, 1989), stealing to fund machine playing (e.g. Chapter 3, this volume; Barham and Cormell, 1987; Moran, 1987; Spectrum Children's Trust, 1988), getting into trouble with teachers and/or parents over machine playing (e.g. Chapter 3, this volume; Moran, 1987), borrowing or the using of lunch money to play the machines (e.g. Chapter 3, this volume; NHTPC, 1988; Rands and Hooper, 1990), poor schoolwork (e.g. Chapter 3, this volume; Moran, 1987) and in some cases aggressive behaviour (e.g. Chapter 3, this volume; Moran, 1987).

From this brief preceding overview it would appear that fruit machine addiction is a bona fide addiction – although evidence for genuine withdrawal symptoms may be considered lacking.

FRUIT MACHINE ADDICTION: A RISK FACTOR MODEL

One consequence of the recent upsurge in research into adolescent fruit machine gambling is that we can now start to put together a 'risk factor model' of those individuals who might be at the most risk of developing pathological fruit machine playing tendencies and also describe some of the signs and 'symptoms' of being a fruit machine addict. Below is a list of factors which when added together indicate that a person might become a fruit machine addict:

- More likely to be male (16 to 25 yrs);
- Begin playing fruit machines at an early age (at around 8 years);
- Less likely to play fruit machines to win money;
- More likely to have had big win on fruit machines earlier in their playing careers;
- More likely to have begun playing fruit machines with their parents or alone;
- More likely to be depressed before playing fruit machines;
- More likely to be excited while playing fruit machines;
- More irrational while playing fruit machines;
- More attracted to the 'aura' of the fruit machine;
- View fruit machine playing as a skilful activity;
- More likely to have bad grades at school;
- More likely to engage in other addictive behaviours (smoking, drinking alcohol, illegal drug use);
- Slightly more likely to come from the lower social classes;
- More likely to have parents who have a gambling (or other addiction) problem;
- More likely to have a history of delinquency.

Although fruit machine addiction is a somewhat 'hidden addiction' with few observable signs or symptoms, there are also a number of possible warning signs to look for. Individually, many of these signs could be put down to adolescence, but if several of them apply to a child or adolescent it could be that they will have a gambling problem. For instance:

- a sudden drop in the standard of schoolwork;
- going out each evening and being evasive about where they have been;
- personality changes such as becoming sullen, moody or constantly on the defensive;
- money missing from the home;
- selling expensive possessions and not being able to account for the money;
- loss of interest in activities they used to enjoy;
- lack of concentration;
- a 'couldn't care less' attitude;
- not taking care of their appearance or hygiene. (This is a common symptom, perhaps due to lack of respect or because they are so preoccupied with their addiction that they simply forget their normal routine.)

These lists are probably not exhaustive but they do incorporate what is known empirically and anecdotally about excessive fruit machine playing.

As research into the area grows, new items will be added to such lists while factors, signs and symptoms already on these lists will be adapted and modified.

FUTURE DIRECTIONS

The general public still know little about fruit machine playing and fruit machine addiction. It is possibly true to say that most people consider fruit machines to be harmless amusement machines on which people occasionally receive a financial reward. Although for most people this may be true, fruit machines are – to an albeit small minority – as problematical, as destructive and as addictive as any number of psychoactive drugs. Although knowledge of adolescent gambling is growing, it is still highly inadequate in the light of the public's general perceptions.

Research is needed to look further into the roots and causes of excessive fruit machine playing, in addition to research into the families of such individuals, the impact of excessive fruit machine playing on schooling, the relationship between excessive fruit machine playing and criminal activity, and its relationship with other 'adult' and 'rebellious' behaviours such as smoking, drinking and drug taking. It would also be useful to study these behaviours in relation to cross addictions or poly-addiction. Preliminary work by myself has already begun in this area (see Griffiths, 1994f; g). The results of these studies suggested that alcoholics who also had a gambling addiction gambled on horse-racing, whereas other gambling cross addicts tended to gamble on fruit machines. The latter was particularly noted among adolescents and young adults. Such a suggestion that particular types of gambers (e.g. horse-race gamblers, fruit machine gamblers, etc.) tend to abuse particular substances requires more substantial empirical support. However, it is interesting that a number of agencies who reported instances of gambling cross addiction should independently report the co-existence of fruit machine playing and solvent abuse among adolescents (nine out of seventy-nine). This is a little documented phenomenon and would make an interesting area of potential study. There is little evidence in the literature to date to suggest addicted fruit machine addicts abuse either alcohol, solvents and/or other drugs. These exploratory studies clearly indicate that adolescents as well as adults can become cross addicts. A number of reasons for the link between fruit machines and solvent abuse and drugs could be speculated. It could be that the arcade subculture in some way 'promotes' deviant activities and is thus utilized by drug dealers. With regards to solvents, it could just be that they are relatively easy to obtain in comparison with other drugs (i.e. they are legally available to buy). Alternatively, it could be the individuals themselves. The sparse anecdotal accounts from the responding agencies reporting fruit machine addiction and concurrent solvent abuse appeared to suggest that at psychological level, addictions were related to social deprivation and isolation, a lack of self-esteem, a lack of communication skills and difficult home circumstances. All of these hypotheses require further support.

Observational research and anecdotal reports from Gamblers Anonymous meetings suggest that excessive fruit machine playing may be age related like other 'deviant' adolescent behaviours (e.g. glue sniffing). There is little evidence of excessive play by people over 25 years of age either from observational research or attendance at GA meetings. However, more research into the developmental path followed by fruit machine 'addicts' is needed. There was some evidence provided in Chapter 7 that excessive fruit machine players 'graduate' on to other forms of gambling (e.g. horse-race betting). However, there is perhaps more evidence that more excessive players stop gambling altogether rather than develop gambling tendencies elsewhere. There is also growing evidence of a link between video game machines and fruit machines, and many fruit machine players are known to play video games also (e.g. Huff and Collinson, 1987; Graham, 1988; Spectrum Children's Trust, 1988; Fisher, 1993a). It may be that there are developmental links between these two forms of gaming. My own research has suggested links (chapters 3, 4 and 7). For instance, in the questionnaire and interview study in Chapter 3, two-thirds of the fruit machine players also played video games and all of the pathological gamblers did so.

One way to conceptualize the links between such activities as excessive fruit machine and video game playing is to study them as 'technological addictions'. So what exactly are technological addictions? My own operational definition (see Griffiths, 1995) is that they are non-chemical (behavioural) addictions which involve human–machine interaction. They can be either passive (e.g. television) or active (e.g. computer games) and usually contain inducing and reinforcing features which may contribute to the promotion of addictive tendencies. The category of technological addictions is not mutually exclusive and contains addictive activities that could be located under other kinds of addiction. For instance, fruit machine addiction (also a gambling addiction) and telephone line sex addiction (also a sex addiction) appear to be obvious candidates. There is little in the way of academic literature on technological addictions but possible activities that could be included under this category are television addiction, computer addiction (e.g. hacking, programming), video and computer game addiction, fruit machine addiction, pinball addiction, trivia machine addiction, telephone sex addiction and in the (near?) future, virtual reality addiction. There is little doubt that activities involving person–machine interactivity are here to stay and that with the introduction of such things as interactive CDs and virtual reality consoles, the number of potential technological addictions (and its addicts) will increase. Although there is little empirical evidence for technological addictions as distinct clinical entities at present, extrapolations from the research into fruit machine addiction and the exploratory research into video / computer game addiction (see Fisher, 1994; Griffiths, 1991a; 1993g; Griffiths and Hunt, 1993) suggest that they do (and will) exist. The 'casualties' of the technological revolution will (if detected and formally identified as a problem) end up in the therapeutic domain of psychologists. Technological addictions are without doubt an issue of concern for psychologists and require further research.

Utilizing and expanding on Brown's (1989b) developmental model of a pathology of man–machine relationships, it could be that 'addicted' amusement machine players (video games or fruit machines) were previously 'television addicts' and possibly go on to be pathological gamblers (see Figure 10.1). In chronological terms, the child may invest an abnormal amount of time watching television because of parent and/or peer deprivation, becoming a continuous passive observer. At some later stage, the child or adolescent may discover that television has an active medium; that is, the playing of video games (at home or at the arcade) in which the child is psychologically rewarded through interaction and decision making via

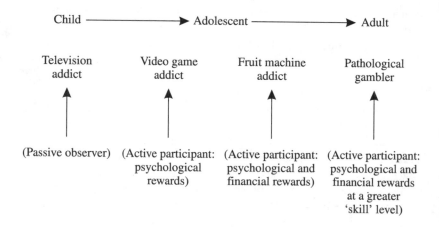

Figure 10.1 A developmental model of a possible route from a television viewer to pathological gambler

the television screen. At the next stage, the discovery of fruit machines is made. At this stage, the rewards during man–machine interaction are both psychological and financial (i.e. the player has the chance to win money). It is in the final stage that the players become pathological gamblers when they discover other forms of gambling (e.g. horse-race betting, card playing, casino gambling, etc.) have both psychological and financial rewards but also require a greater level of skill than fruit machine playing.

Although predictions from this type of model are hard to test, retrospective questionnaire and interview studies could reveal whether fruit machine players were once addicted to television or video games, or whether (non-fruit machine playing) pathological gamblers were once addicted to fruit machines. Such a developmental trend among players would need to be tested against non-addicted controls. In addition, there would have to be an objective (i.e. validated) measure of what a 'television addict' constituted, since many children watch a lot of television and we would not want to class them all as addicts.

This developmental model is admittedly very speculative. However, it may help in identifying vulnerable adolescents or in establishing programmes for clinical intervention. It would also be useful to establish whether children associate fruit machines more with video game machines (because they are both arcade machines) or with other forms of gambling (because they both offer the chance to win money). It could be that there is a developmental difference. For instance, young children might view fruit machine playing as a game, whereas older adolescents might view it as a bona fide form of gambling. Answers to these questions might give further insight into prevention strategies.

Finally, it should be noted that further research into adolescent fruit machine gambling could have a short future. If a future UK government legislates a ban on adolescents playing fruit machines, opportunities to compare the psychological, behaviourial and physiological differences between adolescent gamblers and adult gamblers (or between playing and non-playing adolescents) will be lost or seriously curtailed. Opportunities to follow adolescent gambling development longitudinally will probably become more retrospective than prospective. For these individuals, fruit machine addiction is a social reality. Prevention, intervention and treatment programmes are scarce for both adults and (especially) adolescents. If the problem is not acknowledged this situation is unlikely to change. Fruit machine playing is an important area to study and there is still a relative paucity of data. It is hoped that currently active researchers in the field of adolescent gambling can stimulate other like-minded people to broaden a growing knowledge base.

Appendix 1

CODE OF GOOD PRACTICE FOR AMUSEMENT CENTRES

British Amusement Catering Trades Association

1 Persons under the age of 16 will be totally prohibited from entering the premises.
2 Subscribers will at all times maintain their machines and games in efficient working order and will ensure that any equipment which may be found defective is withdrawn from use until it has been repaired.
3 No subscriber will conduct his business in a manner that is likely to bring it, or the trade generally, into disrepute.
4 No subscriber will do anything that is reasonably likely to cause annoyance or inconvenience to the public or to the occupiers of neighbouring premises.
5 Every subscriber will keep his premises clean and in a good state of repair and decoration.
6 Every subscriber will ensure that all parts of his premises are kept adequately lighted and ventilated.
7 A subscriber will take all reasonable precautions to prevent disorderly conduct on his premises and to ensure that his premises are not used as a place of resort by undesirable persons.
8 Every subscriber will display prominently on his premises a notice indicating his membership of the Association and that he has undertaken to operate within the current gaming legislation.
9 A subscriber will ensure that the premises are always in the charge of a mature and responsible person.
10 A subscriber will ensure that the premises are adequately staffed.
11 A subscriber may require that any person not playing the machines will be asked to leave the premises.

12 No manager will discriminate against, or will permit or aid discrimination against any person on the grounds of colour, creed, race or sex. Every person must be treated fairly and equally. However, no manager will allow any person leniency, undue favouritism or special consideration on the grounds of colour, creed, race or sex.

13 Any member subscribing to this code will display on his premises the name and address of the proprietor or the name of the company and its head office address.

14 A subscriber will comply with the Code of Practice for Health and Safety at Fairs.

CODE OF GOOD PRACTICE FOR BACTA HOLIDAY RESORT MEMBERS

British Amusement Catering Trades Association

1 This code is intended to cover the operation of all kinds of amusement devices, and such other devices as are customarily used in the industry of amusement parks, piers, amusement arcades, prize bingo establishments and similar premises used wholly or mainly for the purposes of amusement catering of coastal resorts, inland amusement parks and holiday camps.

2 Every subscriber will display prominently on his premises a notice indicating his membership of the Association and that he has undertaken to operate within the current legislation and its code.

3 No subscriber will conduct his business in a manner that is likely to bring it, or the trade generally, into disrepute.

4 No subscriber will do anything that is reasonably likely to cause annoyance or inconvenience to the public or to the occupiers of neighbouring premises.

5 Every subscriber will:

a) Keep his premises clean and in a good state of repair and decoration.

b) Ensure that all parts of his premises are adequately lit.

c) Ensure that the premises are adequately staffed and always in the charge of a mature and responsible person.

6 The consumption of alcohol on the premises will *not* be permitted.

7 No subscriber or manager will discriminate against, or will permit or aid discrimination against any person on the grounds of colour, creed, race or sex. Every person must be treated fairly and equally. However, no subscriber or manager will allow any persons leniency, undue

favouritism or special consideration on the grounds of colour, creed, race or sex.

8 Subscribers will at all times maintain their machines and games in efficient working order, and will ensure that any equipment which may be found defective is withdrawn from use until it has been repaired.

9 A subscriber will comply with the Code of Practice for Health and Safety at Fairs.

10 Any member subscribing to this code will display on his premises the name and address of the proprietor or the name of the company and its head office address to whom any important matter may be referred.

Appendix 2

Glossary

PLAY FEATURES ON A FRUIT MACHINE

Feature system

Played by those people who wish to try and match two or three identical symbols to win money (e.g. two lemons). The system is usually favoured by novices who have yet to learn how the number system operates.

Jackpot

The highest pay-out on any fruit machine.

Light oscillation

Often used in combination with the gamble button. For instance, on some machines, certain symbols (e.g. a 10p coin graphic) will flash. If players can press the gamble button as the light flashes inside the symbol, they can increase their winnings.

'Loose' machines

Fruit machines that pay out often and give the owner a small edge over the player.

Multiplier

In some machines (especially in the US), for every additional coin that is inserted before play has commenced, the pay-off ratio increases for each winning combination.

Number system

Many fruit machines have feature symbols which have numbers on them, for instance, a lemon with a number 3 in the centre of it. In this example, if the 'lemon 3' appears in the pay-line, three letters of the machine's name will light up. The more the pay-line numbers add up to, the more letters will light up. The system is often played if the hold button flashes before playing because there is an increased chance that the player can light up all the letters.

Panel lighting

During the playing of some fruit machines, the player is given the chance to light up the panel of letters, which is often the name of the machine they are playing. This is achieved by playing the number system (see separate entry). If a player lights up all the letters they can win a cash prize.

Progressive slots

Machines (mainly found in the US) with no designated jackpot limit. The jackpot increases each time a coin is inserted and no jackpot is won.

Pseudo-skill feature

This refers to any feature which appears to the player to be influencing the outcome but is in fact chance determined (e.g. the gamble button)

Skill feature

This refers to any feature that can genuinely increase the probability of a player winning. For example, hold buttons can technically raise the probability of winning by taking at least one reel out of the next play.

Skill-stop feature

Some machines give the players (rather than the machine's internal mechanism) the chance to stop any of the spinning reels independently. Although it is called a skill-stop feature, it is unlikely that any real skill can develop, as the reels spin too fast for the player to see the symbols properly.

'Straight' machines

Fruit machines that have a designated pay-out according to the listing on the front of the machine.

Symbols

The various markings on a fruit machine. The most popular are fruits, bells and bars. In the US, many casinos put their own logos on the reels for big payouts.

'Tight' machines

Fruit machines that pay out infrequently, thus giving the owner a big advantage over the player.

Tokens

Winnings which have no exchangeable value except the entitlement of free plays on the machine (i.e. they are credits for future plays on the machine). However, it is sometimes possible to win money from a token play.

Well

The bottom metal area of the fruit machine where winnings fall and are collected by the player. Sometimes called the pay-out tray.

Window

The area in front of the fruit machine which shows the line-up of reels and symbols.

FRUIT MACHINE BUTTON FUNCTIONS

Bank button

When lit, the bank button can be pressed to store winnings to either collect when voluntary play is over or to use for further playing once the player has no more money.

Cancel button

When lit, the cancel button can be pressed to cancel any decision made after pressing the nudge or hold buttons.

Collect button

When pressed, the collect button releases all the winnings into the pay-out tray.

Gamble button

When the fruit machine's graphics flash on and off, simultaneous pressing of the gamble button while selected graphics are lit may double the winnings (although the relationship is somewhat spurious; see pseudo-skill features, separate entry). Although this is a 'double or quit' feature, it is subject to variations on a number of machines. For instance, if a player wins 20p, some machines will give the player a chance to gamble winnings up to 30p or to reduce them to 10p. On some occasions, players can keep 'gambling up' to the machine's maximum pay-out.

Hold button

When lit, the hold button can be pressed to keep stationary any fruit machine symbol in a winning position (or position which a player thinks will be to their advantage on the next play) before automatic play has started. This feature increases the probability of winning by removing one, two or three reels from being spun on the next play. However, the final outcome is still chance determined.

Nudge button

When lit, the nudge button can be pressed manually to move any fruit machine reel into a winning position after automatic play is over. A number of recent machines have auto-nudge buttons in which the machine selects the best possible win for the player after automatic play is over without the player having to do anything except press the button itself.

References

Abt, V. and Smith, J. F. (1984) Gambling as play. *Annals of the American Academy of Political and Social Sciences*, 474, 122–132.

Abt, V., McGurrin, M.C. and Smith, J.F. (1985a) Toward a synoptic model of gambling behaviour. *Journal of Gambling Behavior*, 2, 79–88.

Abt, V., Smith, J.F. and Christiansen, E.M. (1985b) *The Business of Risk: Commercial Gambling in Mainstream America*. Lawrence, Kansas: University of Kansas Press.

Acking, C.A. and Kuller, R. (1972) The perception of an interior as a function of its colour. *Ergonomics*, 15, 645–654.

Adkins, B.J., Taber, J.I. and Russo, A.M. (1985) The spoken autobiography: a powerful tool in group psychotherapy. *Social Work*, September, 435–438.

Adkins, B.J., Kreudelbach, N.G., Toohig, T.M. and Rugle, L. (1987) The relationship of gaming preferences to MMPI personality variables. Paper presented at the 7th International Conference on Gambling and Risk Taking, Reno, Nevada, August.

Allcock, C.C. (1986) Pathological gambling (review) *Australian and New Zealand Journal of Psychiatry*, 20, 259–265.

Allcock, C. and Dickerson, M.G. (1986) *The Guide to Good Gambling*. New South Wales: Social Science Press.

Allcock, C.C. and Grace, D.M. (1988) Pathological gamblers are neither impulsive nor sensation seeking. *Australian and New Zealand Journal of Psychiatry*, 22, 307–311.

Amati, B.H. (1981) Juvenile delinquency and habit patterns. *Indian Journal of Social Work*, 44, 405–408.

American Psychiatric Association (1980) *Diagnostic and Statistical Manual of Mental Disorders* (3rd Edition) Washington, DC: Author.

American Psychiatric Association (1987) *Diagnostic and Statistical Manual of Mental Disorders* (3rd Edition – Revised). Washington, DC: Author.

Amsel, A. (1958) The role of frustrative non reward in non continuous reward situations. *Psychological Bulletin*, 55, 102–119.

Amsel, A. (1967) Partial reinforcement effects on vigor and persistence. In W. Spence and J.T. Spence (eds), *The Psychology of Learning and Motivation*. New York: Academic Press.

Anderson, G. and Brown, R.I.F. (1984) Real and laboratory gambling, sensation seeking and arousal. *British Journal of Psychology*, 75, 401–410.

Anderson, G. and Brown, R.I.F. (1987) Some applications of reversal theory to the explanation of gambling and gambling addictions. *Journal of Gambling Behavior*, 3, 179–189.

Antia, C. (1979) Gamblers Anonymous. In D. Lester (ed.), *Gambling Today,* pp. 115–126. Springfield, Illinois: Charles C. Thomas Co.

Arcade Amusement Action Group (1987) Amusement arcades: the case for reforms of law controlling amusement arcades. AAAG Document.

Arcuri, A.F., Lester, D. and Smith, F.O. (1985) Shaping adolescent gambling behaviour. *Adolescence*, 20, 935–938.

Arenson, A.J. (1978) Age and sex differences in the probability of children. *Psychological Reports*, 43, 697–698.

Ashdown, J. (1987) Young people and gaming machines. Unpublished manuscript.

Atari (1982) *A Public Perspective*. California: Author.

Bannister, G. (1977) Cognitive and behaviour therapy in the case of compulsive gambling. *Cognitive Therapy and Research*, 1, 223–237.

Barham, B. and Cormell, M. (1987) Teenage use of amusement arcades in Bognor Regis. Bognor Regis: WSIHE.

Barker, J.C. and Miller, M. (1966) Aversion therapy for compulsive gambling (letter to the Editor), *Lancet,* 1 (7435), 491–492.

Barker, J.C. and Miller, M. (1968a) Aversion therapy for compulsive gambling. *Journal of Nervous and Mental Disease*, 146, 285–302.

Barker, J.C. and Miller, M. (1968b) Treatment of compulsive gambling (letter to the Editor), *Lancet*, 1 (7548), 926.

Bauer, R.H. and Turner, J.H. (1974) Betting behaviour in sexually homogenous and heterogenous groups. *Psychological Reports*, 34, 251–258.

Beck, A. and Emery, G. (1986) *Anxiety Disorders and Phobias: A Cognitive Perspective*. New York: Basic Books.

Beck, E.A. and McIntyre, S.C. (1977) MMPI patterns of shoplifters within a college population. *Psychological Reports,* 41, 1035–1040.

Bell, D.S. and Champion, R.A. (1979) Deviancy, delinquency and drug use. *British Journal of Psychiatry*, 134, 269–276.

Bellaire, W. and Caspari, D. (1992) Diagnosis and therapy of male gamblers in a university psychiatric hospital. *Journal of Gambling Studies*, 8, 143–150.

Bellringer, P. (1992) *Working with Young Problem Gamblers: Guidelines to Practice*. Leicester: UK Forum on Young People and Gambling.

Bentall, R.P., Fisher, D., Kelly, V., Bromley, E. and Hawksworth, K. (1989) The use of arcade gambling machines: demographic characteristics of users and patterns of use. *British Journal of Addiction*, 84, 555–562.

Bergler, E. (1957) *The Psychology of Gambling*. New York: Hill and Wang.

Berkowicz, L. (1970) The contagion of violence: an S-R mediational analysis of some of the effects of observed aggression. In W.J. Arnold and M.M. Page (eds), *Nebraska Symposium on Motivation*. Lincoln: University of Nebraska Press.

Berti, A., Bombi, A. and Lis, A. (1982) The child's conception about means of production and their owners. *European Journal of Social Psychology,* 12, 221–239.

Beverley Area Management Committee (1989) Amusement arcades. Unpublished manuscript.

Bijou, S.W. (1957) Patterns of reinforcement and resistance to extinction in young children. *Child Development*, 28, 47–54.

Birren, F. (1965) *Colour Psychology and Colour Therapy*. New York Hyde, NY: University Books.

Birren, F. (1978) *Colour and Human Response*. New York: Van Nostrand.

Blackman, S., Simone, R.V. and Thoms, D.R. (1986) Treatment of gamblers. *Hospital and Community Psychiatry*, 37, 404.

Blackman, S., Simone, R.V. and Thoms, D.R. (1989) The Gamblers Treatment Clinic of St. Vincent's North Richmond Community Mental Health Center: characteristics of the clients and outcome of treatment. *International Journal of the Addictions*, 24, 29–37.

Blaszczynski, A.P. (1988) Clinical studies in pathological gambling: is controlled gambling an acceptable treatment outcome? Unpublished PhD thesis, University of New South Wales, Australia.

Blaszczynski, A.P. and McConaghy, N. (1988) SCL–90 assessed psychopathology in pathological gamblers. *Psychological Reports*, 62, 547–552.

Blaszczynski, A.P. and McConaghy, N. (1989) Anxiety and/or depression in the pathogenesis of addictive gambling. *International Journal of the Addictions*, 24, 337–350.

Blaszczynski, A.P. and Winter, S.W. (1984) Endorphins and psychiatry: editorial comment. *Australian and New Zealand Journal of Psychiatry*, 18, 111–112.

Blaszczynski, A.P., Buhrich, N. and McConaghy, N. (1985) Pathological gamblers, heroin addicts, and controls compared on the E.P.Q. Addiction Scale. *British Journal of Addiction*, 80, 315–319.

Blaszczynski, A.P., Wilson, A.C. and McConaghy, N. (1986a) Sensation seeking and pathological gambling. *British Journal of Addiction*, 81, 113–117.

Blaszczynski, A.P., McConaghy, N. and Winter, S.W. (1986b) Plasma endorphin levels in pathological gambling. *Journal of Gambling Behavior*, 2, 3–14.

Blaszczynski, A.P., McConaghy, N. and Frankova, A. (1990) Boredom proneness in pathological gambling. *Psychological Reports*, 67, 35–42.

Blaszczynski, A.P., McConaghy, N. and Frankova, A. (1991) Control versus abstinence in the treatment of pathological gambling: a two to nine year follow up. *British Journal of Addiction*, 86, 299–306.

Bolen, D.W. and Boyd, W.H. (1968) Gambling and the gambler: a review and preliminary findings. *Archives of General Psychiatry*, 18, 617–630.

Bolen, D.W., Caldwell, A.B. and Boyd, W.H. (1975) Personality traits of pathological gamblers. Paper presented at the second National Conference on Gambling, South Lake Tahoe, June.

Bornstein, M.H. (1978) Colour vision and pattern vision. *Advances in Child Development and Behavior*, 12, 117–182.

Boyce, P.R. (1975) The luminous environment. In D. Canter and P. Stringer (eds), *Environmental Interactions: Psychological Approaches to our Physical Surroundings*. New York: International Universities Press.

Boyd, W. (1982) Excitement: the gambler's drug. In W.R. Eadington (ed.), *The Gambling Papers*. Springfield, Illinois: Charles C. Thomas Co.

Boyd, W.J. and Bolen, D.W. (1970) The compulsive gambler and spouse in group psychotherapy. *International Journal of Group Psychotherapy*, 20, 77–90.

Braun, C.M.J., Goupil., Giroux, J. and Chagnon, Y. (1986) Adolescents and microcomputers: sex differences, proxemics, task and stimulus variables. *Journal of Psychology*, 120, 529–542.

British Amusement Catering Trades Association (1988) *The Real Facts: Amusement Machines Under Attack*. Tunbridge Wells: Cedar Press.

British Market Research Bureau (1986) *Gambling: Mintel Leisure Intelligence* (Vol.14) London: Author.

Brooks, B.D. (1983) [Untitled]. In S.S. Baughman and P.D. Claggett (eds), *Video Games and Human Development: A Research Agenda for the 80s*. Cambridge, MA: Harvard Graduate School of Education.

Brown, R. (1965) *Social Psychology*. New York: Free Press of Glencoe.

Brown, R.I.F. (1986a) Arousal and sensation-seeking components in the general explanation of gambling and gambling addictions. *International Journal of the Addictions*, 21(9410), 1001–1016.

Brown, R.I.F. (1986b) Dropouts and continuers in Gamblers Anonymous: life context and other factors, Parts 1–4. *Journal of Gambling Behavior*, 2, 130–140.

Brown, R.I.F. (1987a) Classical and operant paradigms in the management of compulsive gamblers. *Behavioural Psychotherapy*, 15, 111–122.

Brown, R.I.F. (1987b) Dropouts and continuers in Gamblers Anonymous: Part 2. Analysis of free style account of experiences with GA. *Journal of Gambling Behavior*, 3, 68–79.

Brown, R.I.F. (1987c) Dropouts and continuers in Gamblers Anonymous: Part 3. Some possible specific reasons for dropout. *Journal of Gambling Behavior*, 3, 137–151.

Brown, R.I.F. (1987d) Dropouts and continuers in Gamblers Anonymous: Part 4. Evaluation and Summary. *Journal of Gambling Behavior*, 3, 202–210.

Brown, R.I.F. (1988) Arousal during play in normal machine gamblers. Unpublished manuscript, Department of Psychology, University of Glasgow.

Brown, R.I.F. (1989a) Relapses from a gambling perspective. In M. Gossop (ed.) *Relapses and Addictive Behaviour*. London: Routledge.

Brown, R.I.F. (1989b) Gaming, gambling, risk taking, addictions and a developmental model of a pathology of man–machine relationships. In J. Klabberg, D. Croowall, H. de Jong and W. Scheper (eds) *Simulation Gaming*. Oxford: Pergamon Press.

Brown, R.I.F. (1990) Book review of *Paradoxes of Gambling Behaviour* by Willem Wagenaar. *British Journal of Addiction*, 85, 420–421.

Brown, R.I.F. and Robertson, S. (1993) Home computer and video game addictions in relation to adolescent gambling: conceptual and developmental aspects. In W.R. Eadington and J. Cornelius (eds) *Gambling Behavior and Problem Gambling*. Reno, Nevada: University of Nevada Press.

Browne, B. (1989) Going on tilt: frequent poker players and control. *Journal of Gambling Behavior*, 5, 274–285.

Burgess, R.G. (1984) *In the Field: an Introduction to Field Research*. London: Allen & Unwin.

Caldwell, G. (1974) The gambling Australian. In D.E. Edgar (ed.) *Social Change in Australia; Reading in Sociology*. Melbourne: Cheshire.

Callois, R. (1958) *Man, Play and Games*. New York: Free Press.

Cameron, B. and Myers, J.L. (1966) Some personality correlates of risk-taking. *Journal of General Psychology*, 74, 51–60.

Capaldi, E.J. (1966), Partial reinforcement: a hypothesis of sequential effects. *Psychological Review*, 73, 459–457.

Carlton, P.L. and Manowitz, P. (1987) Physiological factors in determinants of pathological gambling. *Journal of Gambling Behavior*, 3, 274–285.

Carlton, P.L., Manowitz, P., McBride, H., Nora, R., Swartzburg, M. and Goldstein, L. (1987) Attention deficit disorder and pathological gambling. *Journal of Clinical Psychiatry*, 48, 487–488.

Carmichael, B.G. (1975) Youth crime in urban communities – a descriptive analysis of street hustlers and their crimes. *Crime and Delinquency*, 21, 139–148.

Carr, S.J. and Dabbs, J.M. (1974) The effects of lighting, distance and intimacy of topic on verbal and visual behaviour. *Sociometry*, 37, 592–600.

Carroll, J.S. and Payne, J.W. (1977) Judgements about crime and the criminal: a model and a method for investigating parole decisions. In B.D. Sales (ed.) *Perspectives in Law and Psychology: The Criminal Justice System* (Vol.I) New York: Plenum.

Centre for Leisure Research (1990) *Playing the Machines: A study of Leisure Behaviour*. Edinburgh: Author.

Ciarrocchi, J.W. and Reinert, D.F. (1993) Family environment and length of recovery for married male members of Gamblers Anonymous and female members of Gam-Anon. *Journal of Gambling Studies*, 9, 341–352.

Comess, L. (1960) The analysis of a gambler. Unpublished doctoral dissertation. Southern California Psychoanalytic Institute.

Comings, D.E., Rosenthal, R.J., Lesieur, H.R., Rugle, L.J., Muhleman, D., Chiu, C., Dietz, G. and Gade, R. (1994) The molecular genetics of pathological gambling: the DRD2 gene. Paper presented at the Ninth International Conference on Gambling and Risk Taking, Las Vegas, Nevada, June.

Conklin, H.C. (1968). Ethnography. In D.L. Sills (ed.), *International Encyclopaedia of the Social Sciences*, 5, 172–178. New York: MacMillan and the Free Press.

Cormack, M.A. and Sinnott, A. (1983) Psychological alternatives to long term benzodiazepine use. *Journal of the Royal College of General Practitioners*, 33, 279–281.

Cormack, M.A., Owens, R.G. and Dewey, M.E. (1989) *Reducing Benzodiazepine Consumption: Psychological Contributions to General Practice*. New York: Springer-Verlag.

Corney, W.J. and Cummings, W.T. (1985) Gambling behavior and information processing biases. *Journal of Gambling Behavior*, 1, 111–118.

Cornish, D.B. (1978) *Gambling: A Review of the Literature and its Implications for Policy and Research*. London: HMSO.

Costa, N. (1988) *Automatic Pleasures: The History of the Coin Machine*. London: Kevin Francis Publishing.

Cotler, S.B. (1971) The use of different behavioural techniques in treating a case of compulsive gambling. *Behaviour Therapy*, 1, 579–584.

Coulombe, A., Ladouceur, R., Desharnais, R. and Jobin, J. (1992) Erroneous perceptions and arousal among regular and occasional video poker players. *Journal of Gambling Studies*, 8, 235–244.

Craig, R.J. (1979) Personality characteristics of heroin addicts: a review of the empirical literature with critique – Part II. *International Journal of the Addictions*, 14, 606–626.

Cromer, G. (1978) Gamblers Anonymous in Israel: a participation observation study of a self-help group. *International Journal of the Addictions*, 13, 1069–1077.

Csikszentmihalyi, M. (1976) Play and intrinsic rewards. *Journal of Humanistic Psychology*, 16, 41–63.

Culleton, R.P. (1985) A survey of pathological gamblers in the State of Ohio. Transition Planning Associates, Philadelphia.

Culleton, R.P. and Lang, R.P. (1985) The prevalence rate of pathological gambling in the Delaware Valley in 1984. Forum for Policy Research and Public Service, New Jersey: Rutgers University.

Cummings, S. and Taebel, D. (1978) Economic socialization of children: a neo marxist view. *Social Problems,* 26, 198–210.

Cummings, C., Gordon, J.R. and Marlatt, G.A. (1980) Relapse: prevention and prediction. In W.R. Miller (ed.) *The Addictive Behaviors: Treatment of Alcoholism, Drug Abuse, Smoking and Obesity.* New York: Pergamon Press.

Custer, R.L. (1975) Characteristics of compulsive gamblers. Paper presented at the second Annual Conference on Gambling, Lake Tahoe, Nevada, June.

Custer, R.L. (1977) The gambling scene. Paper presented at the First International Conference of Gamblers Anonymous, Chicago.

Custer, R.L. (1982) An overview of compulsive gambling. In P. Carone, S. Yoles, S. Keiffer and L. Krinsky (eds) *Addictive Disorders Update.* New York: Human Sciences Press.

Custer, R.L. (1984) Profile of the pathological gambler. *Journal of Clinical Psychiatry,* 45, 35–38.

Custer, R.L. and Custer, L.F. (1978) Characteristics of the recovering compulsive gambler: a survey of 150 members of Gamblers Anonymous. Paper presented to the Fourth Annual Conference on Gambling, Reno, Nevada, December.

Custer, R.L. and Custer, L.F. (1981) Soft signs of pathological gambling. Paper presented at the Fifth National Conference on Gambling, Reno, Nevada, University of Nevada.

Custer, R.L. and Milt, H. (1985) *When Luck Runs Out.* New York: Facts on File Publications.

Daley, K. (1987) Encouraging 'habitual' gambling in poker machines. In M.B. Walker (ed.) *Faces of Gambling.* Sydney: National Association for Gambling Studies.

Danzinger, K. (1958) Children's earliest conception of economic relationships. *Journal of Social Psychology,* 47, 231–240.

Darvas, S. (1981) The spouse in treatment: or, there is a woman (or women) behind every pathological gambler. Paper presented at the Fifth National Conference on Gambling and Risk Taking, Reno, Nevada, October.

Dell, L.J., Ruzicka, M.F. and Palisi, A.T. (1981) Personality and other factors associated with the gambling addiction. *International Journal of the Addictions,* 16, 149–156.

Deverensky, J., Gupta, R. and Cioppa, G.D. (1994) A developmental perspective of gambling behavior in children and adolescents. Paper presented at the Ninth International Conference on Gambling and Risk Taking, Las Vegas, Nevada, June.

Devereux, E.C. (1968) Gambling. In D.L. Sills (ed.) *International Encyclopaedia of the Social Sciences,* 6, 53–62. USA: Macmillan / Free Press.

Devinney, R.B. (1979) Gamblers: a personality study. *Dissertation Abstracts International,* 40 (1-B), 429–430.

Dickerson, M.G. (1974) The effect of betting shop experience on gambling behaviour. Unpublished Ph.D. dissertation, University of Birmingham.

Dickerson, M.G. (1977a) 'Compulsive' gambling as an addiction: dilemmas. *Scottish Medical Journal,* 22, 251–252.

Dickerson, M.G. (1977b) The role of the betting shop environment in the training of 'compulsive' gamblers. *British Association of Behavioural Psychotherapy Bulletin*, 5, 3–8.

Dickerson, M.G. (1979) FI schedules and persistence of gambling in the UK betting office. *Journal of Applied Behaviour Analysis*, 12, 315–323.

Dickerson, M.G. (1984) *Compulsive Gamblers*. Longman: London.

Dickerson, M.G. (1989) Gambling: a dependence without a drug. *International Review of Psychiatry*, 1, 157–172.

Dickerson, M. and Adcock, S. (1987) Mood, arousal and cognitions in persistent gambling: preliminary investigation of a theoretical model. *Journal of Gambling Behavior*, 3, 3–15.

Dickerson, M. and Hinchy, J. (1988) The prevalence of excessive and pathological gambling in Australia. *Journal of Gambling Behavior*, 4, 135–151.

Dickerson, M.G. and Weeks, D. (1979) Controlled gambling as a therapeutic technique for compulsive gamblers. *Journal of Behavioural Therapy and Experimental Psychiatry*, 10, 139–141.

Dickerson, M., Hinchy, J. and Fabre, J. (1987) Chasing, arousal and sensation seeking in off-course gamblers. *British Journal of Addiction*, 82, 673–680.

Dickerson, M., Hinchy, J. and Legg England, S. (1990) Minimal treatments and problem gamblers: a preliminary investigation. *Journal of Gambling Studies*, 6, 87–102.

Dielman, T.E. (1979) Gambling: a social problem? *Journal of Social Issues*, 35, 36–42.

Dominick, J.R. (1984) Videogames, television violence, and aggression in teenagers. *Journal of Communication*, 34, 136–147.

Eadington, W.R. (1987) Economic perceptions of gambling behavior. *Journal of Gambling Studies*, 3, 264–273.

Edworthy, J., Loxley, S. and Dennis, I. (1991) Improving auditory warning design: relationship between warning sound parameters and perceived urgency. *Human Factors*, 33, 205–231.

Eissler, K.R. (1950) Ego psychological implications of the psychoanalytic treatment of delinquents. *Psychoanalytic Study Child*, 5, 97–121.

Ellis, A. (1962) *Reason and Emotion in Psychotherapy*. New York: Lyle Stuart.

Ericcson, K.A. and Simon, H.A. (1980) Verbal reports as data. *Psychological Review*, 87, 215–251.

Ericcson, K.A. and Simon, H.A. (1984) *Protocol Analysis – Verbal Reports as Data*. Cambridge, MA: MIT Press.

Estes, W. (1964) Probability learning. In A.W. Melton (ed.) *Categories of Human Learning*. New York: Academic Press.

Eysenck, H.J. (1941) A critical and experimental study of colour preferences. *American Journal of Psychology*, 55, 385–394.

Eysenck, M. (1984) *A Handbook of Cognitive Psychology*. London: LEA.

Ferrioli, M. and Ciminero, A.R. (1981) The treatment of pathological gambling as an addiction behaviour. In W.R. Eadington (ed.) *The Gambling Papers*. University of Nevada, Reno.

Fink, H.K. (1961) Compulsive gambling. *Acta Psychotherapy*, 9, 251–261.

Fisher, S. (1991) Governmental response to juvenile fruit machine gambling in the UK: where do we go from here? *Journal of Gambling Studies*, 7, 217–247.

Fisher, S. (1992) Measuring pathological gambling in children: the case of fruit machines in the UK. *Journal of Gambling Studies*, 8, 263–285.

Fisher, S. (1993a) Gambling and pathological gambling in adolescents. *Journal of Gambling Studies*, 9, 277–288.

Fisher, S. (1993b) The pull of the fruit machine: a sociological typology of young players. *Sociological Review*, 41, 446–474.

Fisher, S. (1994) Identifying video game addiction in children and adolescents. Paper presented at the Ninth International Conference on Gambling and Risk Taking, Las Vegas, June.

Fitchett, S.M. and Sandford, D.A. (1976) Treatment for habitual gambling. In J.D. Krumboltz and C.E. Thoreson (eds) *Counselling Methods*. New York: Holt, Rinehart & Wilson.

Fox, K. (1978) What children bring to school: the beginning of economic education. *Social Education*, 13, 478–481.

Frank, M.L. (1988) Casino gambling and college students: three sequential years of data. Paper presented at the Third National Conference on Gambling Behavior, New York, May.

Frank, M.L. and Smith, C. (1989) Illusion of control and gambling in children. *Journal of Gambling Behavior*, 5, 127–136.

Frankl, V. (1962) *Man's Search for Meaning*. Boston, MA: Beacon.

Franklin, J. and Richardson, R. (1988) A treatment outcome study with pathological gamblers: preliminary findings and strategies. In W. R. Eadington (ed.) *Gambling Research: Proceedings of the Seventh International Conference on Gambling and Risk Taking*. University of Nevada, Reno.

Freud, S. (1928) Dostoevsky and parricide. *The Standard Edition of the Complete Psychological Works of Sigmund Freud* (ed. and trans. J. Strachey), Vol. 21. London: Hogarth Press.

Frey, J.H. (1984) Gambling: a sociological review. *Annals of the American Academy of Political and Social Sciences*, 274, 107–121.

Furnham, A. (1982) The perception of poverty among adolescents. *Journal of Adolescence*, 5, 135–147.

Furnham, A. (1986) Children's understanding of the economic world. *Australian Journal of Education*, 30, 219–240.

Furnham, A. and Lewis, A. (1983) *The Economic Mind*. London: Harvester Press.

Furnham, A. and Thomas, P. (1984) Pocket money: a study of economic education. *British Journal of Developmental Psychology*, 2, 205–212.

Gaboury, A. and Ladouceur, R. (1989) Erroneous perceptions and gambling. *Journal of Social Behavior and Personality*, 4, 411–420.

Galdston, I. (1951) The psychodynamics of the triad. *Journal of Mental Hygiene*, 35, 589–598.

Gallup, G. (1982) The typical American teenager. *Seattle Times*, 19 May.

Gaming Board (1988) *Survey of Under 16 Year Olds in Inland and Seaside Arcades*. London: Author.

Gerner, R.H., Catlin, D.H., Gorelick, D.A., Hui, K.K. and Li, C.H. (1980) Beta-endorphin intravenous infusion causes behavioural changes. *Archives of General Psychiatry*, 37, 642–647.

Gibb, G.D., Bailey, J.R., Lambirth, T.T. and Wilson, W.P. (1983) Personality differences between high and low electronic video game users. *Journal of Psychology*, 114, 159–165.

Gilovich, T. (1983) Biased evaluation and persistence in gambling. *Journal of Personality and Social Psychology*, 44, 1110–1126.

Gilovich, T. and Douglas, C. (1986) Biased evaluations of randomly determined gambling outcomes. *Journal of Experimental Social Psychology*, 22, 228–241.

Glass, C.D. (1982) Differences in internal–external locus of control and tolerance–intolerance for ambiguity among pathological, social and non-gambling groups. *Dissertation Abstracts*, 43, 524.

Glen, A.M. (1976) The treatment of compulsive gamblers at Cleveland Veterans Administration Hospital, Brownsville Division. Paper presented at the eighty-fourth Annual Convention of the American Psychological Association, Washington, DC, September.

Glen, A.M. (1979) Personality research on pathological gamblers. Paper presented at the eighty-seventh Annual Convention of the American Psychological Association, New York, September.

Goethe, J.W. Von (1971) *Goethe's Colour Theory* (edited by R. Matthaei, translated by H. Aach) London: Studio Vista.

Goffman, E. (1967) *Interaction Ritual: Essays on Face-to-face Behavior*. Garden City, New York: Doubleday Anchor.

Gold, R.L. (1958) Roles in sociological field investigations. *Social Forces*, 56, 217–223.

Goldstein, L. and Carlton, P.L. (1988) Hemispheric EEG correlates of compulsive behavior: the case of pathological gamblers. *Research Communications in Psychology, Psychiatry and Behavior*, 13 (1 and 2), 103–111.

Goldstein, L., Manowitz, P., Nora, R., Swartzburg, M. and Carlton, P.L. (1985) Differential EEG activation and pathological gambling. *Biological Psychiatry*, 20, 1232–1234.

Goorney, A.B. (1968) Treatment of a compulsive horse race gambler by aversion therapy. *British Journal of Psychiatry*, 114, 329–333.

Gossop, M.R. and Eysenck, S.B.G. (1980) A further investigation into the personality of drug addicts in treatment. *British Journal of Addiction*, 75, 305–311.

Graham, J. (1988) *Amusement Machines: Dependency and Delinquency (Home Office Research Study No. 101)* London: HMSO.

Graham, J.R. and Lowenfeld, B.H. (1986) Personality dimensions of the pathological gambler. *Journal of Gambling Behavior*, 2, 58–66.

Greenberg, D. and Rankin, H. (1982) Compulsive gamblers in treatment. *British Journal of Psychiatry*, 140, 364–366.

Greenberg, H. (1980) Psychology of gambling. In H.I. Kaplan, A.M. Freedman, and B.J. Sadcock, (eds) *Comprehensive Textbook of Psychiatry* (3rd Edition) New York: Williams & Wilkins.

Greenberg, M. and Weiner, B. (1966) Effects of reinforcement history upon risk-taking behaviour. *Journal of Experimental Psychology*, 71, 587–592.

Greenlees, E.M. (1988) *Casino Accounting and Financial Management*. Reno, Nevada: University of Nevada Press.

Greenson, R.R. (1947) On gambling. *American Imago*, 4, 61–77.

Grichting, W.L. (1986) The impact of religion on gambling in Australia. *Australian Journal of Psychology*, 38, 45–58.

Griffiths, F.V. (1982) A case of compulsive gambling treated by hypnosis. *International Journal of Clinical and Experimental Hypnosis*, 30, 195.

Griffiths, M.D. (1988a) Adolescent gambling: report of a workshop. *Society for the Study of Gambling Newsletter*, 14, 12–15.

Griffiths, M.D. (1988b) The gaming industry: a summary of personal communications. Economic Psychology Research Group Report 88/13, University of Exeter.

Griffiths, M.D. (1989) Gambling in children and adolescents. *Journal of Gambling Behavior*, 5, 66–83.

Griffiths, M.D. (1990a) The acquisition, development and maintenance of fruit machine gambling in adolescents. *Journal of Gambling Studies*, 6, 193–204.

Griffiths, M.D. (1990b) The cognitive psychology of gambling. *Journal of Gambling Studies*, 6, 31–42.

Griffiths, M.D. (1990c) Addiction to fruit machines: a preliminary study among males. *Journal of Gambling Studies*, 6, 113–126.

Griffiths, M.D. (1990d) Arcade clientele and gaming preferences: a long term study. *Perceptual and Motor Skills*, 70, 1258.

Griffiths, M.D. (1990e) Adolescent gambling: an observational pilot study. *Perceptual and Motor Skills*, 70, 1138.

Griffiths, M.D. (1990f) Factors in gambling and sexual behaviour. *Society for the Study of Gambling Newsletter*, 17, 4–9.

Griffiths, M.D. (1990g) The dangers of social psychology research. *The Social Psychology Newsletter of The British Psychological Society*, 23, 20–23.

Griffiths, M.D. (1991a) Amusement machine playing in childhood and adolescence: a comparative analysis of video games and fruit machines. *Journal of Adolescence*, 14, 53–73.

Griffiths, M.D. (1991b) Review of 'Amusement machines: dependency and delinquency (Home Office Research Study No. 101)', *Journal of Gambling Studies*, 7, 79–86.

Griffiths, M.D. (1991c) The psychobiology of the near miss in fruit machine gambling. *Journal of Psychology*, 125, 347–357.

Griffiths, M.D. (1991d) The observational analysis of adolescent gambling in UK amusement arcades. *Journal of Community and Applied Social Psychology*, 1, 309–320.

Griffiths, M.D. (1991e) The social world of fruit machine playing: a note on the practical considerations of observational analysis. *The Social Psychology Newsletter of The British Psychological Society*, 25, 15–19.

Griffiths, M.D. (1991f) Fruit machine addiction: two brief case studies. *British Journal of Addiction*, 86, 465.

Griffiths, M.D. (1991g) Adolescent fruit machine use: a review of current issues and trends. *UK Forum on Young People and Gambling Newsletter*, 4, 2–3.

Griffiths, M.D. (1991h) The acquisition, development and maintenance of fruit machine gambling in adolescence. Unpublished Ph.D. thesis, University of Exeter.

Griffiths, M.D. (1992) Pinball wizard: the case of a pinball addict. *Psychological Reports*, 71, 160–162.

Griffiths, M.D. (1993a) A study of the cognitive activity of fruit machine players. In W.R. Eadington and J.A. Cornelius (eds) *Gambling Behavior and Problem Gambling*. Reno, Nevada: University of Nevada Press.

Griffiths, M.D. (1993b) Tolerance in gambling: an objective measure using the psychophysiological analysis of male fruit machine gamblers. *Addictive Behaviors*, 18, 365–372.

Griffiths, M.D. (1993c) Factors in problem adolescent fruit machine gambling: Results of a small postal survey. *Journal of Gambling Studies*, 9, 31–45.

Griffiths, M.D. (1993d) Fruit machine addiction in adolescence: a case study. *Journal of Gambling Studies*, 9, 387–399.

Griffiths, M.D. (1993e) Fruit machine gambling: the importance of structural characteristics. *Journal of Gambling Studies*, 9, 133–152.

Griffiths, M.D. (1993f) Pathological gambling: possible treatment using an audio playback technique. *Journal of Gambling Studies*, 9, 295–297.

Griffiths, M.D. (1993g) Are computer games bad for children? *The Psychologist: Bulletin of the British Psychological Society*, 6, 401–407.

Griffiths, M.D. (1994a) Beating the fruit machine: systems and ploys both legal and illegal. *Journal of Gambling Studies*, 10, 287–292.

Griffiths, M.D. (1994b) The observational analysis of marketing methods in UK amusement arcades. *Society for the Study of Gambling Newsletter*, 24, 17–24.

Griffiths, M.D. (1994c) The role of cognitive bias and skill in fruit machine gambling. *British Journal of Psychology*, 85, 351–369.

Griffiths, M.D. (1994d) The role of subjective mood states in the maintenance of gambling behaviour. *Journal of Gambling Studies*, in press.

Griffiths, M.D. (1994e) An exploratory study of gambling cross addictions. *Journal of Gambling Studies*, 10, 371–384.

Griffiths, M.D. (1994f) Co-existent fruit machine addiction and solvent abuse: a cause for concern? *Journal of Adolescence*, 17, 491–498.

Griffiths, M.D. (1995) Technological addictions. *Clinical Psychology Forum*, 76, 14–19.

Griffiths, M.D. and Hunt, N. (1993) The acquisition, development and maintenance of computer game playing in adolescence. Paper presented at the British Psychological Society London Conference, City University, London.

Griffiths, M.D. and Swift, G. (1992) The use of light and colour in gambling arcades: a pilot study. *Society for the Study of Gambling Newsletter*, 21, 16–22.

Haertzen, C.A. (1974) An overview of addiction research center inventory scales. DHEW Publication No. (AOM) 74–92. Washington DC: US Government Printing Office.

Haire, M. and Morrison, F. (1957) School children's perception of labour and management. *Journal of Social Psychology*, 46, 179–197.

Halliday, J. and Fuller, P. (eds) (1974) *The Psychology of Gambling*. London: Allen Lane.

Harkavy, E. (1954) The psychoanalysis of a gambler. *International Journal of Psychoanalysis*, 35, 285.

Harris, H.I. (1964) Gambling addiction in an adolescent male. *Psychoanalytic Quarterly*, 33, 513–525.

Harris, J.L. (1989) A model for treating compulsive gamblers through cognitive-behavioural approaches. *Psychotherapy Patient*, 11, 211–226.

Hayano, D. (1979). Auto-ethnography: paradigms, problems and prospects. *Human Organization*, 38, 99–104.

Hayano, D.M. (1982) *Poker Faces: The Life and Work of Professional Card Players*. Berkeley, CA: University of California Press

Heather, N. (1986) Minimal intervention treatment interventions for problem drinkers. In G. Edwards and D. Gill (eds), *Current Issues in Clinical Psychology*. London: Plenum.

Henslin, J.M. (1967) Craps and magic. *American Journal of Sociology*, 73, 316–330.

Herman, R.D. (1976) *Gamblers and Gambling*. Lexington, MA: Lexington Books.

Hess, H.F. and Diller, J.V. (1969) Motivation for gambling as revealed in the marketing methods of the legitimate gaming industry. *Psychological Reports*, 25, 19–27.

Hickey, J.E., Haertzen, C.A. and Henningfield. J.E. (1986) Simulation of gambling responses on the Addiction Research Center Inventory. *Addictive Behaviours*, 11, 345–349.

Hollander, E., Frenkel, M., Decaria, C., Trungold, S. and Stein, D.J. (1992) Treatment of pathological gambling with clomipramine. *American Journal of Psychiatry,* 149, 710–711.

Holmes, W.F. (1985) Video games: concepts and latent influences (Part I) *F.B.I. Law Enforcement Bulletin*, 54(3), 1–9.

Holohan, C.J. (1982) *Environmental Psychology*. New York: Random House.

Hong, Y.-Y. and Chiu, C.-Y. (1988) Sex, locus of control, and illusion of control in Hong Kong as correlates of gambling involvement. *Journal of Social Psychology*, 128, 667–673.

Huff, G. and Collinson, F. (1987) Young offenders, gambling and video game playing. *British Journal of Criminology*, 27, 401–410.

Huxley, J. (1993) Fruit machine use in adolescents and adult women. Unpublished Ph.D. thesis, University of Birmingham.

Huxley, J. and Carroll, D. (1992) A survey of fruit machine gambling in adolescents. *Journal of Gambling Studies*, 8, 167–179.

Ide-Smith, S. and Lea, S.E.G. (1988) Gambling in young adolescents. *Journal of Gambling Behavior*, 4, 110–118.

Israeli, N. (1935) Outlook of a depressed patient interested in planned gambling. *American Journal of Orthopsychiatry*, 5, 1–23.

Jablonski, B. (1985) Locu de controle e o comportamento de jogar. *Arquivos Brasileiros de Psicologia*, 37, 19–26.

Jacobs, D.F. (1985) A general theory of addictions: a new theoretical model. *Journal of Gambling Behavior,* 1, 15–31.

Jacobs, D.F. (1988) Evidence for a common dissociative-like reaction among addicts. *Journal of Gambling Behavior*, 4, 27–37.

Jacobs, D.F. (1989) Illegal and undocumented: a review of teenage gambling and the plight of children of problem gamblers in America. In H.J. Shaffer, S. Stein, B. Gambino, and T.N. Cummings (eds) *Compulsive Gambling: Theory Research and Practice*. Lexington, MA: D.C. Heath.

Jacobs, D.F. and Kuley, N. (1987) Unpublished research report. Jerry L. Pettis Memorial Veterans Hospital, Lorna Linda, California.

Jacobs, D.F., Pettis, J.L. and Linda, L. (1981) The addictive personality syndrome: a new theoretical model for understanding and treating addictions. In W.R. Eadington (ed.) *The Gambling Papers*, Reno, Nevada: University of Nevada.

Jacobs, D.F., Marston, A.R., Singer, R.D., Widaman, K. and Little, T. (1985) Unpublished research report. Jerry L. Pettis Memorial Veterans Hospital, Lorna Linda, California.

Jacobs, D.F., Marston, A.R., Singer, R.D., Widaman, K. and Little, T. (1987) Unpublished research report. Jerry L. Pettis Memorial Veterans Hospital, Lorna Linda, California.

Jahoda, G. (1979) The construction of economic reality by some Glaswegian children. *European Journal of Social Psychology*, 9, 115–127.

Jahoda, G. (1983) European 'lag' in the development of an economic concept: a study in Zimbabwe. *British Journal of Developmental Psychology*, 1, 110–120.

Jones, E.E. and Nisbett, R.E. (1971) *The Actor and the Observer: Divergent Perceptions of the Causes of Behavior.* Morristown, NJ: General Learning Press.

Kahneman, D. and Tversky, A. (1982) The psychology of preferences. *Scientific American,* January, 136–142.

Kallick, M., Suits, D., Dielman, T. and Hybels, J. (1979) *A Survey of American Gambling Attitudes and Behavior.* Ann Arbor, MI: Institute for Social Research, University of Michigan.

Kallick-Kaufmann, M. (1979) The micro and macro dimensions of gambling in the United States. *Journal of Social Issues*, 35, 7–26.

Karpf, D.A. (1973) Thinking aloud in human discrimination learning (Doctoral dissertation, State University of New York, 1972) *Dissertation Abstracts International*, 33, 6111B.

Kass, N. (1964) Risk in decision making as a function of age, sex, and probability preference. *Child Development*, 35, 577–582.

Kazdin, D.A. (1973) Assessment of imagery during covert modelling of assertive behaviour. *Journal of Behaviour Therapy and Experimental Psychiatry*, 7, 213–219.

Kearney, C.A. and Drabman, R.S. (1992) Risk-taking / gambling-like behavior in pre-school children. *Journal of Gambling Studies*, 287–297.

Kiell, N. (1956) The behaviour of five adolescents while playing poker. *Journal of Human Relations*, 5, 79–89.

Keppel, G., Zavortink, B. and Shiff, B.B. (1967) Unlearning in the A–B, A–C paradigm as a function of percentage occurrence of response members. *Journal of Experimental Psychology,* 74, 172–177.

Knapp, T.J. and Lech, B.C. (1987) Pathological gambling: a review with recommendations. *Advances in Behaviour Research Therapy*, 9, 21–49.

Koller, K. (1972) The gambling addicts vs. the gambling professional. *International Journal of the Addictions*, 7, 387–393.

Kopfstein, D. (1973) Risk-taking behavior and cognitive style. *Child Development*, 44, 190–192.

Kraft, T. (1970) A short note on forty patients treated by systematic desensitization. *Behaviour Research and Therapy*, 8, 219–220.

Kroeber, H. (1992) Roulette gamblers and gamblers at electronic game machines: where are the differences? *Journal of Gambling Studies*, 8, 79–92.

Kuley, N.B. and Jacobs, D.F. (1988) The relationship between dissociative like experience and sensation seeking among social and problem gamblers. *Journal of Gambling Behavior,* 4, 197–207.

Kusyszyn, I. (1972) The gambling addicts vs. the gambling professional. *International Journal of the Addictions*, 7, 387–393.

Kusyszyn, I. (1978) 'Compulsive' gambling: the problem of definition. *International Journal of the Addictions*, 13, 1095–1101.

Kusyszyn, I. (1984) The psychology of gambling. *Annals of American Academy of Political and Social Sciences*, 474, 133–145.

Kusyszyn, I. and Rutter, R. (1978) Personality characteristics of heavy, light, non-gamblers and lottery players. Paper presented at the Fourth Annual Conference on Gambling, Nevada.

Kusyszyn, I. and Rutter, R. (1985) Personality characteristics of heavy gamblers, light gamblers, non-gamblers and lottery players. *Journal of Gambling Behavior,* 1, 59–64.

Ladouceur, R. and Gaboury, A. (1988) Effects of limited and unlimited stakes on gambling behavior. *Journal of Gambling Behavior,* 4, 119–126.

Ladouceur, R. and Mayrand, M. (1986) Characteristiques psychologiques de la prise de risque monetaire des joueurs et des non-joueurs a la roulette. *International Journal of Psychology,* 21, 433–443.

Ladouceur, R. and Mireault, M. (1988) Gambling behaviors among high school students in the Quebec area. *Journal of Gambling Behavior,* 4, 3–12.

Ladouceur, R., Gaboury, A., Dumont, M. and Rochette, P. (1988) Gambling: relationship between the frequency of wins and irrational thinking. *Journal of Psychology,* 122, 409–414.

Ladouceur, R., Tourigny, M. and Mayrand, M. (1986) Familiarity, group exposure, and risk-taking behaviour in gambling. *Journal of Psychology,* 120, 45–49.

Ladouceur, R., Gaboury, A., Bujold, A., Lachance, N. and Tremblay, S. (1991) Ecological validity in laboratory studies of videopoker gaming. *Journal of Gambling Studies,* 7, 109–116.

Langer, E.J. (1975) The illusion of control. *Journal of Personality and Social Psychology,* 32, 311–328.

Langer, E.J. and Roth. J. (1975) The effect of sequence of outcome in a chance task on the illusion of control. *Journal of Personality and Social Psychology,* 32, 951–955.

Laufer, H. (1966) Object loss and mourning during adolescence. *Psychoanalytic Study Child,* 21, 269–293.

Lea, S.E.G., Tarpy, R.M. and Webley, P. (1987) *The Individual in the Economy.* Cambridge: Cambridge University Press.

Leary, K. and Dickerson, M.G. (1985) Levels of arousal in high and low frequency gamblers. *Behaviour Research and Therapy,* 23, 635–640.

Lee, J. (1989) *'It's Good Fun Pressing Buttons': Young People and Fruit and Video Machine Use.* Leeds: Leeds City Council.

Leeds Polytechnic (1989) Cited in J. Long, Playing the Machine: amusement arcade ethics. *Leisure Management,* 9(8), 65–66.

Leppard, D. (1987) Scandal of the child gamblers. *Sunday Times,* 3 May, p.16.

Lesieur, H.R. (1979) The compulsive gambler's spiral of options and involvement. *Psychiatry,* 42, 79–87.

Lesieur, H.R. (1984) *The Chase: Career of the Compulsive Gambler.* Cambridge, MA: Schenkman Books.

Lesieur, H. (1988a) Altering the DSM-III Criteria for pathological gambling. *Journal of Gambling Behavior,* 4, 38–47.

Lesieur, H. (1988b) The female pathological gambler. In W.R. Eadington (ed.) *Gambling Studies: Proceedings of the 7th International Conference on Gambling and Risk Taking.* Reno, Nevada: University of Nevada.

Lesieur, H.R. and Blume, S.B. (1990) Characteristics of pathological gamblers identified among patients on a psychiatric admissions service. *Hospital and Community Psychiatry,* 41, 1009–1012.

Lesieur, H.R. and Blume, S.B. (1991) When lady luck loses: women and compulsive gambling. In N. van den Bergh (ed.) *Feminist Perspectives on Treating Addictions.* New York: Springer.

Lesieur, H.R. and Custer, R.L. (1984) Pathological gambling: roots, phases and treatment. *Annals of the American Academy of Political and Social Sciences*, 474, 146–156.

Lesieur, H.R. and Klein, R. (1987) Pathological gambling amongst high school students. *Addictive Behaviours*, 12, 129–135.

Lesieur, H.R. and Rosenthal, R.J. (1991) Pathological gambling: a review of the literature. *Journal of Gambling Studies*, 7, 5–39.

Lesieur, H.R., Blume, S.B. and Zoppa, R.M. (1986) Alcoholism, drug abuse and gambling. *Alcoholism: Clinical and Experimental Research*, 10, 33–38.

Lesieur, H.R., Cross, J., Frank, M., Welch, C., Rubenstein, G., Moseley, K. and Mark, M. (1991) Gambling and pathological gambling among college students. *Addictive Behaviors*, 16, 517–527.

Lester, D. (1980) The treatment of compulsive gambling. *International Journal of the Addictions*, 15, 201–206.

Lester, D., Arcuri, A.F. and Smith, F. (1985) Impact of gambling at two institutions. *Community College Review*, 12(3), 51–56.

Levison, P.K., Gerstein, D.R. and Maloff, D.R. (eds) (1983) *Commonalities in Substance Abuse and Habitual Behavior*. Lexington, Mass: Lexington Books.

Li, W.L. and Smith, M.H. (1976) The propensity to gamble: some structural determinants. In W.R. Eadington (ed.) *Gambling and Society*. Springfield, Illinois: Charles C.Thomas.

Lieberman, M.A. and Borman, L.D. (1979) *Self Help Groups for Coping with Crisis: Origins, Members, Processes, and Impact*. San Francisco, CA: Jossey-Bass.

Linden, R.D., Jonas, J.M. and Pope, H.G. (1984) Pathological gambling and major affective disorders. Paper presented at the New Research Session of the 137th meeting of the American Psychiatric Association, Los Angeles, CA.

Linden, R.D., Pope, M.G. and Jonas, J.M. (1986) Pathological gambling and major affective disorder: preliminary findings. *Journal of Clinical Psychiatry*, 47, 201–203.

Lindesmith, A., Strauss, A. and Renzin, N. (1975) *Social Psychology*. New York: Holt.

Lindner, R.M. (1950) The psychodynamics of gambling. *Annals of the American Academy of Political and Social Sciences*, 269, 93–107.

Ling, T.N. and Buckman, J. (1963) *Lysergic Acid and Ritalin in the Treatment of Neuroses*. London: Lambarde Press.

Livingston, J. (1974) *Compulsive Gamblers: Observations on Action and Abstinence*. New York: Harper and Row.

Loftus, G.A. and Loftus, E.F. (1983) *Mind at Play: The Psychology of Video Games*. New York: Basic Books.

Logan, H.L. and Berger, E. (1961) Measurement of visual information cues. *Illuminating Engineering*, 56, 393–403.

Lorenz, V.C. and Shuttlesworth, D.E. (1983) The impact of pathological gambling on the spouse of the gambler. *Journal of Community Psychology*, 11, 67–76.

Lorenz, V.C. and Yaffee, R.A. (1986) Pathological gambling: psychosomatic, emotional and marital difficulties as reported by the gambler. *Journal of Gambling Behavior*, 2, 40–45.

Lorenz, V.C. and Yaffee, R.A. (1988) Pathological gambling: psychosomatic, emotional and marital difficulties as reported by the spouse. *Journal of Gambling Behavior*, 4, 13–26.

Lorenz, V.C. and Yaffee, R.A. (1989) Pathological gamblers and their spouses: problems in interaction. *Journal of Gambling Behavior*, 5, 113–126.

Lowenfeld, B.H. (1979) Personality dimensions of the pathological gambler. Ph.D. dissertation, University of Kent State, 1979. *Dissertation Abstracts International*, 40, 456B.

McConaghy, N. (1980) Behaviour completion mechanisms rather than primary drives maintain behavioural patterns. *Activas Nervosa Supplement (Praha)*, 22, 138–151.

McConaghy, N., Armstrong, M.S., Blaszczynski, A. and Allcock, C.C. (1983) Controlled comparison of aversive therapy and imaginal desensitization in compulsive gambling. *British Journal of Psychiatry*, 142, 366–372.

McCormick, R.A. and Taber, J.I. (1991) Follow-up of male pathological gamblers after treatment: the relationship of intellectual variables to relapse. *Journal of Gambling Studies*, 7, 99–108.

McCormick, R.A., Russo, A.M., Ramirez, L.F. and Taber, J.I. (1984) Affective disorders among pathological gamblers seeking treatment. *American Journal of Psychiatry*, 141, 215–218.

McCormick, R.S. and Taber, J.I. (1987) The pathological gambler: salient personality variables. In T. Galski (ed.), *Handbook on Pathological Gambling*. Springfield, Illinois: Charles C. Thomas.

McGlothin, W.H. (1954) A psychometric study of gambling. *Journal of Consulting Psychiatry*, 18, 145–149.

McIlwraith, R., Jacobvitz, R.S., Kubey, R. and Alexander, A. (1991) Television addiction: theories and data behind the ubiquitous metaphor. *American Behavioral Scientist*, 35, 104–121.

McMillan, G.E. (1985) People and gambling. In G. Caldwell, B. Haig, M. Dickerson and L. Sylvan (eds) *Gambling in Australia.* Sydney: Croom Helm.

Maccoby, E.E. and Jacklin, C.N. (1974) *The Psychology of Sex Differences.* Stanford, CA: Stanford University Press.

Malkin, D. (1981). An empirical investigation into some aspects of problem gambling. Unpublished Master's thesis: University of Western Australia.

Malone, T.W. (1981) Toward a theory of intrinsically motivating instruction. *Cognitive Science*, 4, 333–369.

Mandell, H. (1983) Dr. Video: NCTV takes stand on video game violence. *Video Games,* February, 97–98.

Marcum, J. and Rowen, H. (1974) How many games in town? – The pros and cons of legalized gambling. *Public Interest*, 36, 26–52.

Markham, R. (1990) Psychiatric nursing and the young problem gambler. *U.K. Forum on Young People and Gambling Newsletter*, 1, 6–7.

Marlatt, G.A. and Gordon, J.R. (eds) (1985) *Relapse Prevention Maintenance Strategies in the Treatment of Addictive Behaviors.* New York: Guilford.

Marlatt, G.A., Baer, J.S., Donovan, D.M. and Kivlahan, D.R. (1988) Addictive behaviors: etiology and treatment. *Annual Review of Psychology*, 39, 223–252.

Marshall, H. and Magruder, L. (1960) Relations between parent money education practices and children's knowledge and uses of money. *Child Development*, 32, 337–338.

Massaro, D.W. (1990) Book review of 'Paradoxes of Gambling Behaviour' by Willem Wagenaar. *American Journal of Psychology*, 103, 290–297.

Matussek, P. (1953) On the psychodynamics of a gambler. *Journal of Psychology and Psychotherapy*, 1, 232–252.

Maurer, C.D. (1985) An outpatient approach to the treatment of pathological gambling. In W.R. Eadington (ed.) *The Gambling Studies: Proceedings of the Sixth International Conference on Gambling and Risk Taking*, 5, 205–217.

Mayne, B. and Tyreman-Wilde, M. (1993) *Playing the Game: A Study of the Attitudes, Perceptions and Behaviours Related to Machine Playing and Gambling*. Swansea: Author.

Mehrabian, A. and Russell, J.A. (1974) The basic emotional impact of environments. *Perceptual and Motor Skills*, 38, 283–301.

Mendelson, J.H. and Mello, N.K. (eds) (1979) *The Diagnosis and Treatment of Alcoholism*. New York: McGraw-Hill.

Milkman, H. and Sunderworth, S. (1983) The chemistry of craving. *Psychology Today*, 17, 36–44.

Miller, L. and Horn, T. (1955) Children's concepts regarding debt. *Elementary School Journal*, 55, 406–412.

Miller, P.M. (1976) *Behavioural Treatment of Alcoholism*. New York: Pergamon.

Miller, P.M. (1980) Cited in H. Milkman and S. Sunderworth, The chemistry of craving. *Psychology Today*, 17, 36–44 (1983)

Miller, P.M. and Mastria, M.A. (1977) *Alternatives to Alcohol Abuse: A Social Learning Model*. Champaign, Illinois: Research Press.

Miller, W.R. (ed.) (1980) *The Addictive Behaviors*. Oxford: Pergamon Press.

Miller, W.R. and Rollnick, S. (1991) *Motivational Interviewing: Preparing People to Change Addictive Behavior*. New York: Guildford Press.

Miller, W.R., Gribskov, C. and Mortell, R. (1981) The effectiveness of a self-control manual for problem drinkers with and without therapist contact. *International Journal of the Addictions*, 16, 829–839.

Mobilia, P. (1993) Gambling as a rational addiction. *Journal of Gambling Studies*, 9, 121–151.

Mok, W.P. and Hraba, J. (1991) Age and gambling behavior: a declining and shifting pattern of participation. *Journal of Gambling Studies*, 7, 313–335.

Montgomery, H.R. and Kreitzer, S. (1968) 'Compulsive' gambling and behaviour therapy. Paper presented at the California State Psychological Association Convention, Santa Barbara, CA.

Moody, G. (1987) Parents of Young Gamblers. Paper presented at the seventh International Conference on Gambling and Risk Taking, Reno, Nevada, July.

Moody, G. (1989) Parents of young gamblers. *Journal of Gambling Behaviour*, 5, 313–320.

Moody, G. 1990) *Quit Compulsive Gambling*. London: Thorsons.

Moran, E. (1967) The problem of gambling. *Psychotherapy and Psychosomatics*, 15, 47–48.

Moran, E. (1969) Taking the final risk. *Mental Health* (London), 21–22.

Moran, E. (1970a) Clinical and social aspects of risk taking. *Proceedings of the Royal Society of Medicine*, 63, 1273–1277.

Moran, E. (1970b) Gambling as a form of dependence. *British Journal of Addiction*, 64, 419–428.

Moran, E. (1970c) Pathological gambling. *British Journal of Psychiatry*, 4, 59–70.

Moran, E. (1970d) Varieties of pathological gambling. *British Journal of Psychiatry*, 116, 593–597.

Moran, E. (1987) *Gambling Among Schoolchildren: the Impact of the Fruit Machine*. London: National Council on Gambling.

Moravec, J.D. and Munley, P.H. (1983) Psychological test findings on pathological gamblers in treatment. *International Journal of the Addictions,* 18, 1003–1009.

Morehead, A. (1950) The professional gambler. *Annals of the American Academy of Political and Social Sciences,* 269, 81–82.

Morris, K.P. (1957) An exploratory study of some personality characteristics of gamblers. *Journal of Clinical Psychology,* 13, 191–193.

Moskowitz, J. (1980) Lithium and Lady Luck. *New York State Journal of Medicine,* 80, 785–788.

Mule, S.J. (ed.) (1981) *Behavior in Excess: an Examination of the Volitional Disorders.* New York: Free Press.

National Housing and Town Planning Council (1988) *The Use of Amusement Arcades: a National Survey.* London: Author.

National Housing and Town Planning Council (1989) *Gambling Machines and Young People.* London: Author.

Newell, A. and Simon, H.A. (1972) *Human Problem Solving.* Englewood Cliffs, NJ: Prentice-Hall.

Nickel, D. (1975) Ski-ing as a natural high. *Journal of Drug Education,* 5, 159–160.

Niederland, W.G. (1967) A contribution to the psychology of gambling. *Psycho-analytic Forum,* 2, 175–185.

Nisbett, R.E. and Wilson, T.D. (1977) Telling more than we can know: verbal reports on mental processes. *Psychological Review,* 84, 231–259.

Nora, R. (1984) Profile survey on pathological gamblers. Paper presented at the Sixth National Conference on Gambling and Risk Taking, Atlantic City, NJ, December.

Nora, R. (1989) Inpatient treatment programs for pathological gamblers. In H.J. Shaffer, S. Stein, B. Gambino and T.N. Cummings (eds) *Compulsive Gambling: Theory, Research and Practice.* Lexington, MA: D.C. Heath.

Ocean, G. and Smith, G.J. (1993) Social reward, conflict, and commitment: a theoretical model of gambling behaviour. *Journal of Gambling Studies,* 9, 321–339.

Odbert, H.S., Karwoski, T.F. and Eckerson, A.B. (1942) Studies in synesthetic thinking: I. Musical and verbal associations of colour and mood. *Journal of General Psychology,* 26, 153–173.

Oldman, D. (1974) Chance and skill: a study of roulette. *Sociology,* 8, 407–426.

Opie, I. and Opie, P. (1969) *Children's Games in Street and Playground.* Oxford: Oxford University Press.

Orford, J. (1985) *Excessive Appetites: a Psychological View of Addictions.* Chichester: Wiley.

Orford, J. (1988) Pathological gambling and its treatment. *British Medical Journal,* 296, 729–730.

Oster, S. and Knapp, T.J. (1994) Casino gambling by underage patrons: two studies of a university population. Paper presented at the Ninth International Conference on Gambling and Risk Taking, Las Vegas, Nevada, June.

Payne, J.W., Braunstein, M.L. and Carroll, J.S. (1978) Exploring predecisional behavior: an alternative approach to decision research. *Organizational Behavior and Human Performance,* 22, 17–44.

Peck, D.F. and Ashcroft, J.B. (1972) The use of stimulus satiation in the modification of habitual gambling. Proceedings of the second British and European Association Conference on Behaviour Modification, Kilkenny, Ireland.

Peele, S. (1979) Redefining addiction II: The meaning of addiction in our lives. *Journal of Psychedelic Drugs*, 11, 289–297.

Perkins, D.N. (1979) A primer on introspection. Paper presented at the American Theatre Association Convention, New York.

Perkins, E.B. (1950) Cited in Cornish, D.B. (1978) *Gambling: A Review of the Literature and its Implications for Policy and Research*. London: HMSO.

Politzer, R.M., Morrow, J.S. and Leavey, S.B. (1985) Report on the cost / benefit effectiveness of treatment at the Johns Hopkins Center for Pathological Gambling. *Journal of Gambling Behavior*, 1, 131–142.

Pratt, M., Maltzman, I., Hauprich, W. and Ziskind, E. (1982) Electrodermal activity of sociopaths and controls in the pressor test. *Psychophysiology*, 19, 342.

Preston, F. and Smith, R. (1985) Delabeling and relabeling in Gamblers Anonymous: problems with transferring the alcoholic paradigm. *Journal of Gambling Behavior*, 1, 97–105.

Prochaska, J.O. and DiClimente, C.C. (1982) Transtheoretical therapy: toward a more integrative model of change. *Psychotherapy: Theory, Research and Practice*, 19, 276–288.

Pruitt, D.G. and Teger, A.I. (1969) The risky shift in group settings. *Journal of Personality and Social Psychology*, 20, 339–360.

Rachlin, H. (1990) Why do people gamble and keep gambling despite heavy losses. *Psychological Science*, 1, 294–297.

Rands, J. and Hooper, M. (1990) Survey of young people's use of slot machines within the Sedgemoor District in conjunction with Somerset Youth Association. Unpublished manuscript.

Rankin, H. (1982) Control rather than abstinence as a goal in the treatment of excessive gambling. *Behavioural Research Therapy*, 20, 185–87.

Reid, R.L. (1986) The psychology of the near miss. *Journal of Gambling Behavior*, 2, 32–39.

Reider, N. (1960) Percept as a screen: economic and structural aspects. *Journal of the American Psychoanalytic Association*, 8, 82–99.

Riley, D. and Shaw, M. (1985) *Parental Supervision and Juvenile Delinquency*. Home Office Research Study No. 83. London: HMSO.

Rosecrance, J. (1985) Compulsive gambling and the medicalization of deviance. *Social Problems*, 32, 275–284.

Rosecrance, J. (1986) 'The next best thing': a study of problem gambling. *International Journal of the Addictions*, 20 (11 and 12), 1727–1739.

Rosenstein, J. and Reutter, R. (1980) Gambling: an adolescent activity. *Journal of Adolescent Health Care*, 1 (2), 180.

Rosenthal, R.J. (1989) Compulsive gambling. Paper presented at the California Society for the Treatment of Alcoholism and Other Drug Dependencies, San Diego, November.

Rosenthal, R.J. and Rugle, L.J. (1994) A psychodynamic approach to the treatment of pathological gambling: Part I. Achieving abstinence. *Journal of Gambling Studies*, 10, 21–65.

Roth, B. (1966) The effect of overt verbalization on problem solving (Doctoral Dissertation, New York University, 1965) *Dissertation Abstracts*, 27, 957B.

Roy, A., De Jong, J. and Linnoila, M. (1989) Extraversion in pathological gamblers: correlates with indexes of noradrenergic function. *Archives of General Psychiatry*, 46, 679–681.

Roy, A., Adinoff, B., Roerich, L., Custer, R., Lorenz, V. and Linnoila, M. (1987) A search for biological substrates to pathological gambling. Paper presented at the Seventh International Conference on Gambling and Risk Taking, Reno, Nevada, August.

Roy, A., Adinoff, B., Roerich, L., Lamparski, D., Custer, R., Lorenz, V., Barbaccia, M., Guidotti, A., Costa, E. and Linnoila, M. (1988) Pathological gambling: a psychobiological study. *Archives of General Psychiatry*, 45, 369–373.

Royal Commission on Gambling (1951) *Report of the Royal Commission on Betting Lotteries and Gaming 1949–1951.* London: HMSO.

Rule, B.G. and Fischer, D.G. (1970) Impulsivity, subjective probability, cardiac response and risk taking: correlates and factors. *Personality*, 1, 251–260.

Rule, B.G., Nutler, R.W. and Fischer, D.G. (1971) The effect of arousal on risk-taking. *Personality*, 2, 239–247.

Russo, A.M., Taber, J.I., McCormick, R.A. and Ramirez, L.F. (1984) An outcome study of an inpatient treatment program for pathological gamblers. *Hospital and Community Psychiatry*, 35, 823–827.

Salzmann, M.M. (1982) Treatment of compulsive gambling. Letter to the *British Journal of Psychiatry*, 141, 318–319.

Saunders, D.M. (1979) Aspects of schedule control within a gambling environment. Unpublished M.Sc. thesis, University of Exeter, Devon.

Schatzman, L. and Strauss, A.L. (1973) *Field Research: Strategies for a Natural Sociology.* Englewood Cliffs, NJ: Prentice Hall.

Scheibe, K.E. and Erwin, M. (1979) The computer as altar. *Journal of Social Psychology*, 108, 103–109.

Schwarz, J. and Lindner, A. (1992) Inpatient treatment of male pathological gamblers in Germany. *Journal of Gambling Studies*, 8, 93–109.

Scimecca, J.A. (1971) A typology of the gambler. *International Journal of Contemporary Sociology*, 8, 56–72.

Scodel, A. (1964) Inspirational group therapy: a study of Gamblers Anonymous. *American Journal of Psychotherapy*, 18, 115–125.

Seager, C.P. (1970) Treatment of compulsive gamblers by electrical aversion. *British Journal of Psychiatry*, 117, 545–553.

Selnow, G.W. (1984) Playing video games: the electronic friend. *Journal of Communication*, 34, 148–156.

Shaffer, H. and Burglass, M. (1981) *Classic Contributions in the Addictions.* New York: Brunner–Mazel.

Sharma, B.P. (1970) Gambling and gamblers in Nepal. *Israel Annual Journal of Psychiatry and Related Disciplines*, 8, 137–142.

Shubin, S. (1977) The compulsive gambler. *Today Psychiatry*, 3, 1–3.

Simmel, E. (1920) Psychoanalysis of the gambler. *International Journal of Psychoanalysis*, 1, 352–355.

Skinner, B.F. (1953) *Science and Human Behaviour.* New York: Free Press.

Skolnick, J. (1978) *House of Cards.* Boston: Little Brown.

Slovic, P. (1966) Risk-taking in children: age and sex differences. *Child Development*, 37, 169–175.

Smith, D.N. and Miller, F.D. (1978) Limits on perception of cognitive processes: a reply to Nisbett and Wilson. *Psychological Review*, 85. 355–362.

Snyder, R.J. (1986) Gambling swindles and victims. *Journal of Gambling Behavior*, 2, 50–57.

Snyder, S. (1975) Opiate receptors in normal and altered brain function. *Nature*, 257, 185–189.

Sommers, I. (1988) Pathological gambling: estimating prevalence and group characteristics. *International Journal of the Addictions*, 23, 477–490.

Spectrum Children's Trust (1988) *Slot Machine Playing by Children: Results of a Survey in Taunton and Minehead*. London: author.

Spradley, J.P. (1980) *Participant Observation*. New york: Holt, Rinehart & Winston.

Stacey, B.G. (1978) *Political Socialization in Western Society*. London: Edward Arnold.

Stark, G.M., Saunders, D.M. and Wookey, P. (1982) Differential effects of red and blue lighting on gambling behaviour. *Current Psychological Research*, 2, 95–100.

Steinberg, M.A. (1988) Unpublished research report. Connecticut Council on Compulsive Gambling, Hamden, Connecticut.

Steinberg, M.A. (1993) Couples treatment issues for recovering male compulsive gamblers and their partners. *Journal of Gambling Studies*, 9, 153–167.

Stevens, W.R. and Foxwell, C.A.P. (1955) Visual acuity. *Light and Lighting*, 48, 419–424.

Stewart, R.M. and Brown, R.I.F. (1988) An outcome study of Gamblers Anonymous. *British Journal of Psychiatry*, 152, 284–288.

Strauss, A. (1952) The development and transformation of monetary meanings in the child. *American Sociological Review*, 17, 275–286.

Strickland, L.H. and Grote, F.W. (1967) Temporal presentation of winning symbols and slot machine playing. *Journal of Experimental Psychology*, 74, 10–13.

Strickland, L.H., Lewicki, R.J. and Katz, A.M. (1966) Temporal orientation and perceived control as determinants of risk-taking. *Journal of Experimental and Social Psychology*, 2, 143–151.

Stumphauzer, J.S. (1980) Learning to drink: adolescents and alcohol. *Addictive Behaviors*, 5, 277–283.

Surrey, D. (1982) 'It's like good training for life'. *Natural History*, 91, 71–83.

Sutton-Smith, B. (1972) *The Folk-Games of Children*. Austin, Texas: University of Texas Press.

Svendsen, R. (1994) Two year summary of the Minnesota Compulsive Gambling Hotline and public awareness projects. Paper presented at the Ninth International Conference on Gambling and Risk Taking, Las Vegas, Nevada, June.

Taber, J.I. (1979) The Breckville inpatient program for pathological gamblers: current directions. Paper presented at the eighty-seventh Annual Meeting of the American Psychological Association, New York, September.

Taber, J.I. (1981) Group psychotherapy with pathological gamblers. Paper presented at the Fifth National Conference on Gambling and Risk Taking, South Lake Tahoe, Nevada, October.

Taber, J.I. and Chaplin, M.P. (1988) Group psychotherapy with pathological gamblers. *Journal of Gambling Behavior*, 4, 183–196.

Taber, J.I., McCormick, R.A. and Ramirez, L.F. (1987) The prevalence and impact of major life stressors among pathological gamblers. *International Journal of the Addictions*, 22, 71–79.

Taber, J.I., Russo, A.M., Adkins, B.J. and McCormick, R.A. (1986) Ego strength and achievement motivation in pathological gamblers. *Journal of Gambling Behavior*, 2, 69–80.

Tan, H.K.R. and Stacey, B.G. (1981) The understanding of socio-economic concepts in Malaysian Chinese school children. *Child Study Journal*, 11, 33–49.

Tepperman, J.H. (1977) The effectiveness of short term group therapy upon the pathological gambler and wife. Ph.D. dissertation, California School of Professional Psychology, Los Angeles, *Dissertation Abstracts International*, 37, 583B.

Tepperman, J.H. (1985) The effectiveness of short term group therapy upon the pathological gambler and wife. *Journal of Gambling Behavior*, 1, 119–130.

Thompson, W.N. (1991) Machismo: manifestations of a cultural value in the Latin American casino. *Journal of Gambling Studies*, 7, 143–164.

Toneatto, T. and Sobell, L.C. (1990) Pathological gambling treated with cognitive behaviour therapy: a case report. *Addictive Behaviors*, 15, 497–501.

Trinkaus, J.W. (1983) Arcade video games: an informal look. *Psychological Reports*, 52, 586.

Trott, J. and Griffiths, M.D. (1991) Teenage gambling: a pilot study. *Psychological Reports*, 68, 946.

Tune, G. (1964) Response preferences: a review of some relevant literature. *Psychological Bulletin*, 61, 286–302.

Turner, D.N. and Saunders, D. (1990) Medical relabeling in Gamblers Anonymous: the construction of the ideal member. *Small Group Research*, 21, 59–78.

Tversky, A. and Kahneman, D. (1971) Belief in the law of small numbers. *Psychological Bulletin*, 76, 105–110.

Tversky, A. and Kahneman, D. (1973) Availability: a heuristic for judging frequency and probability. *Cognitive Psychology*, 5, 207–233.

Unrah, D. (1983) *Invisible Lives: Social Worlds of the Aged*. Beverly Hills: Sage.

Van Ree, J.M. (1983) Neuropeptides and addictive behaviour. *Alcohol and Alcoholism*, 18, 325–333.

Victor, R. and Krug, G. (1967) 'Paradoxical Intention' in the treatment of compulsive gambling. *American Journal of Psychotherapy*, 21, 808–814.

Volberg, R.A. and Steadman, H.J. (1988) Refining prevalence estimates of pathological gambling. *American Journal of Psychiatry*, 145, 502–505.

Volberg, R.A. and Steadman, H.J. (1989) Prevalence estimates of pathological gambling in New Jersey and Maryland. *American Journal of Psychiatry*, 146, 1618–1619.

Wagenaar, W.A. (1988) *Paradoxes of Gambling Behavior*. London: Erlbaum.

Walker, G. (1985) The brief therapy of a compulsive gambler. *Journal of Family Therapy*, 7, 1–8.

Walker, M.B. (1989) Some problems with the concept of 'gambling addiction': should theories of addiction be generalized to include excessive gambling? *Journal of Gambling Behavior*, 5, 179–200.

Walker, M.B. (1992a) Irrational thinking among slot machine players. *Journal of Gambling Studies*, 8, 245–261.

Walker, M.B. (1992b) *The Psychology of Gambling*. Oxford: Pergamon.

Wallach, M.A., Kogan, N. and Bem, D.J. (1964) Diffusion of responsibility and level of risk-taking in groups. *Journal of Abnormal and Social Psychology*, 68, 263–274.

Walton, F. (1990) *A Research Study on Young People and Gambling in Blackpool*. Blackpool: Author.

Waterman, J. and Atkin, K. (1985) Young people and fruit machines. *Society for the Study of Gambling Newsletter*, 7, 23–25.

Webley, P. and Webley, E. (1990) The playground economy. In S.E.G. Lea, P. Webley and B. Young (eds) *Applied Economic Psychology in the 1990s, Vol.2..* Exeter, Devon: Washington Singer Press.

Weinstein, D. and Deitch, L. (1974) *The Impact of Legalized Gambling.* New York: Praeger.

Wexner, L.B. (1954) The degree to which colors (hues) are associated with mood tones. *Journal of Applied Psychology*, 38, 432–435.

White, S. (1989) Against the odds. *Young People Now*, April, 26–27.

Whitman, G.W., Fuller, N.P. and Taber, J.I. (1987) Patterns of polyaddictions in alcoholism patients and high school students. In W.R. Eadington (ed.) *Research in Gambling: Proceedings of the Seventh International Conference on Gambling and Risk Taking.* Reno, Nevada: University of Nevada Press.

Wildman, R.W. (1989) Pathological gambling: marital-familial factors, implications and treatment. *Jounal of Gambling Behavior*, 5, 37–40.

Wilson, G.D. (1966) Arousal properties of red versus green. *Perceptual and Motor Skills*, 23, 947–949.

Winters, K.C., Stinchfield, R. and Fulkerson, J. (1993a) Patterns and characteristics of adolescent gambling. *Journal of Gambling Studies*, 9, 371–386.

Winters, K.C., Stinchfield, R. and Fulkerson, J. (1993b) Toward the development of an adolescent gambling severity scale. *Journal of Gambling Studies*, 9, 63–84.

Wolkowitz, O.M., Roy, A. and Doran, A.R. (1985) Pathological gambling and other risk-taking pursuits. *Psychiatric Clinics of North. America*, 8, 311–322.

Wolpe, J.C. (1958) *Psychotherapy by Reciprocal Inhibition.* Stanford: Stanford University Press.

Wong, G. (1980) The obsessional aspects of compulsive gambling. Paper presented to the Society for the Study of Gambling. Cited in M. Dickerson, *Compulsive Gamblers*, London: Longman, 1984.

Wray, I. and Dickerson, M.G. (1981) Cessation of high frequency gambling and 'withdrawal' symptoms. *British Journal of Addiction*, 76, 401–405.

Wyatt, W. (1988a) Survey on young people and gambling. The Children's Society Youth Link Project. Unpublished manuscript.

Wyatt, W. (1988b) Gambling and school children: a survey by Youth Link. The Children's Society Youth Link Project. Unpublished manuscript.

Zimmerman, M.A., Meeland, T. and Krug, S.E. (1985) Measurement and structure of pathological gambling behaviour. *Journal of Personality Assessment*, 49, 76–81.

Zuckerman, M. (1979) *Sensation Seeking: Beyond the Optimal Level of Arousal.* Hillsdale, NJ: LEA Inc Publishers.

Zuckerman, M. (1984) Sensation seeking: a comparative approach to a human trait. *Behavioural and Brain Sciences*, 413–471.

Name index

Abt, V. 3, 29, 47, 49, 50, 197
Acking, C.A. 206
Adcock, S. 26, 160, 254
Adkins, B.J. *et al.* 15, 82, 213
Allcock, C.C. 4, 7, 13, 15, 212, 220
Amati, B.H. 34, 35, 36, 49
Amsel, A. 12, 23, 201
Anderson, G. 13, 17, 26, 28, 30, 81,
 94, 131, 159, 162, 178, 247
Antia, C. 215
Arcuri, A.F. *et al.* 3, 34, 36, 38, 40, 73
Arenson, A.J. 50
Ashcroft, J.B. 225
Ashdown, J. 56, 66, 102
Atkin, K. 56, 60, 61, 66, 70

Bannister, G. 230–1
Barham, B. 56, 58, 59, 66, 71, 72,
 102, 117, 256
Barker, J.K. 212, 221, 222
Bauer, R.H. 44
Beck, A. 232
Beck, E.A. 27
Bellaire, W. 214
Bellringer, P. 235
Bentall, R.P. *et al.* 56, 57, 66, 68, 96
Berger, E. 206
Bergler, E. 3, 6, 10, 11, 211, 212
Berti, A. *et al.* 46
Bijou, S.W. 12
Birren, F. 205, 206
Blackman, S. *et al.* 214
Blaszczynski, A.P. 13, 19, 20, 25, 27,
 28, 94, 223, 224, 226, 239

Blume, S.B. 21
Bolen, D.W. 9, 11, 15, 27, 214, 215,
 232
Borman, L.D. 213
Bornstein, M.H. 205
Boyce, P.R. 205, 207
Boyd, W. 17, 18, 247
Boyd, W.H. 9, 11, 232
Boyd, W.J. 9, 214, 215
Braun, C.M.J. *et al.* 65
Brooks, B.D. 65
Brown, R.I.F. 13, 17, 22, 26, 29, 30,
 31, 32, 44, 56, 67, 81, 94, 131, 159,
 162, 167, 178, 179, 189, 215, 218,
 218–19, 239, 240, 247, 249, 251,
 253, 254, 260
Browne, B. 9
Burgess, R.G. 98, 99
Burglass, M. 3

Caldwell, G. 110, 205, 207
Callois, R. 47, 48
Cameron, B. 14
Capaldi, E.J. 12
Carlton, P.L. 15, 16, 149
Carr, S.J. 206, 207
Carroll, D. 14, 26, 56, 67, 68, 69, 70,
 71, 72, 128, 133, 248, 253
Caspari, D. 214
Chaplin, M.P. 212
Chiu, C.-Y. 14
Ciarrocchi, J.W. 216
Collinson, F. 56, 57, 63, 66, 72, 82,
 256, 259

Comess, L. 10, 212
Comings, D.E. *et al.* 16
Conklin, H.C. 98
Cormack, M.A. 220
Cormell, M. 56, 58, 59, 66, 71, 72, 102, 117, 256
Corney, W.J. 23, 24
Cornish, D.B. 1, 2, 4, 30, 46, 196, 197, 198, 199, 200, 202, 208, 209, 210
Costa, N. 122, 128, 199, 207
Cotler, S.B. 221, 222
Coulombe, A. *et al.* 26, 248
Craig, R.J. 27
Cromer, G. 217
Csikszentmihalyi, M. 47
Culleton, R.P. 2, 3
Cummings, C. *et al.* 233
Cummings, S. 46
Cummings, W.T. 23, 24
Custer, L.F. 8, 20, 21
Custer, Robert L. 3, 4, 6, 8, 9, 11, 20, 21, 27, 92, 187, 213, 214, 216, 244

Dabbs, J.M. 206, 207
Daley, K. 143
Danzinger, K. 45
Darvas, S. 214
Deitch, L. 3, 196, 198, 204
Dell, L.J. *et al.* 14, 44, 45
Deverensky, J. *et al.* 37, 43
Devereux, E.C. 2
Devinney, R.B. 14
Dickerson, M.G. 3, 12, 13, 26, 27, 30, 131, 160, 167, 178, 219, 220, 225, 226, 235, 239, 247, 254
DiClemente, C.C. 233
Dielman, T.E. 3
Diller, J.V. 122, 128, 198, 205
Dominick, J.R. 65
Dostoevsky, F.M. 10
Douglas, C. 22
Drabman, R.S. 50, 51

Eadington, W.R. 29
Edworthy, J. *et al.* 205
Eissler, K.R. 211, 235
Ellis, A. 230
Emery, G. 232

Ericsson, K.A. 132, 133, 144, 229
Erwin, M. 68, 110
Estes, W. 24
Eysenck, H.G. 206
Eysenck, M. 132
Eysenck, S.B.G. 27

Fink, H.K. 6
Fischer, D.G. 17
Fisher, Sue 52, 54, 56, 57, 61, 62, 64, 67, 69, 70, 71, 72, 73, 82, 97, 102, 128, 145, 146, 169, 203, 207, 248, 253, 259, 260; psychosocial typology of fruit machine gamblers 111–16
Fitchett, S.M. 214, 222
Fox, K. 46
Foxwell, C.A.P. 205
Frank, M.L. 37, 40, 42, 51
Frankl, V. 235
Franklin, J. 213, 214
Freud, S. 10, 47
Frey, J.H. 3, 30
Fuller, P. 1
Furnham, A. 21, 45, 46

Gaboury, A. 20, 21, 22, 94, 143
Galdston, I. 11
Gerner, R.H. *et al.* 19
Gilovich, T. 21, 22, 23, 24, 94, 143
Glass, C.D. 14
Glen, Alida M. 15, 213
Goethe, J.W. von 206
Goffman, E. 21, 47
Gold, R.L. 98
Goldstein, L. *et al.* 15
Goorney, A.B. 221
Gordon, J.R. 227
Gossop, M.R. 27
Grace, D.M. 7
Graham, J.R. 15, 56, 57, 58, 59, 60, 62, 63, 64, 65, 66, 71, 72, 82, 96, 102, 243, 259
Greenberg, D. 12, 224
Greenberg, M. 12
Greenlees, E.M. 121, 127, 205
Greenson, R.R. 3, 10, 20, 211
Grichting, W.L. 2
Griffiths, F.V. 234

Grote, F.W. 201

Haertzen, C.A. 27
Haire, M. 46
Halliday, J. 1
Harkavy, E. 212
Harris, H.I. 11, 44, 212
Harris, J.L. 227, 233, 238
Hayano, D.M. 29, 98
Heather, N. 219
Henslin, J.M. 21, 24
Herman, R.D. 1, 47
Hess, H.F. 122, 128, 198, 205
Hickey, J.E. *et al.* 27, 81
Hinchy, J. 3
Hollander, E. *et al.* 239
Holmes, W.F. 199
Holohan, C.J. 206
Hong, Y.-Y. 14
Hooper, M. 56, 65, 67, 68, 71, 72, 96, 256
Horn, T. 46
Hraba, J. 42
Huff, G. 56, 57, 63, 66, 72, 82, 256, 259
Hunt, N. 61, 260
Huxley, J. 14, 26, 56, 67, 68, 69, 70, 71, 72, 128, 248, 253

Ide-Smith, S. 2, 34, 37, 39, 40, 49, 53, 56, 58, 66, 197
Israeli, N. 10, 20

Jablonski, B. 14
Jacobs, D.F. 13, 27, 28, 34, 36, 40, 42, 45
Jahoda, G. 45, 47
Jones, E.E. 24

Kahneman, D. 23, 24, 201
Kallick, M. *et al.* 2, 3, 42
Kallick-Kaufmann, M. 3
Karpf, D.A. 133
Kass, N. 50
Kazdin, D.A. 133
Kearney, C.A. 50, 51
Keppel, G. *et al.* 12
Kiell, N. 43
Klein, R. 34, 36, 38, 39, 42, 45, 73, 169

Knapp, T.J. 3, 4, 15, 37, 42, 43
Koller, K. 13, 68, 222
Kopfstein, D. 50
Kraft, T. 225
Kreitzer, S. 225
Kroeber, H. 250
Krug, G. 234
Kuley, N.B. 13, 28, 36, 40, 45
Kuller, R. 206
Kusyszyn, I. 6, 7, 14, 45, 47

Ladouceur, R. 2, 13, 14, 21, 22, 34, 37, 39, 42, 94, 131, 134, 143, 169
Lang, R.P. 2
Langer, E.J. 21, 22, 23, 82, 142, 202
Laufer, H. 212
Lea, S.E.G. 1, 2, 12, 13, 34, 37, 39, 40, 49, 53, 56, 58, 66, 197
Leary, K. 26, 131, 167, 178, 247, 254
Lech, B.C. 3, 4, 15
Lee, J. 56, 57, 67
Lesieur, H.R. 3, 4, 5, 6, 8, 9, 15, 21, 27, 29, 31, 32, 34, 36, 37, 38, 39, 40, 41, 42, 43, 45, 73, 82, 92, 169, 187, 214
Lester, D. 38, 215, 221, 222
Levison, P.K. *et al.* 26
Lewis, A. 21
Li, W.L. 42
Lieberman, M.A. 213
Linden, R.D. *et al.* 20
Lindesmith, A. *et al.* 98
Lindner, A. 214
Lindner, R.M. 211
Livingston, J. 7, 14, 20, 217
Loftus, G.A. and E.F. 23, 52
Logan, H.L. 205
Lorenz, V.C. 44, 45, 214
Lowenfeld, B.H. 15, 27

McConaghy, N. 13, 20, 222, 223, 224
McCormick, R.A. 15, 20, 158, 178, 214, 243
McCormick, R.S. 15
McGlothin, W.H. 14
McIlwraith, R. *et al.* 251
McIntyre, S.C. 27
McMillan, G.E. 2
Magruder, L. 46

Malkin, D. 14
Manowitz, P. 16, 149
Marcum, J. 3
Markham, R. 179, 189
Marlatt, G.A. 26, 227, 233, 251
Marshall, H. 46
Massaro, D.W. 24
Mastria, M.A. 240
Matussek, P. 211
Maurer, C.D. 214, 227, 228
Mayne, B. 56, 57, 67
Mayrand, M. 13, 14
Mehrabian, A. 206
Mello, N.K. 45
Mendelson, J.H. 45
Milkman, H. 27
Miller, F.D. 132
Miller, L. 46
Miller, M. 212, 221, 222
Miller, P.M. 26, 240
Miller, W.R. 189, 219, 232, 233, 251
Milt, H. 214, 216
Mireault, M. 34, 37, 39, 42, 169
Mobilia, P. 29
Mok, W.P. 42
Montgomery, H.R. 225
Moody, G. 3, 52, 53, 73, 179, 189, 216, 219, 252
Moran, E. 4, 6, 7, 8, 13, 14, 20, 27, 29, 52, 53, 54, 55, 59, 61, 200, 250, 255, 256
Moravec, J.D. 14, 15
Morris, K.P. 14
Morrison, F. 46
Moskowitz, J. 19, 239
Mule, S.J. 26
Munley, P.H. 14, 15
Myers, J.L. 14

Newell, A. 133
Nickel, D. 249
Niederland, W.G. 10
Nisbett, R.E. 24, 131, 132, 133
Nora, R. 21, 213

Ocean, G. 29
Odbert, H.S. *et al.* 206
Oldman, D. 22, 29
Opie, I. and P. 48

Orford, J. 26, 239, 251
Oster, S. 37, 42, 43

Payne, J.W. *et al.* 132, 133
Peck, D.F. 225
Peele, S. 26
Perkins, D.N. 133
Perkins, E.B. 1
Politzer, R.M. *et al.* 214
Pratt, M. *et al.* 19
Preston, F. 217
Prochaska, J.O. 233
Pruitt, D.G. 44

Rachlin, H. 26, 251
Rands, J. 56, 65, 67, 68, 71, 72, 96, 256
Rankin, H. 224, 226, 235
Reid, R.L. 12, 22, 23, 147, 200, 201
Reider, N. 212
Reinert, D.F. 216
Reutter, R. 34, 35, 36
Richardson, R. 213, 214
Riley, D. 63
Robertson, S. 56, 67
Rollnick, W.R. 189, 232, 233
Rosecrance, J. 3, 8, 29, 98
Rosenstein, J. 34, 35, 36
Rosenthal, R.J. 3, 5, 6, 9, 11, 15, 20, 27, 212
Roth, J. 22, 133
Rowen, H. 3
Roy, A. *et al.* 16
Rugle, L.J. 11, 212
Rule, B.G. 17
Russell, J.A. 206
Russo, A.M. *et al.* 214
Rutter, R. 14

Salzman, M.M. 221, 222
Sandford, D.A. 214, 222
Saunders, D.M. 12, 217
Schatzman, L. 100
Scheibe, K.E. 68, 110
Schwarz, J. 214
Scimecca, J.A. 6
Scodel, A. 215, 217
Seager, C.P. 13, 221, 222
Selnow, G.W. 68, 111, 246
Shaffer, H. 3

Sharma, B.P. 6
Shaw, M. 63
Shubin, S. 6
Shuttlesworth, D.E. 44, 45
Simmel, E. 10, 211
Simon, H.A. 132, 133, 144, 229
Sinnott, A. 220
Skinner, B.F. 11, 30, 200, 201
Skolnick, J. 3
Slovic, P. 50
Smith, C. 51
Smith D.N. 132
Smith, G.J. 29
Smith, J.F. 3, 47, 49, 50
Smith, M.H. 42
Smith, R. 217
Snyder, R.J. 43, 48
Snyder, S. 28
Sobell, L.C. 232
Sommers, I. 3
Spradley, J.P. 100
Stacey, B.G. 46
Stark, G.M. *et al.* 206
Steadman, H.J. 3
Steinberg, M.A. 36, 42, 45, 214
Stevens, W.R. 205
Stewart, R.M. 179, 189, 215, 218
Strauss, A. 45, 98, 100
Strickland, L.H. 21, 201
Stumphauzer, J.S. 94, 240, 242, 249
Sunderworth, S. 27
Sutton-Smith, B. 48
Svendsen, R. 44
Swift, G. 206

Taber, J.I. 14, 15, 178, 212, 214
Taebel, D. 46
Tan, H.K.R. 46
Teger, A.I. 44
Tepperman, J.H. 214, 215
Thomas, P. 46
Thompson, W.N. 48
Toneatto, T. 232

Trott, J. 56, 57, 67
Tune, G. 24
Turner, D.N. 217
Turner, J.H. 44
Tversky, A. 23, 201
Tyreman-Wilde, M. 56, 57, 67

Unrah, D. 98

Van Ree, J.M. 28
Victor, R. 234
Volberg, R.A. 3

Wagenaar, W.A. 21, 23, 24, 26, 29,
   91, 94, 143, 144, 147
Walker, M.B. 13, 14, 26, 143, 214,
   215, 218, 220, 221, 222, 225, 226,
   227–8, 235, 238, 251
Wallach, M.A. *et al.* 44
Walton, F. 56, 65, 67, 72
Waterman, J. 56, 60, 61, 66, 70
Webley, P. and E. 49
Weeks, D. 226, 235
Weiner, B. 12
Weinstein, D. 3, 196, 198, 204
Wexner, L.B. 206
White, S. 202, 204
Whitman, G.W. *et al.* 44
Wildman, R.W. 214
Wilson, G.D. 206
Wilson, T.D. 131, 132, 133
Winter, S.W. 19
Winters, K.C. *et al.* 37, 42, 43, 45
Wolkowitz, O.M. *et al.* 4, 8
Wolpe, J.C. 225
Wong, G. 13, 14
Wray, I. 27, 28
Wyatt, W. 56, 62, 65, 66

Yaffee, R.A. 214

Zimmerman, M.A. *et al.* 7
Zuckerman, M. 13, 16

Subject index

ABC model (functional/behavioural analysis) 240–51
abstinence 213–14, 216, 218, 220, 226, 234, 238, 256
access to machines 53, 58, 193
acquisition: of addiction 39, 47, 75–8, 92, 187, 243–4, 248–9; and development of addiction 2, 8–9, 31–2, 240–1; development and maintenance of addiction 83–95
Action Seekers 115–16
addiction: adolescent 209; fear of 157, 160, 244; fruit machine 167, 251–7; and negative consequences 69–73; qualitative accounts and case studies 169–95; risk of 240
Addiction Research Center Inventory 27–8
'adult' gambling 2, 33–4, 42, 73, 81, 92, 179, 187, 243, 250
advertising arcades 39, 121–2, 124, 128, 210
age: acquisition of addiction 39–40, 44, 62, 64, 76, 78, 84, 88, 92, 128, 243, 248, 256, 259; arcade clientele 97, 105–7, 109, 111–12, 115; gambler 42–3; problem gamblers 53; restriction 2, 34, 64, 109–10, 122, 124–7, 248, 261; risk of addiction 50; size of stakes 202
aggression 10–11, 55, 79, 81, 87, 93, 108, 110, 256
alcohol 3, 42, 79, 92, 240, 257, 258; alcoholism 5, 16–17, 26, 44–5, 73

Alcoholics Anonymous 215–16
alienation 9
alternatives to gambling 30, 32, 77, 84–5, 93, 178, 228, 237
American Psychiatric Association pathological gambling criteria 3–6
'amusement with prize' machines 51–2, 54–5, 58–61
anonymity in research 57, 63, 170, 177
antecedents of gambling 240, 242–4, 248–9
anti-depressants 20
Antisocial Personality Disorder 4–5
Arcade Kings 112–14, 116, 203
arcades 65, 68, 77, 83–4, 96, 179, 198, 201–2, 205–6, 249, 258; inland/seaside 97, 102–5, 107, 109–11, 122–8, 243; observation analysis 99–100
arousal 12, 19, 30, 32, 69, 78–9, 81–2, 93–4, 178–9, 205–6, 222–3, 244, 246–8, 253–5; role of, in addiction 161–8; theory 17–18, 26–8
assessing the problem for treatment 236
atmosphere in arcades 53, 108, 110–11, 115, 154–7, 204–5
Attention Deficit Disorder 16
attraction of fruit machines 87–9, 93, 107, 115, 154–6, 159, 171–2, 178, 194, 204, 257
audio playback therapy 148, 227, 229–30, 241
authority, defiance of 8, 10, 35, 197

auto-ethnography 98
'automatic pilot' 106, 110, 143, 166, 244
availability bias 24–6, 29
aversion therapy 220–1, 238

'bandit beaters' 117, 119–20
beating the machine 108–9, 114, 116–20
behavioural: completion mechanism 223; counselling 220, 225–7; monitoring 162–3, 165–6, 188; treatment 220–7
Bell Adjustment inventory 14
beta-blockers 239, 249
bingo 2, 36, 41, 54–5, 77, 106, 124–5, 127
biological factors to addiction 15–17, 208
birthday money 86, 88–9
blackjack 18, 36–8, 49
blankness of mind 138, 143–4, 184, 187, 244
borrowing money 9, 71–2, 86, 88–9, 173, 256
Brecksville Division of Veterans Administration Medical Center 213–14
British Amusement Catering Trades Association (BACTA) 60–1, 64, 122, 124–7; Code of Good Practice 262–4

California Personality Inventory 14
card playing 21, 35–7, 39–41, 49–50, 54–5, 77, 85, 260
card-flipping 49
case studies 180–95, 238, 241
casinos 36–8, 41, 205, 261
challenge, gambling as 47–8, 89–90, 154–6, 159, 172, 178
chance 1–2, 21–2, 26, 48–9, 79–80, 90, 128, 140, 146, 160, 173, 199–202, 210
chasing losses 8, 35, 71–2, 155–6, 172, 184, 188, 245
cheating the machine 108, 114, 117, 120
cheerleaders 110, 114–16
chemical aversion therapy 221, 223

choice limitation 108, 111, 154–6, 159, 172, 178, 204, 243, 249
Christmas money 80, 86, 88–9
class, social 1, 4–5, 7–8, 39, 45, 64, 198, 257
clientele of arcades 105–7, 109, 111, 112, 128, 201–2
cogbiases 23–4, 25, 94
cognitive: behaviour therapy 232; bias 201, 203, 210, 229–30, 245, 249; bias and skill factors 129–48; biases 21–4, 29, 94; factors in addiction 31, 82, 89, 94, 111, 168, 238, 242, 244, 245; regret 201; restructuring 228–9; theory 21–5; treatment 227–34
coin: fraud 118–19; games 22, 24, 37, 40, 55, 85; pushers 107, 108, 117
colour and fruit machines 206, 209–10
competition machine games 107–8, 111
concealment of gambling 4
confidence 155–6, 236
confidentiality in research 57, 62–3, 111–12, 170, 177
conflict 47, 252, 255
consent to observational methodology 111
context, understanding situational 235
control 7, 93, 108, 111, 114–15, 128, 154–6, 178, 202, 216, 220, 224–5, 242
controlled gambling 225–7, 235
coping 233–4
cost of gambling: money 70, 85–6, 92, 114; time 70, 85–6, 92, 114, 157, 171–2, 182, 257
counselling 9, 213, 232, 236
covert sensitization 220, 224, 231
credit mechanism fraud 117–18
crime 4, 7, 9, 27, 38–9, 42, 73, 81, 83, 171, 178, 258
cross addiction 258
culture 1, 30, 40, 44, 46–8, 50, 206, 243

damage, causing 87, 93
data collection 100–2, 112, 170, 177, 180

debt 9, 80, 86, 88–9, 184, 193, 228, 241
decision making 202
definition: addiction 26–7, 251;
    gambling 1
delinquency 43, 61, 257
dependency, signs of 61–2, 64–5,
    69–73, 93, 247
depression 7, 9–10, 15, 19–20, 27, 31,
    78–9, 82, 108, 115, 149, 151–3,
    158–60, 172, 174, 176, 178, 183,
    185, 187–8, 194, 227, 243–4,
    249–50, 257
development of addiction 75, 92,
    94–5; *see also* acquisition and
    development of addiction
deviance 35, 60, 258–9
dice games 21, 26, 41
diffusion of responsibility 44
discussion, use in research of 75–6
dissociative state 28
diversity of machines 107, 111, 125–6
drug: abuse 26–8, 42–4, 73, 79, 251,
    257–8; selling 38–9
duos, gambling 106, 110

eclectic approach to pathological
    gambling 9, 29–33
economic socialization 45–7
education, lack of 3, 39, 81, 83
educational awareness 249
Edwards Personal Reference Schedule
    14
electrical aversion therapy 221, 223–4
electroencephalographic measurement
    15–16
emotional disturbance 3, 55
employment: self 5; un- 78, 81, 83
empowerment 236
endorphins 18–19, 28, 93, 167, 239,
    247, 249
entertainment, arcade gambling as
    family 109, 122, 127–8
Escape Artists 115–16
escapism as reason for gambling 8, 10,
    17, 47, 78, 82, 94, 108–9, 111,
    143–4, 154–6, 172, 177, 187–8,
    204, 241, 244–5, 250
establishments with fruit machines
    52–3, 77, 84, 92

etiquette, gambling 109–10, 241
euphoria 188, 247, 252–4
excitement 12, 17, 23, 27, 29, 35,
    77–9, 86–9, 93–4, 108, 111, 115,
    131, 152–6, 158–60, 167, 172,
    174–6, 178–9, 184, 187, 194, 201,
    204, 234–5, 241, 246–50, 253–4, 257
exploitation 114, 116, 128
exposure to gambling 8, 39, 76–7,
    172, 182, 187
extroversion 13, 69
Eysenck Personality Questionnaire 13,
    27

family: support 38, 236–7; trouble 8,
    9, 173, 179, 183–4, 189–90
Family Environment Scale 216–17
fantasy 10, 30, 50
fiddling 108, 117
field studies, use in research of 75, 96,
    98, 100, 102
financial help 9, 180, 237
fixed interval schedule 30
food facilities in arcades 121, 123,
    125, 127
football pools 2, 22, 24, 54–5, 77,
    84–5, 200
fruit machine: final overview of
    gambling 240–61;
    functional/behavioural analysis
    240–58; importance of structural
    characteristics 196–210;
    introduction to 50–3; observational
    analysis of playing 96–128; playing
    2, 23, 27; preliminary studies of
    addiction 75–95; qualitative
    accounts and case studies 169–95;
    role of arousal and subjective
    moods 149–68; role of cognitive
    bias and skill 129–48
frustration theory 12, 23, 138, 201
fun as reason for gambling 48, 76, 84,
    92–3, 108–9, 111, 154–6, 159, 187,
    204, 241
future plays 199

Gam-Anon 170
gamble button 141–2, 145–6, 162,
    167, 174, 202, 205

Gamblers Anonymous 52, 170, 179, 186, 188–9, 192, 194, 213, 215–19, 222, 226, 259
gambles, number of 130–1, 134–5, 142
game shows 48
games as precursors to gambling 39, 47–50
gaming 1, 27, 197
Gaming Act (1968) 52
Gaming Board 96–7
gaming machine history 198–9
genetic basis for pathological gambling 17
Gordon House Association 53
guilt 10–11, 122, 129

heart rate 17, 27, 78, 161–8, 241, 247–9, 254
hemispheric dysregulation 16
heuristics 23–6, 30, 94, 129, 138, 144, 147, 204, 245–6
hierarchy, group arcade 106, 110, 113, 116, 203
'high' 28, 78–9, 81, 109, 154–6, 167, 175–6, 178, 184, 188, 194, 246–7, 249–50, 254–5
holiday gambling 97, 109, 111, 125, 128
Home Office report into adolescent gambling 58–64
horse-race betting 1–2, 12, 19, 36–7, 41, 54, 84, 175, 179, 225, 258–60
hospitalization 9
hypnotherapy 234

idiot skill 147, 203, 246
illusion of control 21–2, 30, 51, 82, 129, 142, 147, 202–3
imagery of gambling 122
imaginal desensitization 220–1, 223–4
'in vivo' desensitization 220–1, 224
in-patient treatment 213
incidence of gambling 3, 35, 38–40, 53–5, 57, 64–5, 73, 169
income, use of disposable 58–9, 70
intervention programmes 179, 214, 224, 228, 248–51, 261
interview, use in research of 73–5, 84, 99, 102, 112–13, 129–30, 139, 145, 150, 162, 177

intrinsic association 197, 199
introspection 131–3
involvement of bettor 196, 202
irrationality 12, 24–5, 53, 71–2, 87–9, 100, 144–5, 148, 177, 227, 229–30, 245–6, 248–9, 255, 257

jackpot machines 52, 54, 154–6, 197, 199, 201

knowledge of machines 80, 90–1, 107, 120, 129, 141–2, 145–7, 173–4, 203, 246

learning theory and pathological gambling 11–13
legal socialization 46–7
legislation 3, 34, 38–9, 52–3, 61, 64, 122, 126, 128, 196, 199, 248, 261
leisure activity/gambling 35, 77–8
lifestyle improvement 213
light: effects of machines 205–6, 208–10; oscillation 147
location of arcade 210
locus of control 13–14, 69, 231
loss of money: acceptance 22, 110, 129, 138, 229, 245; big 8, 70, 91, 94, 159, 197; incurring 2; moods 79; as negative consequence 87
lottery 1–2, 22–3, 36–7, 39–41, 54–5, 200
luck 11, 21, 23, 48
lunch money 38, 71–2, 86, 88–9, 171, 178, 256
lying 4, 257

Machine Beaters 114, 116
maintenance of addiction 12, 75, 92, 94–5, 149–68, 187–8, 198, 203, 247; *see also* acquisition, development and maintenance of addiction
marbles 49
marital therapy 214–15
market research 208–9
marketing amusement arcades 120–8, 198
masculinity 48, 81, 111
material gain 8, 30, 35, 48
Matka 35

media 48
memory system 132
men: addiction 27, 42, 78; arcade
  users 96, 103, 106–7, 110, 112,
  114–15; gambling 35, 39–40, 43,
  48–9, 65, 68, 81, 87–8, 92, 131;
  risk taking 50
merchandise selling in arcades 125, 127
methodology: affecting the machine
  outcome 130–4; choice of 54, 75;
  observation analysis 101–2, 122–3;
  practicalities of observational
  analysis 97–9; role of arousal
  149–50, 161–2; use in studies 76, 84
minimal intervention strategies 219–20
Minnesota Multiphasic Personality
  Inventory 14, 27
modelling 242, 249
monoamine metabolites 16
moods 79, 86, 94, 130, 149–61, 169,
  174–5, 206, 255
morality 2–3
motivational interviewing 189, 232–3
multiline pay features 199
multiplier potential 196, 201–2

naming fruit machines 121–2, 124–6,
  128, 207, 209
near wins, effect on addiction of 22–3,
  78–9, 82, 159, 161–3, 165, 167–8,
  179, 200–1, 208–9, 247–8
negative consequences 52, 63, 69–73,
  96, 169, 231, 241, 244–8, 256
neurochemicals 16
neurosis, gambling as 211
neuroticism 27, 68, 227
non-participant observation 74, 98–9,
  102, 112–13
noradrenaline 16
normative decision theory 23–6
number: games 35–6; of machines in
  arcades 123, 125; system of
  machines 138, 147

obscured interiors of arcades 122, 125,
  127
observation: analysis of fruit machine
  addiction 96–128, 241; use in
  research of 73–4, 75–6, 169

one-armed bandit 199
opioids 18–19, 27, 239, 249
opportunity for gambling 3, 30, 39,
  48, 53, 78, 80, 102, 109, 155–6,
  200, 226
optimism 8
outcome of machine, affecting the
  130–48, 202

paradoxical intention 234–5
parents: consent 40, 242–3, 257;
  gambling 39, 43, 44–5, 76–7, 177,
  249, 257; gambling with 85, 107
Parents of Young Gamblers (POYG)
  170, 176–7, 192
partial reinforcement extinction effect 12
participant observation 74, 98, 102, 113
passivity to activity 47
pathological gambling 204, 260–1;
  adolescent 3, 38, 42, 44–5, 73, 81,
  87–8, 90, 122, 128, 169, 197, 243;
  criteria 3–6, 27, 38, 57, 61, 69, 73,
  76, 84, 87–8, 92–3, 150–1, 157,
  171, 177, 180, 188, 204, 248, 252;
  effect on job performance 83; skill
  orientation 129; and social
  gambling 11, 29, 32, 88–90, 93;
  theories 9–33; treatment 211–39
pay-out: interval 196, 200, 209; ratio
  197, 204
peer: groups 7, 32, 35, 38, 43–4, 50,
  63, 65, 68, 96, 112–14, 177, 197,
  207, 243, 244, 249; praise 101;
  pressure 30, 77, 92–3, 154–6, 172,
  187–8, 242
peptides 16, 18–19; neuro 27
'perceived urgency' 205
perceptions, erroneous 22–3, 31, 94,
  130, 139, 156, 158, 160, 174, 196,
  203, 210, 232–3, 244–5, 248
performance: light effects and 205–7;
  speed of 133–4, 142, 163, 166–7,
  246
person-machine interactivity 259–60
personal histories 169–80, 241
personal motivation 175–6, 188–9,
  192, 194, 215, 228, 232–3, 236
personality 68, 73, 233, 252, 257;
  theory 13–14

personification of machine 130,
138–9, 148, 229, 245–6
physiological: factors of addiction 29,
32, 81, 93–5, 149, 161–2, 167–8,
179, 187, 206, 210, 238, 241–2,
244–5, 247–9, 254–5; theory 15–17
pilot research 74, 75
pinball 107, 202
'playing for the sake of playing' 76, 93
pleasure 10–11
pocket money 71, 86
poker machines 18–19, 37, 41, 110
political issues of gambling 58
pontoon 49
pool 40–1
popularity of gambling 2
potting 119
prevention programmes 94, 110, 160,
179, 189, 248–51, 261
prize machines 107
probability of winning 12, 22, 24, 80,
94, 197, 202, 204, 210
problem gambling 5, 8, 42, 52–3, 57,
92, 248
profit as concept 47
progress, measurement of treatment 237
psychiatric disorder 20–1
psychoanalysis: theory 10–11, 30;
treatment 211–13, 238
psychobiological: factors of addiction
149, 161, 168, 179, 247; substrates
16
psychological factors of addiction 29,
31–2, 68–9, 95, 149, 179, 187, 198,
200, 208–10, 241, 260–1
psychology 198, 227; of gambling
1–33; reverse 225; social 232
psychometric theory to pathological
gambling 13–15
psychopaths 7, 14–15, 26, 227
psychophysiological factors of
addiction 17, 30, 32, 149, 161,
246–8
psychosocial: factors 149; typology of
adolescent fruit machine gamblers
111–16
psychotherapy 212–14, 222
psychoticism 26, 69
publication: on beating the machines

117, 119–20; of research 55–6

qualitative research 75–6, 96–7,
99–100, 102, 169–80
quantitative research 75, 96, 100, 169,
195
questionnaires, use in research of 34,
38–9, 53, 61, 66–7, 73–5, 84,
169–70, 176–7, 241

race 1, 3, 46
radio immunassay techniques 19
rational emotive therapy 230–1
re-allocation of wealth, gambling as 1
reasons for gambling 8, 11, 46–8, 76,
85, 88–90, 92, 108–9, 111, 114–17,
145, 154–6, 159, 169, 172–3, 177,
179, 184, 187, 204, 210–11, 241,
243, 256
reels 201; knowledge of 90–1, 146–7,
173–4; multiple 199
regional differences in gambling 45, 58
regularity: arousal theory and 17; of
gambling 2, 57–8, 65, 70–1, 77, 82,
85, 94, 106–8, 110–11, 115, 122;
/nonregularity 129–31, 134–45,
147–8, 161–8, 203, 246;
/pathological criteria 150–61
reinforcement 11–13, 17, 23, 28, 30,
32, 81, 93, 149, 159, 196, 200–1,
241–2, 245–6, 259
rejection 26, 31, 172–3, 185, 187, 193
relapse 188, 215, 218–19, 224, 237,
252, 256; prevention 233
relaxation therapy 179, 186, 188–9,
213, 220–1, 223, 225
reliability of research 138
religion 39
Rent-a-Spacers 114–16
representativeness bias 24, 25
research into adolescent gambling:
addiction and negative
consequences 69–73; case studies
43–5; economic socialization 45–7;
fruit machines as social activity
65–8; gambling as play 47–50;
incidence of fruit machine playing
64–5; prevalence studies 34–43;
psychological factors 68–9; studies

of fruit machine playing 53–64;
studies of risk-taking and gambling-
like behaviour in children 50–1
research into gambling: normal/social
gambling 2–3; pathological
gambling 3–9
researcher, personal characteristics of
99–100
resentment 35
retrospective reports 132
reversal theory 28–9, 94
reward schedules 12
risk taking 1, 13, 44, 48, 131, 155–6,
204, 206
roulette 21

salience 188, 251, 253
sampling for research 56–8, 170, 176
satiation therapy 220–1, 225
schoolwork, impact of addiction on
39, 43, 55, 87, 93, 191, 248, 256–8
seasonal use of arcades 102–3,
109–10, 241
self: destruction 193, 258; esteem
236–7; help treatment 215–19;
reports 34, 44, 68, 73, 76, 94, 96,
142, 149–50, 218, 254
sensation seeking 13, 16, 69
seretonin (5-HT) 16
sex difference in gambling 35, 39–40,
42–3, 48, 51, 241, 256
shoplifting 27, 38
situational characteristics of arcades
121, 123–7, 198–9, 243
size of arcade 103
skill: belief in 21–3, 94, 106–7,
112–15, 155–7, 160, 196, 229, 246,
257; and bettor involvement 179,
202–3; factors 79–80, 82, 90–2,
173–4; factors and cognitive bias
129–48; gambling 1, 47–50; games
36–7, 40–1; level 261; machine as
act of 166, 199; with prize
machines 51–2; as reinforcer 241;
role of 184–5, 187–8; testing 108,
197, 250
smoking 42, 168, 257, 258
social: acceptance of gambling 3;
activity, gambling as 2, 63, 65–8,

77, 83–4, 88–9, 92, 96, 110,
114–15, 143, 154–6, 197, 204, 206,
241, 243, 250; factors of addiction
106–9, 111; gambling 2–3, 8, 122;
learning 51; pathological gambling/
11, 29, 32, 88–90, 93; setting 242;
skill 213, 249; values 43
social sciences 98
sociological factors of addiction 7–8,
29, 30, 32, 69, 77–8, 94, 149, 187,
210, 241, 243, 248
solitariness 2, 63, 65, 68, 83, 93, 96,
106, 109–10, 114, 197, 250
solvent abuse 258
sound: aversion therapy 222; effects
of machines 204–5, 209–10
South Oaks Gambling Screen (SOGS)
42
specialist play 80, 82, 91, 106, 120,
129, 141–2, 145–6, 173–4, 199,
202–3
speculation as gambling 1
spirituality 215–16
sports betting 36–7, 39–41, 54, 77, 84
stakes, range of machine 39, 53, 107,
109, 111, 122–3, 126–8, 196–7,
201–2, 208, 254
state anxiety 227
State Trait Anxiety Inventory 224
status 30, 43, 48–50, 106, 112, 114,
116, 188, 233, 250
stealing 9, 39, 55, 58, 60, 71–3, 81,
83, 86–9, 93, 117, 171, 173, 178,
187, 190, 193–4, 241, 248, 256
stocks and shares 1, 41
stress 4, 7–8, 18, 30, 108, 179, 189,
194, 233, 237, 249
strimming 108, 117–18
structural characteristics of arcades
121, 124, 196–210
structure for change 236
study: acquisition, development and
maintenance of fruit machine
addiction in adolescence 83–95,
241; exploratory study of addiction
among adolescent males 76–83, 241
subordinates in arcade hierarchy
106–7, 112–14, 116, 203
substance abuse 5, 26, 61, 188, 258

suicide 9, 20
support 38, 179, 189, 237
suspension of judgement 197, 207–8
symbol ratio proportions 200–1, 209
systematic desensitization 220–1, 225
systems theory 232

talking as treatment 179, 186, 188–9, 212
tape recording, use in research of 102, 134, 148, 229–30, 249
television addiction 259–61
'ten key aspects' treatment 235–7
thinking aloud method 22, 129, 131–5, 142, 144, 148, 168, 229–30, 241, 245–9, 254
thought stopping 227–8
time: cost of gambling 70, 85–6, 92, 114, 157, 171–2, 182, 257; of day of arcade use 103, 105, 109, 241; stay on machine for as long as possible 79, 83, 129, 143, 158, 163, 166, 185–8, 203, 204, 229, 246
tokens 208
tolerance 159, 167, 188, 247, 252, 254–5
treatment 13, 16, 20, 64, 94, 179, 211–39, 242, 248–51, 261; adolescent addiction 235–7
trivia machines 52, 61
trouble, getting into 87–9, 255–6
truancy 38, 55, 58, 71–2, 81, 83, 87, 89, 93, 191, 241, 248, 256
trust 236, 239
typologies: of adolescent fruit machine gamblers 111–16; of pathological gamblers 6–8

use of arcades 102–5

validity of research 17, 56–7, 131–2, 144, 161, 217
verbalization 22, 68, 106, 110–11, 229–30, 245, 247; irrational 130, 132–8, 143–4, 241
video game machines 51–2, 55, 61, 68, 77, 79, 82–3, 85, 93, 106–9, 121, 123–7, 129, 175, 202, 204, 207, 259–61
videotaping, use in research of 111, 167

wagers 55, 77, 85
wages, use for gambling 37, 71, 86, 171, 182–3, 185
'wheel of change' 233
winners/losers 1
'winning loop' 120
winning money as reason for gambling 46–8, 76, 79, 84, 89, 92–3, 108–9, 111, 154–6, 159, 172, 178, 184, 187, 200, 204, 241, 256, 260–1
wins: effect on gambling of big 8–9, 12, 43, 51, 88, 92, 100, 144, 145, 172, 177, 204–5, 243–4, 246, 257; number of 130–1, 134–5, 142
wish-fulfilment 47
withdrawal 188, 252, 255–6
women: addiction 26, 76; in arcades 96, 103, 107, 110, 114–15; gambling 35, 39–40, 43, 65, 68; middle age 105–7, 109–11, 127; risk taking 50